# SILENCED RESISTANCE

# Women in Africa and the Diaspora

STANLIE JAMES AND AILI MARI TRIPP

*Series Editors*

# SILENCED RESISTANCE

*Women, Dictatorships, and Genderwashing in
Western Sahara and Equatorial Guinea*

Joanna Allan

THE UNIVERSITY OF WISCONSIN PRESS

The University of Wisconsin Press
1930 Monroe Street, 3rd Floor
Madison, Wisconsin 53711-2059
uwpress.wisc.edu

3 Henrietta Street, Covent Garden
London WC2E 8LU, United Kingdom
eurospanbookstore.com

Printed in the United States of America

This book may be available in a digital edition.

Library of Congress Cataloging-in-Publication Data

Names: Allan, Joanna, author.
Title: Silenced resistance : women, dictatorships, and genderwashing in
Western Sahara and Equatorial Guinea / Joanna Allan.
Other titles: Women in Africa and the diaspora.
Description: Madison, Wisconsin : The University of Wisconsin Press, [2019] |
Series: Women in Africa and the diaspora | Includes bibliographical
references and index.
Identifiers: LCCN 2018045756 | ISBN 9780299318406 (cloth : alk. paper)
Subjects: LCSH: Women—Western Sahara—Social conditions. |
Women—Equatorial Guinea—Social conditions. | Women—Political activity—
Western Sahara. | Women—Political activity—Equatorial Guinea. |
Women human rights workers—Western Sahara. | Women human rights workers—
Equatorial Guinea. | Authoritarianism—Western Sahara. | Authoritarianism—
Equatorial Guinea. | Western Sahara—Politics and government. |
Equatorial Guinea—Politics and government.
Classification: LCC HQ1818.5 .A45 2019 | DDC 305.409648—dc23
LC record available at https://lccn.loc.gov/2018045756

*To*

LOGAN, HELIOS, AND MY PARENTS

# Contents

# Illustrations

# Acknowledgments

First, to everyone who gave up their time to share their (sometimes very difficult) stories with me in interviews or less formal conversations, thank you. I am in your debt. Many of these "interviewees" also offered me hospitality, support, and friendship and continue to inspire me.

Manuel Barcía Paz and Richard Cleminson deserve a huge thanks for their encouragement and support, their comprehensive and constructive feedback on my writing, their valuable suggestions, and their always-sound advice. Thanks also to the rest of the staff at University of Leeds Spanish, Portuguese, and Latin American Studies department for their encouragement over so many years and to the wider Arts Faculty and the School of Modern Languages for their support with this project, including the funding without which this book would not have been possible. I am indebted to the Fran Trust, which helped me present this work in Equatorial Guinea, and the Leeds for Life Foundation, which supported me to act on some of the findings of the book in Western Sahara. I am quite sure this book would not exist at all if it were not for Pablo San Martín's teaching several years ago.

In Western Sahara, I would like to give special thanks to Hamza Lakhal, without whom one chapter of this book would look very different, or perhaps would not have been written. Thanks also to Nooni and our two mutual friends for getting me in. In the camps, thanks to Mohammed Saleh, Khalihenna Mohammed, and the rest of the Saharawi Campaign Against the Plunder (SCAP) team, to Limam Mohammed and his family in Auserd camp, and indeed to the Popular Front for the Liberation of Saguia el-Hamra and Río de Oro (POLISARIO) for facilitating my research in the camps. Many Saharawis took real risks to help me and a colleague in Morocco. Thanks is not enough for them. Kristina Andrea Nygaard kept me smiling during a challenging time.

I am very grateful to Trifonia Melibea Obono Ntutumu, who went out of her way to help me with the historical chapter on Spanish Guinea. There are several other women in Malabo who deserve a special thanks, not only for helping me with the project in various ways but also for showing great kindness. Most of them have to remain anonymous. Thanks to all at the Spanish Cultural Center, especially Agueda.

Thanks to Alice Wilson, Enrique Martino, Vivian Solana Moreno, Silvia Almenara Niebla, Hamza Lakhal, Asria Mohammed, Wilf Wilde, Tara Deubel, Shane Doyle, and David and Judith Allan for their readings of my work. Their constructive comments and suggested revisions helped me greatly in forming this book. Thanks also to Rosa Medina Doménech for hosting me at the University of Granada, to Cristina Martínez Benítez de Lugo for her hospitality, and to Igor Cusack, Agustín Velloso, and Nieves Muñoz García for the initial contacts. Igor also helped me greatly by generously posting hard-to-find publications on Equatorial Guinea my way. Thanks to Cate Lewis and Jacob Mundy for their valuable advice on fieldwork. I am grateful to Bartek Sabela and Guillaume Darribau for the wonderful images.

I would also like to thank all at the University of Wisconsin Press for their encouragement and help. I am especially grateful to Dennis Lloyd and the series editors for their initial belief in the book, to Dennis, Amber Rose, Adam Mehring, and Sheila McMahon for their invaluable guidance, and to Mary Magray for helping to make this a better book. Thanks, too, to Mahan Ellison and another anonymous peer reviewer for their detailed readings of my work and their very helpful suggestions, which were a great aid to me in improving earlier drafts of this book.

Thanks to Helios, Frances, Ian, Judith, David, and Logan for their love and support. Thanks to all at Western Sahara Resource Watch (WSRW) and Western Sahara Campaign (WSC) UK for inspiring me.

Thanks to a dear family in El Aaiún for memories that I treasure.

My book does not reflect the views of any people mentioned here, and any outstanding errors in the work are mine alone.

# Abbreviations

| | |
|---|---|
| AU | African Union |
| CAN | African Cup of Nations |
| CDA | Critical Discourse Analysis |
| CEDAW | Convention on the Elimination of All Forms of Discrimination Against Women, or Committee on the Elimination of All Forms of Discrimination Against Women |
| CPDS | Convergence for Social Democracy |
| GDP | Gross Domestic Product |
| JMCM | Youth Marching with Macías |
| LGBT | Lesbian, Gay, Bisexual, and Transgender |
| MAIB | Movement for the Self-determination of Bioko Island |
| MINASPROM | Ministry of Social Affairs and Advancement of Women |
| MONALIGE | National Movement for the Liberation of Equatorial Guinea |
| MUNGE | Movement for the National Unity of Equatorial Guinea |
| NGO | Non-Governmental Organization |
| OECD | Organization for Economic Co-operation and Development |
| PDGE | Democratic Party of Equatorial Guinea |
| PDJS | Party for Social Justice in Equatorial Guinea |
| POLISARIO | Popular Front for the Liberation of Saguia el-Hamra and Río de Oro |

| | |
|---|---|
| PR | Public Relations |
| PUNS | Saharawi National Union Party |
| PUNT | United National Workers Party |
| SADR | Saharawi Arab Democratic Republic |
| SPLA | Saharawi People's Liberation Army |
| UN | United Nations |
| UNMS | National Union of Saharawi Women |
| USAID | United States Agency for International Development |

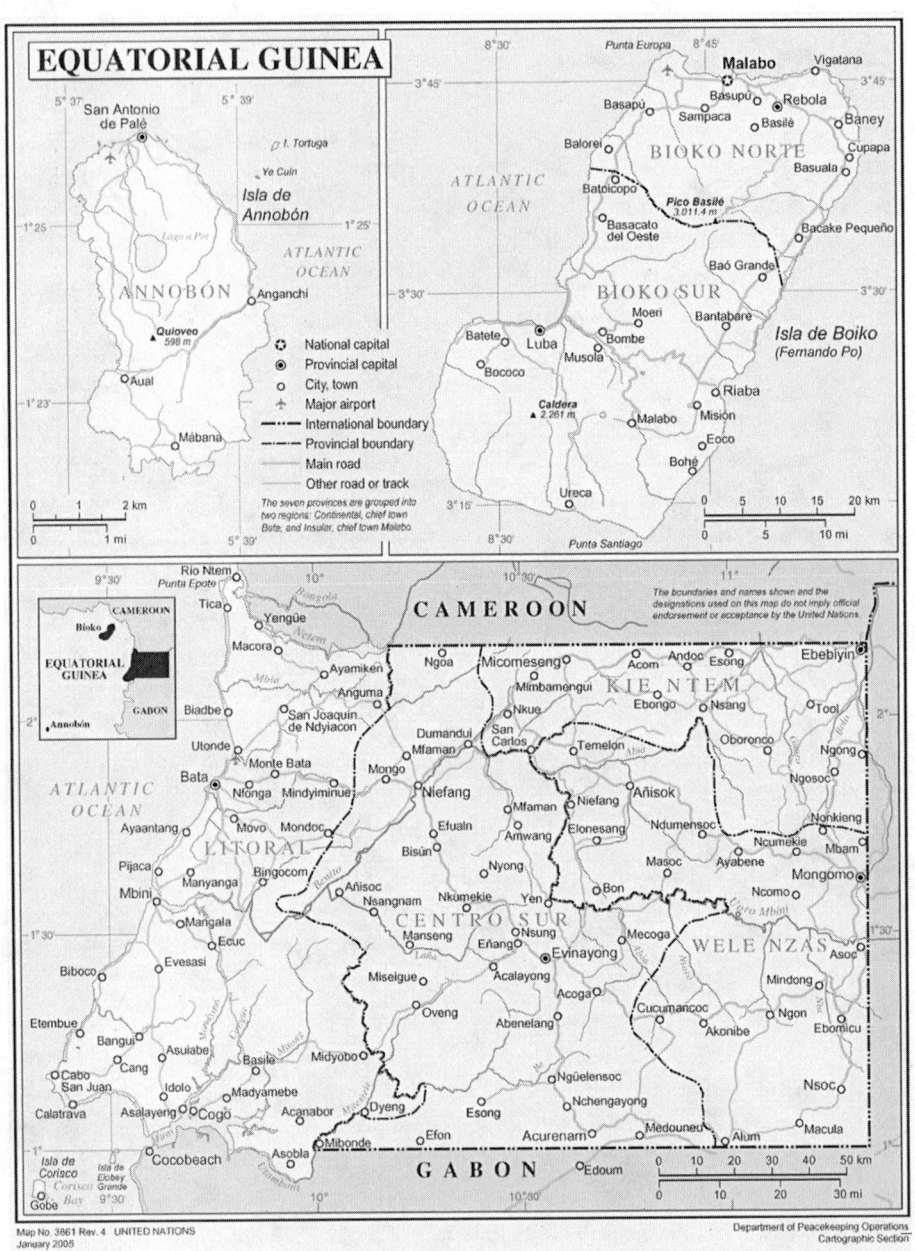

Equatorial Guinea, Map No. 3861, Rev. 4, January 2005, United Nations.

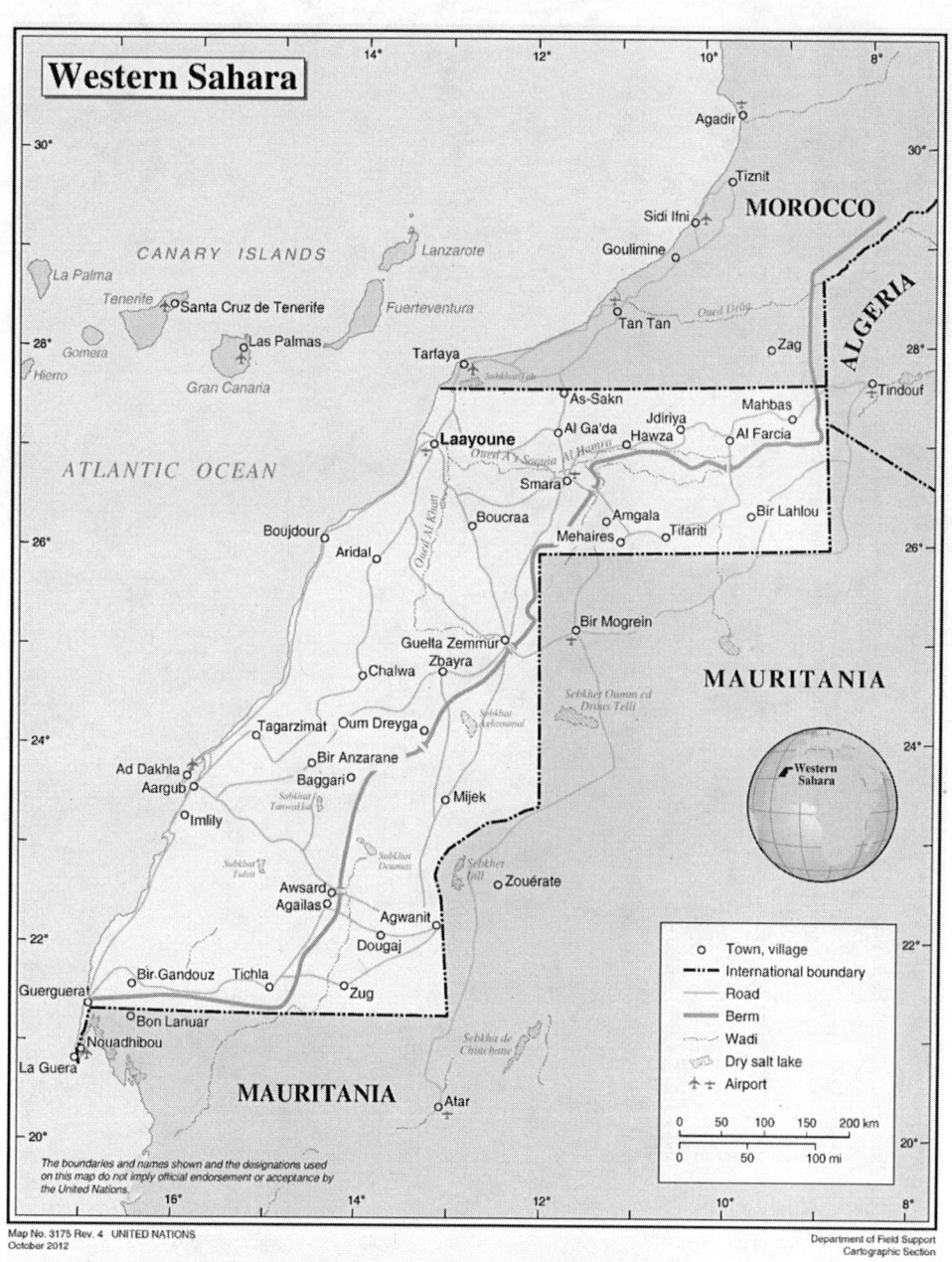

Western Sahara, Map. No. 3175, Rev. 4, October 2012, United Nations.

# SILENCED RESISTANCE

# Introduction

SULTANA TREMBLED. The two policemen had muscled her into the back of the ambulance. She looked down, horrified, at her own eye cupped in her right palm. Sultana tried to keep her balance, a struggle with cuffed wrists, as the wailing vehicle lurched and zigzagged through early evening traffic. Her fellow passengers, the police duo, were arguing over where to take her next. "Let's go to *el garaje*," said one, turning his head to spit on her. *El garaje*, Castilian for "the garage," is the nickname given to a secret detention center in Marrakesh used specifically, Sultana tells me, for sexual forms of torture. "No. She's going to the commission," argued another, before bringing his truncheon down on the back of Sultana's head once more.

As she was dragged across the internal courtyard, her feet ploughing up the scab-yellow dust and congealed blood on the floor, Sultana could hear the tourists outside chattering and laughing, spectators to Marrakesh's most famous square. Red poured from her empty eye socket. Another blow to the head, then darkness.

In the cell, Sultana recognized twenty or so of her fellow Saharawi classmates, men and women, scattered on the bare floor. Some cried, some moaned, some were woefully silent. All had been stripped naked. Colored bruising, lit by a single light source, patterned the prisoners' flesh. Above their heads, dozens, hundreds, it sounded like thousands, of pairs of feet pounded by. All arteries of Marrakesh lead here.

It is easy to miss the architectural understatement of the low-rise, beige Police Commission that sits anemically in one corner of the Djemaa el Fna square. The building's ability to merge blandly into the background is opportune for the Moroccan regime, which shows a heavily made-up face to the country's visitors. The Anglophone guidebooks are an ally to Morocco. They make the best of the story of how the Djemaa el Fna (Assembly of the Dead) got its name: "heretics" and "criminals" were tortured here centuries ago, says Lonely Planet. *Centuries ago.* If the hint of a scream was today to escape from the commission, it would have to fight for attention with the hammers of souq ironmongers, the clashing brass cups of the water carriers, the squeals of dancing monkeys, or the supernatural drone of the snake charmers hypnotizing the guidebook writers. Incidentally, the mouths of many charmed cobras are sewn shut.

Sultana Khaya is a Saharawi, native of Moroccan-occupied Western Sahara. On the day that her right eye was beaten out of her head, 10 May 2007, Sultana, then a student of French, had been attending a peaceful demonstration in favor of Western Sahara's independence at the University of Cadi Ayyad, Marrakesh (there are no universities in occupied Western Sahara, which is why Sultana was studying in Morocco).[1] With her classmates and compatriots, she sat on the floor at the entrance of the halls of residence and made a "V for victory" sign with her fingers. Minutes later, among the confusion of police tear gas, Sultana was dragged outside and into the back of the ambulance.[2]

It was not just any day, but the anniversary of a key benchmark in the Saharawi nationalist struggle. On 10 May 1973 Saharawis formed the Popular Front for the Liberation of Saguia el Hamra and Rio de Oro (POLISARIO), the national liberation movement pushing for the independence of Western Sahara. Spain, the colonial power, sold Western Sahara to bordering Mauritania and Morocco in 1975. While the POLISARIO defeated Mauritania by 1979, the resource-rich part of Western Sahara remains occupied by a brutal Moroccan regime.

Spain's other ex-colony in Africa also faces a heavy-handed regime. According to one group of activists against the Equatoguinean dictatorship, the story of Equatorial Guinea is one of "tragedies and deaths, too many deaths."[3] Personal sacrifice scars the lives of Saharawi and Equatoguinean antiregime activists, yet oppression is met with defiance despite the risks. Says Clara Nsegue Eyi, who was imprisoned for her involvement in the Popular Protest Movement and leadership of the Democratic Party for Social Justice in Equatorial Guinea (PDJS), "[I feel] morally very strong and content."[4] Nsegue Eyi opposes the bloody regime of Teodoro Obiang Nguema, who has ruled over his country since 1979 when he assassinated the previous dictator, his uncle Francisco Macías Nguema. Macías had been elected upon the Spanish exit in 1968.

Nsegue Eyi is a rare woman in Equatorial Guinea. The leadership of the other (estimated thirty) opposition parties is male dominated, and the historically uncommon but increasingly frequent political public protests have been largely masculine environments.[5] On the other hand, in occupied Western Sahara, public protests against Moroccan, and before that Spanish, colonialism have generally been attended by more women than men. It is precisely this contrast in the respective genders of Saharawi and Equatoguinean antiauthoritarian organized public resistance movements that inspires this book, and it is precisely this contrast that makes a comparison between the two cases so urgent. At the same time, the *parallels* rather than the contrasts between the two countries make their gendered histories of resistance comparable. Both faced the authoritarian colonialism of Spanish dictator Francisco Franco, Western interventions owing to the presence of rich natural resources, and ongoing eras of state violence and brutality. Both the Moroccan and Equatoguinean governments have successfully masked heinous human rights abuses thanks to international public relations campaigns that foreground alleged dedication to gender equality.

Drawing on extensive archival and field-based research in Western Sahara and Equatorial Guinea, I analyze the complex relationship between women, feminism, and resistance to authoritarianism in this book. Contrasting the two cases reveals the diverse relationships between discourses of gender equality and radicalism and conservatism: while the Equatoguinean and Moroccan governments use gender equality discourses to support the status quo, the Saharawi government in exile has used them to strengthen revolution. Spain, too, used discourses of gender equality to further its imperial projects in both Western Sahara and Equatorial Guinea. In 1964 the Spanish Falange sent its Women's Section to Spain's African colonies to indoctrinate the indigenous populations with its own perturbed version of gender equality. Yet the nuances of Spanish colonialism in the two countries led to different gendered outcomes among the emergent independence movements. These differences persist today among the communities that fight ongoing dictatorships. In both Western Sahara and Equatorial Guinea, women resist authoritarian regimes, but their tactics differ. Also in both countries, women face challenges such as sexism and racism, breeding a resistance that is as intersectional as the oppressions women fight. In this book I argue that gender is essential to understanding the dynamics of women's resistance to authoritarian regimes. But I also argue that hegemonic Western stereotypes (as well as locally hegemonic Saharawi and Equatoguinean gendered discourses) of the "lack of gender equality" in Africa determine tactics of *oppression* as well as of resistance. In other words, the impact of Western orientalist constructions of "Third World" womanhood, which paint African women as weak, oppressed, and in need of rescue, has hitherto been underestimated. With regard to oppression, while existing research has shown how such negative stereotypes of African (and Middle Eastern) gender relations have been used to undermine women activists and justify Western neocolonial interventions, I argue that these orientalist clichés have further and more specific consequences, down to the level of who African authoritarian regimes punish, how they punish their dissenters, and for how long. With regard to resistance, I argue that African women activists are not merely victims of patronizing Western stereotyping: resourceful activists know how to use even orientalist images to their advantage. I pursue my argument by tracing the histories of Saharawi and Equatoguinean women's resistance to Spanish colonialism and to the authoritarian regimes that came to power after independence.

To understand the different paths that the women of the two countries took with regard to resistance, one must first consider the gendered context of Spanish colonialism in the Sahara and Guinea. Spanish colonial endeavors had different timelines and trajectories in the two countries, and the colonists followed the bloody footprints of other Europeans. From 1472, when the Portuguese first landed on the shores of Bioko Island (formally Fernando Po) and Annobón Island until its liberation from Spain in 1968, Portuguese, Dutch, British, and Spanish colonizers maintained a presence in Equatorial Guinea. While the initial Portuguese colonization was virtual rather than physical, since there were very few Portuguese stationed in the territory, the Dutch exploited Bioko from 1642 to 1648 for trafficking slaves. Later, from the 1820s, Britain used the same island as a base for its challenges to the slave trade. In the 1800s Spain exiled Spanish and Cuban political prisoners to Bioko, effectively transforming the island into an open jail. From 1958 the Spanish began to colonize, in earnest, the mainland part of Equatorial Guinea, known as Rio Muni.

As Justo Bolekia Boleka asserts, the Spanish colonization of Equatorial Guinea was, at least in the first few decades, more "religious and agricultural than commercial and industrial."[6] Spanish Sahara was quite the opposite. The colony was used as a basis for trade and fisheries, and the Spanish attempted to leave Saharawis to their own devices to some extent, at least until the fifties and sixties when the full economic potential of the territory became clear and thus Saharawi workers were needed. These differences in the two colonial projects had important consequences when it came to the development of gendered nationalist movements. However, one similarity in Spanish Guinea and Spanish Sahara was the arrival of the Spanish Falange party's Women's Section in 1964, which attempted to impose its own model of fascist femininity on its colonial "daughters." Thanks to those who wished to sculpt them into Falangist ideals of "native" womanhood, Saharawi and Equatoguinean women faced various overlapping oppressions at once. Yet if one thumbs through the sepia, typed reports, and smudged letters of the Women's Section, and compares the tales found in them with the memories of Saharawi and Equatoguinean women and girls who were once Section students, stories of resistance emerge. The works of James C. Scott and of the Subaltern Studies school of historians are most useful for drawing out these stories. Scott points out that until recently, academics have ignored (and thereby made silent) much of the active political life of subordinate groups because it takes place at a level that is rarely recognized as political.[7] Scott focuses on "everyday" forms of resistance. At first sight these are the innocuous acts undertaken by subordinates, such as foot dragging, arson, sabotage, slander, and feigned ignorance. Such actions often avoid direct confrontation with the authority and also make use of the implicit understandings and networks among the oppressed. According to Scott, these actions are significant in that they require little or no organization, and yet, through them, subordinates are more likely to achieve their goals than by way of more dramatic, mass mobilizations.

In this book, I blend Scott's theory of everyday resistance with Ernesto Laclau and Chantelle Mouffe's reworking of Antonio Gramsci's theory of hegemony to make sense of why resistance emerges. To my reading, Scott sees resistance as inherent to subordinate groups. Laclau and Mouffe, however, do not envisage resistance to subordination or power as something inevitable and inherently human. Subordination, for them, is "when an agent is subject to the decisions of another."[8] Oppression, on the other hand, is when relations of subordination are transformed into an antagonism. This, according to Laclau and Mouffe, happens when an external (counterhegemonic) discourse interrupts the (hegemonic) discourse of subordination.[9] For example, feminist discourse has allowed many women to view their lot vis-à-vis men as one of oppression, whereas others who do not access feminist discourses may see their position of subordination as natural and inevitable. Once an external discourse (such as a feminist campaign) facilitates the conceptualization of subordination as oppression (such as the oppression of women by patriarchal organization of social life), a social antagonism exists around which a social movement can organize. Therefore, while Scott's work allows me to identify "hidden" resistance, Laclau and Mouffe's theories help me to understand *why* resistance emerges. An insight from Frantz Fanon can serve as a further example: "The terms the settler uses when he mentions the native are zoological terms. . . . [The native] knows he is not an animal; and it is precisely at the moment he realizes his humanity that he begins to sharpen the weapon with which he will secure his victory."[10]

Fanon suggests here that it is only when the "native" rejects the colonialist hegemonic discourse that defines him as a barbaric animal and instead begins to identify as a human subject that he will resist.[11] There must have been something that triggers the "native's" change in identification. This "something" was a counterhegemonic discourse. In Spanish Guinea and Spanish Sahara,

I argue in part 1 that it was the development of nationalist ideologies that acted as such counterhegemonic discourses. The effect of these counterhegemonic currents can be felt—with the help of Scott's work—when reading tales of indigenous students' "bad behavior," absenteeism, and "answering back" in the reports of the colonist Women's Section staff.

The Spanish Falange's Women's Section arrived in colonial Guinea and Sahara at a time when the embryonic nationalist movements in both countries were taking full form. If, as I argue in this book, Saharawi and Guinean women resisted the sexism and racism of colonialism through, for example, challenging the schemes of the Women's Section, did they also play a role in the wider proindependence movements or influence the latter in some way? In the case of Equatorial Guinea especially, women's role remains largely invisible in the history books. Although a superficial look suggests that resistance to Obiang and previously to Spanish colonialism is and was male dominated, if I turn my head to see acts of resistance beyond the traditional pillars of party politics and street protests, I find—like so many other feminist scholars have done in other country case studies—that women have their own ways of challenging the political status quo along nationalist, feminist, and antiracist lines. Indeed, just as Kim Crenshaw famously showed that oppressive structures are *intersectional*, that is, overlapping and deeply connected, so too is resistance.[12]

The Sahara/Guinea comparison is most illuminating when I focus on how the nationalist movements in the two countries conceived women's role in a postindependence era. This issue is addressed in part 2, where I focus on the gender politics of today's Saharawi and Equatoguinean societies and look at the role "gender equality" plays in official government discourse. With regard to the Saharawi nationalist movement the POLISARIO, it is arguable that women's key, and very prominent, role in mobilizing against Spanish rule encouraged the male leadership to put the aim of gender equality at the center of its nationalist project. Still today, gender equality retains pride of place in POLISARIO nationalist discourses and is used, ideologically, to further the Saharawi proindependence project and foster women's resistance.[13]

As a revolutionary movement, POLISARIO is not alone in using the promise of gender equality to recruit activists. Focusing on sub-Saharan Africa's independence movements, Joyce Chadya finds that the support of African nationalists for women's rights was merely an empty political strategy to attract women to the nationalist cause. Women, postindependence, remain subordinate, she argues.[14] Cherifa Bouatta notes a similar phenomenon in Algeria, where the female freedom fighters in the war against France were left disappointed at their postconflict marginalization.[15] Both Sherna Berger Gluck and Andrea Khalil suggest that this is a wider "Third World" pattern, in which nationalist movements have made promises to women only to break them upon achieving independence.[16] What are not well researched are the potentially less cynical motivations of the (male) nationalist leaders—is it possible that Saharawi nationalists promised gender equality not only because of political strategizing but also because women inspired them to do so? Aili Mari Tripp has illustrated how violent conflicts in Africa inspire gender equality, since women in war play roles that undermine traditional gender norms. Women then fight to retain their new positions in society after the guns are laid to rest.[17] In this book, I show that greater gender equality can also be an outcome of *nonviolent* movements in that women's actions and demands inspire (male) nationalist leaders. On the other hand, comparing the POLISARIO's case with those of the gendered discourses of the numerous, competing nationalist movements that emerged in Spanish Guinea, and after independence, the nationalist discourses of the Nguema regimes, allows me to ask in more general terms if the ideological employment of gendered nationalist discourse can quell, as well as foster, certain forms of women's resistance.

Using the example of Idi Amin's Uganda, Alicia Decker has powerfully shown how gender is central to authoritarian rule.[18] Other research has more specifically illustrated the centrality of so-called gender equality to the longevity of authoritarianism. For example, Madawi Al Rasheed's discussion of the Saudi case shows how the state uses the fierce debate over gender equality to divert attention away from calls for political reform.[19] Jasmin Lorch and Bettna Bunk illustrate how regimes in Algeria and Mozambique use so-called gender equality as a legitimization strategy, buying international support and thereby increasing the rulers' soft power.[20] Andrea Khalil has noted the same of Ben Ali's Tunisia, while Amina Mama has shown how Nigerian military regimes gained international praise through promising "women's development" but simultaneously reinforced military rule.[21] In the words of Samia Errazzouki and Maryam Al-Khawaja, dictators have acted as "fake feminists" by showcasing a few exceptional, politically powerful women in order to project an external image of progressiveness, while concurrently taking no action to ameliorate the situation of the disenfranchised and marginalized female masses.[22] Research has also shown a similar strategy from Western states and corporates acting in the Global South. Wars, neocolonial interventions, and resource plunder, from Iraq to Afghanistan, are dressed as interventions to "save" women living in misogynous societies, while the militarization of women's lives in reality has devastating consequences.[23] "Gender equality" is likewise at the center of external-facing state discourses in Western Sahara, Morocco, and Equatorial Guinea. While the POLISARIO has arguably made efforts to further gender equality to match the external "progressive" image that helps the proindependence movement build allies abroad, the same cannot be said of Obiang or arguably of Moroccan king Mohammed VI. Applying the concept of *genderwashing* to the actions of Obiang, Mohammed VI, and their partners helps to show why.

Corinne L. Mason developed the concept of genderwashing to show how lip service to gender equality is used to justify imperialist military interventions.[24] I stretch the concept further in this book to encompass not just neocolonial wars but also partnerships of neocolonial states and authoritarian regimes in resource plunder. The idea of genderwashing is rooted in the better-known environmentalist concept of *greenwashing*. This is the process by which green marketing is used deceptively to promote the perception that a company's policies, products, or aims are environmentally friendly. Take Nestlé's "ecobottle," for example. Nestlé gives its plastic bottle a green-sounding name to attract environmentally conscientious consumers. However, its bottled-water industry damages watersheds, adds plastics to landfills, and deprives indigenous communities of access to drinking water sources. I argue that Obiang (and to some extent Mohammed VI) and his Western corporate and state partners use so-called gender equality in much the same way: they abuse women's rights and yet simultaneously convince us that they are promoting women's empowerment in order to attract investment, increase legitimacy abroad, and divert international attention from the women resisting their actions.[25] Indeed, in this book, I aim to further research on genderwashing by, on the one hand, illuminating how genderwashing serves to silence resistance and, on the other hand, showing that these two phenomena—Southern authoritarian regime genderwashing and Western state and corporate genderwashing—need not be treated separately. In the Obiang case, the authoritarian regime works *in partnership* with Western states and corporates to genderwash their collective abuses.

The Equatoguinean economy has, since 1995, relied on oil. By 2005 the country had become one of sub-Saharan Africa's leading energy exporters and was selling more oil per capita than Saudi Arabia.[26] Over the last few years though, falling oil prices globally have accompanied a steady decline in Equatorial Guinea's oil and natural gas production. In 2013, as the country's oil and gas fields matured, resulting in negative production, Equatorial Guinea's gross domestic product (GDP) began to fall and has continued to do so year after year. This has resulted in further cuts to public spending, which was already meager thanks to huge levels of corruption.[27] What is the relationship between this oil industry and genderwashing? Legitimacy, attracting investment, and dampening resistance are the key ideas here, I argue in this book. By unpicking the gendered stitches that hold together Obiang regime discourses, I can show how genderwashing—by Obiang and his Western partners—holds up the dictatorship.

The Western gaze, legitimacy, investment, and the desire to throw a wet blanket on Saharawi resistance also shape gendered tools of oppression in Moroccan-occupied Sahara. Focusing on the gender of the Moroccan occupation helps me build on the theory of genderwashing that I lay down with the Equatoguinean case. This occupation began over four decades ago. In October 1975 Spain contravened the United Nations (UN) call for self-determination of the Saharawi people and carved up Western Sahara between Morocco and Mauritania in exchange for profits from the Sahara's phosphate mine and access to the Sahara's rich fisheries. Morocco proceeded to invade the territory, bombing the terrified Saharawi population with napalm and white phosphorus ahead of the "Green March" of 350,000 Moroccan civilians seeking to "reclaim" the Sahara in a bid of fervent patriotism. This jingoism emerged from a desire to recover a "Greater Morocco," of which Western Sahara was allegedly just one limb. Mauritania, and parts of northeastern Mali and southwestern Algeria, were the other butchered body parts. Hassan II, the late father of the current monarch Mohammed VI, masterminded and orchestrated the nationalist fervor. It was a risky but final chance to breathe oxygen into his ill regime, which suffered from chronic social inequalities, constant political challenges, and general dissent. The king painted the "reclaiming" of the Sahara as an anticolonial endeavor and a symbol of the nation's strength.[28] And indeed, the "retaking" brought a sense of national unity, increasing his popularity and the stability of his position as ruler.

Upon the invasion, dozens of thousands of Saharawis fled to the southwestern corner of neighboring Algeria's desert, where the POLISARIO declared a state-in-exile named the Saharawi Arab Democratic Republic (SADR). This state in exile, as well as serving as a refugee camp, became a place to develop POLISARIO's vision of Saharawi nationhood. These camps are therefore an ideal site for analyzing how, and to what extent, POLISARIO's ideological discourses on gender equality play out in practice. Likewise, this is a space where women mount resistance to the occupation from a distance, while simultaneously contesting sexism and other discriminations. Spain, too, is a diaspora for Saharawi activists, and resistance played out in the ex-colonial metropolis further underlines the intricate relationship between Western hegemonic discourse on gender and gender equality in the "backward" Muslim, Arab, and African world and Saharawi gendered resistance tactics. Paying attention to women's struggles in these diasporas can, therefore, potentially reveal new lessons on the relationship between gender and resistance. Other studies have shown how Western orientalist views of women in the Global

South undermine, underrate, and patronize the latter.[29] Equatoguinean and Saharawi women are also made victims of such condescension, but in this book I show how women activists have sometimes shrewdly managed to use orientalist discourses to their advantage.

By 1979 the POLISARIO was moving toward a checkmate, forcing Mauritania to retreat (Mauritania has since formally recognized the SADR) and pushing Morocco into a small corner: the resource-rich "Useful Triangle" in the north. Yet, with the concealed help of its main allies France, the United States, and Saudi Arabia, Morocco continued in its colonial aspirations, driving back POLISARIO fighters by constructing a large barrier commonly known as the "berm" that bisects Western Sahara.[30] This berm consists of twenty-seven kilometers of defensive walls three to four meters high, patrolled by 130,000 Moroccan soldiers, and is surrounded by minefields for its entire length. It is the longest active military wall in the world, dividing the Saharawis who did not escape during the 1975 invasion (approximately half the residents included in a 1974 Spanish census) from both the Saharawi territories controlled by the POLISARIO and from those who now live in exile in the refugee camps of the Algerian desert.[31]

Currently, the Saharawis remain a people left out in the cold by the international community. The POLISARIO does control a strip of Western Sahara, although it is speckled with landmines. Were the refugees to move there, they might risk bombings from Morocco; thus, while some Saharawis spend the spring shepherding their cattle in the oases of the "liberated territories," the POLISARIO is reluctant to resettle the refugee population.

At the time of writing, eighty-five states have recognized the SADR. Sweden came close to being the first Western state to do so in October 2015, but the need to export flat-packed furniture unscrewed the deal: Morocco counterthreatened to cancel the scheduled opening of the first IKEA on its soil. Sweden dropped its proposal, and IKEA ushered in its first Casablanca customers in March 2016. No state in the world recognizes Moroccan sovereignty over Western Sahara.

POLISARIO, recognized by the UN as the official representative of the Saharawi population, will accept no less than its legitimate right (endorsed by the UN since 1964 when the Spanish Sahara was added to the list of Non-Self-Governing Territories) to a self-determination referendum with the option of independence for its people. Mohammed VI will accept nothing more than limited autonomy for Saharawis. He claims that Western Sahara has always been part of Morocco, referring to it as its "Southern Provinces." Morocco took this claim to the International Court of Justice (ICJ) in 1975, requesting an Advisory Opinion that would help consolidate its invasion legally. However,

Morocco had scarce evidence for its assertions, and the ICJ did not issue the opinion that Morocco hoped for. The court concluded "that the materials and information presented to it do not establish any tie of territorial sovereignty between the territory of Western Sahara and the Kingdom of Morocco or the Mauritanian entity. Thus the Court has not found legal ties of such a nature as might affect the application of General Assembly resolution 1514 (XV) in the decolonization of Western Sahara and, in particular, of the principle of self-determination through the free and genuine expression of the will of the peoples of the Territory."[32]

Nevertheless, Morocco continues to ignore the ICJ, the UN Charter, and numerous UN Security Council and UN General Assembly resolutions, which have all stressed the nonexistence of precolonial sovereignty links between the Saharawi tribes and the Moroccan sultanate and the current international status of the Western Sahara as a Non-Self-Governing Territory.

Today, pro-Moroccan positions on the conflict still focus on the historic existence of a Greater Morocco, in which the peoples that today call themselves Saharawis pledged allegiance to historic Moroccan rulers. As Tara Deubel points out, to comprehend this position, one should bear in mind that notions of nationhood in the Islamic world prior to colonialism were different to those of Europe and, indeed, to today's hegemonic understandings of nationalism. In precolonial Morocco, the sultanate drew sovereignty from tribal allegiance to it and was built on the foundation of a religious bond of Islam. A key task of the sultanate was to collect taxes from allied tribes.[33] Some nomadic *qabā'el* (tribes), whose descendants today call themselves Saharawi, did indeed form temporary allegiances with the Moroccan sultanate, in exchange for goods or assistance against enemies.[34] However, Tony Hodges asserts that such pledges "were both exceedingly rare and of very little and short-lived practical significance" and that "no attempt was ever made by even the strongest of Moroccan rulers to administer or tax these tribes."[35] Contrary to this, Antonio Pazzanita finds that some Tekna *qabā'el*, including the Ait Oussa (who today reside in southern Morocco), did indeed pay taxes to the Moroccan sultan at one time.[36]

Both Morocco and Mauritania cited cultural and ethnic ties with the people of Western Sahara when attempting to justify their 1975 invasion. With regard to the Moroccan claims, philologist Harry Norris argues that there were such ties between the Saharawi *qabā'el* that ventured as far north as the Draa River in southern Morocco and the Berber tribes that lived there. Nevertheless, he also reasons that Mauritania's claim of cultural and ethnic ties between its citizens and Saharawis were far more convincing than Morocco's.[37] Hodges eloquently manages to recognize these links while simultaneously delineating an ethnic and cultural distinctiveness for Saharawis:

As men of the desert, great camel-herding nomads and speakers of the Hassaniya dialect of Arabic, the Saharawis did, in a broad cultural sense, regard themselves as a very different people from the predominantly Tashelhit-speaking sedentary or seminomadic Berbers to their immediate north, in the Noun, the Bani and the Anti-Atlas. The Saharawis were, of course, only a branch of the *beidan*, the Hassaniya-speaking nomads of mixed Arab, Berber and black African ancestry who lived in the vast desert expanses between the Noun and the valleys of the Senegal and the bend of the Niger; but they had a certain distinctiveness, and the *Ahel-es-Sahel*, the people of the Atlantic littoral, an especially arid zone whose *qabael* had never been subservient to either the sultans of Morocco or Mauritanian emirs to the south.[38]

Those today in favor of a Moroccan Sahara argue that Saharawi nationalism is the daughter of Algerian ideological mechanisms and funding. Algeria, of course, would benefit from an allied, independent Western Sahara, which could loan it a route to the Atlantic and counterbalance the power of its regional enemy Morocco. Indeed, many Moroccans see the conflict as a power struggle with an Algerian rival, and thus the Green March lives on in the nation's memory, serving as a rallying point for Moroccan patriotism.[39] Algeria has provided arms and exile for the POLISARIO. However, the leading scholars of Saharawi nationalism find that POLISARIO's genesis was organic and Saharawi led, and they decry the exaggeration of the Algerian role.[40] As will become clear in later chapters, my own research likewise finds little role for Algeria when delineating the factors that push Saharawis toward nationalist activism and sentiment.

Supporters of the Moroccan position draw on *realpolitik* to justify their position. The loss of the Sahara could destabilize the Moroccan regime and, thereby, the entire Magreb region. Furthermore, a Saharawi state could be a failed one—Saharawis have no real experience of rule. Yet Saharawis have attempted to discount such arguments not only in rhetoric but also in practice: the refugee camps are extremely unusual in that they have never been administered by aid agents but always by refugees themselves. The latter have, over the last four decades, shown their ability to run a state in exile in harsh climatic conditions, with very little financial resources. Likewise, the 2010 Gdeim Izik protest camp (discussed in chapter 3) was, said one camp inhabitant, "an experience through which we showed the world that we could rule ourselves. Saharawis can govern. We can lead a country. Because just us, without the POLISARIO, without educated people who practice politics in government, we created a small country. It was disciplined; everyone had his or her rights. We had our own police in the camp. We had medical centers. It was a small country. It was magnificent."[41]

At the time of writing, the diplomatic drain blockage continues. An ineffective UN has been unwilling to impose a solution.[42] It is paralyzed first and foremost by Morocco's closest friend France but also by Spain, which is threatened by Morocco's ability to open the gates of "fortress Europe" as well as tensions over Ceuta and Melilla.[43] Other restrainers of UN action are the United States, which works with Morocco in its "war on terror," and a handful of African states that are offered "development assistance" for supporting Morocco's position on Western Sahara.[44] Morocco has taken advantage of the stagnant waters of UN diplomacy to alter the makeup of the Occupied Territory politically, economically, and demographically, as well as to illegally exploit the territory's immense natural resources.

The postcolonial dictatorial regimes of Macías Nguema and Obiang Nguema are also characterized by stolen treasures. The two dictators are regularly described by international critics as among the worst human rights abusers in Africa.[45] Their form of rule is known by their opponents as *ngueismo*. The reign of terror of Macías, which persisted from the country's independence until 1979, oversaw the collapse of the country's economy, the attempted genocide of the Bubi people, and the executions of thousands of Macías's opponents. A third of the Equatoguinean population fled to exile. In her play *Antigone*, a modern version of the Greek classic, Trinidad Morgades Besari models her tyrannical President on Macías:

PRESIDENT: What does God matter to me? They offended me. To death with the well-being of the people! What they want is power. I have power now, they won't have it. Me, only me, I'm the blessed one, I'm the chosen one, I'm the great one, I'm the father. I will retain power like my life. They will take my life if they want power. They have to obey me. I am authorized to have power.
ANTIGONE: The people have given you power to do good for the people.[46]

Macías's nephew staged a coup and took over power in 1979. For a short while, he was the fool's gold of the many Equatoguineans who hoped for a better future. Feminist Trifonia Melibea Obono Ntutumu describes the mentality of Equatoguinean women upon the 1979 Obiang coup d'état: "At first, the 1979 coup d'état awoke a spectacular interest and a lot of hope for many women; it was thought that both political repression and sexist discrimination had come to an end. But the wait became eternal; the majority of traditional customs that had for years restricted the individual and civil rights of women are still being conserved. The system is maintaining its hold."[47]

Obiang has proved little better than his uncle. While theoretically the country is a multiparty democracy, elections have generally been considered opaque, and Obiang, along with his close family and friends, maintains almost complete control over the political and economic life of the country, funded by the sales of oil to foreign multinationals.[48]

To borrow Clifford Geertz's expression for pithily describing Saudi Arabia, Equatorial Guinea is nowadays "a family business disguised as a state," or a state of family *caudillismo*, in which suspected political opponents are subject to arbitrary arrest and torture.[49] Resistance to *ngueismo* differs from that of Saharawis challenging the Moroccan occupation in tactics and, at first sight, in gender. Unlike in Western Sahara where public streets protests, dominated by women, are a weekly (sometimes daily) occurrence, in Equatorial Guinea loud, highly visible resistance is rare and male dominated. But as in colonial times, that is not to say that women do not have their own ways of challenging the power structures that oppress them. In part 3 I focus on resistance to authoritarianism in occupied Western Sahara and Equatorial Guinea, asking why the most visible forms of resistance are dominated by different genders in the two countries.

But what do I mean by "resistance" and why study it? The term is eloquently defined by Stellan Vinthagen as "acts of defiance or opposition by a subordinate individual or group of individuals against a superior individual or set of individuals."[50] In her pioneering work *Politics of Piety*, Saba Mahmood asks why Western feminists have focused so fixedly on Muslim women's resistance to patriarchy. She rightly cautions against this trend in research interest, since it risks reinforcing the Western orientalist views of Islam that have been recently used to, for example, justify warmongering in Afghanistan (Islam has a "backward" approach to women's rights, therefore the progressive West must wage war in order to "save" Muslim women). Mahmood also highlights the risks in assuming that all women, universally, are naturally inclined to resist subordination. Indeed, her own fieldwork shows how participants in the Egyptian women's piety movement practice agency through promoting, rather than resisting, some patriarchal norms. Given Mahmood's warnings, why select the topic of women, gender, and resistance for this book? I do so precisely because of these Western orientalist norms concerning "gender equality" in the Global South. If we fail to tell the stories of women who resist the Western-backed authoritarian regimes of Morocco and Equatorial Guinea, then it remains easy for the West to continue its harmful role in these regions using precisely the false excuse of "gifting gender equality." Failing to listen and recount makes us complicit in the silencing of women's resistance. Furthermore, the orientalist norms that Mahmood refers to are, as I argue in this book, at the center of how authoritarian regimes are maintained and influence the tactics of women resisters.

But local gender norms, as well as orientalist ones, can determine the strategies of those who resist. Indeed several studies have shown how hegemonic femininity has facilitated activism. One case is that of the so-called mothers and grandmothers of the Plaza de Mayo, who use their status as mothers to protest against, and highlight internationally, the forced disappearance of their children.[51] The Argentinian women's gendered role as mothers inspires their resistance and is at the center of the symbology employed in their activism. For example, the mothers wear white headscarves in recollection of babies' diapers. On the other hand, research on Arab and African contexts illustrates how activists challenge and break down hegemonic gender norms through their resistance to authoritarianism. For example, Nadje Al-Ali has highlighted how women in several countries pushed the boundaries of what was socially acceptable for their gender while resisting authoritarianism during the Arab Spring.[52] Similarly, Samia Al Nagar and Liv Tønessen have highlighted the key role Sudanese housewives played in the overthrow of the Nimeiri regime when they began occupying (hitherto male) political spaces leading street demonstrations.[53] Frances Hasso's research on Palestinian women's resistance to Israeli occupation illustrates that activists have both reinforced and subverted gender roles: women have taken on socially constructed masculine roles in militias while also carrying out traditional "women's work" of nursing the wounded and caring for the relatives of prisoners.[54] In part 3 I follow Hasso's nuanced approach by illustrating that women sometimes conform to, but at other times adapt and subvert, their gendered roles while resisting authoritarian regimes. However, I also add to the debate, first by showing how women use gendered roles as a spiritual defense in the face of the most brutal authoritarian violence and, second, by arguing that activists furthermore react to, and make use of, false Western conceptions about their local gendered roles to further their resistance aims. Before beginning this analysis, I describe below the data collection methods and theoretical framework used to produce this research.

## From a Camel's Green Teeth to a Bonfire of Archives: Methodology

Limam Boicha's father was born in the year of the Camel's green teeth.[55] When his mother was about to give birth, her family's herd fell down with a mysterious dental infliction.[56] This is how older Saharawis mark time, with events instead of calendar years. Likewise, Saharawis have had their own ways of recording history through epic poems and sagas passed from grandparents to little ones, without ink ever meeting a page. As these traditions fade, and the older generations pass, Saharawi history erodes. For the historical parts of my book, then, talking to older people becomes a source as rich as any archive, and a privileged and disappearing one.

When in the camps and occupied Western Sahara, I waited for appointments. Sometimes for hours, sometimes for days. While waiting, I talked to people who had been waiting a lot longer, for whom time, which stretches out in order to contain the hope that is needed to endure over forty years in exile, is elastic. These unlimited and unrushed conversations are precious for a researcher, and thus I draw here on unrecorded informal interviews and conversations (conversations held in the knowledge that they would inform this work and with permission to include the conversations as data) with activists, refugees, "ordinary" citizens, political leaders, and government officials (these are cited as "personal conversations") and email exchanges ("personal communications").

As well as semistructured interviews focused on specific topics, I also used interviews to collect oral histories.[57] The advantages of oral histories are multiple. We can "rediscover" women without the filter of the colonial administration and hear memories with all the (meaningful) emotions and silences that accompany them. On the other hand, the reader receives only my own interpretation of an interviewee's words.[58] Plus, memories are invariably partial and on occasions contradictory and inaccurate.[59] Yet it is possible to cross-check factual information between several interviewees and, where available, written documentation. In any case, as Alicia C. Decker points out, ellipsis and "errors" can still show how women remembered and experienced particular historical events, revealing the subjective aspects of history as meaning.[60]

The majority of interviews and conversations that inform this book were undertaken during fieldwork trips, which also constituted opportunities to carry out participant observation, to the Saharawi camps in Algeria in 2006 (Smara camp), 2008 (Smara and Rabouni camps), and 2015 (Boujdour and Auserd camps); to the POLISARIO-controlled territory (Tifariti) in 2006; to the Moroccan-occupied territory (El Aaiún) in 2014; to Morocco in 2014 (Agadir, Marrakech, and Rabat); to Equatorial Guinea in 2015 (Malabo); and among exiled communities of refugees and economic migrants in Spain in 2013–16 (Granada, Madrid, Jaen, Seville, and Zaragoza). All interviews with Equatoguineans were conducted in Spanish. Interviews with Saharawis were conducted in Spanish, English, and Hassania, depending on the language of preference of the interviewee. Interviews in Hassania were conducted with the help of a translator. The ethical issues associated with this fieldwork, especially the period spent in the risky context of Moroccan-occupied Western Sahara, are vast and profound. I need far more space than a section in this book could offer to discuss these sufficiently. I therefore refer the interested reader to other work on research ethics that takes my fieldwork as a case study.[61]

Because of limits on permissions and questions of personal and participant safety, some of these fieldwork trips were shorter than I had originally planned. This explains my use of an interdisciplinary toolbox of data collection methods. Complementing participative observation with recorded oral histories, social-science-inspired interviews, archival materials, cultural sources, and politically motivated texts provides, I believe, the most watertight data with which to respond to my research questions.

The bibliography lists in full the details of interviews that have made this work possible. The reader will notice that I have been informed by sixty-eight interviews, personal communications, and discussion groups with Saharawis, yet only thirty-two such encounters with Equatoguineans. This bias in data is reflected in the attention paid to the two cases in the chapters that follow. Although there are significant difficulties in carrying out fieldwork in occupied Western Sahara that I have outlined elsewhere, fieldwork and indeed access to Equatorial Guinea is not straightforward for a British citizen at the time of writing.[62] While I have had unrestrained access to POLISARIO's own archives and am fortunate enough to have several colleagues working on the gendered aspects of Western Sahara's history and present with whom to engage and share ideas, some relevant archives of Equatorial Guinea's history have been literally burnt, and memories of some eras of the country's history are still politically dangerous to recall (see chapter 6 for further information). This book is, therefore, not an equally weighted story of two countries.

Nevertheless, despite the drawbacks that such an imbalance brings, I still believe it is crucial to include the Equatoguinean case, which remains, in relative terms, criminally invisible in academia. This book departs from a lonely runway: I know of *no* works that have explored Equatoguinean women's resistance to the Macías dictatorship or to the current Obiang regime in any depth, nor are there historiographies of women's participation in the anticolonial struggle. Like many first efforts, with this exploration and historiography of Equatoguinean women's resistance comes gaps that I hope will be challenged and filled by other researchers as (or if) the political situation improves.

Using archives has the advantage of making fewer intrusions in the lives of Saharawis and Equatoguineans. The majority of archival documents consulted were published in Spanish, bar the POLISARIO schoolbooks that I consulted that were published in Arabic and the English-language documents of the British Consul. An overview of the archives consulted is included in the back matter of this book.

I use critical discourse analysis (CDA) to interpret data collected through my fieldwork. Rooted in theories of hegemony and the relationship between discourse and power, CDA marries well with a theoretical framework informed by feminism and subaltern studies.[63] The concern for the social and political intentions of CDA, and the necessity of allying oneself with those who most suffer from domination and inequality, make it particularly attractive for a feminist project.[64] Indeed, relevant to this methodology is feminist anthropology's favoring of a focus on women, power relations, and sexual asymmetry and its philosophy that the primary purpose of research should be to counter women's oppression.[65]

The principle unit of analysis for CDA is text. Following Laclau and Mouffe, I understand "text" to be not just written texts and speeches and the contexts in which they are produced but rather all social practices, in that discourses as discursive practices are synonymous with social relations.[66] All actions and social practices are understood here as text and as being meaningful, and their meanings are understood as a product of historically specific systems of rules. The social practice of bridewealth is a "text" just as much as a speech by President Obiang denouncing homosexuality. CDA is therefore well suited to the interdisciplinary data collection methods that I employ: ethnographic fieldwork, oral histories, interviews, archival documents, and political propaganda can all be treated as "texts."

CDA involves establishing the context of the text under analysis, including why it was produced, by whom, and—crucially—in what sociopolitical, cultural, and historical setting. Several other factors should be taken into account according to the genre and the format of the text. For example, with an Equatoguinean state news report, grammar features and rhetorical and literary features may be important. Such reports, as well as written transcripts of interviews with activists, can be coded thematically. Once texts are broken down in this way, I interpret them using a feminist framework.

Neither Saharawi women nor Equatoguinean women are homogenous groups, and likewise, the views of Saharawis and Equatoguineans who call themselves feminists are far from unified. To transmit the multiplicity of feminist voices in the two cases, I find it more useful to draw on a flexible mix of feminisms rather than situating myself squarely within one feminist "band." The boundaries of such feminist groupings are blurred in any case.

While postmodern feminism helps me to deconstruct gender, and therefore gender hierarchies, and cultural feminism is useful in illustrating how Saharawi and Equatoguinean women revalue "the feminine" as a form of resistance, so-called Third World feminisms and black feminism, which have criticized the ethnocentricity and racism of white feminism, are also key inspirations.[67] I follow Ranjoo Seodu Herr in recognizing that anti-imperialism is a core value of Third World feminist activism and that, for many feminists or indeed feminist nationalists, the achievement of self-determination is more urgent than overcoming internal gender discrimination. Yet I simultaneously heed Seodu Herr's observation that Third World feminists also face a fight against what she calls "patriarchal nationalists" who attempt to authorize the continued subjugation of women by framing struggles against gender discrimination as "inauthentic."[68] Indeed, one of the challenges of this book is to simultaneously ally myself with women who have very different (often conflicting) views and priorities.

The issue of cultural relativism is also salient here. Laura Zahra McDonald summarizes the debate well for feminists: on the one hand, feminism is "eroded by a relativist trend guilty of condoning misogyny for the sake of inclusivity; or through an embracing of diversity," but at the same time "all too often the feminist academy has failed to divorce itself from racist Orientalism."[69] A relativist approach has the advantage of avoiding ethnocentrism as it assumes that there are no "good" or "bad" cultural practices and therefore the researcher should not judge another culture according to her own moral standards. However, attempting to be value free and condoning all cultural practices to avoid the charge of ethnocentrism brings its own problems. In the words of Deniz Kandiyoti, this could potentially involve condoning "all manner of patriarchal excess under the banner of cultural difference."[70] The result can be the uncomfortable situation described by Saharawi writer Lehdia Dafa who regularly calls out sexist practices on her blog: Western women tell her that her complaints are due to her "lack of understanding of Saharawi culture."[71] Furthermore, while some Saharawi women activists have told me they feel pressured to "tone down" their criticisms of what they see as sexism in their society to avoid "hanging the dirty washing in public," my subject position as an outsider gives me a greater (privileged) freedom to write openly. For these reasons I have rejected a totally relativist approach. Instead, I have tried to ask myself why sexisms exist (and I am aware that most of the criticisms I make about Equatoguinean, Saharawi, and Spanish societies in this book could equally be made about my own). This has allowed me to see the intersections between gender-based discrimination, colonialism, authoritarianism, and orientalism more clearly. Indeed, anthropological criticisms of resistance studies are illuminating in this regard. Sherry Ortner, for example, criticizes existing studies of historic and current anticolonial resistance movements for making invisible the internal politics, power hierarchies, and discriminations within such movements, especially when it comes to gender.[72] She finds that scholars tend to brush over such issues for fear of being accused of reproducing colonial discourse. However, Ortner rightly argues, no amount of internal discrimination, inequality, or violence in precolonized societies would justify the horrors inflicted by European colonizers. But our reluctance to deal with the internal politics of resistance movements serves to "thin" resistance studies research and render it inadequate.[73]

I use patriarchy (or, as some Zimbabwean feminists have nicknamed it with a wink, "Patrick") as a tool of analysis.[74] With the decline of grand, structural social theories and the spread of postmodern ideas in an era of neoliberalism, the use of patriarchy as a conceptual tool has been questioned. Butler has rightly criticized universalist and transcultural ideas of patriarchy.[75] However, patriarchy is, if used as a name for a collective of historical and context-specific discourses and resulting practices that ensure male domination, useful for feminist activism. Patriarchy is to many feminist activists what colonialism and capitalism are to the mobilization of race and class consciousness, respectively. It is a conceptual tool that allows us to *politicize* gender norms. Indeed, if unpopular among postmodernists, patriarchy remains a lens of analysis still widely used by many Middle Eastern and African researchers with an interest in feminism and especially by African (and most importantly, by Saharawi and Equatoguinean) feminist activists.[76]

I understand patriarchy not as an essential structure or monolithic entity that has propped up sexist societies in the same way throughout all of history but as a discursive web of power relations that changes shape from community to community, ensures heteronormativity and feminine submission, and as discourses develop and adjust, morphs its form across time. It is always linked to other systems of power such as racism, ableism, and colonialism, is culturally specific, and is in a constant state of instability: where a feminist or antiracist intervention might chip away at one manifestation of patriarchy, another discourse on gender (for example, an orientalist one) may obtain hegemony and thereby create new patriarchal ways of living and seeing the world. I show in chapter 2 how the Spanish colonial intrusion further entrenched some Fang and Bubi patriarchal norms as well as introduced new sexist practices. These morph to form a *postcolonial patriarchy* that constitutes a steeplechase for today's Equatoguinean feminists. Suad Joseph and Susan Slyomovics describe a similar state of affairs in the Middle East and North Africa, where "contemporary patriarchies are products of the intersection between the colonial and indigenous domains of state and political processes."[77]

Throughout the book, I use the term "feminist" to describe women and men who identify themselves as such. However, when it comes to actions or practices, I use the term more broadly, to describe acts that challenge sexism.

"Gender" itself needs some definition. Ifi Amadiume's research on the Igbo peoples of Nigeria suggests that prior to the colonial intrusion, sex and gender were divorced from one another: a "biological" female could be a husband or son.[78] I follow Amadiume in her assertion that gender has no "natural,

biological" underpinning. Inspired by feminist, queer, and postcolonial theories of intersectionality, I understand gender as a fluxing category that is influenced by, and dependent on, other classification systems such as race, sexuality,
age, and ability.[79] Nationality and ethnicity are especially important in considering the construction of Saharawi and Equatoguinean notions of gender,
respectively. Identity is never singular and unified, but fluid, constantly changing, and constituted by its context. Similarly, an individual may experience
oppression owing to several aspects of her identity. For example, racist and sexist discourses may intersect to oppress a black woman, and indeed racism and
sexism are mutually constitutive systems.[80] In brief, an intersectional approach
to gender requires an understanding of the category's multiple and fluid nature
and a capacity to think in many different dimensions simultaneously.[81] Femininity is raced, classed, and constituted by infinite aspects of identity.

The category of woman is a constructed one, but those who identify, or are
identified by others, as women and/or as feminine suffer consequences because
of this identity due to the patriarchal societies in which we live. However,
recognizing that "woman" is not an essential, objective fact does not mean that
we need to move away from using the identity of "woman" as a rallying point
around which to organize feminist activism.[82] I use the category "woman"
throughout this book despite my awareness that it is a constructed one.

Defining what "gender equality," or indeed the related concept of "women's
empowerment," means is equally problematic. Issues such as the equality versus difference debate within feminism and the problematization of the notion
of (Eurocentric) "equality" are salient here.[83] In this book, then, I understand
both concepts in a similar way and in a very wide sense—as the disruption
of discourses that facilitate the subordination of those who are identified as
women or, put more simply, as challenges to sexism. However, I also analyze
Equatoguinean and Saharawi official state understandings (and usages) of "gender equality." In the section that follows, which begins in Western Sahara's
occupied capital El Aaiún, I move on to define my understanding of the terms
and spellings that are most politically explosive in the contexts of Western
Sahara and Equatorial Guinea.

### Laayoune versus El Aaiún: The Politics of Spelling, Transliteration, and Terminology

We always siesta after lunch. One day, I wake to a chorus of beeping car horns.
It sounds more like the morning mash of a multilane roundabout than the usual
lethargic sighs of El Aaiún's overheated side streets. But then, after a creak, clat-
ter, and slamming of multiple car doors, other voices join in. They indicate joy,
not road rage: women ululating, men cheering and laughing, music, chattering.

Maimouna ushers me to the upstairs room with a smile. The man of the house is somehow still sleeping, his arm peacefully resting on his eyes to block out the early evening's afterglow. Maimouna's two little brothers are kneeling at the altar of the beeswax yellow window, which is frosted and embossed for privacy. They peer through a triangular hole. Was the missing shard born of a rowdy childhood game, or was it fruit of the time police sieged the house, I wonder? On Maimouna's request, the two boys each draw to a side, as if in place of the absent curtains, to make room for me.

Through the triangular frame I'm watching a wedding, or rather, a particular stage of a wedding. The guests have arrived at what will be the couple's home together. They file in to admire the color scheme, the cushions and carpets, the white furniture. Later, they'll head around the corner to the party, and they'll be in no haste about the celebrations: we'll hear the wow-wow of the bass and the hammering drums all through the night.

This is a highly unusual wedding, Maimouna tells me. I can almost hear italics in her words when she explains why: the bride's side is *Moroccan*, the groom's *Saharawi*. But what does "Saharawi" mean? And who decides who is "Saharawi" and who is "Moroccan"? The independence referendum was initially blocked, after all, by thousands of Moroccans "pretending" to be Saharawi in order to win a vote.

Of course, "Saharawi" national identity, like all national identities, is an imagined, constructed, and historically dependent one. Its emergence in opposition to Spanish and Moroccan aggressive nationalisms has been well documented by Pablo San Martín.[84] From an anthropological point of view, ethnic Saharawis derive from not only Western Sahara but also south Morocco, Mauritania, southwest Algeria, and sometimes further along the Sahara caravan routes. Indeed, Morocco's vision of a "Greater Morocco," which would incorporate not only all of Western Sahara but also Mauritania, western Algeria, and northwestern Mali, is partly based on claims to cultural and ethnic ties with the peoples of these Saharan countries.[85] Some who today identify as Saharawi derive from enslaved sub-Saharan Africans. Morocco's attempted provincialization of Saharawi culture, in which Saharawi clothes, language, and way of life is subsumed into a patchwork of identities that make up the wider Moroccan national identity, further complicates matters: some second-generation Moroccan settler colonists now refer to themselves, at least to foreign visitors, as Saharawi on the basis that they were born in Moroccan-occupied Western Sahara.[86] Some settlers join Moroccan authorities in their violence against Saharawis. But relations between Saharawis and settlers on a day-to-day level are mostly polite and cordial. Intermarriage is rare, but as the anecdote above attests, it happens. A few settlers quietly sympathize with the

Saharawi nationalist cause. Scholars have even argued that Morocco fears some settlers would vote for POLISARIO rule over Mohammed VI given the chance. But is there a similar range of attitudes among Saharawis? Certainly, not all of them are staunch nationalists. Tara Deubel's work showcases the plethora of Saharawi political opinions. There are those who are stalwartly pro-Moroccan (such as some members of the Ait Oussa tribe in Assa, some of whom fought for Morocco's independence from France, enjoy a middle-class lifestyle, and today identify simultaneously as members of the Ait Oussa tribe, as Saharawis, and as Moroccans); those who have little interest in politics and do not identify as explicitly pro-POLISARIO or pro-Moroccan; those who privately hold proindependence, nationalist views but express pro-Moroccan views in public to avoid trouble with police; and those who are actively and publicly proindependence.[87] It is also worth noting that not all nationalists are pro-POLISARIO and that there are (as in any political movement) factions and disagreements within the POLISARIO itself, sometimes forged along tribal lines. While POLISARIO, in an attempt to collapse inequalities and unite the Saharawi population, banned the mention of qabāʾel affiliation at the outset of its nationalist project,[88] Alice Wilson has shown how the social structures of, and tensions between, the qabāʾel have not only resurged but are also today essential to the ability of the SADR to govern the refugee citizens.[89] Likewise, Sébastien Boulay has shed light on the situation of the ralliés. These are ethnic Saharawis who are officially presented by Morocco as "escapees" of the refugee camps in Algeria. In return for upholding this image of themselves as "escapees," swearing allegiance to Mohammed VI, and recognizing Morocco's right to the "southern provinces," the ralliés are offered economic benefits such as housing, civil service jobs, and/or a minimum monthly allowance of around 180 euros, and some are awarded high-profile political positions.[90]

Recognizing, therefore, that some Saharawis are in favor of integration with Morocco, it is, however, impossible to know precisely what proportion of Saharawis worldwide support the independence cause, at least without the realization of the self-determination referendum. Pondering this question, Matthew Porges and Christian Leuprecht have tentatively concluded, "Virtually all available evidence suggests that an overwhelming majority of Saharawis living in the Occupied Territory favor independence from Morocco."[91] Likewise, San Martín estimates that he would not be able to find a single Saharawi who would not vote for independence, at least in the camps. He states, "If [a self-determination referendum on independence] ever takes place, no one is in any doubt about the result of a just and fair consultation."[92] While acknowledging that some Saharawis are pro-Moroccan, my ten years' or so experience of researching and working on the Western Sahara issue leads me to the same tentative conclusion as Porges and San Martín.

As is already evident, I refer to the Moroccan-administered part of Western Sahara as occupied rather than as disputed. This is because "occupied" is the legally correct way to describe the territory.[93] Stephen Zunes has highlighted how France and the United States have gradually altered mainstream understanding of Western Sahara from "occupied" to "disputed."[94] Morocco seeks to accelerate this progressive change. For example, in 2016 it expelled the United Nations for the Referendum in Western Sahara (MINURSO) peacekeepers in retaliation at Ban Ki Moon's having described the territory as "occupied."[95] The gravest issue with such a change in language is the legal implications. A "disputed" territory is not subject to all the clauses of Geneva Convention treaties and protocols that an "occupied" territory is. For example, as Zunes says, in a "disputed" Western Sahara it would not be illegal for Morocco to move settlers into the territory or for Morocco to sell the territory's natural resources.[96] The recent (21 December 2016) case of the POLISARIO versus the European Union (EU) in the Court of Justice of the EU found that EU-Morocco trade agreements that include Western Sahara are illegal, thus underlining once again that Western Sahara is "occupied" rather than "disputed."[97]

In chapter 2, I refer to the indigenous peoples as "Guineans," on the basis that the territory in question was referred to as "Spanish Guinea" rather than "Equatorial Guinea" at the time. For proper nouns, I use the English spelling (e.g., the colonial capital of Spanish Guinea, Fernando Poo in Spanish, becomes Fernando Po in English). The first exception is for the names of Saharawi and Equatoguinean liberation movements, for which I use the transcriptions and abbreviations that are in common use in Britain and Spain, for example, Harakat Tahrir, POLISARIO, and MUNGE (Movement for the National Unity of Equatorial Guinea). The second exception is for institutions of Spanish creation such as the Djemaa in Spanish Sahara and the Patronato in Spanish Guinea, for which I use the Spanish spelling. The third exception is place names in Western Sahara, for which I use the Spanish spelling. European colonial place-names in Western Sahara are still highly political, and the United Kingdom follows the French, not Spanish, place-names for towns there (e.g., Laayoune instead of El Aaiún). When Morocco invaded Western Sahara, Spanish road signs were changed to French. Spanish language, and the Spanish colonial heritage, is a "border marker" between Saharawis and Moroccans, which Morocco would like to erase. Saharawis challenge that, and also aim to constantly remind Spain of its debt of responsibility toward the Saharawi people—legally speaking, Spain is still the *de jure* administrative power. The use of Spanish spellings for place-names is therefore a political act for Saharawis.

I act with them. With regard to other words from the Hassania language (not including the aforementioned Harakat Tahrir or Djemaa), I use the Hans Wehr transliteration system for Arabic, except for letters unique to Hassania.

Sultana Khaya works, today, from Boujdour, occupied Western Sahara. She is president of the Saharawi League for Natural Resources and Human Rights. Since I began the manuscript for this book in October 2013, her young cousin, seventeen-year-old Elfayda Khaya, has also had her eye damaged by Moroccan police. She was protesting against Texas-based energy company Kosmos at the time. In December 2014 Kosmos, along with Edinburgh-based Cairn Energy, became the first companies to drill for oil in Western Sahara's waters, joining a host of British corporations that invest in the Moroccan occupation. Also since I began this book, British Gas (before it was bought by Shell) has entered Equatorial Guinea, becoming yet another sponsor of Obiang's terrifying regime.

It is hard to exaggerate the oppression that exists in Equatorial Guinea and Western Sahara. One more parallel that I have yet to mention is that both countries regularly make the nongovernmental organization (NGO) Freedom House's annual top "worst of the worst" list of the least free places in the world.[98] Indeed, although the two case studies are ideal for teasing out the relationship between gender and resistance, they were not only chosen for aforementioned scholarly purposes but also for activist ones. While there are scant studies of Western Sahara and Equatorial Guinea published in English, we cannot deny that Britain, Europe, and the United States, and indeed British, European, and US citizens (on the basis that we consume produce plundered from Saharawis and Equatoguineans), hold a stake in the fates of the peoples of both countries. As I argue throughout the book, this is particularly the case for Saharawi and Equatoguinean women—the United Kingdom and other Western governments directly, and consumers unwittingly and indirectly, contribute to their oppression along gendered as well as racial and neocolonial lines. I hope therefore that this book can make a small contribution to lifting the invisibility cloak that silences the oppression, and resistance, of Saharawis and Equatoguineans.

# PART ONE

# Spanish Colonialism and Indigenous Women's Resistance

# CHAPTER ONE

# Spanish Sahara, Falangistas, and Gendering Subaltern Studies

Tawfa Saleh sits in a smaller-than-usual emergency *ḥaīma* (Saharawi tent), which replaces the adobe house that crumbled to nothing in floods, like sugar dissolving in tea, a month earlier. Empty cardboard boxes from the foreign aid branch of Spanish La Rioja's autonomous region sit piled in the corner, waiting for a new use. Tawfa sprinkles incense on the lisping coals. The scent tangles pleasantly with that of the smoke as she offers blankets to protect from the December cold. White sunlight spills into the tent as Silka Bilaal, Tawfa's sister-in-law, steps through the curtain carrying the clinking tin tea tray, pot, and glasses.

When asked of her past, Tawfa smiles and wipes away a tear. She never got the chance to tell her husband that she had found his hidden POLISARIO pamphlets or that she too was secretly a member of a POLISARIO cell. After her partner died on the front line, Tawfa refused to remarry. She lives today in Auserd camp with Silka.

Silka was also a nationalist activist in "Spanish Sahara." Silka recalls "those days" with a smile that shows all her teeth. "Those days," she says, meaning those of the late sixties and early seventies, those that were marked by studies with the Spanish Falange's Women's Section, those that saw her initiation into political activism, those before the exile, were "a fantastic period in [her] life."[1]

This chapter focuses on "those days" from a gendered perspective. I draw on the archives of the Spanish Falange Party's Women's Section, intriguing as a record of how female colonialists attempted to impose a Falangist model of womanhood on Saharawi women and girls, to reveal a plethora of resistance tactics, from the everyday to organized politics. From the perspective of Western Sahara studies, an analysis of the gender dynamics of the Spanish colonial

period reveals new insights. Perhaps most importantly, it illustrates that Saharawi women not only resisted the racism and sexism of colonialism but also
Saharawi patriarchal elements and, in the case of women and men of sub-
Saharan origin, slavery. This, I argue, makes a small but significant contribution
to correcting a common omission in subaltern studies: the invisibility of, and
resistance to, oppressions that exist among and between subalterns themselves
and how these interacted with the colonial axes of power. Also, the evidence
of these resistances sheds new light on the inspiration behind POLISARIO-
constructed nationalist discourses that emphasized gender equality and eradication of slavery. Studies to date, including my own, have neglected to focus
on the role of Saharawi women in inspiring the feminist, emancipatory discourses formulated by POLISARIO leaders as well as on the effects of these in
inspiring women's public participation in anticolonial activities.

### Spain Arrives in Western Sahara:
### Gendering a Territory

The borders of Spanish Sahara were demarcated between Spain and France in
1900,[2] following the Berlin conference of 1884, in which the European powers
sliced up and dished out Africa as if it were a cake.[3] "Poor Cinderella, still lick-
ing its wounds from the war of independence" in the Americas, Spain was
delighted to have new colonial "children" in the Sahara.[4] However, it took several decades before Spain could establish itself there because of the consider-
able resistance mounted by Saharawi *qabā'el.*[5]

In the eighteenth and early nineteenth centuries, several Spanish, Portuguese, French, English, and North American sailors who washed up on stormy,
foggy, menacing Cape Bojador (part of the coastline of modern-day Western
Sahara) were enslaved by a people whom they called the "wild" and "wander-
ing" Arab pastoralists.[6] These capturers of shipwreck survivors were, significantly with regard to Morocco's historic claims to Western Sahara, "under no
state's control" (as opposed to the settled, "trading" Arabs of the Moroccan
sultanate) and were a presence feared by early would-be European colonists.[7]
As for the Spanish colonists who purposefully landed on the "dangerous" coast
after the Berlin conference, resistance to their intrusions were fierce. For example, Diego Saavedra y Magdalena, ex-commissioner for the Spanish possessions
in Western Africa, describes an attack on the Spanish settlement at Villa Cisneros (modern day Dakhla) in 1885 in which "the rapacity of the indigenous"
caused the death of several Spaniards.[8] Julio Cervera's account of his 1886 expedition to Western Sahara is similarly painted as an ordeal. Cervera's blunder-
ings about the desert ceased dramatically when he and his fellow expedition
members were kidnapped. Saharawi men threatened to rob the latter's camels

and luggage, while the "demands and curses" of Saharawi women metaphorically castrated Cervera.[9]

Spain could only find a foothold in Western Sahara by gradually negotiating with Saharawi *qabā'el* leaders.[10] For example, as the colonial bureaucrat Francisco del Río Joan notes, the founding of Villa Cisneros was only completed thanks to a local *qabīla*. The latter was given twenty houses in return for its support in building a fort, the purpose of which was to protect the Spaniards from the frequent raids of other Saharawi *qabā'el*.[11]

Apart from Cervera's grumblings at the psychological resistance mounted by the Saharawi women in whose camp he was forced to stay, the majority of the colonial pioneers describe Saharawi resistance in terms that construct the latter as masculine. And the construction is of a violent and *uncivilized* masculinity, therefore implicitly justifying a colonial, "civilizing" mission. Río Joan saw the Saharawis encountered during his attempted "commercial and military penetration" (itself a masculine sexual metaphor typically used by European colonialists, as Anne McClintock has highlighted) of Western Sahara as "hostile, war-mongering and ferocious.[12] Saavedra y Magdalena saw "the indigenous" as "strong, vigorous . . . sober . . . [and] maintaining a hatred of Christians," while Soler described them as "virile, tough, even hostile."[13] The geographical territory, on the other hand, was seen through a haze of colonial bravado, eroticism, and machismo. The orientalist brushes of the colonizers painted the desert as an enticing and exotic woman, passively waiting to be seduced (conquered) by an epic, male, white hero: "The dune is welcoming, hospitable, with feminine softness and tenderness, smooth even when the soft wind caresses her crests."[14]

Despite all this bravura, however, even once their hold on the territory was firmly established, the colonizers were cautious of interfering too much with the political and social structures of the Saharawi *qabā'el* lest it lead to more violent conflict.[15] Unlike in Guinea, there had been no missionary presence in the Sahara to colonize minds and subdue the potential of resistance ahead of the entrance of the Spanish army and commercial interests. For example, one indicator of the different levels of enforced acculturation in Guinea and Sahara lies in the field of colonial education: by the end of the colonial period in Equatorial Guinea, more than 90 percent of children were in Spanish schools. In 1975 in Spanish Sahara, on the other hand, just 3,640 Saharawi pupils (of which only 575 were girls) were in the Spanish schools.[16] This was a small proportion, given that the adult population according to the Spanish census of 1974 was 74,000. Most controversially, the Spanish policy of "noninterference" included actively tolerating Saharawi enslavers of sub-Saharan Africans.[17]

From Hidden Tactics to the "Ear-Bite":
Resistance to Enslavement

Shreisher Dahbu, a fictional heroine of Saharawi folktales, faced several obstacles on her adventures. One was a disobedient slave. On a journey in search of Shreisher's long-lost brothers, her slave bathes in a river of milk, turning her black skin white, and forces Shreisher to bathe in a river of tar, making her seem black. When the brothers are finally found, they treat Shreisher as a slave. It is not until meat is served and Shreisher picks the best cuts, while the slave in disguise selects "the insides and the least noble parts of the animal," that the trick is revealed.[18] The brothers carve the guilty slave to pieces.

Of course, the folktale has a racist pedagogy of black "savageness" and seeks to justify one of the most abhorrent manifestations of racism. Read against the grain, though, we also see the story of an enslaved woman (temporarily) outwitting her enslaver and resisting her condition. Such people are the subject of this section.

One factor that encouraged Fang communities to inhabit the continental forests of Equatorial Guinea was "the violent predators," or the "Muslim enslavers," to the north.[19] As early as the fifteenth century, the inhabitants of Western Sahara were trading black slaves with the Portuguese.[20] Later, in Spanish Sahara, says Saharawi writer Larosi Haidar, slavery was an "accepted practice" and the Spanish authorities "did not even lift a finger to attempt to eradicate it."[21] The 1974 census, which avoided publicly demonstrating Spanish complicity in slavery by creating the category "adopted children and poor relatives" under which to lump slaves, found that 4 percent of the population lived in this state.[22]

Sophie Caratini, a French anthropologist who lived among Saharawi nomadic *qabā'el* in 1975, described the status of slaves of sub-Saharan origin in the Saharawi society at the end of the colonial period: "The slave is a prisoner for life. His capacity to work belongs to his owners who use it at their convenience and hold his right to live or die."[23] John Mercer's review of contemporary literature, on the other hand, finds that while some slaves were treated terribly, others were freed after "long meritorious service."[24] According to contemporary accounts collected by journalist Pablo Ignacio de Dalmases, men and boy slaves were used to shepherd animals and gather firewood, while women and girls were used to perform domestic chores and/or were sexually exploited by their owners.[25] Some wealthy Spaniards employed enslaved women as maids in their homes, in the full knowledge that the totality of their wages were passed on to their owners, a pattern that was replicated for enslaved men working in the Nomadic Troops unit of the army, fisheries, and phosphate mines.[26]

If there was not an outright slave rebellion, contemporary accounts suggest that this was because of a combination of harsh discipline and the propagation of a mix of racist myths and religious indoctrination that painted black slavery as natural, inevitable, and the will of Allah.[27] However, the latter of these two tools worked considerably less well on captured slaves (according to Mercer, slave caravans were still passing through Smara as late as 1955),[28] which illustrates the importance of Laclau and Mouffe's modification of Gramsci's theory of hegemony in explaining when and why resistance arises. If hegemony, for Gramsci, is to make power over others seem inevitable and "the natural state of things," Laclau and Mouffe imply that exposure to counter-hegemonic discourses is a necessary precursor to resistance. As opposed to those who were born enslaved, and were therefore indoctrinated from birth into a social discourse that justified their position, captured slaves were of course more easily aware of discourses (from before their capture) that conflicted with the hegemonic ones and saw no natural link between blackness and enslavement. An observation from Caratini illustrates this well: "Escape attempts are mostly carried out by recently acquired captives. Those born in the camps are totally acculturated given that they use the language and respect the customs of their owners, to whom many are sincerely bound."[29]

Indeed, as well as attempted escapes, slaves showed resilience and everyday resistance in the face of their plight. Enslavers feared that slaves (and indeed women) would perform curses on them, which Julio Caro Baroja read as a form of "vengeance" on the part of enslaved peoples and Arab/Berber women resulting from their "inferior" treatment by (enslaving) men.[30] The "ear bite" was another strategy of resistance. An unwritten law among Saharawi enslavers said that, should a slave injure a free person, the owner (enslaver) of the slave must pass the latter to the injured party as a form of reparation. Some enslaved persons used this law to their advantage. If they had a particularly violent owner and met others who treated her or him relatively well, they might injure the ear of the person they wished to become their owner, thus ensuring their own transfer to the property of that person.[31] In a situation of domination, slaves showed resilience with this strategy, finding a way to improve their lives when outright freedom seemed impossible.

Scott, in his theorization of resistance, asserts that while subaltern peoples act in public in ways that seem to endorse and embrace their own subordination (he calls this the *public transcript*), once they are "offstage" and out of the sight of the dominators, the former will mock, bad-mouth, and ridicule their oppressors and the culture that places them as inferior (the *hidden transcript*). A 1935 account from Spanish resident Anicleto Ramos Charco-Villaseñor in Villa Cisneros clearly illustrates the existence of a public and hidden transcript:

"Moors and blacks live, apparently, in perfect harmony, but in their conversations, involuntary perhaps, they show their deep feelings. And upon naming each other, respectively, the scorn of the moor, considering himself superior, is concentrated upon saying, black man! Such scorn is only comparable with the hatred of the black man who, seeing himself humiliated, expresses it when he says, moor!"[32]

Similarly, in 1975 Caratini noted the disparaging opinions of black slaves voiced to her in confidence. One enslaved man said of his enslavers, "They are very racist, very savage and filthy."[33] In the relative security of offstage privacy, slaves voiced their thoughts (the hidden transcript of resistance), but when onstage, they had to maintain the public transcript and show deference to their enslaver to avoid retaliation. At times, when individual slaves could take no more, they openly rebelled (the hidden transcript stormed the public stage, in Scott's terms). There are examples of slaves murdering their enslavers and of enslaved children crying and fighting back when they were mistreated.[34] Others made use of the Spanish population, some of whom were willing to break the official policy of noninterference with what the Spanish authorities called Saharawi "politico-religious customs."[35] Enslaved peoples hid their Spanish-paid wages from their owners to later buy passage on a ship to the Canaries or to pass to a Spanish third party who would buy and then free them.[36]

Slaves found room to maneuver and space to resist throughout the Spanish colonial period and, as the POLISARIO nationalist revolution progressed (at its initiation some POLISARIO members were still enslavers), the perseverance of such a racist institution seemed abominable to the revolutionary movement inspired by the anticolonialist, antiracist, and negritude-influenced currents of the times. As delineated in previous research, the eradication of slavery was another necessary part of the nationalist revolution.[37] Tolerance of slavery was to become something distinctly "un-Saharawi," and the Spanish acceptance of the practice was one more reason decolonization was urgent. In the next section, I look at resistance to gender inequalities in the colonial period, which, coupled with the resistance of the enslaved Saharawis, helps to illustrate how Saharawi women's anticolonial struggles were intersectional, fighting various axes of power at once.

## From Songs to the Courts: Resisting Patriarchies

McClintock argues that colonialism cannot be understood without a theory of gendered power.[38] Colonialism has traditionally been regarded as a male pursuit, in which white women were excess baggage accompanying their adventurous husbands. Some scholars have begun to address this, illustrating that Western women's attitudes toward colonialism ranged from complicity and support to resistance and opposition.[39] Both Equatorial Guinea and Western Sahara prove important studies in this regard, since in both cases, Spain exported its Women's Section for the gendered indoctrination of female colonial subjects by female colonizers. The latter therefore were not mere appendages to male imperialism but rather active colonizers. In this section I ask: how did the Spanish colonialists try to impose their model of what Saharawi femininity should be? Did Saharawi women resist, and if so, how?

The Women's Section of Francisco Franco's Falange Party arrived in El Aaiún in 1964, six years after Spanish Sahara officially became a province of Spain. Although Franco would resolutely avoid it, he was nevertheless aware that the decolonization of the Sahara might be forced upon him (by the UN) in the future. As Andreus Stucki has argued, fostering a sense of belonging to the colonial fatherland among the indigenous population therefore became urgent for the Francoist administration in order to establish preferential industry, commercial, and financial relations for Spain postindependence. But compared to its work in Guinea, Spain was decades behind in its cultural colonization of the Sahara.[40] Women's Section was deployed to help in this work. To put it crudely, Women's Section was there to make Saharawi women more Spanish, contributing to a wider cultural endeavor to coerce the "natives" to replicate the colonists. Publicly though, Women's Section's overarching mission was "the promotion of the Saharawi woman," through "raising awareness of the primordial purpose women have in this life ordered by God: to be a wife, mother and educator of children."[41] In practice, this mission meant molding a role for Saharawi women on the model of the Francoist housewife.

Over the six years between provincialization of the Sahara and the Women's Section's arrival, gradual sedentarization of the Saharawi nomads allowed for increased political, economic, and cultural control. This was an enforced sedentarization: severe droughts, and the colonial constraints that inhibited traditional solutions to such crises, pushed Saharawis to look for work in Spanish urban settlements, which were built around the natural resource hotspots.[42] For example, the provincial capital El Aaiún had just one thousand inhabitants in 1958, but the work opportunities for Saharawis (or better put, imperial plunder opportunities for the colonists) that emerged with the opening of the phosphate mines resulted in great population growth. By 1974 there were eight thousand waged Saharawis in El Aaiún.[43] With the wage earners came their families, and these families in turn constituted a potential audience for colonial education mechanisms, including Women's Section interventions.

However, I should not overestimate the reach of the Women's Section or indeed of the Spanish education system and its other propaganda mechanisms—

I have already argued that these were limited compared with Spanish efforts in Guinea. In this vein, Konstantina Isidoros is right to point out that the extent of coerced Saharawi sedentarization has been exaggerated. She illustrates that the wage-earning opportunities offered by the Spanish administration were, for many of the Saharawis who took them, only temporary responses to the aforementioned droughts, and a significant proportion of the Saharawi population never moved to the cities at all.[44] Nevertheless, although the numbers of Saharawi women who came into contact with the Section were relatively small, the archives of the Women's Section give us an alluring window on an almost all-female site of colonial power and indigenous resistance.

By "Saharawi women," Women's Section generally meant only women of non-sub-Saharan origin, since, in line with the wider colonial policy of the ostrich, the Section made few efforts to challenge the institution of slavery. The archives show but one incident in which Spanish Section staff advocated on behalf of an enslaved woman, and even then it was conditional upon the latter's "good behavior." Describing the first year of the domestic school in El Aaiún, Concha Mateo (the first representative of the Women's Section to arrive in El Aaiún and its subsequent leader for most of the colonial period) notes: "There were two black slaves in this group. The owner of one of them forbade her from attending halfway through the course, the other one came every day and never missed a single class. At the end of the year we brought this problem before the general governor, promising economic support to achieve the freedom of those slave women whose moral behavior was good."[45]

It is clear, then, that at least one black slave woman managed to maintain a public transcript of surface-level collaboration with the Section and thereby secured her own "freedom."[46] Somewhat paradoxically, she appropriated the colonial structures to resist the racism of Saharawi society that enslaved her, and Spanish society that allowed it.

Domestic Schools aimed at adult women initially offered embroidery, cookery, general culture, literacy, machine sewing, hygiene, baby care, and ironing classes.[47] The first was to open in El Aaiún, followed later by schools, or at least "ambulant teachers," in Villa Cisneros, Argut, La Guera, Smara, and Daora. Other initiatives led by the Women's Section included schools for girls, activities circles for girls (members were accompanied on days out to the beach, for example), social workers and health visitors in the major towns, workshops, and a special school for girls with learning difficulties.[48]

While Saharawis, anthropologists, and indeed all other colonialist accounts completely contradict this view of historic gender roles, Mateo claimed that while Saharawi women were responsible for sewing the *āḥīām* (plural of *ḥaīma*, a traditional Saharawi tent) and looking after the children, it was men who did the majority of the cooking and cleaning. Gustau Nerín has highlighted that Women's Section staff also claimed that Guinean men were responsible for cooking and childcare within Guinean society, a conclusion that, he finds, bore no relation to reality (although, significantly, Spaniards employed Nigerian migrant men, whom they called "boys," as domestic servants).[49] Such a conviction was convenient, of course, since it made the case for the Women's Section interventions, which initially focused on domestic chores.[50] Spanish staff felt that a tough job was on their hands in guiding Saharawi women toward "their natural purpose."[51] Indeed, staff were particularly proud of one of their first "great successes": ensuring that their pupils "knew how to clean and iron their respective husbands' suits, if the latter dressed in the European fashion."[52]

Seemingly blind to the inequalities suffered by Spanish women under the regime they represented, the Spanish staff of the Women's Section did not view Saharawi women's position in society with envy.[53] In a brief study on the latter for the central Women's Section office in Madrid, Mateo stated that Saharawi women "had served, throughout their entire history, as nothing more than as gifts for men."[54] Of course, as Enrique Bengochea Tirada points out, such a negative assessment was used by the Women's Section to dubiously justify its colonial intervention in the Sahara.[55] It was an early form of genderwashing, an attempt to make an ugly colonial intervention look selfless and progressive. Just as the British patronizingly espoused in Egypt, for example, Spanish colonialism was necessary to promote "women's empowerment" among the Saharawis, who represented, for the Franco regime, the very picture of "backward," "misogynist" Muslims.[56]

Mateo lamented various perceived gender inequalities surrounding the marriage of girl children to men two to three decades older, restrictions on women's freedom of movement (in particular, it was not seen as proper for girls, once they reached puberty, to continue to take part in sports and other extracurricular activities, while there were very few Saharawi girls compared with boys registered at non–Women's Section, and therefore non-sex-segregated, schools) and unequal custody rights over children after divorce.[57] Mateo, though, did not observe what Sophie Caratini highlights: before marriage in Saharawi society of the early seventies, all girls, reportedly, would have undergone genital cutting, and some would have been fattened in order to ameliorate marriage prospects, practices that the POLISARIO later (and the Spanish never) fought.[58] Nevertheless, in the face of the "inequalities" that she alleged, Mateo noted the constant ability of Saharawi women and girls to negotiate their position, taking advantage of what they could and resisting male domination in their own ways. After listing the problems faced by women, she commented, "It could seem, because of all this, that the woman has no influence in the life of the Sahara.

Well she does. Subterfuges are valued: she pretends to be ill, she escapes, she acts . . . and so she usually gets her own way sometimes."[59] These levers of influence that Mateo identifies are what Scott would call "weapons of the weak," the subtle acts of everyday resistance that are often most opportune for the oppressed in situations of domination, such as was the case for women living in a patriarchal society.[60]

A Women's Section social worker highlighted another case that illustrates Saharawi women's capacity to "play" the traditional and colonial patriarchal systems to reach their wished-for ends. The El Aaiún–based social worker observed:

> In the month of March, the captain chief of the local office of this city sent us a week-old girl who had been abandoned by her mother. The father, who was very old, couldn't look after the baby.
>
> For five days she was kept at the local domestic school, until the mother came to collect her because she had just made an agreement with her husband before the Sharia judge: the ex-husband would have to give her fifteen hundred pesetas every month, so that she could bring up the girl on artificial milk since natural milk wasn't possible. Once this problem had been solved she told us that she had left her daughter because she saw this as the only way that she could get the money she needed.[61]

While Spanish colonialism altered the political landscape in the Sahara, it barely touched the local Islamic judiciary system (legal issues between Saharawis were left for Saharawis to resolve).[62] The Saharawi woman quoted above knew how to manage the two powers. Although the Saharawi mother was economically dependent on her ex-husband, she was nevertheless able to make use of colonial structures just, as we have seen above, like black Saharawi slave women did, to ensure the protection of her baby until she had sought legal justice through the Saharawi judge. Furthermore, she presumably knew the latter would be likely to support her cause since in Islamic law the father must provide *nafaqa* (support) for children in cases where the mother takes custody.[63] She used her knowledge to her own advantage as women in other hassanophone contexts (namely Mauritania) have done. As Majhula Cheikh el Mami told me in an interview, the only schooling she had in Spanish Sahara was in Quranic verse, and yet it "stood [her] in very good stead."[64] Knowledge of the Quran was and is well valued for both girls and boys in hassanophone societies, and mothers, as Corinne Fortier has pointed out with reference to the Mauritanian context, instill in their daughters a strong awareness of their rights with regard to Islamic family law.[65] Caro Baroja noted other cases where a woman used legal structures to claim her rights where *nafaqa* was not paid and where a woman had been mistreated by her husband.[66]

In other cases, when escaping an unhappy situation was all but impossible, there are nevertheless signs that Saharawi women harbored resentment of patriarchal norms and challenges to the same. Coerced marriage is a good example. Although in Saharawi society of the sixties a woman would have more freedom in choosing her second husband if she got divorced, her parents would play a stronger role in selecting her first husband. Marriage was a key guarantor of social cohesion. As Caratini points out, exchanging women in marriage was a crucial form of regulating relations of rivalry, protection, and dependence between men.[67] Well-chosen marriages could keep the peace and forge all-important alliances. That is not to say that all women were content with such arrangements. Some begrudgingly married their parents' choice of husband but showed emotional resistance by harboring secret lovers, by sharing their desires and forbidden love stories with friends,[68] through poetry recited in women-only company, or through music, as the lyrics of this classic song (more than one hundred years old) attest:

Oh mothers and sisters
You married me to an old man
You made my life
A complete misery

Even a young man
Who loves me and whom I love
Why should I marry him
Let alone an old man[69]

Some women reacted more openly. A twelve-year-old Mariam Hassan (who would become one of Western Sahara's most celebrated revolutionary singers), for example, ran away on the day of her wedding when her parents attempted to marry her to an "older man."[70] Mariam was in hiding for three months, her persistent absence eventually pushing her parents to relent. They returned the bridewealth, and Mariam escaped the compromise.[71] Her story has parallels with the successful strategies of women resisting unwanted marriages (purposefully displaying showy symptoms of sorrow and anger such as weeping and refusing to speak to the "culpable" relatives) in the society of the Awlad 'Ali Bedouin shepherds of Egypt, explored by Lila Abu-Lughod. Without wishing to conflate two different cultures, the similarities in the tales of Mariam and the women of Abu-Lughod's study perhaps indicate that Mariam's strategy was no startling exception within Saharawi nomadic society.[72]

Mariam managed a positive outcome for herself, but some parents may have ostracized such a rebellious daughter.[73] We should not forget that patriarchal society (and the Saharawi patriarchal gender norms were reinforced by the colonial ones, as well as by the wage labor economy introduced by the Spanish) made many women somewhat dependent on their male relatives and/or spouses for survival. Outright rebellion in the cases of coerced marriage could mean exclusion by those who provided her sustenance, and so "everyday resistance," quiet and disguised acts such as complaints to a female friend and the cherishing of secret loves, were the best resistance tactics for some women facing coerced marriage.

I argue that Saharawi patriarchal norms were reinforced with those of Francoist patriarchy to make women dependent on their male kin and husbands. However, most of the older women whom I interviewed grew up in the cities of Spanish Sahara. This limits my study: I cannot draw on the experiences of women who lived predominantly nomadic lifestyles during Spanish colonial times. The women I interviewed and their families were incorporated, to varying extents, into the sedentarized and capitalist workings of the Spanish colonial project. Abu-Lughod's research with sedentarizing nomadic Bedouins of Egypt suggests that sedentarization brings increased patriarchal controls on previously nomadic women's freedom of movement, while women's lack of access to the financial resources introduced by the capitalist economy has given Bedouin men a new power over them.[74] While I can estimate that Spanish colonialism had a similar effect, I cannot know this without interviewing a number of women who can recall growing up in a predominantly nomadic family. For example, Caro Baroja's anthropological research carried out among nomadic communities in the 1950s suggests that weaving fabric for the *āḥiām* carried economic importance for "disadvantaged" women.[75] One could estimate that urbanization would lessen the need for *āḥiām*, and therefore the economic opportunities for such women, and that therefore a capitalist economy would impact negatively upon nomadic women's traditional forms of community work and reliance.[76]

It is also important to highlight that Saharawi interpretations of Islam influenced (and influences) their demands for patriarchal practices. In Saharawi society, unlike some other Islamic societies, the *mahr* (bridewealth) is paid by the groom not to his bride but to her father. Nevertheless, as Alice Wilson points out, Saharawi Islam also ensured certain protections for married women. Saharawis practiced the Islamic concept of *rḥīl*, a marriage gift for the new bride. Through the *rḥīl*, the Saharawi nomadic family would give their daughter some camels to take with her when she moved to live with her new husband. Thus, if the woman got divorced, she would have the camels (which remained exclusively hers, not the property of the couple), thereby avoiding her total economic dependency. Furthermore, divorced women had the right to keep their marital tents.[77] Similarly, unlike women living in some other Islamic and Maghreb contexts where a woman who uses her right to inherit property at marriage simultaneously forgoes her right to protection from her natal family in the case of marital dispute, Saharawi women (like their sisters in other Hassanophone contexts) could inherit property at marriage while also maintaining the right to protection from her brothers if needed.[78]

Attendance of the Women's Section itself also represented a space for challenge of patriarchal norms for some women. While Khadijatou Mokhtar attended Spanish schools with the full support of her family, she simultaneously notes that being a girl, her case was rare. She explains: "If the sedentary families didn't tend to send their children to Spanish schools, it was even less common for nomadic ones. And it was far, far less usual for girls to be sent to school. I was an exception because, first, my father is a man with quite an open mind."[79]

Tawfa's case was different to Khadijatou's. She had heard about the Women's Section through female friends and wanted to go to learn "how to write, how to cook, how to speak Spanish."[80] "I wanted to work. I didn't want to remain in a stagnant situation that involved being silent and staying at home," she adds. So in 1972, at the age of seventeen, she defied her parents' wishes and, in secret, began classes. She explains why many girls like her were not allowed to go to Women's Section or other schools: "We lived under a patriarchal system. . . . We girls had the intention of learning more, but at the same time, our fathers were working to preserve values and traditions. They worked for the family and for the girls to protect those values and that system. So my father used to keep a strict eye on me. Men would offer girls all they needed but girls had to stay at home. So, at that time, it was difficult for women to go out and about unless they got married."[81]

Although Tawfa highlights patriarchy as the reason why she was not allowed to go to school, it is possible that families that prevented both girls and boys from attending were resisting colonialism. Indeed, a Saharawi informant of Caratini told her that "[colonial] school means submission."[82] A wry quotation from Mercer is also illuminating in this vein: "If one assumes it is desirable to take the children from the Sahara's delicately balanced nomad society and train them to become a landless urban proletariat dependent upon a highly artificial colonial organization, then it can be said that the Spaniards' recent development of education in the territory has been admirable."[83] While Tawfa feels that her parents' initial refusal to allow her to attend school was because of patriarchal norms, we cannot assume that this was the case for all women.

To summarize so far, Saharawi women challenged sexism through a spectrum of resistance tactics, from the everyday resistance mounted through subterfuge, evasion, and trickery, to seeking recourse through traditional Islamic legal channels and co-opting colonial structures for their own benefit, to the most quiet and disguised resistance at the intimate and emotional level. Saharawi women were to use similar modes of resistance in the face of the Women's Section itself.

### No More Ironing: Saharawi Women's Challenges to the Francoist Housewife Model

Reports on Women's Section activities throughout its eleven years in the Sahara illustrated that Saharawi women were generally resistant to the classes related to good housekeeping, often refusing to attend, making minimal effort, or mocking the teachers.[84] Girls, too, resisted the Falangist indoctrination. Mateo describes the significant difficulties the Section had during the first year of their girls' school in El Aaiún: "Indiscipline, envy, lies, indolence, the most total superficiality, resentment, have been the causes of the tremendous difficulty of giving classes."[85]

On the other hand, cultural and literacy classes were popular.[86] By 1972 there is evidence of Women's Section schools dropping domestic classes in favor of more literacy ones, in response to the demands of Saharawi women.[87] Similarly, the methods by which the Women's Section claimed to achieve its aim of "promoting the Saharawi woman" were widened from teaching them to be good mothers and housewives to stimulating the "intellectual development" of women and girls.[88] The long-term effect of this was that toward the end of their time in the Sahara, Women's Section's understanding of what success meant had changed. The highlights of annual reports sent back to Madrid no longer focused on how many women could iron or sew but rather on intellectual successes. For example, in 1974 Women's Section celebrated first prizes for its students in the provincial theater competitions and a first prize in Spain's Tenth National Literary Competition for the sonnet dedicated to Smara town penned in Spanish by eleven-year-old Fatma Ahmed Abdsalem.[89]

In contrast to the centralized Women's Section policies on nurseries, which deemed their use to be "undesirable," justifiable "only in a pure emergency" since the Francoist women's key role was child rearing, by the end of the colonial period, most of the domestic schools in the Sahara had their own nursery, as did the artisanal workshops.[90] This provision was most likely in response to Saharawi women's pressure on the Spanish provincial government. Indeed, even at the very end of the colonial period, there is documentation of Saharawi women's lobbying efforts for more nurseries as well as for the Spanish government to subsidize learning materials for women.[91]

Saharawi women's Islamic beliefs were tolerated to some extent, with Quranic and classical Arab classes included in the syllabus of Women's Section's schools for adults and children.[92] This too presented a break from one of the main stated aims of Women's Section: to indoctrinate women to be active Catholics.[93] On the other hand, as Bengochea has pointed out, colonial "respect" for Islam was a piece of the wider (self-)image of "benevolent colonizer" that Spain attempted to cultivate.[94]

As the midseventies approached, Saharawi women, many of whom were fluent in Spanish by this time, began to make explicit nationalist and feminist demands on the Women's Section. In October 1974 the Section held meetings with former and current students of the domestic school to research the views of young Saharawi women on their role in society. In one such meeting Embarca Mahamud, Arbía Mohamed Nas, and Fatima Taleb (who was, at the time, working for the Women's Section) asked Mateo and her Spanish colleagues why it was that the Spanish government had only just begun to take an interest in providing educational grants and employment opportunities to Saharawis. They also criticized the Djemaa (a Spanish orchestrated puppet "autonomous government" set up in 1962) for having approved a new teacher training school without having consulted any women, highlighting the sexism of this all-male Saharawi governing structure controlled indirectly by the colonialists.[95] It should be noted that Taleb herself was an exceptional case: she was to become the first Saharawi woman to graduate in medicine (from Granada University, Spain) in 1981, then later played a leading role in establishing the acclaimed health system that now exists in the camps.[96] In 1974 she would have been aware that very few women were benefiting from the scarce opportunities granted to Saharawis to study in universities abroad.

After raising their socioeconomic points, the three Saharawi women then redirected the meeting to raise proindependence demands. The minutes of the meeting record the following intervention by the three: "They proceeded to tell us that they wanted absolute independence. . . . They expressed their wish for women to vote in the referendum."[97] In a second meeting with a similar aim, Saharawi women once again redirected the proceedings. Khadija Abdelmajib said women (including herself) wanted to study but that their families would not let them, and she asked how the Women's Section planned to address this barrier; Fatimetu Abdelahay asked for legislation to prevent parents from marrying off their daughters "and shutting them away in the house" before the age of eighteen; Embarka Mohammed complained that there was no point in the Women's Section encouraging Saharawi women to engage with the Djemaa, since men had no interest in listening to women's political views.[98] On this last point, Tawfa recalls an event organized by Concha Mateo in early 1975 in which Khalihenna Ould Errachid, leader of the Spanish-created and managed Saharawi National Union Party (PUNS), was paraded before Women's Section students and attempted to persuade them to renounce the POLISARIO in favor of the PUNS. Almost all Tawfa's classmates supported the POLISARIO. According to Tawfa, women drew on traditional gender norms to mock Khalihenna:

> At that meeting, only three women spoke, and their response was clear. And they told him, "If you are going to do something good for the Sahara, you have to join the men at the battlefront. That means the POLISARIO. We are just women. We are men's sisters, men's wives." It's like a challenge, when you say to a man that you are just with women. You insult him. He wasn't a man. If he wanted to be a real man, he should join the POLISARIO. They said: "If you want to do something good, you have to discuss it with the men, and if you convince them, we will be ready to follow you."[99]

The overarching goal of the Women's Section was in theory to empower Saharawi women. For the latter, this should have meant fighting for social and political rights, not merely literacy classes and certainly not just the promotion of good housekeeping. In this way, by challenging the colonials for their lack of action on sexism, Saharawi women's resistance could be interpreted as intersectional. It was simultaneously feminist and anticolonialist. Tawfa's explanation of why the POLISARIO movement placed so much emphasis on gender equality backs up this view as well as highlighting how important such Women's Section students, who had challenged (Saharawi and Spanish) society's construction of women's role, were for the success of the POLISARIO's project:

> When I saw the Spanish women working in offices and schools and as nurses, I felt like a guest. I didn't accept this situation. It gave me a lesson . . . motivation. I raised this issue with my husband, my father, my brother. I told them that I would like to be like the Spanish women, or even surpass them. . . . Women developed a sort of confidence. If her husband got sacked from his job, she would go and claim his rights. If her father were sacked, she would do the same. . . . And without those women who had studied under the Spanish, the POLISARIO would not have reached the level that it did. It was the women who studied under the Spanish colonialists who later on became nurses, teachers, and professionals.[100]

Women's Section made at least some sociopolitical efforts that favored individual women (bearing in mind that, in its latter years, the "Women's Section" and "Saharawi women" importantly cannot be considered a dichotomy, since the latter began to be incorporated into employment positions in the former). It bent the rules to provide financial support to at least one woman without means or family, negotiated an educational grant for a girl child who had survived sexual exploitation, personally visited the parents of several hundred girls and young women to convince them to allow their daughters to study, and in its later years, shifted its focus away from domestic chores toward attempting to provide professional-oriented education for women (albeit a heavily gendered and classist one, with training focused on typing, social work, hairdressing, cleaning, and health assistance).[101] This was in direct response to the demands of Saharawi women themselves, especially those left in a precarious financial situation, such as "those divorced and aged over 30," that is to say, significantly, those without a man.[102]

When the Women's Section was notified that the government would be shutting down its dressmaking workshop, it reacted with anger.[103] Nevertheless, the Section converted the workshop into a cooperative, which meant that all funds left in the bank upon its liquidation would have to be divided equally between the twelve Saharawi employees rather than going back to government.[104] Women's Section had further battles with other colonial bodies. For example, the Section had spent time persuading Saharawi families to allow their daughters to apply for a National Identification Document (D.N.I.), which would give them the right to apply for jobs. Nevertheless, the Section complained that the administrative office responsible for preparing D.N.I.s claimed "not to have time" to prepare them for all Saharawi women who requested one.[105] Another is that of the state-owned company EMINSA, later Fosbucraa, which, after several confrontations with Women's Section, was finally persuaded to employ just one Saharawi woman as a cleaner. The reticence of Fosbucraa's management was the result of their racist opinion of Saharawi women: "These women are unreliable, irresponsible as workers, and above all they are not properly trained."[106] Women's Section pressured Fosbucraa, indirectly through lobbying the government, to change its approach. Indeed, in many ways the single and assertive leaders of the Spanish Women's Section staff broke the mold of the Falangist submissive housewife model.[107] In Spain and in the Spanish African provinces, Women's Section leaders had a formidable power: the organization remained independent during the Franco regime and had authority over all Spanish women. Although the Women's Section Falangists extolled a domestic role for women, they themselves enjoyed and practiced much political and social power. As Aurora Morcillo puts it, "Falangist women developed a public persona very different from the private motherly Christian figure their discourse promoted."[108]

It is worth directing the reader to the work of other researchers in this area. Bengochea has highlighted that some Spanish ex-residents of Western Sahara believe that the Women's and Youth Falangist sections may have inadvertently inspired Saharawi nationalism, a view that Mateo herself also held.[109] However, he crucially explains the dark nature of this "inspiration": Spanish Women's Section staff inculcated Saharawi women in Spanish nationalism but simultaneously forever refused to talk of Saharawi women as Spanish: they were merely "natives" or "Muslims."[110] Andreas Stucki, as well as Amalia Morales Villena and Soledad Vieitez Cerdeño (who have carried out interviews with ex–Women's Section leaders), also argue that Women's Section provoked a Saharawi nationalist sentiment in some ways.[111] Indeed, my quotation of Tawfa above indicates that such Spanish women fed her desire for a life outside the domestic sphere, which is quite the opposite of what the Falangists originally set out to do. The insufficient efforts of the Spanish government to support her with these aspirations fueled Tawfa's nationalist sentiments. In what way did Tawfa wish to "be like" or even "surpass" the Falangist women? I would hazard to suggest that she had their public activism, political role, and dedication to the nation in mind rather than the submissive domesticity that Women's Section promoted.

To summarize, Spanish colonialism brought new challenges for Saharawi women. While Saharawi women already had their own ways of bargaining with the patriarchal elements of Saharawi society, Spain imported its own brand of patriarchy. As well as trying to transform Saharawi women into model Francoist housewives, sedentarization and wage labor brought new, gendered problems, not least increasing women's dependency on male relatives and spouses. Nevertheless, Saharawi women bargained with the Women's Section, taking advantage only of the classes that interested them, demanding more of these, and challenged the staff for their lack of political struggle for women's rights to study, work, and participate in politics. During the period that the Women's Section was in the Sahara, Saharawi women resisted both indigenous Saharawi and Islamic patriarchal elements and the new Francoist form of patriarchy that the Section initially tried to impose. (Of course, once Spanish colonialism had infected the Sahara, it became as impossible to disentangle "the Saharawi," "the Spanish," and "the Islamic" as it is to separate out the ingredients of a soup after they have been pureed together in a blender. I merely want to emphasize the point that while huge gender, race, and caste inequalities were enforced by colonialism, they are not totally reducible to the latter in a society where sexism and slavery already existed.) The emerging POLISARIO revolutionary discourses attempted, at least partially, to make a break from these patriarchal elements.

With regard to wider theoretical arguments, these examples illustrate the problem of focusing solely on *colonial* domination in subaltern histories. As Spivak has pointed out, the subaltern is gendered, and yet subaltern studies is not generally informed by feminist theory.[112] Similarly, Sumit Sarkar highlights the dangers of focusing on Edward Said–inspired frameworks while attempting to write subaltern histories. Focusing on colonial domination alone (which Sarkar argues the Saidian frameworks for colonial discourse analysis tend to) risks making invisible other axes of power and, therefore, resistance. Sarkar finds that "indigenous or precolonial roots of many forms of caste, gender, and class domination are generally ignored" in subaltern studies.[113]

As well as patriarchy and racial axes of power, Saharawi women also resisted the colonial administration. They challenged the Women's Section, encouraging it to fight for what could be described as feminist demands, and indeed, they enjoyed some successes in these challenges: on a number of occasions, the Spanish Sahara's Women's Section broke with Franco regime discourse and policy in favor of Saharawi women's interests, but only because of pressure from their colonial subjects. It is also worth noting that by the seventies, a small number of Saharawi women formed part of the Women's Section, and as the example of Fatima Taleb illustrates, they were vocal on the rights of Saharawi women along both gender and nationalist lines. This begs the question (hinted at by Sarkar) whose full response is beyond the scope of this book: to what extent do subalterns themselves shape and influence colonial constructions of gender and gender equality?[114] While the Women's Section Spanish staff may have arrived in their African province with a clear idea of what they aimed to turn Saharawi women into, they no doubt left with a different image of what Saharawi women were, had been, and could be. Did their experiences in Spanish Sahara, and Saharawi women's feminist and nationalist protests, affect the Women's Section staff with regard to their attitudes to gender inequalities back in their Spanish homelands? Such a question is worthy of further research.

Cynthia Enloe has warned political scientists of the dangers of ignoring women's antisexist resistance when analyzing the global political economy. Doing so paints proposals for women's rights as the exclusive brainchild of male "modernizing" elites.[115] In this section, I have applied Enloe's warning to Saharawi history. I argued in previous research that POLISARIO nationalist discourses made gender equality and the eradication of slavery aims, and indeed necessary components, of the independence revolution. I argued that these aims were inspired by other revolutions in which the position of women changed for the better and racist hierarchies were vilified. I also have argued previously that such discourses served several internal and external ideological functions, one of which was to mobilize women politically against Spanish and later Moroccan colonialism. However, our historical focus here, which has brought to light how Saharawi women and enslaved women and men subtly resisted gender and racial inequalities, allows new insights into the formation of POLISARIO discourse. It suggests that not only did black women react to POLISARIO nationalist discourses but they also actively shaped it. Everyday feminist resistances observed as early as 1964 (i.e., before the nationalist movement developed) by the Women's Section suggest that it was perhaps *not only* external anticolonial movements in Algeria, Guinea Bissau, and so on that inspired the (all male) POLISARIO leaders with regard to gender equality. It was also Saharawi women themselves. And it was precisely because of Saharawi women's feminist wants that POLISARIO's pro-women rhetoric was so attractive to the former. The result was the mass presence of Saharawi women and girls, as well as some enslaved peoples, in open resistance to Spanish colonialism, detailed later in the chapter. First, in the following section, we look at why POLISARIO's predecessor independence movement was born in 1969.

### Dangerous Ideas: The Emergence of Saharawi Nationalism

Among the most well off of the Saharawis under the Spanish were those working for the colonial administration, including in the Nomadic Troops (the Saharawi unit of the army) and the Territorial Police. Of course, being "well off" was relative. The Houses of Stones suburb of El Aaiún, where many Saharawi soldiers, police, and their families lived, had an "almost total lack of drains and running water [and a] lack of an organized rubbish collection service."[116] Enslaved families suffered still worse poverty. A Spanish soldier describes how the family of an enslaved colleague in the Nomadic Troops lived: "They usually carry a stick, they are badly dressed and almost semi-naked. Contemplating them reminds us of the olden days, giving the sensation of living in biblical times. After the passing the *haimas* of their owners, you can see behind a type of raised tent with some sticks and a ragged piece of cloth. It's the home of a family of slaves."[117]

The Women's Section observed that Saharawi women were conscious of the luxuries (such as large houses and washing machines) that Spanish women had and wished for the same. Nevertheless, Saharawi women found it hard to obtain the smallest luxuries on their wages: "They work in order to have the money necessary to survive."[118]

In Spanish Sahara, Saharawis provided a cheap labor force for resource exploitation and created artisanal shops to cater for the few Spanish tourists.

Others had jobs in the lower echelons of the colonial administration, mostly with bad pay and few rights. Indeed, Saharawis were well aware that, even if they held the same qualifications, their pay was not the same as that of a Spanish worker.[119] The Spanish authorities themselves recognized the profound racism of most of the Spanish population toward the Saharawis. A government study of the situation of Saharawi youth notes the perspective of the Spanish toward "the natives": "There is an almost total segregation of the native, who is not held in much regard, and a true racism, especially on the part of the Spanish from the peninsula; the Canary Islanders are much more integrated and accepted by the natives."[120]

Even if Canary Islanders integrated with Saharawis, they too noted that the latter were at the bottom of the social pile. One Canary Islander who lived in Spanish Sahara described his perspective: "I felt close to the Saharawis because I'm from the Canaries. Ultimately, we were a type of colonized people too, albeit in a different way. I used to like going to their houses, those of the older kids from school, to take tea amicably. It was well accepted, I felt good with them, better than with the Spanish. In those days Spanish society was extremely closed and hierarchical, and the wives of the noncommissioned officers gave up their places in the queue for the wives of the captains, and the same at church. Just imagine what happened when a Saharawi woman didn't give up her place in line for a Spanish *señora*."[121] These discriminations fed tensions beneath the deceptively calm surface, which were to bubble over with increasing frequency.

Meanwhile, anticolonial fervor burned throughout the African continent, and Spanish Sahara soon caught fire. By the early sixties, the UN's new Decolonization Committee was piling increasing weight on Spain to decolonize Guinea and the Sahara. Spain used similar strategies in both countries to try to shed this weight. First, it created "provinces" of Spain in the Sahara (1958) and Guinea (1959) in an attempt to dodge the label "colonies." Second, as already discussed, Spain created a puppet indigenous government (the Djemaa) in the Sahara and two indigenous governments in the Guinean "provinces" to create the illusion of autonomy. Eventually, after much struggle from its colonial subjects, Spain promised self-determination to the peoples of both countries. In Spanish Sahara, the first leader of said struggle was one Mohammed Sidi Brahim Bassiri.

Bassiri was born in the Saharawi-dominated town of Tan Tan, once in the Spanish province of Sidi Ifni (now known as the Tarfaya Strip), gifted to Morocco in 1958. After many years abroad, he moved back to Spanish Sahara in 1968. Bassiri was an intellectual and moderate nationalist well versed in the socialist, anticolonial currents flowing through Africa in the sixties and seventies. He had studied in Syria and Egypt, where pan-Arabism influenced his political development, before working as a journalist in a newly independent Morocco. Under the guise of his day job as a well-known and highly respected teacher in a Quranic school in Smara, he fostered the spreading of anticolonial political discourses amongst the Saharawi population. Women played an important role in supporting such efforts. Khadijatou Mokhtar explains: "Fundamentally, women's job was to provide logistical support and to change the opinion of the people in meetings, at homes. . . . Their job was to convince their families, not only women but men, their parents, their husbands, to align with Bassiri's embryonic movement."[122]

Indeed, the persuasive role that Mokhtar highlights was key in these early days, as it was later under the POLISARIO. Crucially, as I have argued in more detail elsewhere, in these early days Spanish authorities, who viewed Saharawi women as subjugated and submissive, dismissed the idea that women could be involved in political activities. Ironically then, Spanish sexist attitudes facilitated women's contributions to the nationalist movement.[123]

The revolutionary zeal that these women promoted was further stoked by rumors that Western Sahara would be annexed by Morocco. This was, after all, the fate of the ethnic Saharawi-dominated region of Tarfaya. Spain ceded the Tarfaya Strip to Morocco in 1958 following a Spanish-Moroccan war, in which Morocco invaded the area.[124] Under Moroccan rule, Saharawis living in the Tarfaya Strip suffered intense brutality (pillage, robbery, rape, and summary executions were common practice).[125] As such, it is not by chance that Bassiri as well as subsequent leaders of the Saharawi nationalist movement came from this region. Morocco's violent form of government there only served to feed a Saharawi nationalist sentiment, while Spain's ceding of Tarfaya reinforced the fear that the rest of the Sahara might be next. Announcements in the Spanish national press of possible upcoming agreements between Spain and Morocco that would allow the latter a share in Fosbucraa profits cemented this fear.[126]

As San Martín argues in some detail, the Moroccan specter, the African revolutionary currents, and Bassiri's teachings contributed to the erosion of some traditional forms of nomadic social organization based on kinship in place of a new *national* sense of collective identity.[127] As a 1973 Spanish population survey found, the Saharawis no longer identified themselves along tribal lines, or at least not in a way that the Spaniards could comprehend.[128] Instead, they joked that all Saharawis belonged to a low-caste tribe and paid tribute to the Spanish.[129] The combination of these factors became the placenta for a proindependence movement.[130]

The next section looks at these movements. I begin with a narrative of the Zemla protest. This is a key event in the Saharawi nationalist history, and yet women's experiences of Zemla remain unwritten. It is therefore worthwhile telling the story of Zemla through the memories of women who were there. I move on to look at the emergence of the POLISARIO, women's roles in its cells, the creation of the National Union of Saharawi Women (UNMS), and the parallel feminist and nationalist demands of women activists.

### The Proindependence Protests Begin: Zemla and the Formation of the POLISARIO

On the evening of 16 June 1970, a lizard ran for cover as yet another tire spat rubble in all directions along the main thoroughfare of Las Colominas suburb, El Aaiún. Tawfa and Silka had had been listening curiously to the rumble of Land Rovers all afternoon.[131] Peeking through the doorway of their home, Tawfa noticed "a lot of women on board." She could see that the arrivals were being welcomed by local families. Tawfa called out to a passing neighbor to enquire.

It turned out the convoy had come all the way from the holy town of Smara, meandering through the desert like a black-green serpent. "Don't go to the general's demonstration!" Tawfa recalls her neighbor warning. "There's to be an alternative demonstration—all Saharawis should go." The two girls, aged fifteen and twelve, respectively, listened to their neighbor's arguments regarding the importance of the counterdemonstration and exchanged a smile. They would attend. Tawfa explains that this is how most Saharawis in El Aaiún came to join the protest: "It was spontaneous." But the apparent spontaneity was only possible thanks to the widespread dissatisfaction at inequalities described in the section above—Saharawi ears by now welcomed nationalist arguments with the hospitality typical of their culture. A Spanish government report on Bassiri's movement, produced shortly before the events of Zemla, was correct in its nervous observation that "a Party exists now and, worse still, an idea exists."[132]

The next morning, the dust of Zemla, a barren square in downtown El Aaiún, was awoken early and agitated into the air by people mounting five *āḥīām* and what Tawfa describes as "a tower of rocks and stones." As the sky hoisted the sun up to its full height, five thousand Saharawis gradually gathered in traditional dress, creating a carpet of lapiz lazuli and banded onyx in their gold-fringed, blue or white *ādrārī'* (plural of *derrā'a*, the tunic worn by Saharawi men, in sky blue or white with gold trim around the neck) and new-moon black-blue *āmlāḥaf* (plural of *melḥfa*, a single piece of cloth that covers the whole body worn by women, traditionally in black but today in multi-colors). The atmosphere was expectant, like the warm, close breeze that arrives before thunder.

The colonists had long been planning a pro-Spain demonstration for 17 June (the "general's demonstration," as Tawfa recalls) and had invited international press to come and witness its puppet party's public show of loyalty in a bid to ease the increasing UN pressure to decolonize. Therefore, the much larger and passionate counterdemonstration made Spanish forces panic. They surrounded Zemla square and set up checkpoints in an effort to prevent Saharawis of neighboring districts from joining the protest. But as Ahmed Baba Miské observes, "the militants and above all the women found a thousand tricks to bypass or make it through the checkpoints."[133]

The Vanguard Organization for the Liberation of the Sahara, also known as Harakat Tahrir (Liberation Movement) and founded the previous year by Bassiri and friends, led the Saharawi demonstrators. The protest was a culmination of longer, behind-the-scenes, and, thus far, futile attempts at negotiations with the Spanish. Zemla was a chance for Harakat Tahrir to reach a wider audience, and through informal networks, Saharawis were persuaded to boycott the general's demonstration and head to the counterprotest—there were many who were, like Tawfa's neighbor, spreading the word among trusted friends.

In the square, all eyes were on the bearded young leader as he delivered his speech from the summit of the tower of stones. Tawfa and Silka recall feelings more than words, illustrating the importance of emotions in fueling resistance. Bassiri left the crowds effervescent, they tell me. The electric atmosphere lit up a celebration, and Tawfa and Silka were as eager to party as everyone else. They joined dancers, marking rhythm with their fingers, hips, and shoulders, emptied their lungs with the revolutionary lyrics of the poets, and feasted on the camels sacrificed in honor of the occasion in one of the five fizzing and bubbling *āḥiām*.

Meanwhile, Harakat Tahrir had prepared a petition in favor of gradual independence, to be negotiated with the Spanish colonizers, and asked the governor general to receive it.[134] The latter came but requested that the crowd disperse. Yet, says Tawfa, "the people stayed where they were: enjoying being in the *āḥiām* and singing."[135] Two hours later, the crowds still there, Spanish police began to arrest some of Harakat Tahrir's leaders. In response, Saharawis ran to the tower of stones and grabbed its building blocks, ready to pelt the colonial officers. This unwelcome confetti of rubble further angered the Spanish police, who called on the Legion to exert some discipline. Silka, at this point, was enveloped in the relative safety of the *ḥaīma*, but Tawfa was peeking out of the northern entrance, unsure whether or not to venture out. She recalls seeing a Saharawi woman strike a Spaniard on the neck, then a legionnaire firing three warning shots into the sky. The next moments were a blurred sandstorm of shrieking and pushing as bullets pierced through the skin of the *ḥaima*. There was a woman on the floor. And at least two men. There was the orange glow of angry flames and a surly creeping of smoke. Silka and Tawfa made it outside. They wound around injured bodies, pushed through groups of clashing Saharawis and Spanish, and fled home. The two women remember this as "the Zemla massacre."

Over the following days, severe oppression of Saharawi nationalists ensued. Many were beaten, some arrested, and still others fled the country. The exact circumstances of Bassiri's fate are unknown. He simply vanished. A Spanish provincial government report on Harakat Tahrir dated 12 June 1970 indicated a plan to disappear Bassiri even before the Zemla protest, since Spanish spies were already aware of the "dangerous" nationalist ideas he was spreading. "He should be detained in secret and moved to somewhere outside of the territory and held incommunicado until the situation is normalized," urged the report.[136]

Since the Moroccan invasion, hundreds more Saharawis have joined Bassiri in that dark void of the disappeared. Part of the intended horror of forced disappearance is aimed at those left behind: the not-knowing, the expectancy, and the eternal waiting. Loved ones become human question marks. When there is no definitive truth on offer, people find their own truths. In 1970 rumors abounded, but all nationalists hoped Bassiri would one day return. Some thought he was in a Moroccan prison. Other Saharawis said Bassiri had escaped and was safe and sound in exile, deciding what card to play next. The consensus today, among most Saharawi nationalists, is that Bassiri was kidnapped in the early hours of 18 June from the home of his (male) cousin. Some anonymous Spanish officers have suggested Bassiri was then locked up for six weeks before his final execution. Bassiri's last experiences, according to the officers' truth, would have been the warm July sand under his feet, the cold gaze of legionnaires on his back, the Atlantic's waves whispering in the distance and milky moonlight spilling all around.[137] This desert site of execution and burial was somewhere along the stretch of dunes that lie between El Aaiún city and El Aaiún beach.[138]

Khadijatou, who had been a resident of Auserd refugee camp for forty years when she died there in November 2015, offered a different truth. Her friends recounted to me the story she had cherished telling throughout her four decades in the camps.[139] After giving his speech from the tower of stones, Bassiri skipped the feast and went to Khadijatou's house. He waited there for the Spanish to come for him, ignoring the pleas of Khadijatou and others in the house to hide or to let himself be smuggled to Mauritania. Bassiri was resolute. Others had made sacrifices that day. Some were injured. Died even. He would not resist the Spanish. As night drew close, Bassiri wrote a few final letters, making them a shelter for his memories, and entrusted them to Khadijatou. El Aaiún was sleeping by the time the knocks on the door finally came. They were slow and loud and regular, like a clock sounding the hours.

Khadijatou visited Bassiri in prison every day for weeks. She would take him homemade food, clean clothes, conversation. One day he asked her to bring a razor. He shaved his face and washed, then handed her a pile of clothes, which he said he would no longer need. She cried as they hugged goodbye.

As San Martín has noted in his excellent account of the emergence of Saharawi nationalism, for the Saharawi activists, Zemla meant that the armed, revolutionary struggle was the only route to independence from Spain.[140] What does Khadijatou's story mean? The constructed feminine role of carer and nurturer extended into the prison space, becoming a type of resistance. It means these women, in Auserd camp, have found a way to connect themselves, via Khadijatou, to the celebrated nationalist martyr. The memories meant other things to Khadijatou, no doubt. The way her friends recounted her story gave me goose bumps. Imagine what emotional power it could carry for a Saharawi activist.

After Zemla, the Francoist regime put its repression tactics into a higher gear. On 1 September 1971 the Spanish created the new Domestic Policy Headquarters for Information and Control of the Territory.[141] In practice, this meant increased spying and reflected the growing fear felt by the colonists as a pro-independence sentiment became palpably more apparent among the Saharawi population. Indeed, Bassiri had become the stuff of legend for Saharawis. His photograph was to be seen in the houses and *āḥīām* of most Saharawis. Spain's actions at Zemla would forever be held against it.[142] Four years later Concha Mateo recalled being told by Saharawi women: "The historic moment was 17 June 1970. We can't trust you anymore."[143]

As Tawfa and Silka's singing at Zemla indicates, culture became a womb for resistance. Since protest songs in public spaces were banned by the Spanish, in the early seventies Saharawi women disseminated defiant lyrics by singing anti-Spanish songs and poetry at wedding celebrations and clandestine political meetings.[144] Mariam Hassan (the girl we met earlier in the chapter who avoided an unwanted marriage), for example, was singing at such a meeting in 1973.[145] When Spanish police broke in, she escaped out the window, maintaining her freedom to keep singing revolutionary songs through the final days of the Spanish presence, the exodus to Algeria, and up until her death in 2015.

Mariam, Tawfa, and Silka's singing activities constituted an intersectional challenge to gender norms as well as colonialism. The work of Vivian Solana helps me to explain why. Solana highlights how women activists have challenged the *ḥishma*, a set of social codes associated with modesty. In the prerevolutionary period, explains Solana, it was considered a sexual provocation for women to dance, sing, show their bodies, or raise their voices in front of older men or men who were not blood relations.[146] Women nationalists challenged the ḥishma in the early seventies, and doing so was crucial for the independence cause. Tawfa remembers the motivating effect of songs like Mariam's: "They incited us. This was the way to raise awareness in, let's say, a fashionable way."[147]

Shortly after the massacre and inspired by Zemla and the extinguished Harakat Tahrir, a group of young, male Saharawi university students who had been studying abroad formed the Frente Por la Liberación de Saguia el Hamra y Río de Oro (POLISARIO), led by the charismatic El Uali Mustapha Sayed. Thus the armed struggle began. At first, El Uali and his comrades traveled under cover around the territory to recruit supporters. The recruitment efforts included the establishment of clandestine schools for women. Many trainees were high school students from El Aaiún and other major towns, as well as nomads. Several joined the militant wing of the POLISARIO, the Saharawi People's Liberation Army (SPLA). Women were also empowered, somewhat ironically, by Francoist constructions of politics as a male-only arena: it was relatively easy for women to move freely and hide incriminating evidence under the folds of their āmlāḥaf without attracting suspicion.[148]

POLISARIO influence sent tremors that were increasingly felt by the Women's Section. In January 1974, for example, Saharawi women employees of the dressmaking workshop openly protested for labor rights. When the Spanish decided to reduce the lunch break of the fourteen employees from half an hour to fifteen minutes to promote "better efficiency" as well as to punish the women for their apparent lack of "discipline," eight walked out immediately, six of whom informed their ex-employers that they would be seeking a lawyer.[149] The remaining six demanded a pay rise and inclusion in Spain's social security system.[150] One month later, not just the fourteen women but all Saharawi workers were accorded the right to social security.[151]

Events like the women's walkout made Spain tremble. Tawfa used to buy Spanish newspapers (*El Diario* or *Cambio 16*) every day. There was always a story about the independence movement. She would read in the taxi on the way to work. One day, while nationalist songs blasted out through the car radio, Tawfa thumbed through the sheets to find El Uali's face staring back at her. She recalls: "There were three pictures. . . . In one photo [El Uali] had closed eyes, in the second he had half-closed eyes, and in the third he had open eyes. Each one was subtitled in Spanish. And each one represented something: in the beginning that people haven't become conscious yet, the second that the people are growing in consciousness, and when their eyes are open it means the people are aware."[152]

The Saharawis were opening their eyes and Spain knew it. Incidences, like this, of Spanish media fear gave Tawfa assurance and drive. As POLISARIO grew more confident, so did its activities.

One of the first direct actions of the POLISARIO was to hit Spain where it would hurt most: economically. On the night of 19 October 1974, a group of guerrillas sabotaged two stations of the Fosbucraa conveyor belt.[153] Women, too, were beginning to take direct action. On 20 November 1974, for example, twenty-five women gathered outside the Spanish local government building in El Aaiún, where the Djemaa was holding a meeting. The women proceeded with a nationalist protest. When police tried to disperse them, Arahma Hadir Mohammed and Mina Omar Jilali threw stones and were consequently arrested. The remaining women headed to a Spanish hotel and, from a height, threw stones at the Spanish cars passing below, resulting in six more arrests.[154]

The year 1974 saw the creation of the UNMS. The small-cell organizational structures of the UNMS, formed from the groups of women activists that supported Bassiri's Harakat Tahrir, and the two other unions created by the POLISARIO (the Saharawi Union of Students and the Saharawi Union of Workers) became the principal means through which the guerrilla movement recruited supporters.[155] As we observed in the previous section, Women's Section (ex-)students had told the Spanish management that they wished for a referendum on independence and that women should be included in the voting lists. Concha Mateo did further research. In October 1974 she compiled the findings of a research trip around Spanish Sahara, investigating whether women (and to a lesser extent, men) of different ages, marital status, and education levels had political consciences, and if so, what their views were.

Almost without exception, Mateo found that women of all backgrounds claimed a right to vote, were supportive of a referendum on independence, rejected any sort of integration with Morocco or any other country, held a strong consciousness of the richness (fisheries and phosphates) of Western Sahara, and held the view that, under Spain, this wealth had not been shared with the Saharawi people. However, equally as salient as the nationalist demands were the feminist ones. Concha Mateo summarized her research:

The constants that are repeated in all conversations are the following:
- Women have 50 percent of the votes in her hands
- Women should vote from the age of 14 upward since they get married before this age
- The Sahara should be independent
- The people of the Liberation Front represent the true Sahara
- We have to fight for the liberation of women in order to:

1. Be able to work and study without negative pressure from our families
2. Exercise our own choice when we get married, and to do so at the age that we wish
3. To be able to divorce
4. To take part in decisions and assemblies
5. To access jobs and studies with equal opportunity
6. To access positions of responsibility.[156]

Saharawi women's demands for self-determination were woven together with their own feminist goals. They held the hope that in an independent Saharawi state, the sociopolitical rights that had been denied them by traditional Saharawi society and the Spanish administration alike would at last be theirs. Such hopes are not surprising. Women's equality was a key aim in the emerging nationalist discourses of the POLISARIO.

Point 3 in the above quotation deserves attention. In Saharawi culture and in accordance with Saharawi interpretations of Islam, a woman may initiate divorce by requesting a divorce from her husband (something that scandalized Mateo when she first arrived in Spanish Sahara: in her native Spain, ending one's marriage was almost impossible and carried stigma for women). There was no stigma for divorced Saharawi women (she can remarry), but only a man can realize the divorce. If he refuses, she has recourse to the Islamic judge. If he too refuses, she is stuck. Some Saharawi women today argue for equal divorce rights in the Saharawi state in exile.[157] I would therefore estimate that the women interviewed by Mateo wished either for the right to *realize* divorce as well as initiate it or for more pressure on their husbands to accept women's requests, for an end to the unilateral male right to repudiation, or, indeed, for the overturning of the Djemaa's 1974 decision to enforce women to pay their husbands a fixed sum of money if they wished to divorce.[158]

The views on early and forced marriage expressed in the report are also worth special attention. While women demanded action to help delay marriage, they simultaneously—and no doubt with the nationalist goal in mind—reminded the Spaniards that teenagers, once married, were regarded as adults in Saharawi culture.[159] Thus, argued the Saharawi women, they should have the right to vote. An end to early and coerced marriage was the ideal aim, but ever practical and realizing that the Spanish were unlikely to reverse their policy of noninterference with Saharawi family law, Saharawi women simultaneously raised the demand of enfranchisement for all married girls.

Overall, for the women interviewed by Mateo in 1974, I would conclude that independence meant progress for women's rights. Similarly, black women and girls' support of the POLISARIO depended on its antislavery discourses (which were also most likely shaped by the enslaved peoples themselves, who as we have seen, always found ways to resist their oppression) as well as its fight against a colonial power that had actively tolerated slavery. In other words, women's resistance was intersectional, fighting the unequal power relationships bred of colonialism, patriarchy, and slavery. Pablo Ignacio de Dalmases, a journalist in Spanish Sahara, recalls finding ten-year-old Marrashina, a girl enslaved by the father of one of his Saharawi colleagues, at an anti-PUNS rally in winter 1975: "I found her in the crowd, hidden behind a *melhfa* that was too big for her but with which she tried to cover her face, while, with her little hands, she hoisted the flag of the POLISARIO, surreptitiously extracted from beneath her clothes."[160]

As male members of the POLISARIO militant cells began their attacks on Spanish military targets, other cells were organizing demonstrations in favor of self-determination. Tawfa, Silka, and their husbands joined such cells, but secrecy was a key principle of the POLISARIO. They never informed each other of their political activities. Tawfa recalls her husband arriving home from work late: "He used to tell me he had been playing cards with his friends, but I imagined he was discussing politics. . . . As for me, my cell used to meet on the beach on Sundays, and I'd go without my husband knowing about it. . . . If we went to a protest, I'd keep a change of clothes in another place, demonstrate, change clothes, and then go home."[161]

For many women, such clandestine political activities marked a break with established gender norms. While married and divorced women had more freedom of movement than unmarried Saharawi women, in line with Saharawi interpretations of Islam, the husbands still remained the head of the families and the lead decision makers, at least in theory. Silka, for example, asked her husband's permission before joining Women's Section in 1972, and yet two years later, in line with the POLISARIO secrecy rule, sought the approval of no one before embarking on her political work.

Despite the strict rule of secrecy, there were subtle (gendered) clues between Saharawis to know who was with POLISARIO. Men wore the ends of their turbans with frayed edges, while POLISARIO women would tend not to wear makeup or henna at weddings (as Saharawi women traditionally do) but adorned a bracelet or earrings colored with the red, green, white, and black of the POLISARIO flag.[162]

By the time Tawfa joined her POLISARIO cell in 1974, she had completed her studies and was working as a lab technician in El Aaiún hospital. Making use of her role, she would smuggle out syringes and medicines to send to the POLISARIO soldiers. Indeed, each woman made use of her skills and resources to contribute to the nationalist cause. Silka, who had studied in the Women's

Section's more practical workshops, was responsible for making uniforms and preparing goat skins for carrying water, while Leila Sidi Mahmoud, who joined the first POLISARIO cells in El Aaiún in her early twenties, recalls that literate women would graffiti the walls with slogans such as "Viva POLISARIO."[163] What the Spanish Falangist women's organization had taught these young Saharawis was put to use in ways that the former had never envisioned. I do not mean to suggest that Women's Section empowered Saharawi women. Rather, Saharawi women, in the face of colonial horrors, knew how to take advantage of the smallest of opportunities to empower themselves. Tawfa and Silka joined Women's Section *post Zemla*, after all. They wished to learn new skills and to train, and they did so with their future independent country in mind.

POLISARIO convened the largest nationalist demonstrations to welcome the UN Visiting Mission, 12–19 May 1975, which had been sent to determine the will of the Saharawi population vis-à-vis independence. Thousands of Saharawi women—wearing the traditional Saharawi all-black *melḥfa*—and men lined the streets in all major towns of the Sahara waving Saharawi flags and POLISARIO banners, chanting "Spain out, Morocco out, Mauritania out" and stuffing letters attesting to their support for independence into the hands of the UN Mission staff. Silka and Tawfa emphasize how important the protest was for the Saharawis: "I left my five-month-old son at home in the morning and didn't return to him until after the protest!" says Silka. Tawfa recalls: "All the men—workers, students—joined in the demonstration. And from eight in the morning until four in the evening, no one cared about his mother, his sister, his relatives." For one day, and for the nationalist cause, women halted their gendered role as nurturers and men their role as protectors of their female relatives.[164]

The Women's Section noted the absences in their classes over the few days of the UN visit. It remarked: "During the days of the UN visit there was practically no attendance given that all the women were out demonstrating, although we had a group of 4 or 5 that showed up. All this year it has been clear that in all the riots and demonstrations that happened it was women who performed the most important role, so she has moved from not coming out of the house and being ignored to being the most visible figure of this movement."[165]

Women's Section marveled at what they perceived as a revolutionary change in women's role in Saharawi society. This illustrates the success of the gendered nationalist discourses, which, as Khadijatou Mokhtar told us, Saharawi women were responsible for transmitting, but also how much the Section had underestimated Saharawi women and Saharawi society more generally.

The Women's Section observations also attest to the great extent to which women were the public face of the proindependence movement, organized political actors resisting colonialism and the potential of a new foreign occupation publicly. As we have seen (and Mateo's report backs up the early POLISARIO discourse on this point), it was feminist concerns as well as nationalist ones that mobilized women.

As for Saharawi men, Spanish authorities suspected that their less visible presence was due to worries about losing employment. Indeed, as I argue in chapter 5, Saharawi (and colonial Spanish) constructions of gender that assign the role of breadwinner to men continue to shape the gendered demographics of antioccupation protests.[166] In any case, the women-dominated demonstrations of 1974 to 1975 were a coup for the Saharawi nationalists. The UN report concluded: "The Mission was able, despite the shortness of its stay in the Territory, to visit virtually all the main population centers and to ascertain the views of the overwhelming majority of their inhabitants. At every place visited, the Mission was met by mass political demonstrations and had numerous private meetings with representatives of every section of the Saharan community. From all these, it became evident to the Mission that there was an overwhelming consensus among Saharans within the Territory in favor of independence and opposing integration with any neighbouring country."[167]

Students, too, were involved, and protests, strikes, and walkouts became common in schools, even at primary level.[168] In October 1974 a fifteen-year-old schoolgirl gathered together all her female classmates to plan a break-time protest against the Spanish presence in the territory. In the view of the girls, the Spanish had done nothing in the territory apart from "discovering phosphates" and "taking them away."[169] Another example is the strike of students across three schools in January 1975. The strike was organized in solidarity with three young Saharawis who had been detained because of their proindependence activities. Spanish police took it as a sign of the students' desire for Spain to leave the territory. Seventy students met with the head of education and refused to return to classes until the following demands were met: a new library, more study grants, Arabic-language classes even at primary level, and more professional training courses for women.[170]

Protests continued throughout 1975, up until the Spanish exit. Spanish authorities commented on "the absolute presence of women and children" at such demonstrations, which were often organized to ensure a synchronized attendance in several towns.[171] On 6 July 1975, for example, protests and "violence" broke out in Villa Cisneros, Aargub, Guera, Auserd, and Birnzaran.[172]

Women simultaneously pursued more formal means of resistance, writing letters to the colonial government or appearing in person to present their demands, which included more and better equipped and financed centers for women's training and education, day care centers for mothers who wished to study, respect from the Spanish teachers (which they found lacking), and better conditions for *frigān* (collective of *āḥiām*) and "shacks" surrounding El Aaiún, which were marked by shortages of "provisions, water, health assistance etcetera."[173] Such women who openly complained of conditions or lack of good quality study opportunities were often spied on, which many times revealed that they also pursued clandestine nationalist activities. For example, after she made complaints about the Women's Section, Spanish authorities found out that Suelka Labor Azman had been holding meetings in her house in which "topics of a subversive character" were discussed.[174]

By making hegemonic nationalist discourses that put a spotlight on gender equality and women's empowerment, the POLISARIO mobilized women politically, and as these events of the seventies show, they did so with overwhelming success.[175] Women led walkouts at their places of work, threatened legal action, lobbied (in letters and in person) for social and labor rights, hosted and participated in clandestine meetings supporting men to arrange acts of sabotage, and organized and led mass protests and demonstrations. Saharawi girls, too, led protests as well as organized strikes.

Sadly though, with the exception of gaining the admiration and sympathies of many Spaniards, the Saharawis' resistance did not influence Spain's final act of betrayal.[176] To end her report on the political opinions of Saharawi women, Concha Mateo reminded her Sahara- and Madrid-based Spanish readership of Spain's promise to the Saharawi people: "The Spanish would always be there to defend them from the appetite of any neighbor."[177] One year later, in October 1975, King Hassan II announced his intention to launch the Green March and claim Western Sahara for Morocco.[178] On 2 November, King Juan Carlos, head of state after Franco fell into a coma, traveled to El Aaiún and solemnly promised to defend the Sahara against Moroccan aspirations. Twelve days later, back in Madrid, he signed the illegal Tripartite Agreement (also known as the Madrid Accords), in which the Sahara was handed over to Morocco and Mauritania in exchange for fishing rights and a share of Fosbucraa's profits for Spain.[179]

Back in El Aaiún's Women's Section office, scribbled notes from 23 October reveal the worries of the Spanish women of the threat "coming from the north." Their plan for the 1975–76 school year, in which Saharawi women had been named to take over all roles, would never be put into action.[180] One woman listed the names of all Spanish staff and next to each one indicated what each woman planned to do: while some were determined to stay no matter what, the remainder were described (tellingly) as follows: "Leaving because her military husband is obliging her to."[181] By the end of the month, all Spanish civilians had been evacuated.[182] Its promise broken, Spain—but for a handful

of Spanish-born women and men who stayed and joined the POLISARIO—
left its former colonial subjects to the darkest of fates.[183]

In conclusion, looking at the last years of the Spanish colonial period, when
a half-hearted attempt was made to influence Saharawi culture, allows us to
observe that Saharawi women mounted feminist resistance (both "everyday
resistance" as well as recourse to colonial structures) to Saharawi and Spanish
patriarchal norms long before Bassiri's movement and the creation of the
POLISARIO.[184] The same is true for sub-Saharan enslaved peoples. This offers
new insights into the formation of POLISARIO discourse: it is possible that
women's feminist, antiracist demands influenced the integration of gender
equality and slavery eradication as revolutionary aims in its nationalist discourses. Later, these hegemonic nationalist discourses served to mobilize women
politically, and we see in this period how women's resistance was often intersectional, both feminist and proindependence, challenging Saharawi patriarchy (often reinforced by, or morphed with, colonialism), sexist colonial norms,
slavery, and racist colonialism itself. This illustrates how important it is to analyze inequalities that were not solely a result of colonialism as well as the new
imperial power axes when embarking on any subaltern studies project. This
argument is progressed further in the next chapter with reference to Equatoguinean women's resistance during the Spanish colonial period.

# CHAPTER TWO

# Women's Resistance and
# Gender in Spanish Guinea

IN HIS FAMOUS WORK *How Europe Underdeveloped Africa*, Walter Rodney outlined the anticolonial movements that emerged in various African countries. Rodney regrets finding no evidence of opposition in Equatorial Guinea yet rightly argues that this was a result of the zealous colonial shrouding of the very real resistance: "According to official Spanish sources, it is said that the school system in Spanish Guinea achieved all that the colonizers expected of it. It produced the required Africans who loved Spaniards more than the Spaniards loved themselves, but it produced no opponents of the colonial regime. It is difficult to believe the truth of such an assertion; and the Spanish took good care that no one from outside got wind of what things were like in the small Spanish colonies in Africa."[1] Fortunately, some writers such as Eugenio Nkogo Ondó, Gustau Nerín, Donato Ndongo, Enrique Okenve, Ibrahim Sundiata, Cristina Dyombe Dyangani, Adolfo Obiang Biko, Alicia Campos, and Enrique Martino have now revised the colonial histories to begin to tell the story of the Equatoguineans who challenged colonialism.[2] Nevertheless, except for Cécile Stephanie Stehrenberger, who hints at the use of mimicry among Guinean women dancers; Rosa Medina-Doménech, who illustrates how Guineans (women and men) demonstrated resistance to patronizing colonial psychological tests; and Remei Sipi Mayo and Benita Sampedro Vizcaya, who both tirelessly document the cultural contributions of Guinean women, Equatoguinean feminists regret lonely shelves in the library when it comes to women's resistance to Spanish colonialism.[3]

"Our streets are named after a whole host of heroes from the anticolonial struggle, but there's not one street named after a woman," complained one feminist interviewee.[4] "If you ask any young person to tell the story of proindependence activists, they'll tell you about several men, but none are capable of naming a woman," said another.[5] Francisca Sale, a teenager upon independence, laments that, although women played an important part in the anticolonial struggle, "there is little information about them [and] . . . they have not been taken into account."[6] Equatoguinean women so far remain passive victims to their fates in the history books. As Gayatri Spivak says, "If, in the context of colonial production, the subaltern has no history and cannot speak, the subaltern as female is even more deeply in shadow."[7] The aim of this chapter is to begin to brush the earth off Guinean women's histories of resistance.

A focus on feminist resistance is just as important as revealing women's resistance to colonialism. A criticism made of Western feminist authors is that they have ignored the history of women elsewhere of resisting patriarchy. Mary Daly, for example, has been criticized for representing European women who suffered witch burnings as strong and powerful while simultaneously representing Indian women as weak and helpless in the face of similar patriarchal excesses such as the suttee. Ignoring the history of resistance of Indian (and in the case of this book, African) women is a form of orientalism and posits Western women as the leaders of global feminism.[8] We have seen that Saharawi women found ingenious ways of resisting patriarchy during the Spanish period. In colonial accounts of Guinean societies, and even in contemporary histories of the country, Guinean women are imagined as passive and pitiable, meekly resigned to their status as subordinate to colonial and Guinean men.[9] A second aim of this chapter is therefore to explore Guinean women's resistance to sexisms in the Spanish colonial period.

Other researchers have given an in-depth analysis of the oppressive racial, class, and gender norms established in Guinea by the Spanish.[10] In this chapter, I turn my attention to what women *could* and *did* do in the face of such injustices. First, I focus on women's resistance to patriarchal norms, which of course always intersected with the racism of colonialism. I begin with a focus on Nigerian migrant women and their attempts to find livelihoods to independently sustain themselves and then look at how Guinean women and girls created opportunities for themselves at missionary organizations and nun's schools. I also explore how women attempted to use the justice system to escape abuses and seek custody of their children and how Fang women in particular appropriated a traditional Fang practice to resist unwanted marriages.

In the second section of the chapter I move to women's role in the anticolonial fight. Third, to foreground the arguments of chapter 6 on Equatorial Guinea postindependence, I briefly look at why Guineans elected Macías. Finally, I analyze women's resistance to the Spanish Falange party's Women's Section's efforts in the territory, which, I argue, best illustrates how Guinean women's resistance was intersectional, attacking several axes of power at once.

Before leaping into the analysis, I must make one more disclaimer. Guinean society was (and is) far from homogenous. Colonialism detrimentally affected Fang, Bubi, Ndowe, Fernandino, Annobonese, and other communities in different ways and thus would have been resisted using diverse methods. I do not attempt to delineate these differences here. In the chapter that follows, I make an overview argument that Guinean women *did* resist colonialism, that they *were a vital part* of the proindependence movements, and that we must stop making invisible their contributions in histories of Equatorial Guinea. Far more research is needed on how Guinean women of various ethnicities resisted colonialism (and other oppressions) as well as how these resistances changed over time. I mean this chapter to be a modest initial intervention in what I hope will become a wider field of study.

## Doves of Fire: Guinean Women Resisting Patriarchies

The elder women in Francisca's family always smelt of pipe smoke.[11] They would pack the tobacco into the bowl just right, not too compressed, then take draws while telling little Francisca and her cousins stories of the forests and the spirits. These firelit tales of another world, of a Bubi world before Spain trampled all over it, dazzled her. Years later, the foremothers who inspired Francisca's cultural and feminist activism still linger in her mind like smoke.

We sit together in a bar not far from Banapá, where the Spanish Claretian missionaries first established themselves on the island more than 150 years ago. Behind her, a tropical forest climbs up toward the fog necklace of a dormant volcano. The brightly colored villas of the ruling class form a hem to its green skirts. Francisca reels off the names of women who struggled upward despite the thick canopy of colonialism's multiple oppressions. Trinidad Morgades was the first, she tells me: a Guinean headmistress in a colonial school and, with a literature degree, better educated than the Spanish teachers. Teenage Francisca took Morgades as a "role model."[12] But there was also Fidela Boneke, the "powerful" woman who brought up Juan Balboa, one of Equatorial Guinea's greatest writers (and an ex-minister); *tía* (aunty, used to describe and address respected older women) Watson, who created the first collective for Guinean women of Fernando Po; Amelia, who reaped such riches from her businesses that she (somewhat ironically) became a lender to Claretian missionaries among others; and Montse, who became a mayor in the sixties and pursued policies against domestic violence. I get the feeling Francisca could continue all afternoon, but she has a discussion on women's rights to plan over at the Bubi Cultural Center in Rebola. Her parting wisdom is pertinent: we need to record the achievements of these "powerful" women, but equally important are the stories, lives, and deeds of "normal women: the wives, the *mamas*, the housekeepers."[13] I ask in this section, how did "normal" women take on the intersecting racisms, sexisms, and classisms of colonialism?

The first wave of Spanish settlers in Spanish Guinea, the Claretian missionaries, swept onto the shores of Bioko Island in the 1850s.[14] While colonialism in Western Sahara was delayed and focused primarily on economic profit making rather than on transforming a "backward" culture, the colonial project in Equatorial Guinea was a sociocultural affair almost from the outset. For the Claretian missionaries of Fernando Po, successful colonialism, or rather a successful "divine mission . . . making the sun of civilization shine in the countries enveloped in the dense fog of ignorance and error," meant Hispanicization in every sense of the word: linguistic, cultural, social, and moral.[15] The cultural colonization, which Igor Cusack calls cultural "forced feeding," was pursued far more violently than in the Sahara.[16] This was "cultural assimilation at gunpoint," says Donato Ndongo, who remembers pupils at his school being whipped if they spoke in their native tongue.[17] The enforced Hispanicization of the population paved the way for the Spanish state and economic interests, which at first exploited the local population to labor in their cocoa, wood, and coffee industries.

From the later part of the nineteenth century onward, the Spanish plantations of Fernando Po did well. But they were in desperate need of laborers.[18] Once the local population had been "decimated by disease and forced labor," the Spanish turned to British-ruled Nigeria.[19] Nigerian laborers in Fernando Po numbered around one hundred thousand by 1968.[20] The horrendous working conditions, little different from slavery, were well known across Africa and Europe. Fernando Po became known as "hell's island" or "brutal island."[21] The male Nigerian laborers resisted the draconian conditions through everyday acts of resistance such as stealing from the plantation owners, self-harm, and working slowly as well as more organized forms such as petitioning the British consul (this had been set up in Santa Isabel to, allegedly, protect the rights of Nigerian workers, who were regarded as British subjects) and writing to newspapers.[22] But Nigerian women, too, challenged the colonial pitchforks of "hell's island."

The Spanish did not encourage Nigerian women to go to Fernando Po for plantation labor, but they were "accepted" there as wives for their kinsmen. To travel from Calabar to Fernando Po, women were supposed to carry documents to prove their marriage to a Nigerian laborer. Nevertheless, some single, divorced, and unhappily married women wished to travel to the island to try their luck and look for work. Some got there independently, sidelining the bureaucracy altogether.[23] Others forged papers. A rather fed-up British vice consulate wrote from Santa Isabel back to the labor commissioner in Lagos in

1950 regarding the letters he kept receiving from "irate husbands" demanding their Nigerian wives be sent back. The consulate found "upon investigation" that "nearly always" the said wives had been thrown out by their husbands and thus traveled to Guinea in search of a livelihood.[24]

Some of these women accomplished what they set out to. The observations of the British vice consulate, though most likely overly optimistic, indicated that many found work "collecting coffee and sewing together tobacco leaves," earning, according to the consulate, more than double the average weekly earnings of a Nigerian male wage laborer.[25] We see, therefore, that Nigerian women found ways to circumnavigate the colonial rules that sought to limit their role in Spanish Guinea to that of wife. On the other hand, as in Spanish Sahara, other women appropriated the colonial structures themselves to create opportunities, especially when attempting to avoid individual situations of hardship.[26]

The Claretian missionary church provided one such opportunity. For example, Antonio Aymemí, a Claretian missionary resident in Fernando Po from 1894 until his death in 1941, has recorded the case of a Bubi woman who, facing the death penalty (for adultery, says Aymemí), managed under the cover of night to free herself and run to the missionaries for sanctuary.[27] Similarly, in 1945 the missionaries of Nkue, a settlement in the north of modern-day continental Equatorial Guinea, came under increasing pressure from Guinean village authorities for offering shelter to Guinean women fleeing their husbands. The church was also under fire from Spanish government authorities because of tensions between Guineans and the colonials.[28]

Officially, the missionaries were only allowed to welcome single women who wished for a Christian marriage, or married women who had been given permission to separate from their husbands by their respective village authorities. However, the father superior of Nkue showed little regard for the rules and welcomed several escaped women, letting them live in the mission's boarding school. When their husbands or male relatives tried to process complaints via the colonial administration in an attempt to claim "their" women back, a civil servant writing to the governor general of the territory protested that the father superior gave only "vague and imprecise answers without making [the women] appear at the Summons."[29]

Enrique Okenve's history of the Spanish colonial period, which involved collecting the oral histories of some eighty older Fang citizens living throughout Equatorial Guinea, suggests that the father superior of Nkue's actions became the normal course of action for Claretian missionaries. This "mission as refuge" model provided opportunities for women who had, before then, little room to maneuver at the bottom of the Fang social hierarchy, argues Okenve.[30] The aim of the missions was to convince the women to convert.

Most (but not all) missions also encouraged such women to find a converted husband. When women fleeing unwanted marriages came to them, the missionaries facilitated divorce.[31] This, finds Okenve, was used as a bargaining chip by women and "gave them stronger rights vis-à-vis their husbands."[32] If women were treated badly, they could threaten to leave. Women did not necessarily live up to the missionaries' hope that they would convert and find a Christian husband, but they knew how to make use of the missionaries for their own ends. On the other hand, if a woman did convert and procure a Christian marriage, it became (in line with Catholic doctrine) far harder for her to divorce. The Spanish import of Christianity also impacted negatively on women's sexual freedoms, especially in the Fang case. Unlike other Guinean ethnicities or Spanish citizens for whom premarital chastity was imperative for women, Fang girls were allowed to explore their sexualities before they were married.[33] Yet the arrival of Christianity converted female sexuality into a terrible and dangerous force to be tamed in and outside of marriage.

Okenve argues that conversion to Christianity brought new powers for *some* women, as they could play a more central role in their communities as well as in villages' religious activities.[34] However, this was not universal, and sounds like a common colonial strategy for co-opting indigenous peoples. Some Fang women had, before Catholicization took hold, formed part of all-female religious movements. The most important of these was the Mewungo, which sought to deal with problems faced by women such as infertility, neglectful husbands, and child mortality. Since it was feared by men, it could also serve as a counter to male abuses.[35] Likewise, Fang Bwiti religious practices also provided spaces for women to challenge gendered systems of power: all-women dances explicitly mocked men, while the wider religion served as a spiritual refuge from colonialism.[36]

Christianity also eroded religious power for Bubi women. Before missionary catholicization, Bubi women could be religious specialists in their communities. Such specialists had power over which (male) leader was chosen, which marriages could be made and dissolved, when war and peace could be declared, and what the punishment would be for those provoking the death of another.[37] Indeed, we should in no way conclude that the Claretian missionaries empowered women. The clergymen and women had an agenda: to present an image of "white savior," to recruit new Christians, and to promote a Spanish Catholic nuclear family model (as Remei Sipi Mayo recalls in an interview with Benita Sampedro, the church actively refused rights to those who were not married or born of married parents).[38] Guinean women glimpsed opportunities at the missions and exploited them when they could. If there was empowerment, Guinean women empowered themselves.

Guinean women and girls also took advantage of schools run by Spanish nuns, as is recalled by Ana Alogo Mikue. Born in 1945 in a village in what is today the Kié-Ntem province, Ana and her siblings, whose parents were very ill during her infancy, attended the Casa Cuna, a nun-managed orphanage. At age thirteen, Ana was sent to another boarding school run by nuns in Bata, where she learned how to use a sewing machine. This would stand her in good stead in her later life. According to Ana, some of her classmates at this school had run away from their parents' homes to attend the school. This was because "they wanted to train as maids, because if they could earn a wage as maids they could pay for further education." However, if the young women's intentions were to empower themselves through education (although, significantly, they had to serve in Spanish households in order to afford this), Ana's memories highlight the violent abuse that awaited them at the hands of the Catholic institutions. Although Ana recalls that a few individual nuns did their job well, indeed "they were so kind to [her] that [she] will remember them for the rest of [her] life," in general, the nuns were abusive. "Child abuse was the norm." Ana speaks of one little boy at the Casa Cuna in Mikomeseng who was beaten to death by nuns.[39]

Women also attempted to make use of Spanish judicial authorities, sometimes to challenge sexual abuse. A case brought by a young Bubi woman illustrates this well. She used her better-educated fiancé to represent her in court. When the guilty (Guinean) man was brought before the colonial authorities in Santa Isabel, they gave him a meager wrist slap of a punishment: an informal warning "not to do the same thing a second time."[40]

As for white male rapists, there was impunity. Sexual abuse reached institutional levels. Women prisoners, for example, "were forced by the guards to offer themselves at any moment and especially at nights in the prison house and any woman who refused was completely drowned in beatings, including on her private parts."[41] Maria Jesus Ntutumu remembers with horror what used to happen when, in the early sixties, Spanish soldiers came to visit the town of Ebebiyin where she went to school: "The traditional tribal chief, who had loads of wives, well when the Spanish visited he'd put his wives in a line and let the Spanish captain pick which one he wanted. And the Spanish captain was always accompanied by other soldiers, so they would also . . . well that would be, I don't know, horrific."

Of course, not *all* wives of a polygamist authority would be offered to European partners or soldiers. Furthermore, some of those wives or concubines selected for such a role may have extracted commercial gain. However, as Maria Jesus's emotions of horror indicate, this practice, which still has echoes today, was often a form of institutionalized rape.[42] María Jesus's memories are one manifestation of a wider system, described in detail by Gustau Nerín, of Spanish men's hypersexualization and sexual exploitation of Guinean women (of course, hypersexualization and sexual exploitation are partners: the hypersexualization of black women has a long history rooted in colonialism and served [serves] to banalize sexual abuse and exploitation of black women by white and Arab men).[43]

Moving back to the colonial authorities, the Patronato de Indígenas (a colonial institution ostensibly for "protecting natives," hereafter Patronato) was the main instrument of "justice" for Guineans. It was headed by the church and supposedly aimed to defend Guineans from exploitation by planters. However, it also enforced controversial, discriminatory laws on the indigenous population and attempted to make Spanish morality and culture hegemonic. Spain created the Patronato in 1906, although it did not come into effect until 1928, when the categorization of fully emancipated, partially emancipated, and nonemancipated Guineans came into practice.[44] Nonemancipated Guineans were effectively denied legal status. They could not acquire property and realize commercial transactions. Rather, they remained under the "guardianship" of the Patronato.[45]

Women could only seek emancipated status through marriage to an emancipated man. Through the Patronato, Spain legalized single women's place as third-class (not Spanish, not male) citizens. Among the first things set by the Patronato were the salaries of native workers, which effectively legalized gender discrimination: women were to be paid 50 percent to 75 percent less than men for the same work.[46] Examples from the colonial archives, however, bring to light attempts by women to use the Patronato to resist their situations of sexual exploitation and domestic abuse. For example, in 1937 Ayakaba Nzue began fighting for an end to what she described as her "extremely abusive" marriage, in which her husband, Mba Manga, was beating and forcibly prostituting her.[47] Ayakaba Nzue's case gives us clues as to what strategies women had to resist and escape. According to Ayakaba Nzue's uncle, Fernando Mbo, the girl's father was in prison when he sent a brother in search of a husband for his daughter (who was only eight or nine years old when she was married), hoping the resulting bridewealth would help him to pay off some outstanding debts. Years later, Ayakaba Nzue finally managed to escape from the conjugal home with her young son and sought sanctuary in the home of her sister, Isabel Andame. After six weeks there, she approached the Patronato to ask for an annulment of her marriage on the basis of the abuse suffered.[48]

Other women followed a similar path. The case of Nchama Esono, who asked the Patronato for an annulment of her marriage owing to domestic violence, is emblematic of how such women were dealt with.[49] Several (male) witnesses confirmed that Nchama Esono's own account of how she was abused was true: she was beaten every day, and indeed, her husband confirmed for the Patronato that he did so. A report from the organization's secretary reveals how the colonists resolved the case: "The father of the plaintiff should take into account this inquiry and indicate if he agrees with the marriage being annulled. And in this last case he should return the bridewealth and indicate the quantity that was paid for this."[50]

We can make two observations about the conduct of the Patronato in the cases of the two women mentioned above and others.[51] First, the women's wish for an annulment was not enough for the same to be granted. Several male witnesses were called in each case to testify to the veracity of the women's accusations of abuse. Only if these were proven would there be grounds for the Patronato to pursue an annulment, and even then, this would only be granted upon the mutual agreement of the husband's family and the father of the woman, who would have to pay back the bridewealth in full. Second, even if annulments were granted, domestic violence and sexual exploitation were not regarded as worthy of punishment and, indeed, neither was the coerced marriage of a girl child.[52] Spain institutionalized a gendered hierarchy that made a woman's word worth nothing, stole almost all autonomy from women, and left women and girls vulnerable to astonishing abuses of power.

Ana, whom we met earlier, became trapped for sixteen years in an abusive marriage because of how this justice system operated. After finishing schooling in Bata in 1963, she moved back to the home of her parents, who by then had recovered from their respective illnesses. They proposed a suitor, Roberto.[53] Ana found out he was already married and, on this basis, refused him. "But my father and uncle wanted the bridewealth so I had to marry him. It was a forced marriage. There's no other word for it." Roberto regularly beat Ana, but she was unable to divorce him: "You can't get out of a marriage unless you return the bridewealth, and I didn't even have a cent, and no one to help me with that."

"Next came the babies," recalls Ana. Ana's husband did not provide for their offspring. She could not feed her children sufficiently, nor pay medical expenses when they fell ill. Tragically, one child died. After this, Ana's father bought her a sewing machine. She moved to Bata, where she had her own business as a seamstress and supplemented her income by selling nuts on the street. This way, despite all the hardships she had faced, she managed to save some money. Instead of using it to refund her bridewealth, however, she paid to put her surviving children through school. The Patronato may not have helped Ana end her marriage, but her resilient personality, skills as a seamstress, and a little help from the machine provided by her father allowed her to help her children.

Other women approached the Patronato to seek custody of their children when Spanish fathers attempted to move them abroad. As Pilar Nyangi recalls of mixed raced relationships in her Ndowe community, "The Spanish sometimes went back to Spain with the children from the marriage, leaving the women with nothing, or perhaps with some form of compensation."[54] Such was the case of the late Raquel Ilombé, one of Equatorial Guinea's most celebrated poets. Her father, Raimundo del Pozo, left Raquel's mother, Esperanza Epita of Corisco Island, pregnant, and when the child was born, he took Raquelita to Spain. Terrified at the thought of losing her only daughter, Esperanza appealed to the Patronato but received no support, only the label of being a woman of "loose morals" for having birthed an infant out of wedlock. Throughout her childhood, Raquel was told her mother was dead, and it was not until she was in her midtwenties when she returned to Guinea for her honeymoon that Raquel and Esperanza were reunited.[55]

These cases suggest that the Patronato offered little justice to Guinean women and girls. Rather, it institutionalized the patriarchal norms that ensured their abuse. Nevertheless, by appealing to the Patronato, and escaping to the home of a female relative in one case, these women and girls showed determination in attempting to resist their hardships.

Some Fang women also reappropriated traditional Fang socioeconomic practices to their own advantage. For example, Martino's detailed and nuanced research into how the Fang bridewealth practice altered with the capitalist economy (not least by becoming monetized) highlights how some women and their fathers showed resilience to the changing contexts by hoodwinking Spanish authorities into allowing greater sums, thus increasing the wealth of the bride's blood relations.[56] Other women reappropriated another typical Fang social practice to escape coerced marriage: the *abóm* or in (controversial) Spanish translation, *secuestro* (kidnap). To explore how women used the *abóm*, it is worth drawing on Enrique Okenve's oral history research as well as fiction—specifically, María Nsué Angüe's novel *Ekomo*.

As I have argued elsewhere, *Ekomo* explores how women dealt with the sexual inequalities bred of (intermixed) Fang and Spanish patriarchal norms.[57] The protagonist, Nnanga, is a woman who loves to dance and associates dance with mutiny. She calls herself "Dove of Fire" each time she is tempted to resist a patriarchal norm. Nnanga "personifies," as Nsué Angüe herself says, "rebellion."[58]

One of Nnanga's many rebellions against Fang and Spanish traditions occurs at her marriage. Despite being promised by her family to Lucas, a Christian convert, Nnanga falls for Ekomo. Nnanga hears that Ekomo plans to "kidnap" her on the night of her wedding to Lucas, which means they could be married. The "kidnap" is today seen as an emblem of Fang tradition and is acted out symbolically as part of the wedding ceremony: it allows the "kidnapper" to marry the "kidnapped" woman if he takes her on the wedding night. But Nnanga cannot stomach what she sees as the passivity of being "taken": "Because one thing is not wanting to marry Lucas, and another is letting myself be kidnapped. Do I want to let myself be kidnapped? The question, crept deep inside me. No! No! No! Never."[59]

Although escaping an unwanted marriage by allowing herself to be "taken" by another man does not sit well with Nnanga, being kidnapped would prevent the colonial tradition of being coerced, in a Christian marriage, to submit to a man she does not love. In this way, Nnanga uses the tradition to achieve the best outcome that she can manage in the difficult circumstances.

Okenve's research illustrates more specifically how Fang women used the "kidnap," or better, following Okenve, the *abóm* (the English and Spanish translations of the word indeed remove all possible agency of women) during colonial times as a form of resistance. He suggests that the *abóm* was a tool used by women in the face of socioeconomic changes brought about by the Spanish (capitalist) intrusion. As bridewealths became monetized and expensive during the onset of a capitalist economy, Okenve finds it became increasingly the norm for only older, wealthy men to be able to get married, and to ever younger women, reflecting power imbalances on lines of gender, age, and wealth. The clash with colonial culture illustrated to women that gender-based norms were not necessarily inevitable or "the natural way of things." Some began to rebel against the gendered practices that they disliked. Okenve finds that it became common for women to challenge coerced marriages, something that had previously been unthinkable.[60] The *abóm*, then, was one form of women's resistance. Women rejected unwanted marriages arranged by their parents and "ran away" in the night with their lovers.[61] Nsué Angüe and Okenve both illustrate the resilience and subtle forms of resistance Guinean women, doves of fire, used to get their way. In the next section, we move on to look at how women participated in the fight against colonialism.

## "Silent Political Women?" Women's Participation in the Struggle against Colonialism

"It's a lot of money for some old clothes."

The officer had the stash of money, extracted from the arm of an old shirt, in his palm. Helena's basket, from which the officer had grabbed the shirt, sat next to a stream of mud.[62] The Kie, black and gleaming like a polished stone, had broken its banks again and was laying siege to the defenseless earth in its path.

"I sell good quality clothes."

"They're old rags."

Helena's heart thumped. How could she justify having so much cash on her person? "I sold the good pieces." In truth, she hadn't sold anything.

The rain had sounded like a breeze at first, just a rustle. Now it came down like a waterfall. New muddy streams would burst through the forest soon and make the landscape angrier and angrier. The officer opened his mouth, then promptly shut it again, as if thinking better of it. "Get home quick, you shouldn't be out here."[63] He pocketed the cash. Helena sighed. Typical. She rushed down the path toward home.

The town was the only thing to rupture the unending green for miles. It sat on the corner where continental Guinea meets Cameroon and Gabon, which were the destinations for the money Helena regularly gathered. Rain, don't you ever tire of crying? Vines strangled tree trunks all around. She prayed, under her breath, not to bump into any more officers today. Helena set her thoughts to the following day, to how she would meander through checkpoints and deliver her verbal message to the contact.

Helena was part of a whole network of proindependence women, who went door to door gathering money from Guinean families (often under the guise of selling clothes) to support political activists exiled abroad and/or memorizing messages to pass verbally between activists. "Nothing could be written on paper, you see," Ana, Helena's niece, explains to me. "An officer could search them, and written messages could give everything away." With regard to the collections, selling secondhand clothes was the perfect cover. Ana calls these women "silent political women," because their work was clandestine, anonymous. Women were not the leaders of movements, not the martyrs, but they did quietly form the ranks of the nonviolent foot soldiers. Nevertheless, written out of history, they are still "silent" in the sense that their contributions have not been recorded.

Why were women not the leaders of proindependence movements? The official political sphere of Fang, Bubi, and Annobonese communities was a male one, although in some cases, women invaded it in order to make demands. Fang women, for example, would use the *abbá*, the community meeting place where political decisions would be taken, to reclaim rights accorded to them, especially with regard to marital disputes and rights over children.[64] However, this was a male space that women occasionally entered, not a genderless one. The gendering of political space as a primarily male one was extended and fortified by the Spanish.[65] It is therefore not surprising that, as was the case with the highest echelons of Harakat Tahrir and POLISARIO in Spanish Sahara, no women featured in the leadership of nationalist organizations that emerged to challenge colonialism in Guinea. But as Helena's story immediately shows, that does not mean that they played no role. Below, I sketch (and a rough sketch is all I can offer, when covering more than a century of rich history in a short chapter section) women's contributions to the struggle against colonialism, starting at the point of Spanish colonization, through the maintenance of an anticolonial hidden transcript, to their efforts in the nationalist, proindependence movements of the fifties and sixties.

Nerín has documented Spain's violent military campaigns to gain control over Rio Muni between 1904 and the 1930s and Fang resistance to these.[66] Sundiata has carried out similar work, historicizing the resistance of Bubis to colonialism on Bioko Island.[67] However, perhaps because women's resistance methods were not usually bloody or formally organized, we lack information on their tactics in opposing the efforts of the colonizers. The archives, though, tell a story of women's everyday resistance and hidden transcripts. For an example, a 1904 edition of the Banapá Claretian mission's magazine published the story of a woman who, despite all the missionaries' efforts, would not convert: "Going back to the subject of the woman, we visited her more than five times to give her the key to heaven, but all our efforts were useless and our arguments crashed against a singular and empty answer, 'But, Father, if I am baptized I will live too long and I'll never die; and I no longer want to live.'"[68]

It is hard to tell if this old woman was a philosopher, if she wished to mock the unpersuasive missionaries, or if her words reflected a real weariness at life. Whatever her motives, she successfully resisted the proselytizers' persistent advances. Indeed, Yolanda Aixelà Cabré points out that, after years of failure, the (male) Claretian missionaries had been unable to convert Bubi women on the island of Bioko. It was for that reason that they invited nuns to join them, hoping that, women to women, they might fare better.[69]

Neither were the women of Annobón happy with their Spanish lodgers. The missionaries, who arrived there at the end of the nineteenth century, were insulted, threatened, and poisoned, and they had their crops stolen. Annobonese girl children played an important role in this ostracization of the Catholics. The Spanish nuns, who referred to themselves as "white angels for the black girls," saw their school emptied thanks to a popular boycott by the girls.[70]

As is usual in the case of subaltern peoples, mockery was a key resistance tool for Guineans. Women, of course, participated in this systematic mockery of the colonizers and often led it. The local population had a derogatory nickname for colonial leaders, and anti-Spanish songs were the order of the day.[71] The chorus of one popular song went, "The white man is a wimp. We know that, we know that," while another *sihíri*, a form of Bubi dance and song performed only by women, takes a tone of warning: "The whites have not stopped harassing people. The shark does not usually go back for the scraps."[72] The following traditional Bubi song, popular among women in the 1920s, mocks and undermines the piousness of the Spanish missionaries:

> The priest's thing rises
>> it rises
> the priest's thing rises
>> it rises
> it smells awful
>> it rises
> it tastes bitter
>> it rises
> we say rise up
>> it rises
> we say rise up
>> it rises.[73]

Fang women, too, had cultural weapons. One, arguably, was "The White Lady." This dance, allegedly performed only by women, became particularly popular among Fangs from the forties onward, just as proindependence sentiments were beginning to be incubated in new political organizations and the wider negritude movement was promoting a revalorization of African cultures and rejection of European colonization. Dancers of "The White Lady" wear a mask with four faces. The front face smiles, representing the whites' claims of good intentions, but the faces on the sides and back depict anger and sadness, reflecting the true, malevolent intentions of the colonizers.[74]

"The White Lady" is arguably an example of women's wider role in fostering proindependence sentiments throughout the Guinean population. If (educated and elite) men held the leadership roles in the organized proindependence movements to come, women played an integral part by propagating a counterhegemonic discourse via cultural tools. Throughout the colonial period, women maintained a hidden transcript through traditional song, dance, and the retelling of folktales and oral histories, preserving their own cultures in the face of Spain's aggressive cultural assimilation policies.[75]

Women also maintained the hidden transcript through attempting to cure loved ones through traditional, rather than Western, medicine (such was the case of Nnanga in *Ekomo*) and, as Women's Section archives reveal, through ignoring Spanish attempts to change their culture even at the level of dining room habits: the Spanish headmistress of a Section girls' school in Santa Isabel complained, in 1968, that "with regard to their way of eating, [the girls] have to be continually observed, because as soon as they can, they go back to their primitive customs."[76]

Through these tools, which importantly could speak to large swathes of the local population but which the Spanish could not always understand, women transmitted a counterhegemonic, anticolonial political message. And the increasingly hostile atmosphere created by these messages put pressure on Spain. Thus, women's anticolonial resistance was a true partner to the efforts of the male-dominated organized proindependence movements that lobbied the UN for Equatorial Guinea's decolonization. The actions of these movements are delineated below.

As Donato Ndongo-Bidyogo points out, it is not easy to establish the precise dates of the birth of nationalist movements because of "the oral tradition as the only documented testimony and the necessarily clandestine nature of acts of conspiracy."[77] Nevertheless, we can say that the initial organized movements emerged in the years following World War II, when ideas of freedom were spreading and the UN, along with its Decolonization Committee, was established.[78] Around 1947 Acacio Mañe formed the National Crusade for the Liberation of Guinea (its name was changed in 1954 to the National Movement for Freedom of Equatorial Guinea or MONALIGE). Mañe traveled around Guinea recruiting new members among the relatively small, educated elite—almost all the nationalist leaders were among the minority of Guineans to hold "emancipated" status. Around this time, we see Guineans, women and men, imprisoned for espousing anticolonial views.[79] Several individuals who were discontented with Spanish rule held a small revolt in the Banapá seminary in September 1951. At least twelve were imprisoned, including Enrique Gori Molubela, who would later become president of the Autonomous Government of Fernando Po (now Bioko). When released, most sought exile in Gabon or Cameroon or pursued studies in Spain.[80]

In 1955 Spain was admitted to the UN. This was a crucial step for Spain's reappearance on the international stage after decades of isolation, but as Alicia Campos highlights, it resulted in increased pressure to decolonize.[81] Equatoguinean proindependence activists were aware of this and acted strategically, expending much energy on lobbying the UN.[82] Indeed, Spain's desire to participate fully in international society was a key reason in its eventual decision to cede independence.[83] Another factor was the anticolonial fervor of Guinea's neighbors. As in Western Sahara, the proindependence discourses that were flowing throughout Africa at the time were reaching the territory and served as inspiration.[84] Fang in Cameroon and Gabon as well as in continental Guinea formed a movement known as *alar ayong* (Fang for "unite the clans"), which propagated a Fang nation that would transcend colonial borders.[85]

On 20 November 1958 Mañé was killed by the Spanish Civil Guard in Bata after denouncing the decree that made Fernando Po and Rio Muni Spanish provinces, a manoeuver, as Mañé was aware, by Madrid to avoid UN pressure for decolonization.[86] This murder of a MONALIGE leader gave further impetus to the proindependence movements. The youth of Guinea began "to whisper [Mañé's] name in hushed voices" and, as was the case with Bassiri in the Sahara, his picture was passed clandestinely.[87] Mañé's face, name, and memory became symbols for the hoped-for independence.

Shortly after Mañé's death, on 21 November 1959, Enrique Nvo died in suspicious circumstances in Cameroon, reportedly murdered by Spanish-employed mercenaries.[88] The clouds that surround Nvo's end allow us to once again draw a comparison with Bassiri. Like his Saharawi contemporary, Nvo became the subject of hopeful speculation. While Saharawis assured themselves that Bassiri was in hiding plotting his next anticolonial move, some Guineans spread the rumor that Nvo was away lobbying the UN and would be back soon with good news.[89] The violent treatments of suspected political activists also served to rouse anti-Spanish sentiment. Threatened by the specter of Fang nationalism, Spaniards on the Guinean continent organized armed militias.[90] Ana remembers strict curfews and indeed controls on all movements in her village in Kié-Ntem, plus tortures and killings not just of known activists but also of men merely suspected of activism. Just as the Zemla massacre radicalized Saharawis, the brutality in her village persuaded Ana that "colonialism in Equatorial Guinea, like all colonialism, was a disaster."[91]

On the back of the two martyrdoms of independence, the growing numbers of political exiles in Cameroon, Gabon, and Nigeria began to hold meetings, planning how to harness the support of newly independent African states and to sow nationalism in Spanish Guinea. It was for such people that women like Helena collected money and passed crucial messages. Most of the proindependence strategizing meetings were male-only affairs, but the 22 June 1959 meeting of Guinean residents of Gabon held in Libreville benefited from the contributions of a woman known only as "Madame Pepita," while later meetings in Nigeria were attended by Emma King Renner, Juliet Lisk, and "Keke, Saye and Tuali."[92] Back in Equatorial Guinea, women such as María Ayekaba in Rio Muni and Fidela Boneke in Bioko fought shoulder to shoulder with men, contributing to the clandestine political meetings held by the relatively well-off Guinean elites.[93] Constancia Balbao recalls that women funded the MONALIGE, prepared food for its meetings, and hid wanted men.[94] In this way, women's work provided the foundation of nationalist mobilization. Anita Awaho, a creole woman born in Santa Isabel, owned Bar Anita downtown in the same city. While the main bar served as a watering hole as one would expect, she also kept a secret back room used for meetings by pro-independence activists.[95]

We have already read of the activities of women like Helena, gathering funds and carrying crucial messages on their lips. Crucially, as was the case in the earliest days of the anti-Spanish movement in the Sahara, and indeed of several other contexts where anticolonial movements arose, women were able to carry out this "silent" work because the entrenched sexism of the colonial authorities could not conceive of women being involved in revolutionary efforts.[96] Says Ana, "The officers didn't think that women were capable of being involved in political activities."[97]

Other older Equatoguineans talk of the integral role that women played in persuading their husbands, brothers, and sons to support the movements. Indeed, women's networks and the influence they held over their menfolk were integral to expanding the anticolonial sentiment. Although, as Anne Laurence points out, the idea of "the women behind the men" is difficult from an ideological point of view for those who wish to see women on their own terms, in a time and space where women were relegated from traditional political spaces, purveying influence over their male relatives was an important source of political action for Guinean women.[98]

While MONALIGE was led by Atanasio Ndong, who was forced into exile for his political activities but often came back clandestinely to meet with colleagues in Guinea, other movements emerged, mostly in exile to avoid persecution by the Spanish. These included the Popular Idea of Equatorial Guinea (IPGE), the Pro-Independence Movement of Equatorial Guinea (MPIGE, later absorbed by MONALIGE), the National Movement of Union, the Popular Union for the Liberation of Equatorial Guinea (UPLGE), and the Bubi Union.[99]

In August 1963, under continued pressure from the UN, Spain announced its plans to create a system of autonomy for Guineans, which was put to plebiscite. Guineans voted in favor.[100] New Year's Day 1964 saw the birth of two indigenous-led autonomous governments, one for Rio Muni and another for Fernando Po. Both worked under the "supervision" of a Spanish government advisor and the General Metropolitan Commission, which replaced the governor. Defense, foreign affairs, and budget remained under Madrid's control.[101] Enrique Gori Molubela became president of the Autonomous Government of Fernando Po, and Bonifacio Ondó Edú headed up the Autonomous Government of Rio Muni. Both had returned from exile to take up these positions.[102]

The Movement for the National Union of Equatorial Guinea (MUNGE), which dominated the autonomous governments created in 1964 (Gori and Ondó were members), was created at a Congress in Bata on 30 November 1963.[103] The Movement's aim was to negotiate, peacefully and gradually, independence from Spain in partnership with the "Caudillo," recognizing "how much Spain had given [the Guinean] people."[104] Gradual decolonization was the best option, thought its affiliates, in order to give time to train the population for the new responsibilities that independence would bring. It is unsurprising, therefore, that, as Alicia Campos has highlighted, a strategic "double language" emerged among the Guinean nationalists: one used abroad, based on discourses of self-determination and anticolonialism *de vogue* on the international stage, and one used at home, which emphasized the "civilizing" influence of the Spanish and the links with Spain that would be achieved postindependence.[105]

Following the creation of the autonomous governments, the atmosphere in the country became "extremely tense and difficult."[106] The most collaborative of the Guinean elites became gradually less popular. Of Abilio Balboa, the mayor of Santa Isabel, Maria Nieves Sunyer of the Women's Section, for example, remarked, "He's the most intelligent and most European, but it seems that because of that, the natives don't like him."[107] Okenve notes clashes in rural areas between the general populace and the village "tribal chiefs," who, reminiscent of Djemaa members in the Sahara, had been selected and imposed by Spain, replacing the more democratic traditional systems of political control. Aware that a Spanish exit would not be in their immediate personal interest, these "tribal chiefs" were among the minority that was not proindependence.[108]

In 1965 the UN, in response to the demands of the Guinean nationalists, asked Spain to give a date for the concession of independence.[109] The MUNGE began its path to radicalization. This was particularly so following a civil service strike, by which time it had become clear, as Campos argues, that autonomy was not serving the interests of Guineans.[110] It is important to note that many of the MUNGE's leaders had previously been in trouble with Spanish authorities owing to their proindependence activism. As such, upon seeing that autonomy was not a gradual "training period" to prepare Equatoguineans for taking over all institutions and assuming independence, as they had expected, but rather a strategic transition to neocolonial rule, it is not surprising that MUNGE affiliates became increasingly proindependence.

The tense situation that characterized the midsixties saw many sectors of the population palpably fed up with their lodgers. This was partially thanks to women's efforts to transmit an anticolonial hidden transcript of resistance through cultural tools, as described above. By February 1968 resistance to Spanish rule was becoming increasingly violent. Carmen Obón, a Spanish Women's Section teacher, wrote from Bata: "No one is scared here, but in the forest they are. All the white women have left, those ones who had a ticket for a date before

June. There's no tickets left for the boat. . . . In Santa Isabel they've killed two white women."[111]

Finally, on 14 April 1968, Spain committed to the international principles of decolonization and began preparations for an election.[112] On 12 October 1968, Francisco Macías became president following his successful election campaign. Yet unlike Bonifacio Ondó or Atanasio Ndong, Macías, a civil servant under Spain and, after provincialization, mayor of Mongomo, did not have a history of having suffered repression or exile, or like Acacio Mañé and Enrique Nvo, of risking life and limb for self-government.[113] Why, then, was Macías the preference of the Guinean people? I argue below that, in some ways, his election indicated the failure of a hegemonic project in Laclau and Mouffe's sense.

For Laclau and Mouffe, a theory of "equivalence" can help those struggling against an oppressive power. In colonial contexts, a movement struggling for independence often uses the constructed idea of the nation to unite oppressed peoples against the colonialist foe. Each of the struggling parties' complaints is, to use Laclau and Mouffe's terminology, made equivalent: women survivors of domestic violence offered no justice by the courts, victims of forced labor and those denied dignity on account of their color are encouraged to recognize their common concern with independence from the colonial power. An imagined nation—they are all *Equatoguinean* and are all oppressed by *Spanish*—they can join their hands. I do not mean to suggest that the idea of "nation" is universally empowering for colonized peoples. But in the struggle for hegemony, nationalist discourses are commonly employed to rally support and solidarity in anticolonial contexts, just as a constructed understanding of womanhood is often used in feminist struggles.

Eugenio Nkogo Ondó, one of the proindependence activists of the fifties and sixties, argues that Equatoguinean nationalism failed even before independence was achieved.[114] Murray Steele, who highlights that a grassroots nationalist movement never emerged (we should highlight here the discrepancy between the anticolonialism of the masses and the lack of nonelite representation in the organized movements), echoes this view.[115] Similarly, Campos asserts that "fragmentation was a main feature of the Guinean nationalism."[116] Nze Nfumu explains the face of this fragmentation: "The lack of an objective nationalism, of an effective nationalism, ensured that the Equatoguineans of pre-independence did not speak of a single country, but of a type of ripping into parts so that each group, along ethnic, regional, or other criteria, did its bit for whoever would best serve its interests."[117]

In other words, the proindependence movements did not create a chain of equivalence to unite the different groups, ethnicities, and regions of Guinea. Using the "divide and rule" policy so typical of European colonialism, Ndongo argues that Spain created ethnic divisions intentionally. Spain brought the "spirit" of civil war to Guinea, he states, and did so by "presenting the country not as a unity but as a fragile amalgam of antagonistic tribes, some poorer and more 'wild' and others more 'civilized' and rich, whose coexistence could only be guaranteed by Spain; the objective was to invoke suspicions and rivalries that had not previously existed."[118]

A letter to Madrid penned by Edmundo Bosio, candidate for the Bubi Union party, and his colleague Ricardo Bolopá illustrates well the effect of Spain's strategy. Their words, scribed shortly before the elections, beg for Spain's intervention in favor of an independent Fernando Po for the Bubis in order to prevent "slavery . . . , civil war, and genocide."[119] Bubis, the preferred ethnicity for the colonizers, greatly feared discrimination and violence at the hands of the, until now, less privileged Fangs. Other ethnicities had their own parties that relied on ethnic support bases, such as the Democratic Fernandino Union and the Ndowe Union. It is true that the Spanish attempted the same strategy of division in the Sahara with the creation of the Djemaa and the PUNS, structures that "represented" the "heads of tribes" and thereby emphasized the heterogeneity of a tribal society. Nevertheless, the POLISARIO arguably had a far easier task in uniting the population, given the largely shared language, religion, and culture with which Spanish authorities had actively avoided interfering and the relatively short period of time in which the Saharawi population had become urbanized and in which they lived under direct Spanish rule.[120] Conversely, the major indigenous ethnic groups living in Spanish Guinea spoke different languages, practiced different religions (before Spain's enforced Catholicization, at least), and had very different cultures, popular histories, and social and political practices.[121] Arguably then, each of these ethnic groups had a latent potential to develop their own nationalist conscience and pursue their own, individual nationalist projects, and Spain had several decades to foster a sense of difference between these groups.

In the presidential elections, Ondó Edú was seen as the candidate backed by Spain's barely hidden hand, which damaged his popularity in some communities. Atanasio Ndong, on the other hand, had lived in exile so long that he was not well known by "the people." His campaign lacked confidence, and he seemed to focus on how he could form a coalition with the winner rather than ever envisioning himself as the victor. Edmundo Bosió was the product of the ethnic differences discussed above, and while a welcome candidate for many Bubis, for obvious reasons his Bubi Union party had less appeal for the Fang majority and other ethnicities. Macías, the remaining candidate, was not Spain's first choice but one that the colonial power nevertheless felt comfortable with in terms of its future options for influence.[122] As Cusack has pointed out, Macías, Obiang, and several high members of both their regimes had been among the Equatoguinean elites under the Spanish system and had studied on the mainland.[123] Furthermore, Macías possessed a natural forte for public relations. As Nze Nfumu points out, he knew Fang culture well and took advantage of this when carving out his public image.[124] He fashioned himself as the people's leader, and indeed this is what he became: he won the democratic election and became president on 12 October 1968.

What happened after October 1968 and the gendered shape of the Macías regime will be subjects for chapter 6. First, though, I go back to 1964. In the following section, I take a magnifying glass to the resistance of one small sector of the Guinean female population: women who had contact with the Spanish Falange party's Women's Section. The archives of the latter provide an insight into how Equatoguinean women showed resistance to colonialism, racism, and sexism simultaneously.

### Intersectional Resistance: Fighting the Racism, Sexism, and Colonialism of the Spanish Women's Section

In 1964 a nineteen-year-old Ana was not happy with her parents' birthday gift to her. "What a present! An abusive husband!" Indeed, it was on her birthday that she married Roberto. Ana never came into contact with the new Spanish arrivals of 1964, who were ostensibly supposed to be "empowering" women like Ana: the Falangist Women's Section.

The Women's Section arrived in Guinea at the invitation of Gori Molubela, who was the president of the Autonomous Government of Santa Isabel, Fernando Po.[125] The MUNGE and the increasingly radical Guinean elites associated with the Autonomous Government envisaged a role for women in constructing a future independent Guinea. For this they needed to train women. Yet the role would be in line with the Falangista model: women would be good housewives and mothers. Unlike the POLISARIO, then, the MUNGE did not incorporate feminist demands into its nationalist rhetoric, even when it radicalized from 1966 onward.

Unlike in Spanish Sahara, Women's Section staff arrived in Equatorial Guinea fully aware that their destination was set to become an independent country. Their aim, from the outset, was not only to impose the Falangist construction of femininity on the colonized subjects but also to ensure the longevity of this construction. The Section sought to train "native" teachers to reproduce Francoist housewives postindependence.

As was the case in Spanish Sahara, one of the initial and necessary tasks of the organization was to genderwash: to justify colonialism by lamenting the "subordinate and backward" position of the "native" woman. In a 1964 research report aimed at mapping the situation of the Guinean woman and how the Section could "organize [itself] in benefit of the women of the territories," Dolores Bermúdez Cañete finds that "up until now, the woman has been no more than man's slave, and is valued less than any animal. She does all the work, no matter what type."[126] The Women's Section aimed to "correct" this. An information leaflet aimed at Guinean women explains the role of the Section: "Our goal is to *train women*, making them essentially feminine and . . . also managing to convert them into wives and mothers who truly are companions to men."[127]

The structures installed by the Women's Section in the two provinces of Rio Muni and Fernando Po were much the same as those in the Sahara and in Spain itself: domestic schools for women, primary and high schools for girls, and ambulant teachers to reach out to the rural areas. However, the Women's Section of Spanish Sahara was exceptional in terms of how its curriculum gradually took on a more academic face. In Guinea, apart from literacy classes, the curriculum was entirely focused on exporting Falangist womanhood. Reports sent back to Madrid on the achievements and work of the Section focus on progress made by pupils in flower arranging, table setting, eating habits and Spanish cookery, cleanliness, personal hygiene, hospitality, house decoration, and even the arts of conversing like a lady, laughing delicately, and behaving appropriately on trains and other forms of modern transport.[128] Maria Luisa Iriarte, headmistress of Ewaiso Ipola school, writes in her 1967–68 report of a particular incident that illustrated how far she felt "her" girls had come in their hospitality skills. When a group of white French students from Cameroon came to stay and one told a Guinean student that she did not much care for the latter's skin color, the latter "reacted very well and did nothing but smile."[129] Women's Section students were expected to know their place and accept such racist comments. Indeed, Sipi Mayo, who attended this school, recalls the everyday racism: "The indigenous girls (that was what we were called in those days) and the European girls wore different uniforms. . . . They sat at the front, we sat at the back. . . . If we spoke Bubi, we were forced to wear a necklace of foul-smelling snail shells, and we couldn't take it off until another girl spoke Bubi and then we'd have to pass the punishment on to her. . . . On the bus, the indigenous girls sat at the back with no cushions, the whites sat at the front with cushions."[130]

Women's Section also attempted to impose on Guinean women and girls the strict sexual controls to which they themselves were subjected in Francoist society. Single Spanish women moving to Guinea were only permitted to do so if they could prove they would live in the household of someone who could attest for their "morality."[131] They tended to become upset at signs of sexual activity among their students: "Imagine our displeasement," Purita García Morales wrote from Bata to her colleague in Madrid. "Irene . . . was going around with men and in a bad way. . . . A great girl, clever, a wonderful presence . . . and look what she does."[132] Sexual activity and being a "good student" were mutually exclusive for the Women's Section, and so, when selecting which girls would have the opportunity to study in Spain, girls regarded as promiscuous or who had had abortions were overlooked.[133]

The Section always had the aim of incorporating "natives" into its staff, and in 1965, a summer training program in the peninsula for sixty Guinean women was proposed as "fundamental" by Maria Nieves Sunyer, one of the leaders of the Section. Selection of the women would be easy. Sunyer proposed simply picking "the wives and sisters of the Autonomous Government's authorities."[134] Indeed, as Anne Foot has argued, Spain ruled through a system of patronage that favored loyal (significantly, mainly ethnic Bubi) Guineans.[135] The practices of the Women's Section in choosing which women and girls would receive study grants, who could access opportunities for education and work experience on the Spanish mainland, and who would be employed back in Guinea are a microcosm of this wider system. Women's Section archives house much correspondence between Section staff and male Guinean autonomous government representatives and civil servants regarding study grants for the latters' daughters and sisters, and they show a preference for women married to Autonomous Government politicians when recruiting "native" teachers.[136] A quotation of a letter from the Fernando Po delegation of the Section back to the Madrid office helps illustrate how things worked: "We also have two *mulatas* that did a few domestic courses for three months in Las Palmas and although they're not much good, since their father is the secretary of the Police Station, we had to give them a post somewhere."[137]

The female elite after independence would be hand-picked, thought Spain, from among the female relatives of the Guinean male civil servants. Yet this female elite, in line with Francoist ideology, would always be kept subordinate to men. The types of studies to which women had access helped to ensure the future of this unequal gender power dynamic. Few were the Women's Section students who were allowed to go on for a university degree after completing high school. Most were sent to Women's Section's own training centers in Spain and the Canary Islands to study vocational courses in traditionally "feminine" (the traditionally Spanish construction of feminine, that is), underpaid, and undervalued fields such as home economics, dressmaking, or nursing.[138]

And yet Guinean women, even those hand-picked by the organization to be sent to Spain, resisted Women's Section indoctrination in a number of ways.

Academic reports of schoolgirls, for example, illustrate a lack of interest in the syllabus and/or a will to defy the authority of the Spanish teachers. Adela Ntang Nbeng, for example, "[did] things reluctantly and always protest[ed]," while Carmen Eyenga Mba-Oyana, "[was] a very apathetic girl and live[d] her life in the School without making an effort to fit in with School life."[139] Angela Nefiri Bacale Usuru, who was later to become a physical education teacher for the Section, showed "indifference," Florentina Ntutumu Nchama showed "apathy" and "evasion" of her duties despite her noted capabilities, and Rosario Tomo Coffi found it "very hard to obey."[140] These school reports also revealed teachers' concerns that Guinean girls tended to mix with each other exclusively rather than with their Spanish classmates.

But aren't the Women's Section staff right to interpret these reports as Guinean "bad behavior"? How can I confidently suggest this is resistance? Scholars of student resistance such as Daniel McFarland recognize jokes, whining, and private socialization as passive forms of everyday resistance, and as part of a hidden transcript, and open challenges to the teacher or refusal to work as "active resistance."[141] Ties in the classroom, or cliques, such as those of Equatoguinean girls studying in Spanish peninsular schools, give resistant students a network of support, enhancing their ability to rebel repeatedly in class.[142]

An advantage held by scholars of African independence movements is that they can talk to surviving activists. During a visit to Malabo, I showed extracts of the above school reports to a woman who had attended a Spanish nun's boarding school. I asked what she thought of the reports. Her response highlights how girls resisted, yet at the same time showed further agency via maintaining a veneer of collaboration in order to create advantageous opportunities: "My reports were like that. I think they show resistance. I got told off for not following orders and things like that, but these nuns were militants! They'd have us doing the laundry, scrubbing the floors all day, and I was in a nun's school but the Women's Section schools were just the same, and we tried to rebel against all that. But me, I won the nuns over because I was clever and nice and I studied hard, so they helped me to get a study grant to go to Spain. So you could say I collaborated. Yes, in a way we collaborated with the system. But it was only to get ahead."[143]

Girls who studied in Spain did so under strict supervision. At the discretion of the Women's Section branch where they stayed, girls were or were not allowed to attend functions organized by other bodies and to go on excursions at weekends. Many girls lived in religious establishments, and on the occasions when girls were allowed out with friends, strict curfews were imposed. But again, Guineans resisted such regimes, ignoring restrictions on freedom of movement.[144]

Significantly, as independence drew closer, discipline in the Women's Section schools of Guinea, as well as among Guineans in Spain, worsened. By late 1967 discipline had become "deficient," and by February 1968 schoolgirls in Bata openly told their Spanish teachers that, while Spain pushed for autonomy, a "war" of independence was imminent and that, therefore, Women's Section courses would come to a halt within a matter of weeks.[145] Postindependence, in early 1969, a Spanish Women's Section teacher found her pupils "more difficult," since they no longer felt they needed to show any obedience to their white teachers.[146] The increased "bad behavior" of schoolgirls as independence approached speaks of the objects of resistance: efforts to undermine the Spanish teachers and the Falangista syllabus were as much anticolonial as antisexist.

As well as the classroom disciplinary problems, Spanish Women's Section staff faced added challenges. The adult domestic classes, which were never popular anyway, were increasingly afflicted with a "dying interest" among attendees as independence neared.[147] Furthermore, staff were frustrated when young Guinean women returning from Spain refused to take the jobs that had been set aside for them. Said one staff member, "It hurts me that they behave like this when they are being helped so much in Spain. . . . Is this what they want for their country?"[148] Despite pressure from Women's Section, some Guinean women took advantage of the training opportunities to pursue life paths of their own design.

Concha Tentor, one of the Spanish leaders of the Women's Section, complained that the organization's locally employed staff did not possess the proper Falangist "spirit."[149] This was despite the efforts, by some of these Guinean teachers, to provide a more varied program for the Section. In 1968 Trinidad Morgades, for example, proposed and led a study about women's role and position in Guinean society to present at an International Women's Conference.[150] Morgades was one of very few Guinean women who managed to complete a literature degree despite the racism and sexism of the colonial system. Later to become one of Equatorial Guinea's foremost authors, vice rector of the University of Equatorial Guinea, and today, an advocate for Guinean girls' education, she worked as headmistress in a secondary school in the sixties. Although Morgades has since defended some of the Falangist Women's Sections values and methods, at the time she challenged some of the Spanish leaders.[151] The latter cautiously noted Morgades's "communist" "political ideas."[152] These "subversive" political views had come to the fore in a disagreement with Spanish staff member Angeles Mallado in spring 1964. Mallado had unilaterally decided which girls would be sent to Spain without any discussion with Morgades. An argument "on racial lines" ensued, and Morgades, according to Mallado, "attacked Spain, the Women's Section, and Jose Antonio

[Primo de Rivera], and she even said some things about the Bible. . . . She even said I should go to her house to submit myself to what she had to say, since this is Africa and I'm a European."[153]

We can see, then, that as in Western Sahara, Guinean women who worked for the Women's Section harbored oppositional views. Collaboration and resistance in colonial times were not a dichotomy. Women showed resilience to colonialism and patriarchy by whittling study and employment opportunities for themselves from the rotten wood that the colonial administration offered. They also reimagined and reappropriated traditional cultural practices to avoid unwanted marriage and attempted to use the colonial justice system to escape abuse. Yet women also outright resisted colonialism, as the cases of Morgades and Helena powerfully illustrate. They subverted notions of the "appropriate" role for women on both sides of the colonial/independence struggle: Spanish authorities' underestimation of Guinean women as political actors allowed the "silent political women" to successfully get on with their proindependence work, while the Guinean elite leaders of the anti-Spanish organized movements, who failed to see the potential of incorporating women into the leadership, nevertheless relied on women for funding, food, safe houses, communications, and safe meeting spaces. Undoubtedly, the proindependence struggle would have looked very different without the contributions of these "silent political women."

Furthermore, the focus in this last section on the hidden transcript maintained by Women's Section pupils, and by those women and girls who refused Women's Section's offers of training in the Francoist housewife model, illustrate the intersectional nature of Guinean women's resistance to Spanish colonialism. Like Saharawi women, they resisted traditional and colonial patriarchies as well as (racist) colonialism itself.

One difference between the POLISARIO and the Guinean proindependence movements is the former's success in linking the grievances of all sectors of Saharawi society to colonialism (from the enslaved, to women oppressed by patriarchy, to the underpaid workers of the phosphate mines), discouraging hierarchies and differences between Saharawis and thereby uniting almost the entire population under one nationalist movement. On the other hand, while there was widespread discontent with, and resistance to, colonial rule in Guinea, the organized political movements were fragmented, elite dominated, and never successful in mobilizing the population behind a unified vision of a future Equatoguinean nation. And I highlight nationalism precisely because a nation was the aim of the proindependence movements, whether it be a Bubi nation on Bioko Island, a merger with the Cameroonian nation, or an Equatorial Guinea composed of all the regions of Spanish Guinea.

With regard to women's oppression, unlike the POLISARIO, none of the movements made a real attempt to discursively address women's specific gender-related grievances. This greatly limited the extent to which women could be mobilized and, indeed, is emblematic of how the movements failed to take advantage of the masses that supported the anticolonial aim. Even if many hearts and minds were anticolonial, they were not united behind one vision of the future but were, rather, struggling against the specter of a new domination by a community other than "one's own." Furthermore, although women have played a strong if forgotten role in the fight against colonialism, the failure to envisage a rupture with the colonial-imagined role for women has also had far-reaching consequences even to the present day with regard to women's role in organized political resistance movements (see chapter 6). This failure plays into the hands of the current dictator Obiang, who, as detailed in part 2, reinforces enduring sexisms while publicly and loudly declaring that he champions gender equality.

# PART TWO

# The Politics of Gender in the Saharawi State in Exile and Equatorial Guinea

# CHAPTER THREE

# Saharawi Women's Resistance in the Diaspora

Four-year-old Zuenana lay still alive among the flames beside her dead parents. The brother of Leila Sidi Mahmoud scooped up the little girl and ran toward the lonely tree on the hill.[1] Zuenana's arm was blown off, yet according to the doctor who gave her first aid, the napalm had possibly provoked hemostasis, which prevented her from bleeding to death.[2] Zuenana remembers her grandfather cutting off the part of her arm that hung loose from the elbow and, later, the doctor treating her. Today, she wishes she could know where her parents are buried.[3]

Zuenana and her family had been sheltering at Um Draiga refugee camp when the Moroccan air force smothered it with the black, building, rolling clouds of napalm and the white, billowing, garlic-scented clouds of phosphorus in February 1976. The other civilian camps of Guelta, Tifariti, and Amgala, all in Western Sahara, suffered similar attacks. Leila remembers clearly that the first tent in flames was that one marked with the Red Crescent symbol on its canvas roof—the hospital tent.[4]

Between the start of the Black March in October 1975 and Spain's official exit in February 1976, city-dwelling Saharawis had been fleeing by car or on foot toward the open desert to the east. It was not an organized exodus provoked by the POLISARIO, however, but a displacement forced by terror.[5] Chilling rumors were rapidly spreading of human rights violations and the military planes, heavy artillery, and rattling tanks of the invasion.

People of the south fleeing the "Black March" (known to Moroccans as the "Green March") headed to the oasis of Um Draiga, a traditional nomad camp, located at the summit of a hill east of Dakhla. Zuenana's family had envisaged a temporary stay at this camp, a safe refuge until a solution was found. Saharawis had expected to be able to return home—they left with "the keys in the bag," as Saleh Lbujali puts it—but the napalming of a civilian population incinerated these hopes.[6] Realizing that no Saharawi was safe in her own country, the refugees headed silently and by night from here to the Tindouf region of Algeria. The POLISARIO had convinced its neighbor and ally to offer the Saharawis a piece of barren, desert wasteland to stay until they could go home.

Tindouf is an Algerian military outpost that sits where the Moroccan, Algerian, Western Saharan, and Mauritanian borders collide. Its defensive army buildings look over the yellow and vast Saharawi refugee camps that begin a few kilometers away. As in Um Draiga, the new camps at Tindouf were populated mainly by children, disabled and old men, and women and were run by the latter. Silka remembers the heavy but willingly realized labor of making and laying bricks, while Tawfa, volunteering as a nurse, recalls the excruciating sadness of having "ten children die every day to epidemics like cholera or tuberculosis or malnutrition" and the silent heartbreak of working on and pushing back tears as news of passed husbands and brothers reached the camps from the frontline.[7]

To this day, these camps in Tindouf remain the dwelling place of some 175,000 Saharawis. Other exiles live elsewhere in the diaspora: Latin America, the Middle East, and Europe, especially Spain, but the camps of Tindouf are unique in having been declared, since February 1976, as the Saharawi state in exile. This is a space, or "social laboratory," where the POLISARIO have been able to realize to some extent (taking into account the very harsh conditions and meager funds) their model of Saharawi society.[8]

The first task of this chapter is to discuss the place of so-called gender equality in POLISARIO nationalist discourse. I then turn to the camps to see how hegemonic discourses on gender equality are used or challenged. These camps were largely a feminine space during the war but have undergone dramatic socioeconomic changes since the end of conflict, the en-masse return of male soldiers, and the now decades-long stalemate. They are therefore the ideal site for analyzing feminist (nationalist) resistance and women's efforts to improve their position in a POLISARIO-imagined Saharawi society. I use a theoretical framework informed by feminist nationalism throughout this chapter.

The scholarship on feminism and nationalism is characterized by a dichotomy of viewpoints. On the one hand, some researchers argue that feminism and nationalism are, like oil and water, immiscible, since nationalism undermines women's rights.[9] On the other hand, some researchers find that feminist nationalism is a possibility, sometimes the *only* possibility. Not only can feminism redefine nationalism to put women at the center but nationalism also has the potential to further feminist causes, especially in cases of foreign occupation, neocolonialism, and capitalist globalization.[10] Nadje Al-Ali and Nicola Pratt move away from this dichotomy. They note that the tensions and harmonies between feminism and nationalism, particularly in postcolonial communities, are complex and dependent on historical and sociopolitical context.[11] I follow their nuanced approach to feminism and nationalism, and in this chapter focus on these themes in Saharawi exiled communities. I find that Saharawi women's rights activists take a feminist nationalist path at times but equally pursue separate feminist and nationalist aims in tandem when the particular women's rights issue demands such an approach. Saharawi women see the benefits of a feminist nationalist struggle, since independence would be to the advantage of Saharawi women in a number of ways, but are also aware of moments when Saharawi feminism and hegemonic Saharawi notions of national identity clash, namely, when women's behavior is seen to encapsulate the "national culture." I argue here that their astute and nuanced approach, which both marries and divorces feminism and nationalism at particular moments, is a recipe for assuring Saharawi women's rights.

With regard to the structure of this chapter, I first analyze the role of "gender equality" in the official nationalist discourses of the POLISARIO. Then, I turn my attention to the situation of women in the Tindouf camps, the seat of the Saharawi government in exile. I explore how the UNMS uses traditional gender norms, hegemonic in Saharawi society, to lobby for women's increased participation in the highest echelons of political power. Third, I look at how the UNMS, as well as Saharawi feminists acting as individuals, envisage a new construction of Saharawi masculinity that encapsulates mothering. Fourth, I focus on efforts of the UNMS and other Saharawi women to make sure that women are included in, and benefit from, the emerging market economy in the camps. Fifth, I turn my attention to a case where the West has undermined the struggle for women's rights in the camps by focusing on the case of the so-called kidnapped women, that is, women allegedly forced to remain in the camps against their will. Sixth, I look both at women's "everyday" forms of resistance in the camps, and how they take advantage of Islamic norms to support their position, in cases surrounding gender-based grievances in the arenas of marriage and divorce. Next, I look at Saharawi attitudes toward lesbian, gay, bisexual, and transgender (LGBT) rights in the state in exile. Finally, I shift the focus away from the camps as a space of feminist nationalist activism in exile and look at two cases of how such activism is played out in the other Saharawi diaspora, Spain.

## "Gender Equality" in the Early Nationalist Discourses of the POLISARIO

A traveller asks me
what is the meaning of Galb.
I tell him, for example,

that Miyek is a blemish
in the belly of the earth.

That Ziza, for example,
is the Berber for breast,
and that the wing of a dune
can touch the sea of the sky.

I say, for example,
that in the high peaks
of prismatic dawns
there is much sleeping life
rubbing its skin.

That in the transient stone
there are stationary craters,
islands emerging
from an ocean of nothing.

For example, a Galb might be
the name of a girl
engraved
into the eyelashes of a cave.

As Tiris is the navel
of the Sahra,
Galb is a heart,
a heart of stone.[12]

In Limam Boicha's imagination, Western Sahara is personified as a woman,
just as she was by the colonial pioneers whose exploits were told in chapter 1.[13]
However, Boicha's Sahara is not just a beguiling object of desire (as she was in
the eyes of the colonists). The image of a lovesick figure declaring his eternal
devotion by carving his darling's name in rock, and the play on *galb*'s double
meaning in the final stanza, suggest that the poetic voice is in love: Western
Sahara is his sweetheart. How do people come to *love* their nation in this way,
often so deeply that they would sacrifice everything for it? In his classic work on
nationalism, Benedict Anderson responds to this question with the concept of
*imagined communities*. Anderson sees nations as invented entities distinguished
from one another not by authenticity but by how they are imagined.[14] That is,

a nation is not something authentic, material, and timeless but rather something based on a shared (imagined) sense of belonging, of perceived commonalities, between a group of people. The "imagined community," the national identity of those who group themselves together, is forged largely through narratives of national culture, through nationalist discourses. I understand "discourse" not just as speeches or written material but also as organizations, institutions, historical events, and so on that function to foster common perceptions and understandings for specific purposes.[15] The Gramscian concept of hegemony, where various ideologies or discourses come into conflict until the victor is propagated through society at all levels, is central to my understanding of how discourse works.[16] The hegemonic discourse governs people's behavior, to the point that its ideological character is hidden and appears as common sense or natural. No physical force is needed to ensure that individuals submit to the ideological system. For example, it is because of hegemonic constructions of gender in the United Kingdom that many British people insist that little girls should wear pink and boys should not wear skirts. The very maintenance of the boy/girl dichotomy is also the result of hegemonic ideas about gender. As for the Saharawi nation, certain ideas, practices, and attitudes become understood as "naturally" Saharawi, if they enjoy hegemony. In this section, I look at the idea of gender equality, the idea that "women have always enjoyed equality in Saharawi culture," in POLISARIO's official nationalist discourses. I argue that gender equality is seen to be just as intrinsic to Saharawi national identity as are the geographical features of Western Sahara's landscape, so lovingly and patriotically evoked by Boicha.

Since its formation in 1973, POLISARIO discourse has been influenced by the revolutionary vogue of the period. Indeed, founding members of the POLISARIO were followers of the Vietnamese, Palestinian, and other African causes as well as of revolutionary thinkers such as Fidel Castro, Che Guevara, Gamal Abdel Nasser, and Mao Tse-tung.[17] They were particularly keen observers of the revolutions of Guinea Bissau and Algeria, in which the position of women changed as their participation in the armed struggle increased.[18] The influence of the socialist and revolutionary ideas of the time was central in early POLISARIO discourses and the articulation of their vision of society in the Laclauian sense.

According to Ernesto Laclau, society is incomplete. Thus nothing can be said about its "truth" or "totality" since these are impossibilities. Society is merely an attempt to cover a lack. We use convenient fantasies provided by political ideology in an attempt to fill this void.[19] An ideology creates such a fantasy by way of *articulation*, which is the act of giving a partially fixed meaning to various signifiers within a discourse. This implies that meanings are never

inbuilt but, rather, contingent.[20] For example, the signifier "freedom" is usually articulated very differently in authoritarian ideologies than in liberal ones.
By combining together a complex web of articulations, ideology engenders
a certain way of understanding society and produces the fantasy that should
the ideology be followed and acted upon, then society will be realized.[21] Empty
signifiers, concepts that are present through their absence, help to create the
fantasy. For example, an empty signifier used in POLISARIO ideology is *liberation*: liberation from Moroccan colonialism. Liberation, owing to its absence,
is desired, and if it were to be achieved, Saharawi society would be complete.
As such, in the early years forging the nationalist movement, POLISARIO
ideology was articulated in opposition to what it conceived to be "Moroccan
Nazism,"[22] that is, on the basis of revolutionary, socialist discourses that emphasized the centrality of the role of the popular masses for social (revolutionary)
change, the need for unity of the "heroic people,"[23] and the principle that
collective interests should always precede those of the individual. I argued
in chapter 1 that (black) women themselves also greatly influenced emerging
POLISARIO ideology. Their relentless and varied resistance strategies in the
face of gender and racial inequalities arguably inspired the leaders of the nationalist movement, who realized that emancipation from gender, racial, and colonial oppressions had to be incorporated into the nationalist movement in order
to mobilize the entire population.

POLISARIO therefore came to envisage an egalitarian, communal society
in which slavery was abolished and the emancipation of women and their full
participation in society was an aim.[24] Saharawi nationalist discourses launched
a reading of the social that, following what Laclau and Mouffe have named the
"logic of equivalence," attempted to divide the field of discursivity into two
opposing and antagonist ideological blocks able to deny each other (and, therefore, constitute each other and delineate their mutual contours), while "decon-
testing" and making equivalent a whole series of more particular discourses,
conflicts, and grievances.[25] The discrimination of Saharawi employees in the
Fosbucraa mines, the lack of access to education of Saharawi women, the impossibility for younger generations to participate in the political process (blocked
by the Djemaa puppets), and the racial discrimination of the enslaved and ex-
slave black population were all made equivalent and acquired their meaning
as different expressions of a single oppression: the oppression of the Saharawi
people by a colonialist foe—Spain in the first instance and Morocco and Mauritania later. The emancipation of women, therefore, became one more (necessary) step in the process of national liberation.

Focusing on POLISARIO publications from around the time of the beginning of the nation-building process, "the masses" are often addressed as

"brothers and sisters," creating an image of gender equality through language by choosing not to use solely the hegemonic male form of the noun in question and occasionally putting the feminine noun before the male, "women and men," reversing traditional male superiority commonly reflected in grammar.[26] The zealous participation of women as well as men was seen as vital to the success of the liberation movement, and POLISARIO called for "all Saharawi men and women" to stand firm in their roles in the revolutionary process.[27] One 1974 publication ironically states that "Spanish colonialism prohibits our women from going to cultural education centers, perhaps to conserve our customs!"[28] The irony here nods to Spanish orientalism as well as underlines that women's emancipation was necessary for the realization of Saharawi nationhood. According to a 1976 POLISARIO publication, the Saharawi woman "deservedly faces the enemy alongside men" and should receive "a cultural and political education" in order to help her carry out her "decisive . . . role in the revolution."[29]

Aside from making women's emancipation a central component of its nation-building project and, in fact, succeeding in introducing a whole new gender discourse and language in official documents and publications, the POLISARIO also claimed, and continues to claim, that "the Saharawi woman has the same rights as the Saharawi man" and enjoys "all the freedom that she deserves."[30] That is, POLISARIO claims success, not only in changing the discourses but also in reversing the previous (Spanish-enforced) situation of women in society. For example, a 1985 issue of *Free Sahara*, one of the official publications of the POLISARIO, focused on the first UNMS conference. In the lead-up to an article titled "The SADR Has Established the Conditions of Total Freedom for Women," the UNMS alleged that "the Saharawi woman has achieved equality, social freedom, the freedom of the Saharawi woman lies in her maturity, in the grade of her attachment to national identity, to the values of her people."[31] As a revision of the official POLISARIO publications from the mid-1980s onward shows, the story of Saharawi women is constantly presented as a "success story" that demonstrates the "special" character of the Saharawi nationalist revolution, while the UNMS continues to use the positive voices and achievements of Saharawi women to tell the same story internationally.[32]

But what are the benefits for the POLISARIO of presenting such images of women and creating a metonymical sliding between themselves and gender equality?[33] First, the images of women presented by the POLISARIO serve the internal function of giving coherence to political discourse in the formation of national identity. The representations of women delineated above serve to underline the egalitarian, left-wing, progressive, modern "spirit" assigned to Saharawi society. Second, imagining the nation as a woman and seeing women as symbols of the national "essence" serves to strengthen the POLISARIO's construction of masculinity and thereby recruit men for the army. If the nation is a woman, then she must be protected from invasion/rape by foreign males.[34] Thus, men must protect their own masculinity by defending women/the Sahara from the virility of the enemy and by maintaining their control over the feminized nation/body. The POLISARIO highlights the "calamities suffered by thousands of women" and calls on men to exhibit their masculinity by protecting them.[35]

Second, representations of women serve an external function by detaching Saharawi society from Western orientalist stereotypes of backwardness normally associated with Arabic, Islamic countries. One of the ideological "mentors" of POLISARIO's historical leaders was Frantz Fanon, who argued in his seminal work *Black Skin, White Masks* that white Westerners had imprisoned black non-Westerners by hegemonizing the inferior, patronizing stereotypes and pejorative images of the latter.[36] Similarly, in part 4 of his classic work *Orientalism*, Edward Said examines how Western popular images create a certain negative stereotype of the "Arab."[37] It is these Western-fabricated stereotypes from which the POLISARIO attempts to distance itself in order to attract international interest and support.

But as I argued in previous research, instead of questioning the constructed character of Western gazes toward Muslim and "Third World" women, this Saharawi *external-facing* nationalist discourse (internal debates are very different, as is discussed below) accepts such stereotypes in order to present Saharawi women as an exception to the norm.[38] Fiddian-Qasmiyeh has subsequently made a similar argument concerning POLISARIO's externally projected images of gender equality. She asserts that this picture functions as a form of ensuring support from Western aid agencies, which insist on "women's empowerment measures" as a condition of funding.[39] The question that we must bear in mind is what other choice does POLISARIO have? In a decades-long situation of neither peace nor war, with very limited financial resources to sustain the refugees and fight its cause, in a world ruled by an orientalist "West" obsessed with "saving" Muslim, African, and "Third World" women from their own men, POLISARIO is playing the only game there is.

Finally, in a more post-Marxist and critical discourse analytical fashion, we can see how such images of women play a part in the formation of Saharawi identity, constructed around the antagonism with Morocco. A crucial part of nationhood, of "imagined communities," is determining who is "in" your community and who is "out." In other words, the borders of nations are not just geographical but imagined, ideological. The POLISARIO's representations of gender equality reinforce what it means to be Saharawi in the face of Morocco, which during times of conflict is crucial in uniting and mobilizing "the people" against the "oppressors." Women, as signifiers of Saharawi democracy, freedom, and equality, are the border markers that differentiate Western Sahara from "dictatorial," "feudal," and "backward" Morocco, where women are represented in POLISARIO's discourses as subjugated and weak.

But how does the POLISARIO validate and solidify the construction of such images? Above, the quotation from a 1974 POLISARIO publication stated that Spanish colonization reversed the emancipation of women, implying that traditionally, Saharawi women enjoyed equality. This suggests that POLISARIO's discourses of gender equality do not emerge from a vacuum but, on the contrary, are presented as rooted in a deeper tradition, which was only subverted and challenged by the colonialist foes. The narration of Saharawi collective history/story therefore becomes a central field for increasing the plausibility of the discourses concerning present revolutionary achievements. Furthermore, it adds weight to the depiction of the Saharawi nation as a "natural entity" rather than a constructed concept. Indeed, what is in fact an invention can only appear natural and attract mass loyalty by "seeming to persist through time and by being linked to imagined, mythic pasts."[40] As Hayden White points out, historical narrative, far from being merely a neutral discursive form, entails "ontological and epistemic choices with distinct ideological and even specifically political processes."[41] Histories are constructed in hindsight, with the personal opinions and motivations of the writer subconsciously or consciously influencing the final product. The brief history of the position of women in Saharawi society, as seen from the point of view of the POLISARIO, serves the function of justifying and giving coherence to its current ideology and political project. Three main epochs emerge in this history: the romantic precolonial period that illustrates how women have "always" been powerful and equal in Saharawi tradition and culture (the Golden Era of the Saharawi people); the disastrous Spanish colonial period that forced the Saharawi woman into a subordinate position and caused widespread ignorance and retrocession among the population (the time of crisis); and finally, the modern period, beginning with the resistance movement in the late sixties and early seventies when women started to reclaim their "historical" and "truly Saharawi" emancipated position (the moment of reconstruction, of "recovery" of the lost arcadia). In other words, regression and sexism are linked to colonialism and completely removed from Saharawi agency, while gender equality is a natural and historical characteristic of Saharawi society, with deep roots in a distant and idyllic Golden Era.

To summarize then, ameliorating the position of women was a central tenet of POLISARIO nationalist discourse in the midseventies. These discourses also painted gender equality as a "naturally" Saharawi phenomenon, which had been eroded by colonialism before the state in exile successfully reinstated it. Such constructions of "gender equality" served (and serve) the internal function of recruiting women and men to the revolutionary cause. Externally, it aims to secure Western allies for the POLISARIO and draws a cultural border with Morocco. But if POLISARIO has put gender equality at the center of its nationalist discourses in order to further its revolutionary aims, how does a regime determined to *prevent* revolution put the image of gender equality to use? In the next chapter, I will use the case of Obiang to explore this question. For the rest of this current chapter, I look at how these POLISARIO nationalist discourses are reflected, used, and/or contradicted in the everyday life of the Saharawi state in exile.

### Reworking Gender Norms: The UNMS and the Fight against Sexism as a "Naturally" Saharawi Pursuit

Addressing an audience of mostly distinguished sub-Saharan African women at a 2015 conference hosted by the Pan African Women's Organization, Baida Embarek Rahal, Saharawi minister for women and social affairs at the time, noted the tendency of independence movements to, first, see women as the incubators of "national culture" and, second, to put women's emancipation from certain restrictive gender norms second to the goal of national independence.[42] Her paper was illustrative of the UNMS's wider consciousness of women's experiences of struggling for a national cause elsewhere: when the national question is "resolved," the national victory is not equally open to women in that their gender-specific demands are too often ignored. The case of the Algerian revolution is particularly noted by UNMS leaders. There, women struggled hard and made huge sacrifices in the war for independence from France. After independence, however, the emerging Algerian state enacted a family code that Cherifa Bouatta describes as "institutionaliz[ing] the inferior status of women."[43] The UNMS therefore envisages its mission as a blend of overlapping, but sometimes parallel (and therefore double), struggles for national independence *and* women's rights. In other words, because of its awareness of historic "betrayals" of women nationalists postindependence, the UNMS does not assume that women's participation in the national struggle will automatically result in hegemonic gender norms that are more beneficial for women. I argue in this chapter, then, that Saharawi feminist nationalism teaches us that feminist nationalist approaches (the two intersect and oftentimes overlap) *sometimes* involve tackling feminist aims and nationalist ones in tandem.

How does the UNMS approach this "double" mission? I argue that, even though the UNMS is acutely aware that work is needed outside of actions to forward the independence cause to ameliorate women's position, it largely uses nationalist discourses to frame its feminist activities. The UNMS thereby draws greatly on the above-delineated official discourse of the wider POLISARIO. This makes the UNMS's actions more likely to be well received and, therefore, successful among even the most conservative elements of Saharawi society.

Before looking at the UNMS's work in more detail, it is worth describing the geographical and political structures of the camps in brief as well as giving a short overview of how UNMS membership functions. The camps' population is divided into five *wilāyāt* (provinces)—Aaiún, Dakhla, Smara, Auserd, and Boujdour (formally 27th February camp, which emerged to accommodate students of the women's school located there)—each symbolizing provinces of occupied Western Sahara. These are further divided into six *dawāir*, or municipalities, named after Saharawi towns. For example, Smara is divided into Bir Lehlú, Mahbes, Echdeiría, Farsía, Hausa, and Tifariti. Each *daira* (singular form of *dawāir*) is composed of four *barrios* or districts, where *āḥīām* are lined up. The latter are not numbered, but rather each is known by the name of the woman who runs it. As well as these five residential *wilāyāt*, there is Rabuni camp, which is the political and administrative center of the state in exile. Rabuni houses the principal government institutions and several nongovernmental organizations (NGOs) as well as the sleeping quarters of their employees.

UNMS membership nowadays works much as wider POLISARIO membership does. Every woman living in the camps who considers herself a member and/or contributes to the UNMS in some way is a member. To clarify then, throughout this work, by "UNMS" I mean its leadership, unless otherwise stated. Some of the UNMS's key efforts in the camps are focused on increasing women's political participation. Indeed its work in this area has been fruitful. In 2008 the SADR introduced a quota system, which has further increased Saharawi Arab women's already relatively high political participation.[44] At the time of writing, according to the UNMS representation in Spain, 33.7 percent of seats on the Saharawi National Council (SNC), or Saharawi parliament, are held by women. Of the Council of Ministers, 24 percent of seats are held by women. As for the National Secretariat, the executive organ of the POLISARIO, women hold 7.5 percent of seats. At a local level, one of the five *wilāya* governors is female. Internationally, three of the SADR's five deputies on the Pan-African Parliament are women. Yet the UNMS aims for full gender parity at all levels of government. Says UNMS president Fatma Mehdi in this vein, "At the top levels of government, they are always talking about the role of women, but we need to bridge the gap between ideology, or theory, and practice."[45]

Smara camp at dusk, 2014. Photo by Bartek Sabela.

Mehdi and her colleagues pursue methods beyond the quota to work toward their goal of gender parity in government. Above I noted that POLISARIO uses a constructed feminist nationalist history to argue that women have "always" played a strong political role in Saharawi society.[46] The UNMS uses this history to give strength to its push for political parity: Women in government is "normal" in Saharawi culture, and feminine political participation is "naturally" Saharawi.[47]

The UNMS also makes use of Islamic feminism by, for example, engaging religious scholars to make theological arguments in support of women's empowerment, employment, and political participation.[48] I observed this directly at a UNMS event titled "Women, Communication and Media" held on 1 April 2008 in Boujdour camp. Among several (mostly women) speakers discussing research on Saharawi women's access to media, the history of Saharawi women's communications roles in anti-Spanish resistance movements, and the need to formulate programs for collecting women's life histories, an Algerian imam was invited to give a feminist interpretation of women's roles as communicators in the Quran. Prioritizing a greater role of women in Saharawi media would be well within the spirit of Islam and would lead to increased participation of women in the wider social, political, and economic life of the camps, according to the imam. Similarly, the UNMS draws on women's traditional roles as carers and nurturers to encourage the electorate to vote for women. It regularly organizes events to this end at local *daira* level. Again, it is worth quoting Mehdi to illuminate what arguments the UNMS employs:

> If I have a problem, who should I contact for this problem? My woman neighbor, my sister, my woman friend. If you want to sew your tent, who will help you? Women. If you have a problem and you want someone to talk to, to understand and advise you on your problem? Women. Who cares for society, I mean our children, our neighbors? Women. And government is responsible for society, for people. So who is always in the camps? Who has the capacity to solve the problems of everybody in the camps? Everyone says women! Because men are not here. They don't know about our daily problems. So why are you voting for men to be your representative in parliament?[49]

In this way and, it could be argued, in the spirit of cultural feminism, the UNMS builds on the highly respected role of women as carers and nurturers in Saharawi society. As Mehdi explained to me, UNMS also uses this argument to undo efforts by some men to have the hard-earned aforementioned quota reversed on the basis that "women shouldn't participate in government because they are too busy with the children and housework."[50] The UNMS pushes for increased participation of women at the highest levels *precisely because* of their mothering experiences.

Yet the UNMS is shrewd. While always celebrating the importance of women's work as carers and leaders of the *āḥīām*, the UNMS simultaneously calls on men to take on a fair share of the housework and child rearing. While always astutely recognizing that, until the present day, women have inspirationally led the important and historically recognized work of motherhood (and indeed, care for the elderly, the disabled, and social affairs more generally that are linked to the portfolio of the minister for women and social affairs), the UNMS simultaneously rejects biological determinism in calling for male mothering. In the next section, I look at the UNMS's efforts, as well as those of other Saharawi women living in exile, in this arena.

## Imagining New Masculinities: The Politics of Mothering

Motherhood is an intellectual discipline that requires judgment, reflection, and emotion and involves the acts of nurturing and caring. In most readings, from diverse cultural and ideological contexts and historical times, motherhood encompasses not just looking after children but also caring for other family members, such as the elderly, and domestic work such as cooking and cleaning. In hegemonic Saharawi gender discourses, the role of mother is reserved for women.[51] The *āḥīām* are assigned to women, not men, and, apart from on trips to the *bādīa* or in the preparation of meat sacrificed at a wedding celebration,[52] it is rare to see a Saharawi man carrying out domestic labor, except perhaps "helping" to clear away the dirty plates, sacrificing a goat for a feast with distinguished guests, or playing with the children.

In pre-exile, nomadic Saharawi society and indeed during the war, feminine mothering roles formed part of a division of labor in which men would be away for long periods of time grazing livestock or raiding, for example, or latterly fighting at the front line. Before 1975 a woman's role would also depend on whether or not she was enslaved or enslaved other women. Since the return of men from the front line in 1991, however, there is a shining contrast between the packed days of women and girls while men and boys watch on, sometimes with little do if they have finished their studies and have not found employment. As Fatima Zrug Yomani, member of parliament representing the Youth Union at the time of our interview, explained to me, the problem of this unilateral (and very heavy, in the difficult conditions of the desert refugee camps) workload for women is that some women and girls drop out of education early to be able to cope.[53] These unequal, gendered responsibilities are provoked, in many ways, by the situation of neither peace nor war generated by the international community's failure to force Morocco to abide by international law. In the years of armed conflict, women were responsible for all tasks in the camps, many of which would have traditionally fallen on men. We have seen that since its constitution, the POLISARIO has supported this diversified role for women in its nationalist discourses. The result, in the current stalemate of neither peace nor war, is that while men do not encroach on "women's work" of mothering, "[women] do all women's tasks and sometimes also take charge of the men's ones," as Maimona Sayed, head of a Smara camp *daira* at the time of our interview, put it.[54]

Yet encouraging men to take part in care work makes nationalist sense in another way: it makes it easier for Saharawi mothers to enthusiastically participate in the demographic struggle. The womb as a weapon of war is a phenomenon common to prolonged national conflicts, and Western Sahara is no exception. POLISARIO must pursue demographic policies that foster birthing children as an act of patriotism (and that deprioritizes the issue of access to contraception) to ensure the continued existence of a Saharawi population that can claim its right to nationhood.[55] If men would share the long hours of work that mothering requires, women could be better encouraged to expand their families.

Saharawi women politicians and the UNMS are conscious of the need to encourage male mothering if their policies of fostering population growth and women's education, employment, and political participation are going to continue to grow in success. How, then, do women respond to this need? After all, as R. W. Connell has shown, the hegemonic form of masculinity changes over history and according to context: new Saharawi masculinities are possible.[56] At the level of the home, we can see elements of a hidden transcript of some women, who, once out of the earshot of family members, might complain of the "laziness" of their brothers, express sympathy for girl friends who have had to drop out of school to help their mothers, and voice wishes that men would "help out" more. Others might ask (and my subject position becomes salient) if European men divide responsibility for household tasks, to which my response would be to point out the "double burden" or "second shift" phenomenon among the majority of heterosexual couples in Western culture, which puts into question women's so-called liberation, and without the barriers of colonialism, occupation, and exile with which Saharawi feminists have to contend.[57] Of course, the fact that we call this phenomenon the double shift or burden in Europe and North America reflects another important difference between these contexts and that of the Saharawi state in exile: while in the West, the work of mothering has been and is demeaned and looked down upon, in the Sahara, many women would not wish for this valued role to be lowered in public discourse to the status of a "shift."

When it comes to the UNMS, there have been awareness-raising initiatives including dressing the external walls of its headquarters with slogans such as "the *ḥaīma* work is men's work too." Like Equatoguinean feminist Remei Sipi Mayo, who declared, with humor, at the launch of her recent anthology of Equatoguinean women's writing that "[men] make perfect assistants, but they don't *work with us* [on the household chores]," the UNMS reminds its audience that these are not "women's" tasks that men should "help" with but, rather, a responsibility that, these days should be equally shared (the division of labor during the war and before was, the UNMS would argue, far more logical).[58]

Saharawi women writers such as Agaila Abba have highlighted to the audiences of their blogs and websites the roles of exceptional men who have practiced what I have called "male mothering."[59] Indeed, Abba's grandfather's actions date long before the aforementioned UNMS campaign. It is worth quoting her extensively to illustrate how she relates his actions, and its positive impact on her, to the nationalist cause:

When I was growing up my mother left to visit my father's side of our family in a different city. The visit lasted for six months. While she was gone I was under the care of my grandfather. He was the one who made sure I didn't need anything and he also made sure I was going to school everyday as well as doing my homework. My grandfather had a large part of raising me because I was with him in this important stage of my life. He was with me when I needed a person to be my father, mother, and my teacher. He was all this and more, not only for these six months, but for all of my life. I call him the foundation of my life because I have built my life on the principles that he taught me and for this I am so very thankful to him and I admire him dearly.

He wasn't only the foundation of my life, but also he was a freedom fighter for my country. In 1976 he fought in the war between the Western Sahara, and Morocco. He left his family and his new bride when he went to war. This war cost him his sight, his legs, and his health. He made this sacrifice because of his belief in freedom for my nation, and for my people. He also fought for the rights of women in our society as well as in my family. He instructed the elderly men of our family and tribe to release the young women from arranged marriages, and encouraged the women to pursue their dreams and to study no matter if it was in the refugee camps or abroad.[60]

Abba strengthens her arguments, for a Saharawi nationalist audience, by emphasizing the sacrifices her grandfather made for the struggle. This man deserves Saharawi respect, thus his actions in favor of women's rights and men's support in child rearing carry weight. Other women with a strong public profile in the Saharawi nationalist cause in the camps and abroad, such as Asria Mohammed, write with a view to specifically engage men in the debate. Mohammed encouraged her young nephew to make a photo essay to depict her life as a woman in the refugee camps. He shadowed her tending to the goats, washing clothing, preparing the meals, cleaning, and so on. She published the pictures along with the following statement on her Facebook page:

Since we were kids my sisters and I we were always encouraged to study and that we can be anything we want, but we were always reminded of our role as women and what our family and society expect from us.

Because I am the only girl in the house now, I have to make breakfast, clean after them then clean whole house then make lunch then clean after them then carry heavy bags and feed the goats then come back and wash dishes, clothes or anything they think it is dirty (I do same things every day from 9 morning to evening).

It wouldn't have bothered me if I am only serving my mother and my sisters, but it kills me to see how much work women have to do here while men are lying down not helping me. My own brother, uncles and neighbours.

It bothered me when my friends call and ask why didn't you go back to your old job while you are here. Most of them are guys, they think I have so much time and freedom as they do.

It bothered me when men stand in meetings and blame women for not being "active" or present in meetings. Even if we manage to be present physically in meetings, but mentally we are not. Half of my brain would be thinking of the bread I left in the oven or the family and the animals that still waiting for me to feed.

I never felt how difficult daily life for women here until I experience it myself. Years ago I used to work away from home, but my sisters were here covering my absence. Today I am alone and I am hating that I am woman. I am hating how friends and family telling me that I should accept the fact that I am woman and all the responsibility and expectations come with my gender. That I stop complaining and do my job as other girls here.

My mom every single day asks me, no actually begs me to get married. My strongest argument against her proposal is: I would rather be slave for you than for a man.

Daily life is small thing if I compare it to more complicated things.

I asked my nephew to follow me three days in row. Here is my daily work.[61]

Mohammed not only taught her little nephew about the importance of men sharing the mothering work, she called out to her male Saharawi colleagues and, by posting in English, put into question for foreign solidarity activists the notion that all social battles within Saharawi society are resolved. This is significant since, as Mohammed told me, she believes the largest threat to gender equality is believing that it is achieved before the event.[62] Furthermore, she highlights the contradiction between the POLISARIO-supported Saharawi emphasis on women's education and participation in "the cause" and the difficulty of this if one is responsible for running a ḥaīma. In this way, like the UNMS and Abba, she shrewdly links reworkings of gender norms to the nationalist cause while simultaneously challenging hegemonic POLISARIO nationalist discourses that paint a picture of a society enjoying full gender equality.

### Women's Place in the Emerging Market Economy: Social Changes, Resilience, and Economic Independence

"Coca-Cola," scribed in Arabic, decorates the red plastic door handles of Mohammed's mint green grocery shop. His business sits next to El Corte Ingles, a clothes shop named, with a wink, after Spain's most prestigious department store. On the other side of Mohammed's place, a young man sells jewelry. He has fashioned soft metal into sun-frosted bracelets, all emblazoned with a miniature SADR flag and displayed as gleaming treasures in alluring bowls of polished, dark wood.

Women from all over Auserd camp color the shops of Mohammed and his neighbors every day. They arrive on foot or by taxi. The international community's aid provision is no longer anywhere near sufficient. Thus state-administered rations of rice are supplemented with bought goods when a family falls on relatively good times. Women with a little more spare cash might also visit a hairdresser's, even a Turkish bath, while at the market.

Since the 1991 ceasefire and the subsequent realization that a return home was not yet in sight, a market economy has emerged in the camps. Running a shop, taxi, or another business is considerably more lucrative than a public sector job. The POLISARIO, with its limited funds, cannot offer competitive salaries. Thus the communal labor that characterized what Wilson calls "the early revolutionary period," when all were equally impoverished and worked for nothing but rations and hope, diminishes as the market expands.[63]

Men run the majority of these small, private businesses, in line with their gendered roles as breadwinners.[64] But women, too, have netted opportunities. The UNMS supports such efforts by, for example, opening a pizza shop as a social enterprise in Dakhla camp, with posts reserved for single mothers.[65] It has also established a micro-credits program exclusively for women.[66] Also, we should not forget here the economic safeguards afforded to married women, discussed in chapter 1, thanks to Saharawi interpretations of Islam.

In April 2016 four women successfully pitched for external funding to open a women-only driving school in Dakhla camp. With the school, the founders aim to ensure that women are increasingly able to move around without depending on men, but it is also expected to further challenge social attitudes that see driving as intrinsically unfeminine.[67] Ambarka Mohammed Salem has also used entrepreneurship as an opportunity to carve out opportunities for women. She is the director of a factory in the camps that employs eighteen women to produce *āmlāḥaf* from cloth imported from Mauritania.[68]

Women continue to work in the public sphere, which today accords symbolic salaries in line with the POLISARIO's reduced resources. Indeed, Vivian Solana Moreno has highlighted an extraordinary and innovative pro-women policy: When the state's Youth Union lacks resources to remunerate all its volunteers, women are prioritized on the basis that they have less time and opportunity to pursue economic activities.[69] As for "feminine" fields of work, women dominate the primary teaching sector and the running of the local councils. The woman-only field of midwifery is also a sphere that, according to Errer Bouzeid, allows women to pursue some level of economic independence that facilitates increased decision-making over their own lives.[70] Several women also work in government and NGO posts in Rabuni camp.[71]

We have seen so far how the UNMS and activists such as Abba and Moham-med increase the likelihood of attaining feminist goals by linking them to the nationalist cause. In the sections below, I explore areas of Saharawi women's lives where groups of Saharawi women's rights, and invariably also nationalist, activists work beyond the UNMS's areas of focus. The UNMS leadership, and indeed the POLISARIO leadership more widely, has to strike a careful balance between conservative and liberal elements of exiled Saharawi society in imple-menting the "social revolution" that began in the early seventies. Wishing to maintain unity behind the nationalist cause, it must avoid alienating the more conservative elements of Saharawi society. Sometimes, this results in less action from the political elites on certain gender-specific issues than the more liberal aspects of Saharawi society would expect. This is not unusual in postcolonial, nationalist struggles. As al-Ali and Pratt highlight with regard to the Iraqi case, and Frances Hasso shows in relation to the Palestinian one, nationalist move-ments have been open to integrating women into the public sphere but face an uphill struggle when it comes to challenging gender norms associated with the private sphere (marriage, divorce, children, and other aspects of life associ-ated with family law in some countries) and violence against women.[72] Below I explore how Saharawi women tackle such issues outside the state framework, but I also follow a key theme of this book in exploring how globally hegemonic, Western constructions of gender and gender equality in the "Third World" affect Saharawi women's efforts.

### The "Kidnapped" Women: When the West Invades the Debate

Tikrit looks dissatisfiedly at her mobile phone and rolls her eyes. It has run out of battery again. She won't recharge it today because she needs to save the energy from the solar panel to power the TV later, ready for the weekly broadcast of *Star Academy*. The music and dancing show, in which youths from all over the Arab world (minus Western Sahara, significantly) compete for the grand prize of a record deal, enthuses Tikrit, herself a talented singer. Her family can afford the relative luxuries of a TV and solar panel not so much because of her sister's job as a schoolteacher or her brother's role as a soldier (both are paid a symbolic salary by the POLISARIO, which has only very limited financial resources) but to her younger siblings' relationships to Spanish families.[73]

Through the Holidays in Peace program, thousands of children spend the stifling summer months away from the camps with Spanish "parents." Close relationships develop summer after summer, and Spanish "parents" oftentimes send back money to their Saharawi counterparts via the children. The well-intentioned program has resulted in positive relationships for Saharawi and

Spanish families alike on an individual level. More widely, it has at times helped garner visibility and support for the Saharawi cause in Spain and other countries where similar programs have existed. However, at other times, and especially over the last few years, some unforeseen results of the program have served to erode support.

While the issue has existed for much longer, the cases of the so-called "kidnapped" Saharawi women has caught the attention of the Spanish media over the last few years.[74] The case of Mahjuba Mohamed Hamdidaf was the first to receive significant long-term visibility in national print, radio, and television media coverage in Spain. Hamdidaf's story is illuminating with regard to gender relations but also in terms of how foreign policy and media can overshadow, even prevent, an open discussion regarding women's position in the camps.

Hamdidaf was born in the refugee camps in 1991. In 1999 she traveled to Spain for the first time as part of the Holidays in Peace program. After spending three consecutive summers with her Spanish "family," the latter invited her to stay permanently with the consent of her Saharawi family. In August 2014 Hamdidaf went to the camps to visit her family, as she had done many times. Nevertheless, on this visit, her family hid her passport and told her that from then on she would be living with them in the camps. Hamdidaf telephoned her Spanish family to ask for help, expressing that she wished to return to Europe. Significantly, she had just finished studying and had a job offer in the pipeline.[75]

According to Hamdidaf's Spanish family, they spent three months attempting to resolve the situation "quietly," but by October, with negligible cooperation from the POLISARIO, they went public through the Spanish press, television, and radio, which widely reported the "kidnap" of a Spanish citizen with outrage.[76] As Hamdidaf holds Spanish citizenship, Spanish government figures intervened. Finally, on 29 October Hamdidaf left the camps in secret (without the consent of her parents) and returned to Spain. It is unclear what the POLISARIO's role was in her exit. Suspecting that it played an active role, dozens of Saharawis reportedly demonstrated against the POLISARIO for colluding with Spain against the rights of Hamdidaf's biological parents. Other Saharawis drew on human rights discourse to decry the POLISARIO and the UNMS for not explicitly supporting Hamdidaf or other women facing a similar situation. Hamdidaf said of her experience:

> It's about family honor. My biological family is under a lot of social pressure: I am their only daughter and I have six other brothers. For them and for the community that they live in, I should stay here. I have already studied, so they believe that my place now is in the camps. There are people that tell my parents

that I don't even have a right to speak. . . . I love my biological family a lot, but
if I have to decide between going back to Spain or staying here for ever, I pick
going back, it's my decision and they can't cut my freedoms this way. . . . This
isn't a political decision, it's not about attacking the entire Saharawi population,
it's about human rights and gender: if I were a man they wouldn't have done this,
I'm sure.[77]

Let's now analyze some of the diverse Saharawi voices that commented on
the case.

On 20 October, the founder and president of the Saharawi Women's Association in Europe stated that Hamdidaf was happy to be in the camps with
her family and that she was better off with her biological parents.[78] In a comment directed at concerned European solidarity groups, Khadijatou Mokhtar,
UNMS head of external affairs, stated that one can't support Hamdidaf's
individual cause and simultaneously call oneself a supporter of the Saharawi
cause.[79] Other Saharawi feminists such as Aminetou Errer Bouzeid and Lehdia
Dafa, who call out solidarity activists and foreign academics for maintaining a
silence over problematic women's rights issues within Saharawi society, counter Mokhtar's view.[80] Another counter is from solidarity groups, many of which
count Saharawi women among their members. Such groups argue that they
have lobbied for respect of the human rights of Saharawis for decades and find
their arguments against the brutality of the Moroccan occupation undermined
by increasing questions from the targets of their lobbying about the rights of
women in the camps.

The then-POLISARIO ambassador to Algeria has asserted that POLISA-
RIO had attempted, in Human Rights Watch's words, to "negotiate with the
Saharawi family to 'persuade them' to allow Hamdidaf to leave the camps, and
that while the goal was for Hamdidaf to exercise her choice in the matter,
Saharawi 'patriarchal society' with its 'traditions,' 'culture,' and 'complex fam-
ily ties,' required them to handle the matter carefully."[81]

Indeed, we have seen that, upon Hamdidaf's return to Spain, POLISARIO
faced complaints from both "sides" of the debate. The chief POLISARIO
diplomat in Spain announced that the POLISARIO was working to ensure
that Hamdidaf would be able to return to her work and studies but commented that "one thing is the host father, and another is the father."[82] His view
is that the biological father should have the final say in Hamdidaf's destiny.

On the other "side," some Saharawi women took (and take) to social media
blogs and Facebook to support Hamdidaf and subsequent cases. For example,
via Facebook Shaya Deh called for more Saharawi women to join her in speaking out: "When I put myself in Mayuba's shoes I swear this issue is making me

see red. . . . Unfortunately this isn't the first case of Saharawi women held against their will . . . , but if we fight . . . , if we make ourselves heard we'll achieve what we want."[83]

Hurria Salama stated simply, via Facebook, "Free Sahara and the women too."[84] One Saharawi-led proindependence group based in the Spanish autonomous community of Aragón quoted the SADR commitment to the rights of the individual in its statement on the issue. In doing so, it highlighted that, for that group, the Saharawi nationalist cause and the prioritization of a Saharawi woman's *individual* rights were not necessarily mutually exclusive. In sum, with Hamdidaf's case there was potential for a worthwhile debate among Saharawis concerning traditions, values, and women's changing position. However, I argue below that this chance for debate was undermined, at least to some extent, by the reaction in Spain.

At the peak of tensions between Spain and the POLISARIO, the Valencian autonomous government pulled its aid to Saharawi refugees. This was an affront to many Saharawis in the camps, who felt they were being subjected to collective punishment by the power that they see as culpable for their exile. Of course, it was also a disaster for the poorest families, taking into account that the camps receive nowhere near as much aid as is needed in the first place.[85] Furthermore, as several Saharawis have pointed out, the cases of Spanish Saharawis (Saharawis in the Occupied Territory that hold Spanish citizenship) who have been subject to human rights abuses committed by Moroccan authorities have never caused so much interest among Spanish press and politicians as Hamdidaf's case and the subsequent cases of other "kidnapped" women. Also largely absent from Spanish media are Saharawi complaints concerning Spanish families who have unofficially "adopted" Saharawi children without parental consent—this, too, is surely a form of "kidnap." As such, while some Saharawi women tried to harness this issue in order to provoke a debate within their own society regarding women's rights within the family, they faced difficulties as the issue became increasingly framed as one of Sahara versus Spain rather than a question of Hamdidaf's rights and wishes or her biological family's rights and wishes. Hamdidaf's own statement ("it's not about attacking the entire Saharawi population") is telling in this context. She had to make this statement precisely because the Spanish government and media reaction provoked the framing of the issue, in Saharawi society, as one of Spain versus Sahara, not one of a woman's individual rights versus parental authority over their offspring.

On a more positive note, since the Hamdidaf case, young Saharawi women are carving out space online to debate similar issues. The statement from Hurria Salama, "Free Sahara and the women too," has been subsequently reused by other Saharawi women, applied to other issues. This slogan pithily highlights that the nationalist and feminist struggles are seen as necessarily *parallel* rather than *integrated* by some Saharawi women, which constitutes a counterhegemonic challenge to the official POLISARIO nationalist discourses on gender equality that I outlined in the first section of this chapter.

At the time of writing, the most recent campaign where the slogan was used is #NoSoyMenosSaharaui/#I'mNotLessSaharawi.[86] In March 2016 women began to upload to social media photographs of messages written in the sand, on paper, or on their bare arms, such as "I'm not less Saharawi for doing what I want with my life," "I'm not less Saharawi for dressing how I want," or "I'm not less Saharawi for being *sayba* around the world," thereby linking their (nontraditional) life choices with their subjective national identity.[87] Saharawi women launched this campaign in response to an online attack in which a man uploaded photographs of women to the internet who had chosen not to wear the *melhfa*.[88] He accompanied the photographs with a diatribe making use of sexist terms designed to police women's behavior.[89] The man in question, and some other Saharawi bloggers and online voices, decry certain practices by women as "unsaharawi."

Once again, women's burden of bearing the national culture in times of conflict, in which national honor is reflected in women's and girls' behavior and women's roles as biological reproducers of the nation, comes into question.[90] Nevertheless, the women campaigners chose not to dismiss the role of cultural reproduction. Rather, they reconceptualize what constitutes "honorable" behavior for Saharawi women. The activists highlight that their life choices (to live abroad, to travel alone, to upload photographs of themselves to Facebook, to avoid early marriage, and/or to not wear the *melhfa* every day) and decisions to decry certain sexist norms (such as pressure to marry, to travel only with a male guardian, to remain silent about incidences of sexual violence in the camps) are not "unsaharawi."[91] Indeed, in this way, campaigners draw on POLISARIO and UNMS nationalist discourses that make women's empowerment and struggle for equality "naturally" Saharawi, even if they simultaneously challenge the hegemony of the idea that gender equality already exists in Saharawi society. The campaigners say there is nothing "unsaharawi" about challenging the patriarchal control of women. They note that if a Saharawi man today engages in practices that decades ago would have been unusual and/or taboo in Saharawi society, such as making it publicly known that he has a girlfriend, this is not usually cause for questioning his national and cultural identity.[92] The women of "#I'mNotLessSaharawi," the leaders of whom are, significantly, strong advocates for the independence cause if not with official positions in the POLISARIO or UNMS, demand the same right. As well as this public campaign, these activists also have closed-access (invited women only) online groups that provide safe space to discuss what they call "Saharawi modern feminism." Other Saharawi women have set up the open forum "Undressing Taboos" (*desmaquillando tabúes*) to initiate collective action on issues of discrimination on the basis of gender. As Silvia Niebla Almenara has highlighted, other women, while maintaining "untraditional" life choices and dressing habits when studying away from the camps, avoid social conflict and gossip altogether by having two Facebook profiles—one directed at an audience of relatives and neighbors in the camps, one at their friends in Spain.[93]

The growing online resistance of Saharawi women is provoking debate. This is a positive development for women of previous generations, such as the Wurud Asahra anonymous blog writers, who gave up their feminist blog (the first Saharawi one to draw attention to the issue of the so-called "kidnappings") after online misogynist backlash became unbearable.[94] Nevertheless, the hyperbole of the Spanish media, the decision of the autonomous government of Valencia to cut its aid program to the camps, and the hypocrisy of Spanish politicians who were fast to criticize Saharawi society for its denial of Hamdidaf's rights when they have been silent in the face of thousands of heinous human rights abuses by Morocco against (Spanish) Saharawis, resulted in an understandably defensive attitude among several elements of Saharawi society. This was exacerbated by the obvious pain suffered by hundreds of Saharawi families who, knowing that their children may have more opportunities outside the camps, allow them to live with Spanish families and subsequently suffer the anguish of missing a cherished child for years on end. As such, when Saharawi women such as Dafa, Deh, Salama, and others attempted to launch debates concerning the rights of women in the camps on the back of Hamdidaf's case, Saharawi responses largely focused on the crimes of Spain rather than the rights of women. In this way, the foreign policy of Spain, its silence regarding Moroccan crimes against Saharawis, and its long history of what is seen as the betrayal of Western Sahara have served to create an additional barrier to the efforts of some Saharawis to encourage debate on women's rights concerns.

### Bargaining and Resilience: Relationships, Marriage, and Divorce

Soumaya, with whose family I stayed during my third visit to the camps in 2015, scrolls through memes on her smart phone, received and shared via Whats App.[95] She shows me a cartoon of a woman and man embracing, his hands on her buttocks. Both wear tight shorts, his showing the Saharawi flag and hers the Moroccan. He is victorious, to be admired. He has seduced (conquered) this woman. She, on the other hand, is shameful, deserving of some unmentionable label.

I am reminded immediately of the (heterosexist) slut versus stud dichotomy of British culture, in which a man who has several sexual partners wears a badge of pride, while a woman who engages in any sexual behavior perceived as falling outside traditional expectations is slut-shamed.[96] Slut-shaming is a social stigma applied in Britain to women who, for example, are *perceived* to dress in a sexually provocative manner, who have casual sex, or who engage in prostitution, for example. In the Saharawi case, the sexual double standard embodied in the cartoon is linked to the context of threatened nationhood and, thereby, entangled with the history of occupation and colonialism. As Valentine Moghadam argues, Anderson's perspective of the nation as an imagined community can explain this.[97] If the nation is a community or, rather, an extended family at large, then women, as the nurturers and child bearers, must therefore be symbols of the community's values.[98] This is true of the Western Sahara, which, as the logo of the UNMS depicting a Saharawi woman wearing the colors of the national flag illustrates, is gendered as feminine.

Errer Bouzeid has described in much detail how society polices unmarried girls and women in the camps. According to Bouzeid, this ranges from the ritual of *legfil* (closing), which is designed to protect girls entering puberty from losing their virginity before marriage, to the sociolinguistical concept of *sayba*, the state punishment of imprisonment for women who fall pregnant before marriage (it is officially called a "Maternal Assistance Center," but it is compulsory to stay there until a husband is found for the disgraced woman). There is also the more exceptional (and indeed widely criticized and socially taboo) cases of men and boys beating female relatives who may have done something that has put the family's honor under question.[99] Wilson finds that at some weddings in the camps the blood-stained sheets of the wedding night will be displayed at the nuptial celebrations to evidence the bride's so-called honor.[100]

As for the "Assistance Center," the UNMS stops short of criticizing the punishment of unwed mothers and instead lobbies for better conditions at the center.[101] This is perhaps a consolation to the more conservative elements of Saharawi society, and as discussed above, the UNMS is a state body and therefore subject to such political pressures: it must carefully balance the spectrum of views of a religious society in a bid to maintain national unity in the face of colonialism and exile.

In any case, the UNMS position is arguably one of resilience—if women are to be treated in this way, then at least let there be better conditions. On the other hand, Bouzeid has argued in the strongest terms that such a position is one of complicity with the worst kind of gender discrimination. While Dafa, Bouzeid, and others like them lobby for a change in policy, women who are in danger of being sent to the center have also found a way to undermine the system: they head to the *bādīa* with their families, away from the dangerous gossip networks of the camps, and wait there until the baby is born.

Marriage itself could also be read as an avenue of resilience to the social policing of chastity. Once married, or indeed divorced, a woman can escape many of these pressures. Marriage affords her social status and increased freedom of movement. If the fulfillment of certain roles is expected of her once married, for example, responsibility for the nurture of children and domestic duties, this is also true of her husband, who is obligated to respect and provide for her and her children. In this respect, marriage could be interpreted as a form of "bargaining with patriarchy," a concept developed by Deniz Kandiyoti to facilitate analysis of how women in any given community strategize within the constraints imposed on them by that community's particular model of patriarchy.[102] The "bargain" in this case is as follows: a woman (publicly seems to) meet the demand of premarital chastity and later to comply with the responsibilities of a wife in order to achieve an "eligible" husband who will be able to provide well for her and her children.

As noted in chapter 1, Saharawi women (like Hassanophone women in Mauritania) enjoy certain rights and privileges in marriage and divorce that women in other Islamic societies do not: Saharawi interpretations of Islam allow them protection and certain avenues for resistance. She can take her inheritance (*rhīl*) and still rely on the protection of her family in the case of a dispute with her husband and/or his family.[103] Furthermore, whereas an Equatoguinean woman divorcée may be seen by society as a failure and even disowned by her family,[104] a Saharawi divorced woman will not face stigma and she can marry again. On the other hand, in line with hegemonic Saharawi interpretations of Islam, a Saharawi man can unilaterally repudiate his wife without "just" cause and without her consent. After the first, early years of marriage, during which a woman may initiate divorce by returning the bride-wealth, a woman may only divorce without her husband's consent if a (male) imam finds she has "just cause" to do so. With men's unilateral right to repudiate, coupled with their unilateral, if rarely practiced, right to polygyny (also fruit of Saharawi hegemonic interpretations of Islam), comes the problem of women who are *mu'alaqa*, women left "hanging" by a refusal of divorce by their husbands, who themselves remarry. This is another issue taken up as key by the aforementioned Saharawi "modern feminists" (to use their terminology) active on social media, and one on which some call for state intervention. Likewise, some UNMS members lobby for a "family code," which those in favor argue would protect against cases like those of the *mu'alaqat*.[105]

If Saharawi legal interpretations of Islam afford men with some unilateral rights surrounding marriage and divorce, Saharawi women have their own unilateral strategies for wrestling back power at a day-to-day level. Before exile and the proclamation of the SADR, a woman could become angry (*muġtāḍa*) with her husband, for example, if he married a second wife, which would cause *qabīla* elders from both the husband and wife's families to become involved to resolve the matter. Often, the husband would have to make reparations, including material gifts, to win his wife's favor.[106] While some women attempt to prevent future polygyny by demanding ever higher bridewealths from husbands-to-be so that they will not be able to afford to remarry, Saharawi women also have a long pre-exile history of inserting clauses into the marriage contract in an attempt to preclude polygyny.[107] Solana Moreno has also highlighted that many Saharawi women today see the bridewealth both as a protection against repudiation and an avenue for initiating divorce should the marriage not work out.[108] In the early days of the exiled period, before soldiers returned to the camps and the justice profession became staffed with Saharawis who had been able to study law abroad, women formed the Popular Justice Committees, with one male advisor on religious law to guide them. These women focused on disagreements caused through male polygyny or men refusing their wives' requests for divorce.[109]

Still today, in response to the "hanging" situation, we find a type of resistance in the form of the divorce party. While journalists have written of this party as an event held by all divorced women with a view to inviting possible new suitors, other Saharawis have described it to me as a more intimate affair, held not with suitors but with close friends and family, to cheer up the newly single divorcée.[110] However, Dafa presents another view of the party: it is a celebration only for formerly "hanging" women, giving them the opportunity to rejoice in their newfound freedom following a period of anguish.[111] If Dafa's perspective on the celebration is correct, it is possible to read the party as a form of women's resistance to patriarchal legal norms that control her sexuality.

The forms of resilience and everyday resistance outlined in this section could be described as feminist but less easily as nationalist. They have little to do with the pursuit of independence. Yet the double standards in the realm of sexuality that women cope with and resist are nevertheless linked to the state of the nation. If we accept what numerous researchers of gender, women, nation, militarism, and conflict consistently point out, that in times of conflict the nation's "honor" is sewn into the sexual behavior of "its" women and that religious norms are generally (re)interpreted to further justify this couture of gender roles, we must also accept that Saharawi gender norms are firmly tied up with the more than four-decades-long state of exile and occupation to which Morocco and the international community have subjected Western

Sahara. Women's resistance and resilience in the face of patriarchal practices in the realm of sexuality, marriage, and divorce may not be explicitly nationalist, but the longevity of these practices is arguably prolonged by the irresolution of the national conflict.

### "Western Imports": Challenging Gendered Sexual Norms?

With the exception of a brief but rich study by Laura Limón Rivas, one vastly underresearched area in Western Sahara studies are nonheterosexual practices and attitudes toward them.[112] The lack of attention is perhaps due to the taboo status of the issue within Saharawi society. The hegemonic view is that nonheterosexual practices are intrinsically un-Saharawi and therefore simply do not exist. However, some (supposed or openly) gay solidarity activists have come under fire for their sexualities among some sectors of the Saharawi population.[113] On the other hand, one POLISARIO leader indicates that the state would not oppress LGBT rights activists, if they existed. Omar Mansur, the governor of El Aaiún camp, has stressed that there is nothing in the statutes of the POLISARIO or the constitution of the SADR to prevent the creation of an association defending the rights of homosexuals. However, no such attempt has as yet been made because, in Mansur's opinion, society is not "prepared."[114] The UNMS representative to Spain explained to me that there is no homosexuality (or indeed abortion) in Saharawi society, and so it is a nonissue. However, she emphasized, the UNMS stands in solidarity with women struggling for LGBT rights and on pro-choice campaigns elsewhere in the world.[115]

Saharawi informants prepared to make comments that surpass the line of "there is no homosexuality here" explain that nonheterosexual practices are tolerated as long as no reference is made to them publically.[116] In other words, "open secrets" are possible as long as appearances are maintained. However, a literary example from the Equatoguinean case helps to illustrate the limits of such invisibility for claiming LGBT rights. Says the character Jesusín in Trifonia Melibea Obono's groundbreaking and brave novel about the persecution of gays and lesbians in Equatorial Guinea: "If you are invisible you can't vindicate any right."[117] Those who might be most likely to fight for such rights— those who have suffered from oppression because of their sexual inclination— are under pressure to hide their identities and desires.

Another issue that cements the image of nonheterosexual practices as un-Saharawi is their construction as a Western invention or Western perversion. This is easily deconstructed, and indeed, we should not understand homophobia as something "traditionally" Arab or intrinsic to Islam. Several scholars have powerfully argued that there is no evidence of condemnation of homosexuality in the Quran.[118] Brian Whitaker has highlighted that homosexuality and homoeroticism abound in classical Arab literature and that their absence in modern Arab literature along with the insistence that nonheterosexual practices "do not exist" have more to do with an Arab state policy of othering itself from the imperialism of the West through recourse to "cultural purity" (which in the Saharawi case involves the affirmation of patriarchy and compulsory heterosexuality) than they do with any long-standing historical tradition. Indeed, Whitaker also makes the point that Britain, over several centuries, waged a war on homosexuality on a scale that arguably surpassed the discrimination and abuse that happens in Arab countries today.[119]

Western states arguably do little to help the process of deconstruction of nonheterosexual practices as intrinsically Western by modeling themselves as the global leaders in LGBT rights. Melanie Richter-Montpetit has shown how Western states have used so-called LGBT equality as a benchmark for measuring their own relative civilization against the "backwardness" of the rest of the world and of migrant cultures within their own countries.[120] This strengthens the accusation of "Westoxication" against which LGBT activists in the Arab world and elsewhere must fight.

Women in times of war, exile, and imperial encroachments become the cultural bearers of the nation. In the Saharawi context, sex outside marriage for women and nonheterosexual sex become "licentious" and "Western imports."[121] I have argued here that homophobia cannot be separated from the wider Western colonial history of the Middle East and Africa. Furthermore, for Western Sahara, still colonized by Western-backed Morocco and the subject of constant Western scrutiny in the state in exile, the stakes for maintaining an "authentic" Saharawi culture are high. The challenge for those Saharawis who are keen to foster more positive attitudes toward nonheterosexual practices and identities is to initiate a debate that moves away from the decadent (accepting of homosexuality and female "promiscuity") Western versus "pure," "authentic" Arab-Muslim dichotomy. With regard to the wider argument of this chapter and indeed the book, the case of LGBT rights once again illustrates that the relationship between Saharawi gender norms and resistance cannot be separated from the national situation of occupation and exile, on the one hand, and patronizing, neocolonial attitudes on the part of the West on the other.

So far in this chapter I have looked at how Saharawi feminists and feminist nationalists in the camps have worked to challenge gender roles that are seen to restrict or oppress women and girls and how these challenges have related to the nationalist cause to varying degrees. But what if we look at Saharawi women's activism in the diaspora from the point of view of the nationalist cause first? And what if we focus on activities realized in a different diaspora, that is, Spain rather than the camps? In the next section, I focus on two prominent cases of Saharawi women's resistance to the Moroccan occupation mounted in the Spanish diaspora. Doing so furthers our discussion of Saharawi resistance and feminist nationalism by illuminating how Western, globally hegemonic discourses on Muslim, Arab gender roles influence Saharawi feminist nationalist resistance.

### Orientalism, Resistance, and Mother-as-Martyr: Aminatou Haidar and Tekbar Haddi

Researchers have drawn attention to the role of orientalist discourses (where "orientalism" refers to the patronizing attitudes of the West that see Eastern countries as backward and undeveloped, thereby justifying colonial interventions) in the POLISARIO-projected image of "gender equality" in the Saharawi state in exile.[122] The situation in the Moroccan occupied part of Western Sahara has, on the other hand, received little attention, something that I have tried to begin to address in chapter 5. My aim, in the following section, is to show how orientalist imaginations of Muslim, Arab women and men impacts upon Saharawi protest in the diaspora. I do so using two examples: the hunger strikes of Aminatou Haidar in 2009 and Tekbar Haddi in 2015, both staged in Spain.

Aminatou Haidar, known as the "Saharawi Gandhi," is perhaps the most famous figurehead of the Saharawi nonviolent, antioccupation movement. She is one of hundreds of Saharawi victims of forced disappearance and spent 1987–91 in a secret prison before being incarcerated again in 2005–6 because of her independence activism. In 2009 her protest against Moroccan authorities brought her—and the wider Saharawi nationalist cause—unusual levels of international attention.

On 14 November 2009 Haidar was deported from El Aaiún after being detained by Moroccan authorities. Returning from the United States, she had referred to "Western Sahara" rather than "Morocco" as her home on her landing card. The authorities then confiscated her passport and forcibly flew her to Lanzarote.[123] With no travel documents, she was bound to the airport. There, on 15 November, she began a hunger strike to demand her right to return to her home in El Aaiún, Western Sahara. Partway through the protest, in a show of feminine solidarity, eleven other Saharawi women residing in Lanzarote joined her in the hunger strike.[124]

Thirty-three days later, Haidar was finally allowed to fly back, making both the Spanish state and the Moroccan regime bow to her will in the process. Morocco had initially refused to allow her to set foot in Western Sahara again unless she requested a pardon from the king, while Spain offered her refugee status and then Spanish citizenship, stating that it would be impossible for her to return to El Aaiún. (Spain also imposed a court fine for "disturbing public order," which she refused to pay, and indeed Spain's decision to "let her in" despite her lack of travel documents is highly suspicious, suggesting a pre-meditated collaboration with Morocco.) Yet with huge media coverage and public outcry in Western Sahara, Morocco, and Spain (the Spanish state, desperate, had pleaded for diplomatic help from the United States and France and for Ban Ki Moon's mediation), Spain and Morocco ceded to the demands of Haidar, who was finally flown home on a private plane. One Moroccan-run blog quoted by Vivian Solana Moreno put it perfectly when it pointed out, with disappointment, that "a woman is stronger than our state."[125]

In the narratives beside pictures of Haidar's weakened body and stoic face, Western newspapers repeatedly chose to draw attention to the human rights defender's status as a (single) mother of two in their basic descriptions of who she was.[126] The few Western journalists who interviewed Haidar during the strike foregrounded her status as a mother in their narratives and asked leading questions about her children.[127] This was despite Haidar's own efforts to focus coverage on the wider human rights and political issues surrounding the demands of her protest.[128] Indeed, after cajoling Haidar to talk about the suffering of her children, one journalist admitted, "She finds it hard to talk about her feelings and prefers to emphasize her struggle."[129] While Haidar positioned (and positions) herself first and foremost as a human rights defender, the Western journalists covering her hunger strike positioned her first and foremost as a distraught and suffering mother.

The newspapers' construction of Haidar is significant, bearing in mind orientalist discourses that tend to victimize Arab, Muslim women and paint them as bound to the domestic sphere as well as wider discourses of conflict and wartime that tend to paint women as weak and in need of protection.[130] The image created of a starving and physically weak but morally strong mother, willing to die rather than be kept apart from her children (a feminine archetype in many ways), was an emotionally provocative one for a Western public. In this context, Haidar's case was attention grabbing. The Spanish politicians letting her starve, normally so full of rhetoric regarding their efforts to "empower" women in "backward," "Muslim" countries, became hypocrites in the eyes of the Spanish public. In other words, orientalist constructions of gender helped to create international support for Haidar. The Western press deployed certain constructions of feminine gender and motherhood to create a sensationalist mother-as-martyr capable of appealing to the emotions of their readership.

Activists in the occupied zone, Spanish solidarity activists, and the UNMS have watched the media episode surrounding Haidar's successful hunger strike in Lanzarote, which made her into a heroic mother-as-martyr figure capable of awakening emotions in a foreign public. In a world where Western models of activism often incorporate the same discourses on Arab, Muslim women as discussed with reference to Spanish media above, some Saharawi women have had to adapt their own activism when Western audiences are the target audience.[131] The case of Tekbar Haddi highlights how lessons surrounding Haidar's hunger strike have been learned and, perhaps, strategically incorporated into subsequent campaigns.

Haddi's son, Mohammed Laimine Haidala, died in February 2015, days after a group of Moroccan settlers stabbed him in the neck. Moroccan authorities confiscated his body. Haddi staged her hunger strike in May–June 2015 outside the Moroccan consulate in Las Palmas, Gran Canaria, demanding the

Tekbar Haddi's campaign poster, 2015. My son, my heart! #JusticeforHaidala.

return of her son's body, an autopsy, and an independent investigation into the circumstances surrounding his death.

Haddi has—unlike Haidar—consciously and explicitly identified motherhood as central to her hunger strike. Much like the Argentinian mothers of the Plaza de Mayo, motherhood is what inspires her resistance, and "mother" is an active, claimed, and political position for her.[132] Saharawi and Spanish activists, as well as the UNMS, have worked together in a transnational campaign to support her, and "mother courage" is its slogan. "My son, my heart, justice for Haidala," reads a campaign poster. If the mothers of the Plaza de Mayo invented "revolutionary motherhood," then their solidarity demonstration for Haddi in Argentina on 1 June 2015 and the scores of Saharawis visiting Haddi's own mother (who was beaten in her home in El Aaiún by police during Haddi's strike) indicate the practice of a transnational revolutionary motherhood.

The latter visits to Haddi's mother are significant for another reason. The numerous visits by Saharawis, and the visits by distinguished Saharawis such as Haidar and renowned activist Hmad Hammad to Haddi in Las Palmas, offer public recognition of Haddi's sacrifices (both as a mother losing her son and as an individual risking her physical well-being) as supreme acts of resistance for the wider cause.[133] In Western Sahara, Haidala, like all Saharawis killed by Moroccan settlers or security agents, is now known as a "martyr," and Haddi, like all Saharawi mothers of murdered children, has earned the respected label of "mother of the martyr."

June saw solidarity protests in many Spanish cities, and public messages of support from celebrities such as Kerry Kennedy, Pilar Bardem, and Viggo Mortensen helped to increase the press coverage, ample in Spain at local and national levels (and also making the UK press, albeit quietly).[134] Indeed, the case provoked far more media attention than any other incident after the 2010 Gdeim Izik protest, much as was the case with Haidar's hunger strike in 2009 after four years of near silence in the international media. If, as Stephen Zunes and Jacob Mundy suggest, engaging international civil society is key to the success of the struggle in the Occupied Territories, then Haddi's case builds on that of Haidar's to illustrate the vital importance of deploying certain constructions of gender in ensuring that success.[135]

In Haidar's case, the press *imposed* the identity of mother and played on orientalist constructions of Arab, Muslim women to strengthen the emotional power of its stories, which arguably worked in Haidar's favor. Haddi, on the other hand, actively claimed the identity of mother, and her supporters used this strategically, helping to ensure that the press used the same emotionally charged angle as was the case with Haidar. While in the Sahara Haddi is the respected "mother of the martyr," in Europe she is mother-as-martyr, almost a

Virgin Mary archetype of sacrificial femininity, and this provokes passion. The strategic recourse to the traditional (and malleable) Saharawi feminine gender role of mother, at least in Spain, increased interest in the Saharawi cause exponentially, even if only temporarily. The importance of this interest is illustrated by Morocco's reactions of fear: Haddi's family was offered (and rejected) €90,000 in hush money followed by the (also rejected) offer to return Haidala's body if the requests for autopsy and inquest were dropped.[136]

If mobilizing international civil society is a key success factor in the nonviolent struggle, then Saharawi "mothers" have proven to be the point of the blade on two occasions. Haidar and Haddi do not just influence but also actually lead the nonviolent, nationalist resistance movement. Their activities in the diaspora of Spain were nationalist first and foremost, and yet their practices, as well as their effects, are inextricably linked to Western, orientalist gendered discourses. On the one hand, Haidar and Haddi's political leadership and resistance challenge Western prejudices about Arab, Muslim womanhood. On the other hand, we have seen how Western media attempted to impose a primary identity of single, divorced "mother" on Haidar during her hunger strike, an identity she attempted to resist in favor of her chosen primary identity as human rights activist. Nevertheless, Western media's emotional framing of the Lanzarote protest as the struggle of a starving mother arguably fostered further coverage and support for Haidar, precisely because of the prejudices held about Arab, Muslim feminine gender roles and, indeed, about feminine archetypes in Western cultures held by Western audiences. Later, Haddi actively claimed her identity as primarily one of mother, and the Western media framing of her struggle has been, much like that of Haidar's, an emotionally charged one that capitalizes on the identity of mother to better engage Western audiences. Saharawi women's resistance cannot be untangled from hegemonic Western discourses on Arab, Muslim, and African gender norms.

Likewise, Saharawi women's resistance cannot be untied from the situation of exile. A common Saharawi joke helps illustrate the pervasiveness of exile: "On judgment day, God was deciding where to send the peoples of each country. Some went to heaven, others to hell, according to God's whim. When the turn of Western Sahara arrived, God said, 'I can't decide what to do with you. Why not pitch up some tents and wait around until I've made up my mind?'" This joke makes light of the excruciating, endless waiting and exile to which the international community has subjected Saharawis in the diaspora. The stories and perspectives of Saharawi women told in this chapter indicate a view that national liberation and gender equality are mutually dependent, thereby reflecting the official POLISARIO nationalist discourses forged in the seventies that I analyzed at the outset of this chapter. Saharawi women organize themselves in the diaspora to achieve the double aims of independence and gender equality. Some women, such as Haidar and Haddi, have pursued activism in Spain with a tremendous impact. While their professed aims were pro–human rights and nationalist, a by-product of their campaigns has been a public challenge of Western, colonialist understandings of Muslim, Arab, African women as submissive and in need of saving from "their own" men. At the same time, such Western stereotypes arguably provoked a certain fascination with their cases that perhaps furthered media interest abroad. While Haidar was resistant to Western media's attempt to prioritize her identity as "mother," Haddi and her informal network of supporters used this identity actively and politically, illustrating a Saharawi brand of active maternalism that I will explore further in part 3.

If Haidar and Haddi prioritize the nationalist and human rights struggle in their campaigns abroad (albeit with the arguably feminist and antiracist outcome of challenging orientalist understandings of Muslim, Arab women's role), in the camps of Algeria the UNMS follows a firmly feminist nationalist path, pursuing both these intertwined and mutually necessary goals sometimes at once, sometimes in tandem, sometimes drawing on official POLISARIO discourse, sometimes not. They work shrewdly. With efforts for men and boys to take on domestic tasks, the UNMS takes an antiessentialist position on nationalist gender norms. It challenges the hegemonic nationalist view that *ḥaīma* work is women's work. At times though, the UNMS uses essentialisms *strategically*. For example, it makes use of the essentialist construction of care and nurturing work as traditionally feminine to argue that such responsibilities make women ideal carers and nurturers of the national community, and therefore ideal political leaders.

However, the UNMS is a POLISARIO and state body, and it plays two more vital roles in attempting to maintain unity among the Saharawi population of the camps, on the one hand, and on the other, presenting the flawless view of Saharawi society (including in the realm of gender equality) that the West demands in return for foreign aid and solidarity. These two crucial responsibilities mean that the UNMS must remain quiet on some of the more contentious issues that affect Saharawi women's lives in exile, such as the alleged "kidnappings," LGBT rights, or the double standards surrounding chastity. This is where other Saharawi women, often the younger generations and often online, take the baton. Such women pursue a parallel, feminist and nationalist struggle, fighting for the nationalist cause but also against the silencing aspects within it. Indeed, in terms of theoretical discussions on feminist nationalist resistance, the Saharawi case demands a departure from a dichotomy of understandings. We have seen that Saharawi women's resistance in the diaspora is, at different moments, feminist (particularly women's "everyday" and historical strategies for preserving power in the face of patriarchal practices), feminist nationalist, nationalist with feminist outcomes, feminist but framed in the discourse of nationalism, and feminist and nationalist in parallel.

The flexible, multipronged feminist-nationalist resistance strategies of Saharawi women are well suited to the latter's struggle against multiple oppressions. But we have seen how Saharawi women's feminist struggles can also be undermined by the actions, or lack thereof, of external states. Returning to the aforementioned most contentious issue of sexuality, we see that such gendered problems cannot be viewed in isolation from international geopolitics. It is hard to think of a single culture, internationally, where double standards regarding sexuality do not exist. However, ample research in various contexts has illustrated that women's sexual behavior reaches new, national importance in situations of conflict. Likewise, my gendered analysis of resistance in the diaspora illustrates that the Sahara is no exception.

Similarly, we have seen that, in the case of the alleged "kidnappings," younger Saharawi feminists acting independently of the UNMS tried to raise a debate over Saharawi women's individual rights to autonomy and freedom of movement and their families' traditional right to decide what is best for their daughters. The chance for fruitful discussion was undermined, I have argued, by the actions of the ex-colonial power, Spain. A Spanish autonomous government effectively enforced collective punishment on the Saharawi refugee population by cutting much-needed aid when the Saharawi "daughter" of a Spanish host family was "kidnapped" by her Saharawi parents. This, coupled with the Spanish state's neglect of cases of Spanish families "kidnapping" Saharawi children, and their wider indifferent gaze on Saharawis violently abused in the occupied zone, muffled the debate initiated by Saharawi feminists and gave the microphone to those who see the Spanish state's interference in the case of "kidnapped" Saharawi-Spaniards as yet another example of Spain's betrayal of the Saharawi nation. The fate of the "kidnapped" women is tangled in the net of international geopolitics, and it is the women, their Saharawi families, their Spanish loved ones, and the aid-deprived Saharawi refugees who suffer. The only beneficiaries are to the West, where the Moroccan lobbyists cannot believe their luck. The Moroccan state eagerly gathers up all coverage of the "kidnapped" women, much-needed ammunition for its propaganda war in which the camps are painted as "gulags" where all refugees are retained against their wishes. Such an unrealistic portrait paints over the achievements of the remarkable nation in waiting, built by the hands of women like Tawfa and Silka, retained by women like Asria and Agaila, and defended externally by women like Aminatou and Tekbar.

# CHAPTER FOUR

# Constructions of Gender in the Nationalist Discourses of the Obiang Regime

D OLORES MOLUBELA is an elderly cleaner in Malabo. The establishment where she works is popular with ex-pat oil industry members. Despite laboring all day, six days a week, she struggles to feed her orphaned grandchildren on her wages. "They say that there is petrol here. Well, the petrol is just for a few people. They fill their stomachs and get fat, and leave the rest of us to starve."[1] In this chapter, I explore the relationship between gender constructions, oil, and Obiang regime discourse on gender equality, which together have caused and perpetuated the daily struggles of Dolores and others like her.

Discourses, understood here as systems of meaning production, construct a "reality" from a specific sociocultural perspective. As discussed in the previous chapter, the Gramscian concept of "hegemony" sees dominant power groups in a culture exert their power over others by projecting their representation of the world. However, I should make clear that Gramsci made a key distinction between hegemony and domination, which proves relevant for the Obiang case. If a discourse is hegemonic, it is seen by the majority of the community as entirely natural and common sense. However, for Gramsci, where force has to be used to ensure the community behaves according to the dominant power group's discourse, domination exists.

In this chapter, I deconstruct the images of gender that are projected in the nationalist discourses of the Obiang regime and attempt to explain the ideological functions of such imaginations. This serves to add to wider research on African examples of "state feminism."[2] By focusing on Obiang, I show how an oppressive authoritarian regime employs constructions of gender (equality) to further its own ends. I compare this with observations of the previous chapter, to illustrate how similar mechanisms of discourse can be used for very different purposes. That is to say, POLISARIO used particular constructions of gender and "gender equality" to strengthen the national liberation movement and has been largely successful in making these part of hegemonic nationalist discourse. Obiang uses similar discourses on gender equality to oppress his population, often through domination rather than hegemony.

First, I describe how Obiang came to power and how he has attempted to build a national identity, with himself as its foundation. I also explain how the Equatoguinean government is structured. This helps us establish the extent to which Obiang and government discourse are one and the same. Then, I move on to deconstruct gender and gender equality in regime discourse, before exploring the internal and external functions of such constructions. Finally, taking into account that the oil industry today dominates the economy of Equatorial Guinea, I look at what oil has meant for women's socioeconomic opportunities.

### The Myth of Inevitability: Obiang, the Predestined Leader

Early in the morning of 24 September 1979, thousands of Equatoguinean citizens formed a queue outside the Marfil cinema, Malabo. They were not eager to catch the latest Hollywood offering, however, but rather to witness the trial of Francisco Macías, the self-proclaimed "One True Miracle of Equatorial Guinea" and conductor of a miserable orchestra of poverty and terror since winning elections in 1968.

The first five hundred citizens in the queue were permitted entry. The rest spilled out and splashed through the neighboring streets where loudspeakers transmitted the proceedings. Four days later Macías was found guilty of genocide, mass murder, embezzlement of public funds, material injury, systematic violations of human rights, and treason.[3] On the evening of 29 September he was taken to Black Beach prison, the site of the torture and death of some of the more than fifty thousand Equatoguineans killed by Macías, where he was shot dead by a Moroccan firing squad.[4]

When the Macías verdict was announced through the loudspeakers, the crowds outside the cinema (the condemned dictator had left few functioning state institutions and thus the cinema was used as a courthouse) erupted into spontaneous cheers and applause. Obiang took power. Even though he had ordered deaths and headed the hellish Black Beach prison under Macías and, once the ruler, installed former torturers as ministers in his new government, collective temporary amnesia allowed a climate of elation in Equatorial Guinea and abroad.[5]

Ever since his successful coup, Obiang has put on an annual celebration of Macías's overthrow, thereby reminding Equatoguinean citizens that they are united in their adversity to this past, tyrannical regime.[6] State media channels maintain that Obiang, "the country's God," has rescued Equatorial Guinea, "a country whose development grows day by day," and is working hard to end all the grievances caused by Macías and colonialism.[7] That is to say, Equatoguinean national identity is articulated in opposition to past oppressive forces. Equatoguineans are now "free," and freedom carries Obiang's face.

Aside from attempting to make a metonymical slide between Obiang and freedom, regime nation builders have also drawn on other tools to hoist and wave the Equatoguinean flag. Just as the POLISARIO (and, arguably, all nation builders) makes use of a constructed history to bolster its current nationalist ideologies, the Obiang regime, as Cusack argues, creates and draws on an ancient history of "the Bantu people and culture of Equatorial Guinea."[8]

Equatorial Guinea is made up of different ethnicities. Eighty percent are Fang, a people of Bantu origin, concentrated in the continental region of Rio Muni, and 6.5 percent are Bubi, living principally on Bioko island. There are the smaller groups as well: Ndowe (also known as Playeros and made up of Kombe and Benga) on Rio Muni's coasts and the islands of Elobey Grande, Elobey Chica, and Corisco; Bissio, from the coasts of Rio Muni; Fernandinos, living mostly in Malabo and Luba on Bioko Island; Krio also living on Bioko; Annobonese on Annobón Island; and around two hundred Pygmies in the forests of Rio Muni.[9]

Not only are Fang dominant in numbers but they also make up the ruling elite, itself headed by members of Obiang's Esangui clan, based in the town of Mongomo, Rio Muni. Therefore, as Cusack points out, Fang culture, constructed as having roots in the ancient Bantu traditions of Equatorial Guinea, is the model to which other ethnicities are likened and around which other ethnicities are homogenized. Obiang is the metaphor for the homogenized nation of what Cusack—nodding to the natural resource wealth that funds the regime—calls the Mongomo "nationalist entrepreneurs."[10]

One key part of the regime myth of a shared and ancient Bantu heritage is the emphasis of the Bantu belief in destiny. In this history/story, Obiang was destined from birth for his role as president, and the regime admits that predestination acts as "a brake to [their] intentions of arriving at pluralist democracy."[11] In other words, the inevitability of Obiang as dictator is made part of a national belief system in regime discourse. The belief that a dictator's rule is inevitable or destined, argue Gene Sharp and Steven Lukes, is a key barrier to mobilizing resistance.[12]

At the center of Obiang regime-constructed national identity is the personality cult of Obiang himself, savior of the Equatoguinean people and deliverer of their "freedom."[13] When I arrived in Malabo in June 2015, Obiang had just celebrated his birthday. National and multinational corporations had hired the many billboards around the capital to publicize messages wishing the president a happy birthday.[14] At every roundabout, along every thoroughfare, gigantic Obiangs were pictured next to corporate greetings. To do well in Equatorial Guinea, big business directs its advertising campaigns very publicly to one person only. But mini Obiangs also looked at me from the desks of offices, the counters of cafés, even from behind the soot-blackened barbeques of one-woman eateries. In Equatorial Guinea, as is the case of Mohammed VI in Morocco and occupied Western Sahara, Obiang looks down on his subjects from the walls of every establishment. The pair are ever present in their respective territories watching citizens both symbolically, through said photographs, and literally, thanks to the vast plain-clothes police and civilian informers, the all-seeing tentacles allowing the two dictators to look well beyond their protective shells without having to extend their heads.

The next section of this chapter looks at the articulation of gender within Obiang nationalist discourses. First, let's consider to what extent the government of Equatorial Guinea can be said to act as a mouthpiece for Obiang. There are three branches of government: executive, legislative, and judicial. The executive is led by Obiang as the head of state plus, since 2011, his two vice presidents; the head of government (the prime minister) and his three deputies; and a cabinet of eighty-six ministers, vice ministers, delegate ministers, and secretaries of state. These cabinet posts, which are numerous for a country with a population under a million, are well described by Freedom House as "a ready source for patronage appointments."[15]

Obiang's family members enjoy high posts. His sons Teodorín and Gabriel are first vice president and minister of mines and hydrocarbons, respectively, his nephew Baltasar Engoga Edjo is minister of state, as is his brother Antonio Mba Nguema.[16] Family members also sit on the boards of multinationals active in the country and establish their own individual "national" companies, thereby ensuring their hands remain in the country's till.[17] Constitutional reform in 2011 limited the president's seven-year terms to two.[18] Obiang did not honor this. On 24 April 2016, after announcing the elections by presidential decree, Obiang was reelected with 93.7 percent of the vote, although opposition parties might dispute use of the word "elected."[19]

The legislative branch is made up of two parliamentary chambers. The Senate has seventy seats, fifty-five of which are (in theory) directly elected and fifteen appointed by the president. The House of People's Representatives, or the Chamber of Deputies, holds one hundred seats, held for terms of five years by representatives who are (also in theory) directly elected. Obiang's party, the Democratic Party of Equatorial Guinea (PDGE), dominates both. However, since the constitution invests all executive authority in the head of state, parliament has little power.[20]

The judicial branch was, until May 2015, formed by the Supreme Court (judges appointed by the president) and the Constitutional Court (five members appointed by the president, two of which were nominated by the Chamber of Deputies). There were also a number of subordinate courts. Judges working on sensitive cases often consulted the president's office before issuing a ruling.[21] In May 2015 Obiang temporarily dissolved the entire judiciary on the basis that it was "corrupt" and a "hindrance to foreign investment."[22]

Elections in Equatorial Guinea are neither free nor fair. The country is among the most censored in the world, and media censorship reaches new levels ahead of elections.[23] In the weeks and days leading up to the April 2016 elections, hundreds of opposition campaigners and supporters suffered illegal arrest and detention, brutal beatings, attacks on their homes and families, and robbery.[24]

Given the political oppression and nepotism rife in Equatorial Guinea, it is fair to equate "government" with "Obiang regime," and I do so throughout this chapter. This is not to say that the regime consistently speaks with one single and unified voice. Indeed, I consider contradictions in how the government articulates gender and gender equality below.

## Hollow State Feminism:
## Gender Equality in Obiang Regime Discourse

In Malabo Central Market, a woman hangs her wares from a wooden rail. The dresses and skirts are emblazoned with the bright colors of the national flag, geometric patterns emblematic of current central African fashions, slogans such as "Thank You," and the face of Obiang and his most famous wife, Constancia Mangue. The vendor herself wears a picture of Obiang on her shirt. Another has Mangue's face on a dress, which is also decorated with the words "International Women's Day," and "Thank You." She links Mangue to the struggle for women's rights and is far from the only person attired this way. Whether they are being sincere or whether their clothing is a precaution against regime harassment, many Equatoguinean citizens choose to silently but openly thank the president's wife for her "efforts" for gender equality when they get dressed each morning.[25]

Researchers have illuminated the ulterior motives of state "feminism," where states co-opt the language of feminism (often with the first lady[ies] as the figureheads) for purposes that are anything but feminist, elsewhere in Africa. Amina Mama illustrates how the Babangida and Abacha regimes in Nigeria used the language of "women's development" to neutralize the potentially subversive power of women's liberation and normalize military rule.[26] For these regimes, argues Mama, populist measures that were in theory designed to empower the most underprivileged women in rural areas actually fostered a role for women limited to the home and petty trading that "perpetuated rather than challenged patriarchal traditions."[27] Although Mama points out that the two regimes did not seek to win international support with their so-called pro-women policies, she does highlight that the latter resonated with the interests of international financial institutions keen to see marginal groups incorporated into capitalist development. Similarly, Dzodzi Tsikata has chartered how the "NGO-ization" of Ghanaian feminism has seen the promotion of national and global neoliberal agendas at the expense of women's ability to take mass action against gendered discrimination.[28]

In this chapter, I add to the work of Dzodzi Tsikara, Mama, and others by exploring how the global neoliberal agenda, particularly the thirst for oil, influences the use of state "feminism." While POLISARIO's centering of "gender equality" in its nationalist discourse has indeed played an external, West-facing function, some "real" dedication to the aims of tackling sexism and indeed racism was, as I have argued, nevertheless crucial for recruiting (black) women to the revolutionary struggle. Contrastingly, I argue now that Obiang and his neoliberal allies work together *as a partnership* in formulating a *false* state feminism in which the regime, so-called gender equality, and oil are tangled together like spaghetti. First, I contemplate the regime-painted picture of "gender equality."

According to Equatorial Guinea's Press and Information Office, "Today, young and mature women excel in all sectors," and, "[their] presence can already be seen and heard in all areas."[29] Likewise, on International Women's Day 2011, the minister of promotion of women declared, "At present we all have the same rights."[30] When asked to what extent there is gender equality in Equatorial Guinea, one government representative explained, "If I had to give a mark between 1 and 10, I'd go as far as a 9. . . . There's a level of equality here that's higher than many countries."[31]

To whom do Equatoguinean citizens owe this happy state of (alleged) equality? According to government propaganda, the heroine is the first lady, Constancia Mangue.[32] In almost all communications concerning "women's progress" published by the official government news website, she, and frequently Obiang, are thanked for their great personal efforts toward this cause. Indeed, Obiang's and Mangue's role in women's empowerment is woven into the nation's constructed history. In its second and third periodic report to the Convention on the Elimination of All Forms of Discrimination against Women (CEDAW), the Equatoguinean government states: "On becoming a sovereign national State, Equatorial Guinea suffered a bloody dictatorship from 1969 until August

1979. Following the *coup d'état* of 3 August 1979, the country experienced true freedom, thanks to H. E. Obiang Nguema Mbasogo, the President of the Republic, who recognized women's rights for the first time in the history of our people."[33]

Officially then, Obiang is the savior of the oppressed Equatoguinean woman, supported by his wife. According to her government-penned biography, the first lady is "a fundamental figure for the evolution of women of Equatorial Guinea," and she is, at the time of writing, honorary chairwoman of the ruling party's women's organization.[34]

Nevertheless, despite the picture of gender equality painted in official government discourse, the regime simultaneously boasts of its numerous efforts to work *toward the achievement* of the same. That is to say, official discourses on gender equality are somewhat contradictory, since there would be no need to work toward an ideal if said ideal had been realized.

So what has the regime done to further gender equality? A ministry for social affairs and women's promotion does exist. According to researchers and interviewees, Obiang has modeled the ministry on the Falange's Women's Section.[35] State news reports describe government-organized events celebrating women and their achievements. These are marches, high-level receptions, roundtables, and beauty pageants, the effectiveness of which are questionable. As the CEDAW Committee has noted, there is no evidence of the results and impact of such events.[36] Indeed, Equatoguinean feminist interviewees complained of the lack of government action on issues such as violence against women and girls, sexual violence, sexual exploitation and human trafficking for the same, polygyny, teenage pregnancy, and homophobia.[37] Said one feminist interviewee when asked her views on the key problems faced by Equatoguinean women today: "There are various. But the main one is that women are overlooked. . . . They are disregarded by everyone, the political parties . . . , the institutions."[38] Said another: "We have a ministry that focuses exclusively on gender issues . . . , but tell me what we are supposed to do when the political leaders are all sexists? . . . Calls for rights on specific days and events are not enough."[39] Although international rankings are problematic, a cursory look finds Equatorial Guinea at the depressing position of 138 on the UN Development Program's Gender Development Index.[40]

If, in anonymous interviews, feminists criticized the government for failing to tackle sexism, their ability to lobby is curtailed by the justified fear of oppression. One feminist who attempted to lobby by engaging the government with direct and overt criticism and by suggesting policy changes received very serious threats to her freedom and well-being from cabinet members.[41]

However, feminists push for change in other ways, as is outlined in the final section of chapter 6.

I turn now to the views of key figures on what gender equality means and the barriers that exist to its achievement. In her 2012 acceptance speech on being "elected" honorary national chairwoman of the ruling party's women's organization, Mangue outlined her ideas for creating a "more just society" with respect for women's position by "focus[ing] her thoughts on . . . the abandonment of evil vices that stain the image of women."[42] Such vices, according to Mangue, include "alcoholism, drug addiction, [and] promiscuity."[43] If Mangue advocates for women to abandon drugs, alcohol, and nonmonogamous sex in order to reach full gender equality in Equatoguinean society, her fellow regime mouthpieces on equal rights also see women's behavior as the key success factor. Eulalia Envo Bela, when minister of social affairs and promotion of women, implied that gender inequality was the fruit of women's reluctance to overcome "their weakness."[44] According to Obiang himself, "empowering men" is the key, because in his view, empowering men will automatically lead to the empowerment of women, since the two genders "should complement each other, and act in solidarity."[45]

Then minister of women's affairs, Jesusa Obono Engongo, representing Equatorial Guinea before the CEDAW Committee, blamed women's lack of political participation on "local custom" and "women's own traditional attitudes."[46] Another government representative explained the low representation of women in government with the assertion that women are "reluctant to [participate] because they [are] clinging to tradition."[47] Indeed, the resounding tone throughout most Equatoguinean government submissions to the CEDAW Committee is one that is simultaneously righteous and hopeless— righteous since the government has made every effort possible and "there are no barriers as such" to gender equality apart from the obstinate and backward attitudes of the female population, and hopeless since the government can do nothing to change such attitudes.[48] For example, in response to CEDAW Committee's concerns about the high prevalence of human immunodeficiency virus (HIV) among Equatoguinean school girls, the Equatoguinean government representatives' responses were that "the Government could not possibly do more." They explained that "truckloads of condoms had been sent into the countryside; it was not the Government's fault if the population did not use them."[49] It is fair to say therefore that, according to official regime discourse on gender equality, the government has made every effort possible to realize gender equality, and as such, if the latter does not exist, the government is not at fault. However, it is hard to identify any meaningful or successful measures led by government to tackle sexism.

### Insider Reworkings: The Construction of Gender Roles in Regime Discourse and Challenges from Civil Servants

Regime discourse has a dichotomous view of sex and gender. There are "natural biological differences between men and women," and the two sexes are assigned different roles culturally.[50] Women should seek marriage and procreation, and strive to support their male partners throughout life. Indeed, in official speeches, Mangue places importance on the role of woman "as mother, wife and companion of man."[51] Meanwhile, the members of the Women's Solidarity Association for the Promotion and Protection of Human Rights are made up of "the wives of Government members."[52] Government-issued news articles on high-profile events tend to report the attendance of ministers and other politicians "and their wives."[53] The presence (or otherwise) of the husbands of the few female politicians at such events is never deemed worthy of comment. Woman is articulated as the supporting actor to man's leading role.

The government neglects to challenge existing hegemonic masculinities, which determine the identities of many Equatoguinean male citizens and serve to entrench gender inequalities. The lack of a discursive effort by government to change said constructions raises yet more questions about the dedication of government to promoting equality. One aspect of hegemonic masculinity proves to be particularly problematic: sexuality. Men should be virile heterosexuals. Paying (female) minors for sex is normalized through state television, and the unilateral right for men to have multiple wives was included in a draft law in 2002.[54] Homosexuality is not tolerated by the regime, and there is no protection against discrimination based on sexuality or indeed on gender identity. Government television has paraded men arrested for "homosexual acts" on air.[55] In one example of this, state television interviews a detained "transexual [sic]" in the police station. In an attempt to explain his (the program uses male pronouns) "crime," the seventeen-year-old boy states, "I need to feed myself. I don't know. I don't have anyone who can feed me."[56] The fact that the child, selling sex in highly risky circumstances in exchange for food, is painted as a perturbed criminal owing to his perceived sexuality reveals the extent to which sexual "deviation" is reprehensible.

Through this construction of those who deviate from compulsory heterosexuality as criminal, the hegemony of binary gender roles and heterosexuality is maintained and enforced through fear and violence. Similarly, Obiang's rule, in more general terms, is maintained through fear: state media broadcasts "observations" such as "[Obiang] has the right to kill without anyone calling him to account because it is God himself [sic]."[57] As Sharp has noted, the fear of sanctions and the belief that the ruler possesses superhuman qualities are two further ways to prevent resistance (another one is patronage, of which, as we have seen, Obiang makes heavy use).[58] More widely, not only gender norms but also Obiang's rule are maintained through a combination of hegemonic discourses, force, and fear. This dynamic of oppressive fear is further explored in chapter 6.

On the other hand, there are moments when civil servants have subtly criticized the government, most often for blocking or refusing funding for their gender equality initiatives. Said an anonymous author in a report to the CEDAW Committee in 2004: "A draft law designed to regulate customary marriages attempts to provide a legal framework for the dowry, consent, inheritance, widowhood, and other highly important matters, which up to now have left women at the mercy of the husband or his family. This text has been in the drafting stage for almost three years and, unfortunately, seems to represent a threat to some men, who are doing everything possible to prevent its adoption."[59]

In the same report, the author describes planned services to support women in prostitution and women vulnerable to HIV/AIDS and comments that "unfortunately, the necessary funds have not yet been provided."[60] In another report, the CEDAW Committee is informed by the Ministry of Social Affairs and Advancement of Women (MINASPROM) as to why there has been little progress on providing health care for women in rural areas of the country. The failure is attributed to "the dearth, or late availability, of funds for the various plans, programs, and projects, resulting in little or no implementation."[61]

Wherever a criticism of government is hinted at, it is done from the position of a low and subservient bow: Obiang must be simultaneously flattered and distanced from whatever government inefficiency is under question. The individuals quoted here implicitly wish to take effective action (that is to say, not beauty pageants) to ameliorate the position of women. Although part of the regime themselves, they resist it from within, questioning the lack of funding and sexist government attitudes that make action on gender inequality impossible. The fact that these individuals' criticisms are couched in praise for Obiang does not prevent them from being acts of resistance, nor is such couching unusual in cases of resistance. With reference to peasant resistance to the will of the elite classes, Scott argues, "The success of de facto resistance is often directly proportional to the symbolic conformity with which it is masked. Open insubordination in almost any context will provoke a more rapid and ferocious response than an insubordination that may be as pervasive but never ventures to contest the formal definitions of hierarchy and power."[62]

The slightly dissatisfied individuals quoted here are not peasants. They represent the regime, often speak its voice, and are employed by it. Nevertheless, they are still subordinate to Obiang, and indeed, my fieldwork in Malabo suggested that not all high-ranking civil servants work for the regime of their own free choice. In any case, coerced into employment or otherwise, a few critical voices subtly challenge the regime to which they belong without ever criticizing the overall hierarchy that their dictator chairs. They are not publicly oppositional or pushing for emancipatory change, but rather, to use Cindi Katz's terminology, they attempt to *rework* aspects of the regime from within the system.[63] This shows that complicity with authoritarianism is not a clear-cut, black-and-white matter. An Equatoguinean citizen may, at times, comply and collaborate with the regime, or even be a part of it. At other times, that citizen may attempt to challenge it through subtle resistance or otherwise.

## Why Gender Matters: The Benefits of Painting a Picture of Gender Equality

There is much research on how states and nations use certain constructions of gender for a variety of ideological purposes.[64] What purposes do Obiang regime constructions serve, internally and externally?

So far, I have argued that government discourses perceive a need to empower women and promote gender inequality in Equatorial Guinea. Nevertheless, there is a serious lack of meaningful policies and actions to realize these aspirations. Regime figures' understandings of barriers to equality belie the lack of government commitment: backward citizens and jealous and underconfident women are blamed for the lack of equality, but the government is accorded no fault or role. It is fair to conclude, therefore, that the focus on gender equality within Obiang regime discourse does not reflect any material commitment on the part of the government. Not only does this keep woman in a subordinate place, it also suggests that perhaps the achievement of gender equality would not serve the regime. Sharp argues that the absence of self-confidence among a repressed people is fostered through subordination. This absence of self-confidence in turn prevents efforts at resistance or revolution.[65] I suspect, therefore, that maintaining women in a subordinate position and fostering their lack of confidence is within Obiang's interests. Conversely, then, feminist activism is perhaps in the opposition movements' interest, an argument that I develop further in chapter 6.

Gramsci differentiated between hegemony, where the people consent to their rulers, share their world vision, and abide by their constructions of identity because they view the latter as natural, and domination, where those in power maintain it by force. Since coming to power, Obiang has made use of both to sustain his power. His regime has attempted to make hegemonic an Equatoguinean national identity that places his own personality cult at the center. Obiang is the Equatoguinean people's freedom. Obiang *is* Equatorial

Guinea. He propagates the idea that his dictatorship is inevitable, which blends hegemony and domination. It is a hegemonic project, since his rule is painted as natural, yet it is also an attempt at domination, since his rule is not based on winning hearts and minds but rather on fear and therefore force. This is a strategy to quell resistance, since even if Obiang's rule is regrettable, there is no point in fighting something believed to be inevitable. The depiction of Obiang as all-powerful and godlike only adds to this veneer of inevitability, while threats to "unpatriotic" dissenters are pure domination. Obiang-orchestrated Equatorial Guinea is a nation in which the imagined community and its "distinctly" Equatoguinean identity have been forged as a foundation for the moneymaking venture of the dictator's clan and those whose patronage they buy. This venture is supported by external-facing discourse that promotes Obiang's dedication to "gender equality" as a concept.

At a roundtable debate of feminists held in Malabo, June 2015, the participants and audience laughed with irony as one of the Equatoguinean panelists announced, shaking her head, that Equatorial Guinea had just been awarded an international prize for its efforts toward gender equality.[66] Others have noted Obiang's attempts to fashion himself as a philanthropist and his penchant for pricey "prestige projects" such as the new luxury towns built for the 2011 African Union Summit and hosting of the 2015 African Cup of Nations (CAN).[67] I argue below that so-called gender equality plays a central role in this wider soap opera of Obiang regime affluence, prestige, and "charity" acted before the world.

Simon Anholt describes branding as "a technique for achieving integrity, and reaping the reputational benefits of integrity."[68] Just as the POLISARIO promotes its policies for achieving gender equality as a "success story" to garner external support, the Obiang regime attempts to brand itself as a champion of gender equality to match the current international trend for supporting, at least in theory, women's empowerment in the "developing world."[69] As Reem Mohamed puts it with reference to the discursive focus on gender equality in the Zine Ben Ali, Muammar Gaddafi, and Hosni Mubarak regimes, "Reflecting the image of 'supporters of gender equality' earns the state international praise with little emphasis on either implementation or budgetary allocation."[70] This image making and its political objectives are encompassed by the term *genderwashing*.

Genderwashing, a concept developed by Corinne L. Mason, can be explained by first focusing on the better-known concept of *greenwashing*.[71] It refers to marketing efforts by corporations to project an image of being "environmentally friendly." Big businesses co-opt the language and imagery of environmentalism to address the concerns of environmentally conscious consumers without cleaning up their practices and/or to divert attention from the environmental degradation that they cause. With regard to "gender equality," states and their corporate partners market their policies and practices in a similar fashion. To quote Mason, who, like Abu Lughod, notes that in recent years women's empowerment has been placed at the forefront of US foreign policy in order to justify foreign intervention, genderwashing is "the way that feminist and liberal concerns for equality and women's rights are co-opted for imperialist projects."[72] I argue in this section that the concept of genderwashing is applicable beyond imperialist foreign policy. We see Western corporations employ genderwashing in the form of "corporate social responsibility" to distort their support for authoritarian regimes. We also see Western states genderwashing their foreign aid and international development policies and budgets. They do so to veil the donor state's use of foreign "aid" to further its own business interests. For example, the UK Department for International Development (DfID) under the center-right Conservative government has stated that *the key aim* of its aid is to *make a market* for British business abroad.[73]

Some brief background to overseas aid in Equatorial Guinea, historical and current, is helpful to contextualize the arguments that follow. Equatorial Guinea's reliance on foreign aid peaked in 1989 when it constituted 54 percent of the country's GDP. This has progressively decreased to 0.5 percent in 2007.[74] Put another way, Equatorial Guinea currently receives a 0.1 percent share of overseas aid donated from the Organization for Economic Co-operation and Development (OECD) members to African states.[75] Spain has been the main donor to Equatorial Guinea since independence, with its funds constituting approximately 31 percent of aid received. France comes second, followed by the European Commission.[76]

The only systematic, evaluative study of the contribution of overseas aid to Equatorial Guinea has found that, until the discovery of oil, external aid "fed" corruption, a lack of transparency, and the persistent inefficiency of state institutions.[77] After the oil boom, the study's conclusions on the effects of foreign aid are equally damning. The latter has "intensif[ied] the unjust political system and the lack of liberties."[78] More specific findings are as follows: there has been questionable direct impact from aid, especially since deadlines and quantifiable outputs and outcomes have not been specified;[79] foreign aid passes into the hands of the ruling family; aid is channeled into the ruling PDGE party; aid donated to ministries and other "official" entities is appropriated by individuals and/or the PDGE and does not help the wider population at all; places on training courses are reserved for "nguemistas"; educational grants and technical assistance benefit "nguemistas" and the "Mongomo clan"; and corruption is also alleged with regard to money donated to some NGOs and churches.[80]

Turning to corporates, foreign investments in the mammoth Equatoguinean oil sector constitute "an enormous financial contribution" to Obiang's military spending as well as to his family's personal wealth.[81] Put bluntly, Obiang's trade partners are key backers of his regime. As Mario Esteban highlights, for state partners of Equatorial Guinea (principally the United States [which reopened its Malabo embassy in 2003 in response to oil industry pressure], Spain, and France but, lately and increasingly so, the United Kingdom), doing business with, and making diplomatic concessions to, a regime as corrupt and brutal as Obiang's can "badly affect the popularity of the authorities."[82] Take as an example the furor in the Spanish press and among Spanish civil society when news broke that the Cervantes Institute was hosting a reception for Obiang in Brussels in 2014, and a year earlier, upon the participation of the Spanish national football team in a friendly match with Equatorial Guinea in Malabo.[83] Indeed, in Spain at least and in the United States to some extent, civil society is mobilized against Obiang, and thus, government courting of Malabo is politically contentious. Through loss of moral authority in the eyes of their politically engaged citizens, Spain and the United States risk diminishing their own soft power.[84] A loss of moral authority in turn puts their investments in Equatorial Guinea at risk. As one employee of Stratfor, a company that provides intelligence to several US government agencies, asked in 2011 following a "negative PR spree" on Obiang in US media, "At what point will bad PR affect UK/US oil companies [sic] investments?"[85] If the United States, UK, and Spain wish to maintain access to Equatorial Guinea's resources via its gatekeeper Obiang, they must improve the latter's image in their own media channels. If they succeed, they will suffer less pressure from their own citizens and less damage to their self-cultivated image as "responsible international actors." I am therefore suggesting that Western corporates *encourage* Obiang to improve his image abroad. Indeed, as we will see below, some actively invest in his image, which, as we have seen, is one of "champion of women's empowerment." When at all possible, I argue below, corporates draw on additional help from state actors. This helps the West's investments to look "cleaner" to the general public.

Constancia Mangue is personally responsible for stealing millions from her people in oil revenue. For example, in the 2004 American Riggs Bank scandal, through which around $700 million from oil companies, mostly ExxonMobil, was paid, in the full knowledge of the bank, into the personal accounts of Obiang and close family members in exchange for access to Equatorial Guinea's oil, five of the accounts and three of the deposit certificates were in her name.[86] Nevertheless, her alleged efforts (I can find no evidence of the fruits of these) to support the most vulnerable women have earned her an honorary doctorate from the European School of Management (Spain), the Center for the Studies of Popular Democracy (Chile), and the Euro-American Forum of Educational Development.[87] She also received the 2013 Women's Progress Award from the US charity Voices for African Mothers.[88] This illustrates that regime discourse that constructs Mangue as the engine behind women's empowerment in Equatorial Guinea is indeed used in a bid to increase her legitimacy (and collaterally that of her husband and the wider regime) in Europe and the Americas, at least in some academic and third-sector circles.[89] Meanwhile, Obiang continues to garner support in high places in the United States.

Obiang was received as "a good friend" by Condoleezza Rice and has posed for photographs with the Obamas.[90] The United States offers friendship to Obiang in order to access Equatorial Guinea's hydrocarbons, which, according to 2015 estimates, count for roughly 90 percent of the country's economy.[91] Following the events of 11 September 2001, the United States was keen to redirect its oil supply from the Middle East to the Gulf of Guinea. Soon, the United States became "the largest single foreign investor in Equatorial Guinea."[92] Oil companies, including American Marathon Oil, Chevron, Exxon-Mobil, Hess, and Texaco, have poured billions of dollars into the country. As the US embassy put it in 2009, "We (via U.S. oil companies) pay all the bills—and the EG leadership knows it."[93] Meanwhile, the United States has allowed the quasi-governmental US Overseas Private Investment Corporation (OPIC) to fund a $450 million methanol plant (reportedly OPIC's largest Agreement in sub-Saharan Africa) and given permission to Military Professional Resources Incorporated (MPRI), a private corporation, to develop a coastguard to protect Equatorial Guinea's oil fields.[94] Sandra Barnes delineates a wider pattern of the US government providing military assistance to African dictators in order to support US oil companies, backed by what she calls "strategic philanthropy."[95] In Equatorial Guinea, she finds US military expertise has been used specifically to protect Exxon Mobil's oil fields in the territory.[96] A leaked US embassy cable explains the reasoning behind such activities: "Taking away U.S. energy imports from North America (i.e., those from our immediate neighbors Canada and Mexico), we find that over 30 percent of our imported oil and gas comes from the Gulf of Guinea region—more, for example, than from the Middle East. The largest portion of the Gulf of Guinea maritime territory belongs to little EG. To ignore the security implications associated with the country at the heart of this key region would leave a gaping hole in the map of our national strategy."[97]

The US oil companies themselves have also invested in Obiang and, more importantly, in his image. Mobil made a $65,000 donation to an organization Obiang set up in Virginia to improve his image abroad, while Marathon contributes $13,000 per month to the Equatoguinean embassy in Washington, DC.[98] Other companies have sponsored events praising Obiang and the virtues of his government and funded its lobbying campaigns abroad.[99] As Mario Esteban points out, Spain has followed a similar pattern to the United States, with Spanish oil giant Repsol-YPF encouraging the government to make concessions to Obiang.[100] Indeed, June 2014 saw the first visit by a Spanish president to Malabo in twenty-three years.[101] Thus, we see that (unsurprisingly) US oil companies and the US embassy in Malabo share common interests. We see that they want to keep Obiang in power to maintain access to oil. We see that the companies invest in Obiang's image abroad to spin their support for an authoritarian dictator before a domestic audience that could otherwise be critical, while the US state has invested in the security infrastructure surrounding Equatorial Guinea's/the Obiang family's oil fields.

The oil companies and the US embassy receive help in their efforts from the United States Agency for International Development (USAID). According to the Equatoguinean government, USAID provided support and technical assistance for setting up the country's Social Development Fund.[102] This provides substantial funding for MINASPROM and, thus, activities in theory dedicated to gender equality but in reality, as we have seen, dedicated to *painting a picture* of dedication to gender equality.[103] As the US embassy in Malabo tellingly put it in an internal communication in 2009, US technical assistance would be "effective in giving EG the future we want it to have."[104] That was an Obiang-led future that would avoid, the embassy said, "revolution that brings sudden, uncertain change and unpredictability [and] potentially dire consequences for our interests, most notably our energy security."[105]

USAID has also prioritized other projects associated with women's empowerment, including technical support for the Self-employment for Rural Women Project.[106] This same project has also received technical assistance and funding from the Canadian Cooperation Agency.[107] Equatorial Guinea's two NGOs that focus on promoting gender equality both receive funding from the United States and German embassies, while other projects carried out in partnership with Spain, Morocco, and others allegedly focus on promoting women's empowerment.[108] In Spring 2013 Washington-based reputation-management firm Qorvis began a PR push on behalf of its client, the Republic of Equatorial Guinea, on the so-called outcomes of such programs and other policies.[109] As such, the story of the Obiang regime's "aggressive" progress toward achieving gender equality was echoed around relevant US online news circles.[110]

The USAID focus on social programs and especially on projects that promote women's empowerment reflect a wider trend among the Western powers to brand themselves as global leaders in the fight for gender equality.[111] As Bruno

De Cordier argues, international aid has become part of a wider security and control agenda in which neoliberal development models (almost always with a gender equality or "women" chapter) are implanted in "beneficiary" countries.[112]

To summarize this section, internally, nationalist discourses on gender and "gender equality" are potentially aimed at curbing women's ability to resist the dictatorship—precisely the opposite aim of POLISARIO's centering of "gender equality" in its nationalist discourses, which were designed to encourage resistance to colonial foes. As for the external function of these discourses, we have seen that key corporate backers of the Obiang regime are concerned about the PR implications of backing a violent dictatorship. As for the United States, its oil companies and the US embassy have invested in Obiang's image (an image that heavily incorporates an idea of the ruler as "gender equality champion") arguably to avoid criticism from the US public. Yet they have been supported by their international development arm, USAID, which has channeled funding to the ministry responsible for gender equality, a ministry that has had, at best, a questionable level of impact on the lives of ordinary Equatoguinean women and girls. This pattern is replicated on smaller scales by other countries and their corporates. The role of overseas aid to Equatorial Guinea in general terms has received a damning judgment: the only systematic, independent evaluation available finds that aid has been used principally for the personal and political advantage of the ruling regime, while having no positive impact on the lives of the poorest Equatoguineans. My key argument is that mirages of gender and gender equality contribute to maintaining the rule of the Obiang regime. Crucially, I argue that both Obiang and his Western partners *know* that their "gender equality" measures are hollow, merely for show. This is not one-sided. This is *collaborative* genderwashing.

The effects of the Obiang regime on women's lives in terms of oppression, violence, and poverty are further explored in chapter 6. But what are the socioeconomic effects of this oil economy on women?

## Oil and Inopportunity? Women, Gender, and the Oil Industry

Michael Ross argues that oil maintains patriarchy. In an oil economy the wealth generated in oil sales raises the real exchange rate, making it cheaper for locals to import traded goods from abroad than to buy them from domestic producers. This causes a decline in the traded-goods sector (agriculture and manufacturing), which, argues Ross, tend to be gendered feminine in most developing countries. Thus, an oil economy reduces the incorporation of women into the labor market, which in turn means fewer women in political positions.[113] With respect to Equatorial Guinea, since the oil boom began in 1995, the economic reliance on petroleum has certainly provoked a decline in agriculture, a woman-dominated profession. In that sense Ross's argument is applicable. I argue here, however, that the oil economy sustains *multiple* oppressions in Equatorial Guinea, and not only because the oil economy undercuts the local traded-goods sector.

Oil, the mainstay of the Equatoguinean economy, burrows under the skin of gender, race, class, and age inequalities and feeds on them. With regard to race, Hannah Appel's excellent ethnographic research into the offshore oil industry and its (onshore) executives reveals the worries of the poorly paid, overworked Equatoguinean men on the rigs and juxtaposes this with the luxury lifestyles of the white executives living in enclaves on the mainland.[114] Sexual transactions, however, are a key indicator of the multiple inequalities fostered by the oil economy.

Equatoguinean interviewees complained of the sexual relationships between young Equatoguinean women and girls and white, wealthy, middle-aged oil company executives, among others.[115] In Malabo, Bata, Mongomo, and Oyala especially, there are incidences of sex trafficking of children and women from neighboring countries as well as from China, a phenomenon that the US Trafficking in Persons Report explicitly links to the oil economy.[116] Also, some Equatoguinean parents encourage their daughters to engage in prostitution, "especially with foreigners," in exchange for groceries, housing, and money.[117] As one Spanish retired television executive boasted in the Spanish Cultural Center café in Malabo before trying to grope me, "I can have five young wives here. I can do things that I wouldn't get away with in Spain."[118]

These sexual encounters are enacted along a spectrum between women's agency at one end down to rape and sexual exploitation at the other. One interviewee saw this spectrum as a "system" that submits girls and young women to "sociosexual slavery."[119] Another thought most girls and women showed agency in these relationships yet simultaneously identified the men involved as abusers. His comments are worth quoting *in extenso* as they helpfully point to the wider socioeconomic and political context:

> It's really normal for, for example, a fifty- or sixty-year-old North American to go out with a fourteen- or fifteen-year-old girl. First, at the cultural level, Equatoguinean girls see it as a form of gaining status, you know? That they are going out with "a white man," so to speak. But if you reflect, if you think about it, this would be a crime in other societies. It's a crime. But in Guinea as much her family as the girl herself see it as progress. And the bad thing is, the problem is, . . . why are we going to lie? They do it knowing it's a crime, these men, that it's morally inconceivable. This is an everyday thing in Equatorial Guinea. It's an everyday thing. And apart from the whites (I can't blame just the foreigners) the

typical thing in Guinea is that a member of parliament, a minister, men who are high up in the government or whatever, men with money, they leave their wives at home and go out with fifteen- or sixteen-year-old girls. It's complex. What saddens me most is that Guineans ourselves do this, but it's not the fault of the girls in any way. They are innocent, they see it as a good thing, or they do it because of need. And sometimes their families. . . . But the economic factor enters into play here. The father sees it as in his interest that his daughter brings resources to the home, so that the family can eat.[120]

The encounters described here are neocolonial in the sense that the wealthy, white executives are benefiting sexually and economically from gender and racial inequalities in a neocolonial setting but also in the sense that their actions build directly on deeply rooted patterns of sexual exploitation practiced by the Spanish colonials, as we saw in chapter 2.[121]

But oil is not simply something that "happens" to women. Women have found ways to take advantage of the oil boom.[122] Most foreign companies bring their workers with them, but some have employed a handful of locals, and government employs a few (PDGE member) women in management positions in the industry (figures are scarce, but overall, covering all ministries, only 14 percent of employees are female).[123] Interviewees linked the "economic independence" that such women enjoy to small and gradual social changes. This nascent middle class of women need not put up with machismo, explained feminist interviewees: if such a woman cannot find a man who is prepared to be monogamous, carry out domestic chores, and treat her as an equal, she can choose not to marry.[124] For feminists, this is revolutionary, since, as one explained to me: "If you are not married you are worthless. . . . In our society, no matter what you achieve professionally, if you are a woman who does not get married and have children, you have no status. . . . It's like in other countries where they call unmarried women 'spinsters,' but it is much more intense here."[125]

This handful of women in management level jobs are able to use their relative wealth as a form of resistance to sexist social norms. In time, feminists hope, this will force changes in attitudes, and unmarried women will no longer face stigma. However, we must underline that such women with management roles are rare. As Alicia Campos highlights, women are generally excluded from technical, operational, and management jobs in the oil sector as well as in the associated construction and transport fields.[126]

Further down the social scale, some women who have worked abroad for years have returned to Equatorial Guinea. With their savings, they open grocery shops and cafes, drawing on oil and construction workers as their clientele.

Other women work as cleaners for foreign companies, or sell their smallholder produce near the ports. That is not to say that such women are able to make enough to live on, as Dolores's case shows, but, ever enterprising (indeed, "enterprising," *emprendadora*, was the one key word that Equatoguineans chose again and again when talking of women in their country), they prepare themselves for the grayest days through savings arrangements.

Reminiscent of the concept of tontine in Francophone African countries, Equatoguinean women use the Ndjangui, Esuan, or Alason.[127] As Yolanda Aixelá Cabré explains, through these systems, women embark on informal arrangements with women friends or relatives, in which each woman pays a regular sum into the tontine and can take out a portion when she faces exceptional financial difficulties (for funeral costs or hospital treatment, for example). This system of feminine solidarity and support relies on mutual trust and bypasses the "official economy" as well as interventions from the likes of foreign embassy assistance programs, the World Bank, and development agencies. In some cases, shows Aixelá Cabré, the tontine extends beyond the group of investors and can be a source of microcredits for the wider community.[128]

Migrant women, too, mostly from West and Central Africa, have tried to take advantage of the oil wealth, getting jobs in cafés, restaurants, and shops or trading in the markets. They face systematic xenophobia from authorities, however, in the form of regular extortion and racist insults, the arbitrary closure of their shops, and expatriation, beatings, and rape.[129] One such woman is Claudette Kendo, who moved to Malabo alone from Cameroon. The first time we met, she was working in her snack bar, one eye on the hob, one eye on the door. The police come here regularly to extort money from her—if she doesn't pay, they will deport her. She explained, "I come to work, I go back to my house, and that is all. I try to avoid going out as much as possible, to avoid problems."[130]

On balance then, a small handful of women today earn a fair salary thanks to the oil industry, and their resulting economic independence gives them tools to challenge some manifestations of sexism. Poorer women, always enterprising, have also responded to the oil economy by carving out opportunities for themselves. But "poorer women" constitutes the vast majority of women. This is trickle-down economics with next to nothing trickling down. Sexual politics are indicators of who is benefiting most from the oil economy. The wealthy, white oil executives and their regime partners benefit sexually, as well as economically, from the oil wealth, and they foster gender, race, age, class, and neocolonial hierarchies in doing so.

To conclude part 2, both the Obiang regime and POLISARIO put so-called gender equality at the center of their nationalist discourses, with external and internal ideological functions in mind. In Western Sahara, the so-called kidnappings, as well as the Maternal Assistance Center, the unenviable situation of the "hanging" women, and other societal problems discussed in the previous chapter beg an uncomfortable question: given that its official nationalist discourses declare the existence of full gender equality, is POLISARIO guilty of genderwashing? These discourses benefit POLISARIO by securing foreign, Western allies and recruiting Saharawis to the revolution, after all. However, my definition of genderwashing requires that claims of commitment to gender equality be used to the benefit of the state when the latter's actions in practice work *against* gender equality. Although questionable policies and laws remain in the state in exile, these should be judged with POLISARIO's difficult task of keeping the peace between conservative and liberal elements of society. Furthermore, POLISARIO, especially through the UNMS, does actively pursue the rights of women in political, economic, and social fields. The analysis of Saharawi feminist nationalism shows that POLISARIO's official discourses on gender equality are, at times, put to use both by the UNMS to offer discursive support to its feminist nationalist policies as well as by the self-described "modern Saharawi feminists." The latter, thanks to these POLISARIO official discourses, are able to paint their feminist actions as "naturally" Saharawi, even if they simultaneously tackle the hegemonic view that gender equality has already been achieved.

Like POLISARIO, Obiang has the West in mind with regard to external-facing discourse, but Equatoguinean state discourses that focus on gender equality are not constructed to entertain Western allies but rather are constructed in partnership with them. The United States actively seeks to keep Obiang—the United States' gatekeeper to Equatoguinean oil—in power and sees its "technical assistance" and "development" programs as tools to help ensure this. USAID has arguably focused its efforts on so-called gender equality. Yet Obiang has not attempted to hegemonize new gender roles. By failing to challenge the binary gender roles that make women subordinate, and by promoting fear and oppression, Obiang attempts to dampen women's resistance efforts. Through their support of Obiang, Western states and corporates are undermining gender equality and, indeed, respect for human rights and democracy more widely, despite their PR claims to the exact opposite. Meanwhile, some of the oil executives on the ground foster gender, raced, and neocolonial axes of power through exploitative sexual encounters with children (mostly girls) and women. The outcome of this collaborative genderwashing project with Obiang is, on the one hand, the lubrication of oil transactions between the two partners and, on the other, the continued subjugation of women like Dolores Molubela, who works hard all day cleaning up after oil elites and yet barely has the wages to feed her grandchildren.

# PART THREE

# Resistance to Authoritarian Dictatorships since Spain's Exit

# CHAPTER FIVE

# Women, Gender, and Resistance in Moroccan-Occupied Western Sahara

I MAGINE THE AIR as Fatima felt it on her skin on 8 January 1976. Imagine the biting cold of winter near the sea, the eerie half-light that dusk casts on us, the dead quiet and paranoia of streets already invaded. Imagine the terror of a lonely car engine humming behind you, the eyes burning into your back as you gather pace, the car doors creaking open, the four men leaping out, their hands all over you, over your mouth—don't bother screaming!—then the smallness and blackness and airlessness of a shut boot. Saharawis saw police bundle Fatima into the back of a black Renault 16. They didn't see Fatima again for fifteen years.[1]

As the Moroccan army descended on Western Sahara, it attempted to clear the southern regions of Morocco, which were once part of Spanish Sahara, of suspected POLISARIO sympathizers. Among the first to be taken was twenty-four-year-old Fatima Ghalia Leili. Fatima was well known in Tan Tan, her hometown. Despite her youth, she had a high-profile civil service job and was a leader of a local women's group. Indeed, it was on the walk back from work that she disappeared.

Until her arrest, Fatima's public façade was far from an activist one, yet she had been secretly proindependence for years. When the POLISARIO was formed, Fatima had become a double agent, collecting information from her place of work and passing it to the Saharawi nationalists. She also trained women and men in protest techniques.[2] On top of this, she had a brother who was a POLISARIO founder. In other words, Fatima was dangerous. She had to go.

After Moroccan agents had disappeared her, they came back a month later to disappear most of Fatima's extended family, which was common practice.[3] "They also kidnapped her father, her sister, most of her brothers, her mother, her aunt, and her uncle," says Soukaina Yaya, who, when a small girl in Tan Tan, watched the events of 2 February 1976 from her window with dread.

Police broke down the door of the Leili family home and took all who were there, pulling Fatima's father, ill with asthma, from his bed. His crime was having relatives linked to the POLISARIO.[4]

Yaya, now a human rights activist in El Aaiún, finishes her former neighbor's story: "When [Fatima] came out of jail, she had suffered a lot. She married, but she wasn't able to have children due to injuries inflicted through torture. They tortured her very, very badly."[5]

In her summary of Leili's post-prison life, Yaya emphasizes her compatriot's marital status and inability to procreate. In our interview, Yaya explains the fate of one other female friend, the novelist El Bataoul Mahjoub Lmdaimigh. El Bataoul, also known as "the woman with the black pen" because of her refusal to follow the conventions of the Moroccan education system by writing in black rather than blue ink, witnessed the kidnap of her father and other relatives. Says Yaya of El Bataoul: "When they took her father and other members of her family, her childhood stopped. This was in 1977. And she decided then that she would never marry, because the regime had taken all the male members of her family, so from then on she would accept males only as friends but not as a husband."[6]

Again, El Bataoul's marital status is part of the primordial information given in the brief summary of her life. I have previously argued that the role of mother and caregiver in Saharawi society is constructed as feminine in hegemonic discourse and that marriage is a key aspiration for women.[7] Yaya, indeed, has given motherhood and marriage central importance in her recounting of women activists' life stories. While Leili is unable to pursue what is seen (in hegemonic Saharawi nationalist discourses) as her role as a woman owing to the torture inflicted on her, El Bataoul resists her gender role in the name of the nationalist cause. In this chapter, I further explore the relationship between marital status, compulsory heterosexuality, gender, and resistance in occupied Western Sahara.

I tell the story of Saharawi resistance to Moroccan colonialism chronologically, thereby setting the complicated and nuanced relationship between resistance and gender in its wider historical context. During the Moroccan and Mauritanian invasion, we see how Morocco made use of Saharawi constructions of gender to traumatize its victims. Focusing on the years of war, I illustrate how everyday resistance (the tool so important to Saharawi and Equatoguinean women resisting patriarchy and, for black Saharawis, slavery in the Spanish colonial period) resurfaces as the main arm of Saharawis opposing the Moroccan occupation.

The first major public protest in 1987 of Saharawi nationalists under Moroccan rule allows us to use and develop Scott's theorization of when the hidden transcript becomes public. I then use a testimony of a former disappeared woman, captured in the 1987 demonstration, to argue that Morocco's policy of targeting mothers backfires as women make their status as mothers a site of, and spiritual fuel for, resistance.

Moving to the time of the 1991 ceasefire, the nonviolent movement grew when hundreds of former disappeared emerge from Moroccan dungeons. I analyze the intifadas of the nineties as well as the bolder 2005 intifada. This section is largely narrative, but some knowledge of the diplomatic intrigues that helped provoke the intifadas is essential for understanding the wider story of gender and resistance. Furthermore, a look at the story of Embarka Hassan, whose first street protest was in 2005, helps us understand why young women decide to become activists.[8]

Next I move to the 2010 Gdeim Izik protest, by far the largest protest in Saharawi recent history. I build on arguments made in chapter 1 concerning the external ideological function of state constructions of gender equality in a world where the West is currently prioritizing women's "emancipation" in "backward" countries. I look at how pressure from the West influences Moroccan oppression of resisters and how this, in turn, affects the gendered makeup of Saharawi public protest. I also explore how Saharawi femininities and masculinities affect who resists.

A look at how Morocco tortures Saharawi prisoners and detainees reveals how constructions of gendered sexuality are used not only to invoke trauma and horror but also to prevent the reproduction of Saharawi nationalism itself. However, I also argue that Saharawi women have found ways to resist even the most terrifying types of torture. The centrality of female chastity in Saharawi culture, and how Morocco darkly takes advantage of this in its prisons and secret detention centers, leads us to a discussion of Saharawi women's reactions to current gender inequalities in Saharawi society. Finally, I conclude that while the relationship between gender and resistance is dependent on the idiosyncrasies of Saharawi gender norms, which affect greatly who resists, why, and how and which also determine Morocco's response, the relationship is, as in Equatorial Guinea, inseparable from the globally hegemonic Western orientalism and its constructions of gender.

## The Invasion: Tortured Mothers and a Disappeared Father

One day in early November 1975, a sweaty Spanish soldier wiped his brow after plunging yet another post into the ground. Fences were to entirely hem in the Saharawi suburbs of El Aaiún and were intended to help prevent resistance to the ensuing invasion. The barriers' disciplinary role was made more violent by the presence of tanks.[9] The colonial government hoped the Moroccan takeover would go smoothly, without incident. From a Spanish perspective, perhaps it did. Most of the troops left the Sahara in time "to spend Christmas at home."[10]

It was a different story for Saharawis. POLISARIO sympathizers living in the Tarfaya Strip were already disappearing. Indeed, it was November 1975 when nine-year-old Aminatou Haidar heard the news that her father was dead. Officially, he was accidentally "hit by a lorry" somewhere between Tan Tan and Guelmin. Unofficially, he was murdered.[11]

Back in El Aaiún, as soon as Khadijatou, whom we met in chapter 1, realized that the Moroccans had crossed the Northern border, she fled by car to the east. Tawfa waited a little longer—long enough to receive the certificate confirming the completion of her studies, but also long enough to see her former Spanish colleagues handing over the hospital, her place of work, to Moroccan troops. As the latter and their Mauritanian counterparts trod further into Western Sahara, scores of arbitrary arrests of anyone suspected of involvement with the POLISARIO began "on a massive scale."[12] The International Federation for Human Rights describes the horrors: "The soldiers of the two occupying countries have butchered hundreds and perhaps thousands of Saharawis, including children and old people who refused to publicly acknowledge the King of Morocco."[13]

At this time, further members of the UNMS began to join the Saharawi People's Liberation Army (SPLA). Their roles included guarding prisoners and helping to evacuate and hide Saharawis living in the desert settlements during bomb attacks and building and securing a life in exile in Algeria for the swelling refugee population.[14] In La Güera Saharawi women also served temporarily as combatants in the standoff against the Mauritanian army.[15] Others served on the battlefront as nurses.[16]

Women who tried but did not make it to the frontline or the rear guard of the camps beyond often suffered a horrific fate. Maayifa Ment Ehseina, for example, was captured and taken to the military detention center in El Msayed, near Tan Tan, along with six of her young children. Ehseina, released in 1978, was the only woman ever to emerge from El Msayed. The six children died. Today, fellow Saharawi El Batal Lahbib, disappeared on 27 October 1975 in Lebuerat, is the only surviving ex-captive of El Msayed. Lahbib remembers two large earth trenches, probably dug out by a tractor. One was used for torture and interrogations. The other served the double purpose of the prisoners' cell and a pit for half-dead bodies. Corpses—Saharawis were shot, stoned, beaten, or whipped to death in the first of the two trenches, or dissolved in what Lahbib describes as a "huge iron bucket . . . with something inside that destroyed flesh"—were taken elsewhere.[17]

Lahbib's testimony indicates gendered forms of torture. As well as losing his own testicles, he remembers the women and girls being repeatedly gang raped by guards while male prisoners were forced to perform sex acts on each other.[18] The gendered implications of sexual torture will be further discussed later.

On 27 February 1976, a day after the Spanish officially left the territory and a day before the Spanish military lowered the last Spanish flag in El Aaiún, the POLISARIO filled the political vacuum by declaring the Saharawi Arab Democratic Republic.[19] Meanwhile, Moroccan occupiers were detaining, arresting, and disappearing not only women suspected of links to the POLISARIO but also others selected at random, often, like Ehseina, in the company of their children. The aim was to create a climate of terror among the population—anyone could be next.[20] Mahjouba Ment Issa Ould Douega, for example, was arrested in 1976 along with approximately fifty other women, all with their children. Douega witnessed the death, in prison, of her one-year-old daughter, Taghla. When she gave birth shortly after being released, the newborn died twenty-four hours later. Douega's pregnant sister Khadijatou was also imprisoned. She miscarried following torture.[21] Over the course of 1976 in the town of Smara, thirty-one mothers with infants still at breastfeeding stage were imprisoned. Only two of the babies were to survive.[22] Likewise, in the Saharawi-dominated town of Tan Tan, southern Morocco, forty-two women and their babies were kidnapped and tortured just ahead of the Green March.[23] Moroccan torturers were capitalizing on the Saharawi women's role of primary caregivers. The targeting of nursing mothers, the beating of pregnant women, and the practice of torturing babies in front of their mothers are gender-based forms of abuse in that they deny women's gender-ascribed role as carers and protectors of their offspring.[24]

Of the young, able-bodied male Saharawis who escaped capture by Moroccan authorities, most departed their homes to join the SPLA. Some became soldiers. Others were captured on the way. When asked why they are today political activists despite the risks to their lives, Mahfood Dahou's and Mohammed Mayara's responses recall these departed men. Says Dahou: "I was born here in El Aaiún in 1975. My father, who was a soldier, died in the Saharawi refugee camps. I never met him. He left my mother pregnant. So, like most Saharawis in the Occupied Territories, I've grown up without a father."[25] Explains Mayara:

My father was one of four brothers who were kidnapped by the Moroccans and put in jail, and he died there. My cousin also died in prison after torture. So of course I, like all Saharawis, we suffer. We are born into sufferance. At this time, part of my family joined the POLISARIO. And so they fled from the planes and the crimes of that time committed against the Saharawis. Other members of my family were then put in secret prisons and others faced the terror and horror committed by Moroccans. So I want you to see, in a patriarchal society like the Saharawi, growing up in a family where there is no father . . . the father isn't there. . . . All my cousins, my uncles, were also absent.[26]

Moulay Ahmed Leili, the asthmatic father of Fatima, who we met in the opening of this chapter, took it upon himself to wash and pray for the bodies of those who died while in detention at the ancient Moroccan forts of Agdz and later Qal'at Mgouna. He was released on 21 June 1991. He died the next day. With his last breaths, Moulay managed a final effort for his former Saharawi inmates: he recited the names of the deceased and the dates and locations of their deaths. He recalled that Heiba ould Mayara, Mohammed's father, passed on 28 September 1977 at Agdz fort.[27]

When asked when and how they first become involved in activities resisting the occupation, Mayara and Dahou both highlight how the actions of the Moroccan regime have left them fatherless. As Mayara says, Saharawi society is patriarchal, and as explored in previous research, gender roles within the family are binary and clearly defined, each carrying its own importance.[28] The father is the head of the family, is responsible for providing sustenance for his wife and children, and, once male children approach puberty, must begin playing a greater role in the latter's upbringing. To decapitate a generation of Saharawi boys of their fathers was, for Saharawis like Mayara and Dahou, not just to leave them with the emotional and psychological burden of lost loved ones but also to take from them what Saharawis see as an integral part of the family unit, strongly structured as it is (in hegemonic discourse) along binary gendered lines. The sense of injustice at such a loss fed Mayara's and Dahou's wills to resist.

A Saharawi man's role, as in many cultures, also encompasses caring for and protecting women. If we go back to Agdz fort, where Heiba ould Mayara was held and died, a testimony from a Moroccan political prisoner helps us to understand how prison guards made use of such constructions of masculinity to add to the suffering of Saharawi men.

Mohammed Nadrani was a politically active philosophy student at Ibn Zohr University in Agadir when he was captured in 1976 and taken to a secret detention center in Rabat. A year later, with nine other Moroccan political prisoners, he was transferred to a fort in the town of Agdz, a popular tourist destination famous for being, as *Lonely Planet* puts it, "a classic caravanserai oasis with a still-pristine *palmeraie*, ancient mudbrick kasbahs, and a secret desert prison."[29]

We pick up Nadrani's story at the point of his first night in the detention center. It is worth quoting his testimony *in extenso*, since as well as revealing the gendered dimensions of torture infliction, it hints at the lost stories of those men, such as Heiba ould Mayara, who never came back:

> We heard women's voices—we couldn't make out what they were saying, but they had a southern accent. We got close to the door to look through the cracks. There weren't many of them, draped in the black chadors of the south. They were hurriedly washing their faces and hands from pitchers in the yard. Then there was another creaking lock, shouts and insults hurled at the women, and they ran back into their cells. . . .
>
> Then the Sahrawi women were moved to an annex and we were given their cell, which was cool and infused with an intoxicating smell of women. It made us nostalgic. . . . It represented lust but also the families we had lost. A sort of mother awoke in us all. We felt the women's presence, their sufferings and hopes. They had suffered the same lot as the men. They were there to sustain the men but also to be a source of suffering for them, of torture. Sahrawi men could not accept the suffering of their women. However, women bear suffering, privations and nightmares well. In prison they are stronger than men. They were beaten and insulted because the guards knew how it hurt the men. We could not bear them to be traumatized and thought of them as our sisters. . . .
>
> Then they left the door open—we didn't understand, it was the Sahrawis who came to us, it was very warm, embraces, so we mixed with them for about twenty days. There were all classes, peasants, herders, civil servants. They said that twenty-five people had died in that center—we didn't understand how people died, we'd been thinking of a trial and then prison, in prison we'd be able to study—and now this was another reality which was completely new. Then we realized that we were outside Moroccan reality—everything they had said about democracy—the reality was worse.[30]

As Nadrani points out, prison guards hurt women *specifically* to cause men pain psychologically. Moroccan security officers prevent Saharawi men from fulfilling their masculine role of protecting the women close to them. Particularly in the case of the sexual torture of female loved ones, the abuse arguably takes on tones of imperial conquest.[31] As Libby Tata Arcel points out, the abuse of women in a patriarchal society in a situation of conflict symbolizes defeat for men.[32] The function of sexual violence against the female relatives of political prisoners is further explored in chapter 6, where I will compare the gendered practices of Moroccan and Equatoguinean authorities. Of course, gender norms aside, the pain of knowing a friend's, loved one's, or even fellow human being's intense suffering is also inflicted by such abuses.

Another important point raised in Nadrani's testimony is his description of his situation and that of his fellow inmates as "outside Moroccan reality." Keeping political prisoners in secret detention centers such as Agdz rather than official prisons had, and continues to have, advantages for the authorities. Most importantly, such centers do not officially exist, and the detainees are not officially detained.[33] I will return to this detail later in the chapter, as it has shown, since 2010, to have important consequences in terms of gender and resistance.

The War Years: Offstage Resistance and<br>How Motherhood Powers Revolution

During the war, the words "POLISARIO" and "Saharawi" became publicly unpronounceable. Yaya explains, "If police caught you calling a Saharawi in Las Palmas just for a chat, they'd take you and throw you in jail," while Hamza Lakhal indicates that oppression was such that public protest was unthinkable: "You can't even imagine that you *can* protest."[34] Dahou, too, underlines this sense of impossibility with regard to publicly challenging Morocco, yet he points to the climate of resistance that persisted behind the scenes: "All our work had to be secret. If they saw two or three Saharawis together in the street, they would beat you. We had to do something. There were no mobiles then, no internet. We had to work using the intelligence of the Saharawis."[35]

James C. Scott would see such draconian conditions as ripe for breeding a *hidden transcript*, that is, resistance that "takes place 'offstage,' beyond direct observation by powerholders."[36] Under such levels of oppression, Scott would argue, the Saharawis had "a vested interest in avoiding any *explicit* display of insubordination" in order to avoid the tyranny of the Moroccan occupiers.[37] If in the streets Saharawis appeased the authorities and avoided trouble, in the relative safety of their homes more subtle kinds of resistance flourished.

As a young child in the offstage privacy of her parents' living room, Sultana Khaya remembers listening to the POLISARIO's news via the radio that was buried under a warm womb of blankets to ensure the waves would not reach the ears of informers outside.[38] Not only was this an example of the everyday resistance that Scott discusses but it also points us toward the presence, in that living room, of a counterhegemonic discourse. As I argued in the introduction, Scott implies that resistance is inherent to all subalterns, yet the Saharawi case illuminates how it was ideology that made their actions possible. The POLISARIO had begun to hegemonize a Saharawi national identity long before the Moroccan invasion. Of course, the terrible injustices committed by

the occupiers pushed the Saharawis to reaction, to develop a hidden transcript, but it was the nationalist discourse of the POLISARIO (and Bassiri
before it), and its reaffirmation of the unspeakable identity of "Saharawi," that
made resistance possible. In Gramscian terms, Saharawis did not see Morocco's takeover of the Sahara as something "natural" and "inevitable." If they had
done, the Saharawis would not have resisted: the will to resist is not an innate
characteristic that subalterns are born with. A Saharawi national identity as
distinct from Moroccan was hegemonic among the Saharawi population, and
being able to listen to the POLISARIO via the radio gave Khaya courage.

Soukaina Yaya also recalls the sound of her nation in waiting. After moving to El Aaiún, she would be startled, now and then, by the crash of gunfire
in the desert. She knew the POLISARIO was near. This armed her with hope,
an emotion that fuels resistance. Also inspired by this hope, Saharawis found
ways to play out their nationality in public spaces. For example, some teenagers would subtly but defiantly shut their mouths when pupils were called to
sing the Moroccan national anthem at school. Other activists were clandestinely distributing pro-POLISARIO information. The most daring took part
in what Saharawi youth called "operations": writing Saharawi slogans and painting Saharawi flags on the walls of Moroccan administrative buildings, swap-
ping Moroccan flags for Saharawi ones, and hiding and smuggling wanted
Saharawi activists.[39]

These youths were challenging Morocco's domination and feeding the idea
of an independent nation in the Saharawi social imaginary order. Although
tremendously risky, as long as the perpetrators were not caught, these activities
remained anonymous and therefore preserved some level of safety. So what
would it take for these activists to take off their masks and publicly challenge
Moroccan domination? Scott argues that those who resist will only "storm the
public stage" when "the pressure [of indignation] rises or when there are weak-
nesses in the "retaining wall" holding it back."[40] He asserts that "the greater
the disparity in power between dominant and subordinate and the more arbi-
trarily it is exercised, the more the public transcript of subordinates will take
on a stereotyped, ritualistic cast."[41] This explanation works for many cases of
subordinated peoples, but although infrapolitics are used by Saharawis, there
is also ever greater public resistance despite continued violent oppression. The
strategic need to perform resistance to an audience (and thereby further disseminate a counterhegemonic discourse) is crucial to the nonviolent movement.
This movement focuses on delegitimizing Morocco and its allies in front of
external *onlookers*, as well as on recruiting international supporters. Therefore,
the movement's actions *must* be public, no matter how tough the repercussions.
I suggest that the hidden transcript storms the public stage in the presence of

one or more of the following factors: following Scott, mounting indignation on the part of the oppressed peoples; again following Scott, a reduction in the practice of discipline and punishment by the dominant; and when performing resistance before an (internal or external) audience could bring strategic benefits.

This third point highlights rational thinking and strategy: the oppressed take a *decision* to make resistance open and public. Here, studies of contentious politics, as developed by Doug McAdam, Sidney Tarrow, and Charles Tilly, can help us understand why and when such strategic decisions are made. By contentious politics, McAdam, Tarrow, and Tilly refer to episodic, public, and collective interactions among and between claim makers and their objects, between activists and government, for example.[42]

Within the school of contentious politics, the idea of political opportunities and constraints/threats is helpful. Political opportunity structure is the framework in which people decide whether or not to mobilize. It refers both to features of regimes that facilitate or inhibit a political actor's action and to changes in those features.[43] Political opportunities and threats help us understand the ebb and flow of a resistance movement or, in the Saharawi case, why activists moved from using Scott's "weapons of the weak" to mounting outright intifada. In 1987 one such opportunity arose for the Saharawi nonviolent movement.

On 20 November 1987 a joint UN Technical Commission arrived in El Aaiún. Its aim was to evaluate the conditions for organizing a self-determination referendum for the Saharawis.[44] Activists realized that this visit presented an opportunity worth risking everything for. With a public demonstration, they could display Saharawi enthusiasm for self-determination as well as raise awareness of the appalling human rights situation before a key international actor. But Morocco also saw the opportunity. The latter advertised the date of the commission's arrival as one day earlier than it was. Thus when hundreds of Saharawis amassed near the airport to welcome UN staff and illustrate their support of independence, Moroccan authorities could catch their targets.[45] Four hundred activists, known as the "Commission Group," were unofficially imprisoned, most in the Mobile Intervention Unit Headquarters, a secret detention center in El Aaiún.[46] The stories of women survivors of the Commission Group help to illuminate the relationship between constructions of gender and resistance.

The testimony of Fatma Aayache of the four years she spent disappeared is striped with a theme of (prevented) motherhood. It is valuable as an example of how mothering activities are dramatically brought to the fore precisely because of their enforced halt. Mothers, their children, and the metaphorical umbilical cords that link them are constantly present throughout the entire narrative.

The text illustrates how the context of war and colonialism have shaped a specific mother's experience, in which her motherhood is actively employed as a source of emotional strength that helps her to bear, psychologically, years of physical and mental torture. Aayache's was a spiritual and emotional resistance, in which she attempted to maintain her dignity and sense of humanity in the face of the torturers' efforts to dehumanize, degrade, and destroy her.

Aayache's narrative illustrates, first, the important and high status that the mother figure has within the family unit and in wider Saharawi society. The first line of the testimony reads, "My name is Fatma M'barek Mohamed Aayache, born in 1968 in El Aaiún, Western Sahara [W.S.], mother of Lhalla Charafu, 19 years old, and Abdelaziz Elbachraoui, 7 years old."[47] Thus, among the first (and therefore primordial) pieces of information that the reader receives about the author is the fact that she is a mother of two, which serves to emphasize the pride associated with her position.

A reference to Aayache's own mother also serves to illustrate the sacred status of the mother figure in Saharawi families. When Moroccan police enter Aayache's home to kidnap her, they use violence against all her relatives, yet she specifically highlights the abuse of her mother as the single most shocking action, giving "a great fright to all [her] family members."[48] This abhorrence at the ill treatment of Aayache's mother shows the inviolable respect that mothers enjoy in Saharawi narratives. Furthermore, the constant focus on motherhood throughout the testimony is in itself illustrative of the central importance that this role has in the eyes of the writer. She is much more than a Saharawi nationalist kidnapped and tortured; she is a kidnapped and tortured *mother*, whose fate illustrates the dehumanized nature of a Moroccan aggressor willing to cross all the lines.

Second, the testimony illustrates how the bonds between mother and child inevitably become a source of suffering in a context of imprisonment yet simultaneously a birthplace of powerful resistance to the Moroccan's objective of "minimizing dignity or of being a human."[49] When Aayache focuses on the personal story of the still disappeared Mohamed Lkhalil Aayache, it is always in relation to the reactions and emotions of his mother Salka. Salka, "who had to endure both her and her son's torment," now suffers mental illness as a result of her son's disappearance.[50] Yet at one stage while they were in prison, Mohamed gives his mother strength: "His mother was facing his groaning with patience. He was inspiring her and us to cling to resistance and life."[51] Aayache gains a similar strength from the thought of her own daughter: "My angel, Lhalla, was helping me endure the torturers' violence. . . . I was handcuffed, but I was embracing her in my mind, playing with her beautiful hair."[52] In this way, Aayache shows motherhood to be intertwined with political resistance. The motherhood of Fatma and Salka Aayache, in the context of resistance to Moroccan colonialism in the Occupied Territories, takes on revolutionary power.[53]

Third, the testimony reveals the power to resist derived from maternal solidarity and support. In the case of Fatima ment Saaid who left behind a baby of two months when she was kidnapped, Aayache writes: "Feeling sad for her, we took turns sucking her breasts to alleviate the pain that the bursting of milk breasts were causing her."[54] Here, the women are united by the maternal action of breastfeeding. Through the emotional bond of empathy, the women suck Fatima's breasts to comfort her and thus give her the strength to continue resisting. Fellow Commission Group detainee and nowadays probably the most famous and loved Saharawi activist Aminatou Haidar (the girl whom we met earlier who lost her father in 1975) also practiced this "communal" motherhood while in prison in 2005–6. Hundreds of Saharawi citizens came to visit her, but the Moroccan police would only allow her two children entry. Haidar refused to see anyone unless she could see everyone, thereby illustrating that in her eyes all Saharawis were her immediate family.[55] This illustrates Haidar's use of her role as mother *ideologically*. With such actions Haidar was symbolically showing that the fight was for everyone's children, not just their own individual child. In contrast to the Western idea of nuclear family, she was socializing motherhood.

Aayache's text, with its focus on maternity, feminine solidarity, the female body, and mother-daughter bonds, can be read as an example of cultural feminism.[56] It reclaims personal, lived women's experience as intensely important and makes motherhood central to a testimony of political resistance. Her struggle in the Moroccan jails, which is narrated with metaphors derived not from stereotypical male experiences such as warfare but from motherhood, symbolizes the suffering of a people. The ideological use of her experiences as a mother makes Aayache's testimony a strong example of what Caron Gentry terms active maternalism. Gentry describes her concept further: "Politically active mothers, in this context as dissidents or agitators, are self-identified as mothers. There is a strong history of women whose politicisation is owed to their motherhood, typically because something happened to their children. . . . This is an active and claimed maternalist position."[57]

Nevertheless, the Saharawi example is a distinctive form of active maternalism. Unlike the active maternalism of one of Gentry's examples, the Mothers of the Plaza de Mayo, who took to the streets to protest against the Argentine military dictatorship following the disappearance of their children, Saharawi mothers, in their majority (the case of Tekbar Haddi, explored in chapter 3, is a significant exception), do not cite their status as mothers as the primary reason for their politicization but rather highlight discrimination along national, ethnic, and economic lines.[58] This is a crucial point. Whereas other women political actors, such as the Argentinian mothers, used active maternalism to legitimize their political activism in a culture that may have otherwise rejected such a role for women (but where the link to motherhood made the activism sufficiently "feminine" as to be acceptable), in Western Sahara political activism is as "naturally" feminine as it is masculine, thanks to hegemonic POLISARIO nationalist discourses, and Saharawi women have no need to find such justifications.[59] Their maternalism is active and claimed, but neither Aayache nor Haidar state that their activism is "owed" to it.

In Aayache's story, motherhood is key to her identity as a revolutionary. As a tool of emotional and spiritual resistance, it helps her to survive. Yet motherhood is never identified as the trigger for her activism. On the contrary, it is her desire to achieve "self-determination" and the need for "pinpointing and unveiling the flagrant human rights violations daily perpetuated by the Moroccan regime" that explain her engagement.[60] Similarly, Haidar's motivating cause is "to contribute to a better society for all; constructive, lawful, nonviolent, and based on principles of equality and equal opportunity."[61] Saharawi mothers could be said to practice an active maternalism, in that they are politically active mothers and self-identify as such. Yet, transcending Gentry's definition of active maternalism, motherhood is not named by these women as the seed for their political consciousness. Neither is motherhood always the source of their resistance. Rather, Saharawi mothers' identification as mothers *facilitates* their resistance.

The next section focuses on the intifadas that followed Aayache and Haidar's exit from prison. It is mostly narrative, yet it is essential to understanding the historical development of the Saharawi resistance movement as a whole and, therefore, in turn, the wider relationship between gender and resistance in the Occupied Territories.

### The Ceasefire and Intifadas of the Nineties: When the Disappeared Come Back

In 1991 the UN brokered a ceasefire between Morocco and POLISARIO promising a self-determination referendum for Saharawis. Coinciding with this, Morocco released three hundred Saharawi prisoners, including surviving members of the Commission Group and Saharawis who had disappeared in the seventies and early eighties.[62] Adjusting to life outside of prison was hard, not just because the ex-disappeared continued to be monitored and harassed by police but also because of the physical and emotional scars. Haidar emerged "a shadow of [her] former self, a ghost, a living dead, a young woman back from a kind of hell that bears no name."[63] Aayache faced struggles of her own: her daughter, now five years old, had forgotten who she was, while Aayache's own mother was dying.[64] Nevertheless, both women continued with their pro-independence struggle, becoming two of the handful of unofficial "leaders" of the resistance and role models for Saharawi girl activists.

The liberation of these political prisoners helped to inspire a younger generation of Saharawis, while the new presence of the UN in the territory also gave many activists renewed confidence to go public in their acts of resistance.[65] As I argued earlier, the strategic need to perform resistance before international actors can encourage activists to take the risk of directly challenging the regime, and Saharawis at that time also hoped that the gaze of the UN would bring protection.[66]

But Saharawi activists were proved wrong. MINURSO, the UN mission to the territory, is highly unusual in that it is a peacekeeping mission with no mandate to monitor human rights. This is mainly thanks to France's threat to veto such a mandate. Nevertheless, protests led by Saharawi youths in favor of independence and the release of political prisoners and against the holding of Moroccan parliamentary elections in Western Sahara continued to take place throughout the 1990s.[67] During these intifadas (much smaller in participation and shorter in time than the more famous intifadas of 1999 and 2005 but identified as intifadas by Saharawis nonetheless) hundreds of youths were arrested. Some, such as Kelthoum El Ouanat, a young woman caught protesting in Smara during the Intifada of Three Cities (Smara, El Aaiún, and Assa) in 1992, received twenty-year sentences issued by military tribunals.[68] This context of protests met with heavy repression followed by further protests created a pressure cooker of tension, which was to explode when the political situation changed in 1999.[69]

When the UN originally brokered the ceasefire, both Morocco and POLISARIO agreed that voter eligibility would be based on an updated version of the 1974 Spanish census. But the Moroccan state encouraged dozens of thousands of Moroccans to apply for a vote and to launch appeals when rejected, effectively blocking the referendum for years on end, with the UN unable or unwilling to take action.[70] By 1999, losing faith in the referendum process, Saharawi frustrations exploded.

In early September 1999 students launched a sit-in in the streets of El Aaiún, raising the issue of student unemployment and the meager bursaries and transport services. The sit-in began with around three hundred to five hundred protesters sleeping in tents in a smaller-scale, urban precursor to 2010's Gdeim Izik protest but grew over the following days as Saharawi workers, including swathes of women employed in low-skilled, underpaid employment and disabled people denied the opportunity to work, gradually joined the students.[71] As well as opposite the Nagjir hotel where UN staff are based, *āḥīām* (Saharawi tents) were erected in the Maatalla residential district, where the first site of Saharawi nationalist uprising at the square of Zemla once lay.[72] The location and symbology therefore drew on the Saharawi collective memory and added historical continuity to the protest.

Police eventually destroyed the camps. Almost two hundred Saharawis had been detained and brutalized by Moroccan police by the end of October 1999.[73] As Stephan and Mundy have reported, it was this violent repression of a peaceful, organized sit-in that sparked a spontaneous intifada, which spread across Western Sahara and the Saharawi-dominated Tarfaya Strip.[74]

Although the public demands of the 1999 intifada focused on economic issues, students' rights, and human rights, many activists were involved in clandestine, proindependence activities, including spreading pro-POLISARIO information. Proindependence slogans were not used publicly, though, since this was seen as too dangerous.[75] Nevertheless, the protests of the first intifada had seen unprecedented numbers of Saharawis on the streets. After 1999, human rights activism strengthened. "People gradually lost their fears. Each generation is more fervent, more patriotic, more nationalist than the last,"

A Saharawi woman sits beside a building adorned with paint-smothered proindependence graffiti, El Aaiún, 2014. Photo by Bartek Sabela.

explains one of the leaders of the 1999 intifada, Malainin Lakhal.[76] By 2005 activists were ready to publicly raise the banner of independence.

In the next section, I explore these diplomatic anguishes, but we must also explain Lakhal's point. If each generation is more fervent than the last, despite POLISARIO's base being on the other side of a military wall, despite the long-ago end of the war, and despite no living memory of a time before Moroccan occupation, why is this? And also we must ask, does gender play a role (as I have argued it did in Spanish Guinea and Spanish Sahara) in inspiring nationalist activism in women? I address these questions in the next section. I do so by using the story of Embarka Hassan's initiation into the proindependence movement.

### The 2005 Intifada and Embarka Hassan:
### Why Girls Become Activists

Nine-year-old Embarka left school with the *V* of a frown on her face and ethnic discrimination in her satchel.[77] Her teacher, once again, had put it as starkly as white chalk on a blackboard: "You're lazy, you Saharawis, lazy and stupid." Embarka was young, still at primary school, and yet had already learned that being a Saharawi girl was not the same as being a Moroccan one.

Her route home was usually an unremarkable, short walk past house fronts of pastel greens and purples, mole hills of rubbish and dust, and smells of sewers, baking bread, fresh mint, and charcoal fire smoke. The king's portrait was so ubiquitous that it smudged into the background, as did the green star on red hanging from every lamppost, clanking in the wind. Some days, though, Embarka's eyes would land and linger on "Viva RASD" graffiti.[78] Such slogans tended to live short lives scrawled in black or blue on some crumbling wall, shouting their messages until authorities found the time to smother them in paint.

On this particular day in 1999, El Aaiún's sky was overcast. Out toward the *bādīa* (desert countryside) darkness was gathering, like the Saharawi *qabīla* leaders used to in times of trouble. Embarka could hear shouting. She sped up.

Rain fell as Embarka turned onto the street where home waited. She could still make out human screams despite the racket of droplets pelting the nearby car roofs. Looking down the avenue to her right, Embarka spotted a swarm of smart, gray-suited men kicking three figures with relish, as if to hammer them into the ground and out of sight. The three human marks could not rise from the muddy, wet earth for the constancy of the blows. Nearby, abandoned on the edge of the path like road kill, lay three flags of white, red, green, and black. "Why do the soldiers torture and beat the Saharawis?" Embarka remembers asking herself.

That evening, Embarka's father met with a storm of questions from his daughter. "[He] started to explain to me that we are Saharawis, that Morocco occupied us, that we're divided into two parts, there are people in the refugee camps and others in the Occupied Territory, and 'your mother is in the camps,' he said," recalls Embarka. "That's when I began to comprehend that we are an occupied people."

From then on at school, Embarka took note of the older Saharawis who arrived late, missing the morning recital of the Moroccan national anthem. She made new friends. Together they made plans. In time, they would become a student movement, one capable of taking the baton from the police-hounded 1999 veterans. Embarka explains:

> We organized demonstrations, we wrote on walls, we fought, we complained, and we demanded freedom for political prisoners. We started making leaflets to hand out among other students. Little by little we developed, we deepened our understanding, we improved our fight, and we had a better consciousness of what we were doing. . . .
>
> Later, in that school, most of our companions had gone up to study the baccalaureate and there was just Hayat and I left at school. We were the only ones left there out of our big group! So we started to make new contacts and to raise awareness among the new students just starting at school, encouraging them to join the struggle too, so that we wouldn't be alone.[79]

Embarka's story reinforces what Mundy has argued: Moroccan oppression breeds Saharawi nationalism.[80] Or as activist Ahmed Baba puts it, "Through suffering discrimination you become nationalist without anyone having to tell you anything about the case."[81] Indeed, Embarka's story is typical of young women activists I interviewed. The reasons why they became activists are not gender specific. Life histories of discrimination and violence are the midwives to young Saharawis' nationalism in the Occupied Territories.

Embarka also shows us how she and her friend Hayat—like Fatima Ghalia Leili, whom we met in the opening to this chapter—have actively scouted for new recruits, ensuring that there is always a nonviolent army to keep the struggle going. These women chose to reproduce the nation not only through procreation or maintaining a traditional culture but also through training the next generation of foot soldiers.

The first public demonstration for Embarka Hassan was during the 2005 intifada. "I was fifteen," says Embarka. "I remember that the first slogan I learned was "Poli Po Poli, viva POLISARIO." The movement of a political prisoner from El Aaiún's Black Prison to Morocco on 21 May triggered the uprising.

The new location would make it harder for his family to visit and provide him with food and medicine.[82] But like in 1999, the Saharawi frustrations that culminated in the 2005 intifada followed UN diplomatic failures.

James Baker, former US secretary of state and UN envoy responsible for negotiating a peace process in Western Sahara, resigned in spring 2004.[83] Baker left his post exasperated by the Moroccan rejection of his Autonomy Plan II. Baker's first plan had envisaged granting Western Sahara the status of autonomy within the Kingdom of Morocco. Yet this so-called solution was seen as unacceptable not only by the Saharawis but also by the UN Security Council since it did not include a referendum on independence. This contradicted the entire UN discourse on decolonization and was scrapped. Baker's second plan offered a period of limited autonomy for the Sahara, which would be followed by a referendum with the option of independence in which Moroccan settlers as well as Saharawis would be entitled to vote. In a surprising diplomatic move, the POLISARIO accepted the plan, yet equally astonishing was Morocco's rejection of it (it has been suggested that Morocco feared its own citizens would prefer POLISARIO rule to the decadent and corrupt Moroccan monarchy).[84] Baker's resignation, and the diplomatic stalemate that it once again signaled, provided the spark for the explicitly nationalist, proindependence uprising that mobilized thousands of Saharawis across Western Sahara and the Saharawi-dominated areas of southern Morocco.[85] However, sustained oppression in the form of forced disappearances, long prison sentences, and the politically motivated murder of activists eventually watered the fire of the uprising, although, suggests Elliana Bisgaard-Church, the afterglow was not fully extinguished until 2008.[86] In any case, as is explained in the next section, it would not be long until the frustrated Saharawis rose again.

## The Gendering of Protests and Custodial Punishment Post–Gdeim Izik: Female Demonstrators, Male Prisoners

The indignation that finally exploded at the Gdeim Izik camp was growing rapidly from 2009 onward, when an abuse of a Saharawi's rights became relatively major news in a Western country, which is a highly unusual occurrence. This incident—Aminatou Haidar's deportation to Lanzarote, Spain, and her subsequent monthlong hunger strike (explored in chapter 3)—which Stephen Zunes has highlighted as one of the two key successes of the Saharawi's nonviolent struggle, was a crucial factor in the outbreak of the protest.[87]

The press coverage that Aminatou garnered having come close to starvation in Lanzarote airport had an important effect on Saharawis back in the Occupied Territories. Not only were they indignant at the treatment of their heroine, but as Carmen Gómez Martín points out, the international press attention to the conflict after four years of oblivion (events in Western Sahara had barely even made the Spanish press since the 2005 independence intifada) also breathed oxygen into the struggle.[88] Protests were resuming with ever-increased intensity, and it was not long before Saharawi youths attempted to create a new form of protest: the occupation of the *bādia*, the traditional lands of the Saharawi nomads.

They began to pitch their *āḫiām* on 10 October 2010 in the countryside fifteen kilometers from El Aaiún, at a place called Gdeim Izik, meaning *the tendon of Izik*. "But the protest was the Achilles tendon of Morocco, not the Sahara," poet and political activist Hamza Lakhal aptly puts it.[89] Over subsequent days, Saharawis of all ages joined the youths. They demanded socioeconomic rights, independence, and an end to the exploitation of Western Sahara's natural resources.[90]

When the camp gathered to its full size, it boasted 15,000 to 20,000 inhabitants.[91] As Alice Wilson has pointed out, the current Saharawi population of Western Sahara is unknown, and the latest available UN estimates cite the adult population at (a probably modest) 41,150.[92] As Wilson rightly argues, this helps us understand the immense size of the camp in proportional terms.[93] Indeed, it isn't for nothing that Noam Chomsky argues that this camp was the start of the Arab Spring.[94] Wilson's excellent research explores the relationship between the latter movement and Gdeim Izik, illustrating how, despite the Saharawis' perception that their camp held strong similarities with the wider regional movements, the Saharawi uprising has effectively been disappeared by most analyses of the Arab Spring.[95]

On 8 November 2010, after threatening an invasion for days, Morocco finally razed the camp to the ground. Gdeim Izik ended in tragedy, but it left a defiant mark on the hearts and minds of the Saharawi population. It also left its mark in the Spanish (and indeed British) newspapers and in the reports of various international human rights NGOs, which led to lasting consequences in terms of gendered oppression and resistance.

Since Gdeim Izik, women have organized a regular protest on the fifteenth day of each month on Smara Street, El Aaiún, demanding freedom for Saharawi political prisoners and an end to natural resource plunder.[96] If we search on YouTube, we can find short films of protests by Saharawi-led media organizations (forcibly unregistered by Morocco) that are active in Western Sahara. We will see, at least in videos of the smaller, regular protests, just a handful of Saharawi men among a sea of the brightly colored *āmlāḥaf* (plural of women's traditional dress). As political activist Hassana Aalia states, "The reality is that in the Occupied Territories the women go to protests more than men and that's the end of it. The women go out and fight more than the men. And I am seeing that and you can see in the videos that women are out on the streets more than men.[97]

We know that Saharawi women have been an active presence at demonstrations since the Spanish colonial period. Indeed, they dominated the protests of the colonial period. Yet it would be unfair to claim that women dominated the 1987, 1999, 2005, or 2010 uprisings to quite the same extent as they have since Gdeim Izik. So what has changed? Izana Amidan explains:

> There's a difference between the period following 2005, and after Gdeim Izik. . . . Of course, the Moroccan regime still attacked us always, in savage ways. They'd take us and put us in prison. However, before Gdeim Izik, women and men were treated the same. There were many women political prisoners as well as men. However, since Gdeim Izik there has been a lot of pressure on Morocco from NGOs and the UN about the imprisoning of women. So Morocco has since been more cautious about making political prisoners of women, but that doesn't mean they don't beat us in the street and incarcerate us for short periods of time for torture. But now, when associations and organizations reprimand Morocco for its repression of women, Morocco turns around and says, "But we haven't arrested any women." You see?[98]

Gdeim Izik brought Western Sahara under international eyes once again. Respected organizations with an international reputation such as Human Rights Watch and Amnesty International drew attention to the atrocities committed during and after the destruction of the camp. Yet, although dozens of women (including Izana Amidan, quoted above) were detained, tortured, and kept incommunicado for varying periods of time, few women featured among the hundreds of Saharawis who were officially arrested and imprisoned (with the exception of Nguia El Haouasi, Hayat Rguibi, and four other women, who spent several months in the Black Prison).[99] The so-called Gdeim Izik Group of twenty-three political prisoners who remain incarcerated at the time of writing on mostly twenty-year-to-life sentences are all male.

The decline in official custodial punishments for women is linked to orientalist constructions of gender. As in Equatorial Guinea, we can see how the West's construction of "African" masculinities and femininities impact the lives of Saharawi men and women in the Occupied Territories. Just as Obiang has in Equatorial Guinea, Morocco has noted the PR importance of "gender equality" in the development portfolios of Western governments and of "saving" African women as key US and British foreign policy priorities (the "victimized" and "oppressed" Muslim woman is still a legitimate "rescue project" for the West, just as she was in colonial times).[100] Morocco has also felt the weight of pressure from NGOs especially concerned with women's mistreatment. Indeed, other researchers have noted that Mohammed VI's "commitment" to women's rights is the result of pressure from NGOs and international agencies alike.[101] As discussed in chapter 3, this is in line with genderwashing policies and funding programs of governments, which must disguise their support for authoritarian regimes by wearing the clothes of "modernization," "progress," and "women's empowerment."

In 2011 Morocco enacted a new constitution for gender equality. It also developed, crucially under the strict supervision of the World Bank, a National Youth Strategy after the 20th February uprisings earlier that year (Morocco's answer to the Arab Spring). This was drenched in the language of gender equality and human rights.[102] Maria Cristina Paciello, Renata Pepicelli, and Daniela Pioppi highlight that Morocco borrows such language from international agencies pushing a Western neoliberal agenda. They argue that this marks a new strategy for managing political dissent. In their words, "Moroccan authorities were sophisticated enough to parallel pure coercion with a new kind of social policies [sic] enshrined in the neo-liberal framework (and inspired by international agencies) that aimed (and at least partially succeeded) at integrating the disadvantaged in the system, without of course questioning, and at times even reinforcing, the unequal system itself."[103]

Like Obiang, Mohammed VI has been held up by international organizations as a women's empowerment champion. He has received much praise for the limited reforms of family law (the Mudawanna, further discussed below). The EU, for example, has showcased Morocco as an example of "good practice" when it comes to gender equality.[104] According to the EU, "Similar to the European Union, the promotion of gender equality is a political priority for the Moroccan government, and . . . it is very clearly committed to equality."[105] Morocco is the EU's largest recipient of funding through the framework of the European Neighborhood Policy, and indeed in 2012, it received approximately €38 million of EU funding to address sexism.[106] Similarly, since 2009, thirteen Moroccan ministries have received funding from UN Women, UN Population Fund, UNICEF, UNESCO, UN High Commissioner for Refugees, the Food and Agriculture Organization, the International Labour Organization, and the UN Programme on HIV/AIDS to tackle violence against women.[107] It is also noteworthy that the EU has various trade agreements with Morocco that fail to explicitly preclude occupied Western Sahara.[108] Katja Zvan Elliot powerfully argues that Morocco has carefully cultivated an image of progressiveness with regard to women's rights for international consumption. But this is just a mask disguising a reality, argues Zvan Elliot, of regime-supported and unabated patriarchy.[109] Likewise, Samia Errazzouki shows that working-class

Moroccan women in particular remain marginalized despite the state's projected image as women's emancipators.[110] Although not as blatant as the case of the Obiang regime and its Western allies, a brief analysis here suggests that Morocco relies, to a certain extent, on genderwashing to maintain itself.

By punishing women activists for short periods in secret detention centers rather than dragging them through the courts and officially imprisoning them for long periods, Morocco strategically attempts to make invisible the mistreatment of women and therefore to participate in the collaborative project of genderwashing with its Western allies. Yet reputation is not such a concern when it comes to imprisoning men. The demonization of Muslim men as terrorists and/or extremists in the West is well researched.[111] The proliferation of terrorism-centered Hollywood films that reinvigorate orientalist discourses comes at a time when the Muslim man as the violent and uncivilized Other permeates not only Western media but also domestic politics, religion, and foreign policy.[112] The imprisonment of some disobedient Muslim men in Morocco, a key Western ally in the so-called war on terror, is unlikely to create outrage internationally. The Saharawi man is not a victim worthy of rescue. Although Saharawi women activists know they may face violence and possibly torture in secret detention centers, the knowledge that, unlike male activists, they are unlikely to face long prison sentences is one reason Saharawi interviewees give to explain women's proliferation relative to men at demonstrations.

Yet Morocco's gendering of judicial punishment is not the only reason why Saharawi women are more visible at public political demonstrations than men, although it is the key reason for explaining the post-2010 change. Saharawi women's traditional gender role as mothers and carers based in the *ḥaima* has facilitated their political participation in very practical terms over the years. On the prominent role of women in protests, Saharawi activist Salaam explains: "Of course we take part in demonstrations, we must! It is our land as much as the men's. And a lot of the men can't take part because they will lose their job if they are seen at the demonstrations."[113]

Salaam's reasoning is just the same as that of the Spanish colonizers cited in chapter 1. Similarly, activist El Ghalia Djimi explains, "It's about the space provided. . . . Women stay at home and get more involved; at the same time, men don't want to lose their jobs."[114] Traditional gender roles, in which men are breadwinners and women take charge of the domestic sphere to practice mothering, allow women to participate in public acts of political resistance such as demonstrations. Many Saharawi men fear losing the employment that sustains their families financially should they be caught publicly demonstrating. This would interrupt their masculine role as breadwinners. If women are not in employment, there is no such danger for them. Furthermore, as Loveday

Morris argues in the same vein as Djimi, Saharawi women's role as mothers in the private sphere gives them the time and flexibility to protest very publicly.[115] This "time and flexibility" as mothers is, of course, the result of the socialized model of motherhood practiced in Saharawi society. If an activist who is also a mother has the time and flexibility to participate in public resistance activities, it is because other women (her sisters, aunts, mother, cousins) take over her domestic duties. In this way, we see how the traditional gendered division of labor derived from the patriarchal organization of society actually facilitates women's leading role in the resistance.

Djimi also draws on women's historic role in traditional Saharawi society to justify their primordial role in the protests: "The key role of women in the independence movement can be partially attributed to the Sahrawis' nomadic background. . . . Until the early twentieth century, women were often left to run camps while men traveled, putting the women in control of household finances and community management."[116]

Here Djimi echoes POLISARIO's hegemonic construction of Saharawi history outlined in chapter 3, which draws a continuum between women's current public, politically active role and her past responsibilities in a nomadic existence. Public politics, whatever its form, is constructed as a natural part of Saharawi femininity and by no means a transformation in gender roles brought on by the current situation.

At the same time though, women's participation in public protests also involves some challenges to traditional gender and age hierarchies. Understandably, some families often do not wish for their daughters to become activists because of the very real dangers that such roles bring. Says Sultana Khaya when she began to protest publicly in 2005: "I had problems with my family, because they didn't want the Moroccans to put me in prison."[117] Similarly, Hayat Rguibi tells me: "Conversations within our families always emphasized that we shouldn't talk about [the Saharawis' problems] outside the home. And why shouldn't we talk about it outside? Because they are afraid of what might happen to us, that we might be detained, disappeared."[118]

Dafa has argued that Saharawi women never come of age, in the sense that they are expected to obey their parents until they get married, at which point the husband becomes the head of the family (of course, this is a contested view and women's capacity to maintain power through bargaining and "everyday resistance" should never be underestimated).[119] In the Occupied Territories, we see that women challenge and defy the wishes of their families in order to play active roles in the resistance. Once the women become activists and bear the consequences on behalf of the nationalist cause, they become heroines. Initially though, some women defy the head of the family to attend these protests, and in this way, gender norms are (successfully) challenged by women activists to benefit the fight for independence.

Linked to gender norms that demand female chastity before marriage, most unmarried Saharawi women avoid sharing pictures of themselves online. "My brothers would accuse me of encouraging boys to look at me," explained one Saharawi woman when I asked.[120] Nevertheless, like Mariam Hassan in the Spanish period, Saharawi women activists today continue to challenge the *ḥishma* when doing so will further the nationalist cause. Women who have suffered violence brush aside the unwritten rules and publish photographs of injured and bruised heads, limbs, chests, and buttocks on social media. With regard to the latter especially, women face a backlash from some sectors of the community who see the sharing of such pictures as *ḥarām* (forbidden in Islam).[121] This negative reaction, taking into account the added trauma that survivors of violence can experience if they tell their story and are not supported, only underscores the courage of such women. For them, denouncing the brutality of the Moroccan occupiers comes before maintaining gendered cultural practices.

Gender discrimination and how Saharawi women maneuver around it are further considered later in this chapter. First, though, given how it links to gender inequalities surrounding chastity in Saharawi society and its significance in terms of gender constructions more widely, we must consider what exactly happens to Saharawi men and women when they are detained by Moroccan authorities.

### The Unsaid, Trauma, and Testimony: Resisting Gendered Torture

In recent years, the sexual violence that has been used as a weapon by the Moroccan state since the run-up to its 1975 invasion of Western Sahara has gradually become more visible. This increased visibility is thanks to the small but growing number of testimonies of male and female survivors of sexual violence. Following are a few short quotations from Saharawi testimonies that describe events that took place in 2014:

> They insulted me with very rude words and told me that they were going to rape me. My husband tried to rescue me, but they hit him too, as well as his friend. They then told us they would take my daughter and rape her too. She was eleven years old at the time.[122]

> I've suffered from torture. The police are always beating me and . . . what can I say? They are trying to make me stop protesting. They beat me in places that,

you know, are very fragile for a woman. They . . . you know what I mean. But it won't stop me. I believe we will achieve independence one day. . . . When I go to protests I know that I might die, but I don't care.[123]

They started hitting me on my face and all over my body with their batons. And I heard them saying, "We will rape you." So they took off my pants and they raped me with a baton.[124]

They took off all our clothes and made us lie, face down, on the ground, then the police started to torture us in a very savage way. They raped us with sticks, while asking who it was that had painted the UN vehicle. At first, we didn't tell them anything, but they kept raping us brutally and beating us until finally we all confessed. Police told us that if we continued such acts of protest, they would kill us in the future. They said, "We don't want to see your faces in any protests, in cafes, or in the street." Then the police took us again, three of us in each of the two cars, and dumped us on the eastern bank of the Red Canal River.[125]

In this section, we look at gendered experiences and effects of torture before exploring how Saharawis who suffer torture manage to show resistance, both during periods of detention and in the face of trauma afterward.

For some individual Moroccan security officers, the belief that Saharawi political activists are socially inferior to Moroccans loyal to the regime arguably feeds their sense of entitlement to violate Saharawi bodies and minds.[126] More generally though, Morocco's systematic use of sexual abuse most likely serves the same purpose as states' use of sexual torture in other countries: to "hurt, control, and humiliate," to violate the Saharawi victim's "mental and physical integrity," and to provoke, in the victim, "an experience of disintegration and *a changed view of the world*," which "may, of course, also affect the political identity of the prisoner."[127] I argue here that Morocco makes use of social constructions of gender to further these aims.

When I have asked Saharawi women activists in the Occupied Territory about their life stories, the experience of secret detention and torture is ubiquitous. Almost as ubiquitous are their laconic accounts of sexual abuse while in detention. When they tell of the nature of the tortures endured, the "threat of rape" might be briefly mentioned, or a woman might say, "you can imagine what happened," before moving to the next chapter of her story. Sometimes, a friend and fellow listener might fill in some of the gaps. Below is one (Izana Amidan) activist's story of short-term disappearance, followed (in italics) by the comment of our mutual friend:

In 2005, they kidnapped me and tortured me in savage ways. They used a lot of unimaginable forms of torture. For example, they took my clothes off and put me in the "roast chicken" position, in which I was suspended from my knees, with my wrists tied over my legs, and tortured me like that. I think they do this to discourage women from protesting. They think that if women know this will happen to them, they won't protest anymore. As you know, we are a Muslim society, and we have many values between family members, between women and men, between women and her sons, her society. So these acts of torture, if people know about them, they . . . you can imagine. So it's a problem. It's a problem not to tell my story because Morocco will still torture people in this way. Morocco has done this to a lot of women, not just me. If I don't tell my story, it won't stop Morocco from doing it anyway. But if I do tell my story, many women might be discouraged. So it's confusing. But in the end I decided to tell my story.

There are still some Saharawis who don't know about politics. I mean, they are all Saharawis, they know we are Saharawis and they want independence for Western Sahara, but they don't know a lot about politics. And when they find out what happened to me, they tell their daughters not to be friends with me. They do this because of the police, because they are afraid that the same thing will happen to their daughters. And you can imagine the psychological effect of this on me and on other women who have been abused, but I also know that these Saharawi parents are just scared for their daughters. The Moroccans do many dirty things.

*Izana hasn't told her whole story. They didn't just take her clothes off. She was raped. They put a blindfold on her eyes, she was naked, and they tortured her this way for three days without stopping. Three days!*[128]

The first Saharawi woman to speak out publicly about the systematic rape she suffered in detention was Kelthoum El Ouanat.[129] Kelthoum's brother Mohammed explains how he feels about her breaking the silence: "My sister said it publicly. She is a reference when people talk about the rape of Saharawis and activists, they mention her as an example. And I've always said it's an honor, because they didn't rape her in a bar or in a brothel, they raped her in the Resistance."[130]

While the division of rape survivors into "good" ones and "bad" ones is always highly problematic as it builds on the subtle social controls of sexuality that attempt to justify sexual violence, we should take into account here the observations of psychologist Carlos Beristain Martín and political scientist Eloísa González Hidalgo. The two academics interviewed 261 Saharawis (over half women) as part of a two-volume study of human rights violations. They found that most Saharawis have not talked of sexual abuse because (in Beristain and Hidalgo's view) of the fear of stigma. They further explain: "While people who have been killed are considered 'martyrs,' or victims of torture can have a status as resisters, there is no similar designation for women that have suffered rape. That is the same for men, where it is considered an attack on their masculinity. In this way, the suffering of the person and the family is not recognized and it can't be validated socially. Also the cultural or religious value placed on 'purity' and sexual privacy can make affected women or their families feel especially knocked by this experience."[131]

In the light of Beristain and González's insights, we can better understand some aspects of Mohammed Laabeid's statement. Not only should women who survive rape in detention not be stigmatized; they should also be honored and supported if they decide to share their stories.

Let us return now to Amidan's more recent experiences. Amidan highlights the psychological torture that pursues her as a result of telling her story. The public knowledge of her ordeal has led some to isolate her, although she is understanding of the reason why. While one can easily argue that many loving parents would use any means to discourage their daughter from activities that will likely result in her torture, it is significant here that Amidan contextualizes her stigmatization by making references to the important norms surrounding interactions between the sexes in her culture. Parallels can be drawn here with the Algerian and Palestinian liberation movements. In both these cases, women activists who have been imprisoned and tortured have been celebrated as heroes, and at the same time have faced painful challenges when returning home owing to compatriots' suspicions about sexual violence.[132] In Saharawi society female chastity before marriage is idealized. A practical consequence of this in the Occupied Territory, as well as Amidan's problems with some female friends' parents, is that women who are known to have been raped by Moroccan security officers often face difficulties if they wish to get married since they are no longer "virgins."[133] This is one more factor in explaining Morocco's ubiquitous use of the sexual torture of women activists. Through rape, Morocco maintains Saharawi patriarchal structures that make the nonvirgin woman, including the rape survivor, unsuitable for marriage and motherhood. Sexual torture helps prevent the reproduction of the Saharawi nation.

While the rape of women in situations of conflict has begun to receive much scholarly attention, the sexual torture of men is regretfully less well researched.[134] Of the four quotations that appear near the beginning of this section, two are from Saharawi men. Sexual torture is still suffered by male political prisoners as well as by men secretly detained for short periods.

As in all cultures, Saharawi men's gendered experiences of rape depend on Saharawi hegemonic constructions of femininity and masculinity and on what is and is not acceptable in Saharawi culture with regard to sexuality. Despite increasingly open and positive debates, Saharawi society is still, generally speaking and like most societies, homophobic, and this impacts on constructions of hegemonic masculinity. Sandesh Sivakumaran argues that sexual violence against men is often perpetrated with the purpose of destroying the victim's sense of masculinity, to "feminize" them, and, particularly in cultures where homosexuality is taboo, to strip victims of their heterosexual status.[135] Inger Agger's research has also highlighted how the torturer plays on hegemonic constructions of masculinity and compulsory heterosexuality to maximize humiliation.[136] Indeed, the torturers of Saharawis are, significantly, exclusively male. Oppression, in this context, has a male face, and the prison cells are a space for torturers to play out a violent masculinity.

As well as humiliation, sexual torture commonly results in severe trauma and long-term sexual problems for both men and women, including, sometimes, a fear of one's partner or spouse when it comes to sex.[137] These traumatic effects of sexual torture, coupled with the forced sterilization and forced miscarriages of Saharawi women in detention (we observed, earlier in this chapter, that these were common practices in the seventies, yet unfortunately they remain so to this day) have important effects when an increased birth rate of the Saharawi population is seen as crucial for the nationalist cause.[138] Indeed, it has been argued that the key purpose of sexual violence in situations of conflict is to destroy a population.[139]

Aside from rape, it is worth noting briefly how other types of torture used by Moroccan security officers are gendered. Given the importance of nice teeth and long, healthy hair for women in Saharawi culture (every culture and time has its own hegemonic construction of beauty), the practice by Moroccan security officers of knocking out women's front teeth and subjecting them to waterboarding with chemicals and electrical torture (both of which cause alopecia) are noteworthy.[140] The practices are designed to cause women psychological suffering (as well as the obvious physical pain and long-term health problems) by partially destroying their ability to conform to Saharawi notions of feminine beauty. In the case of men, the common method of applying electrical currents to the genitals, which can result in sexual dysfunction and testicular atrophy, seems designed to attack an important facet of a Saharawi man's sense of masculinity through threatening his future ability to reproduce or enjoy sexual pleasure.[141]

Faced with these situations of imprisonment or incommunicado detention and physical defenselessness against sexual torture, or the threat of finding oneself in such a situation once again in the case of ex-prisoners and ex-disappeareds still living in the Occupied Territory, how could Saharawis possibly resist?

Ahead of detention, Sébastien Boulay has argued that the aforementioned YouTube videos of women protesting are in themselves a form of resistance.[142] When these films show the violent response of police, they loudly make visible what Morocco has tried so hard to hide: male violence against women is state policy. During detention, I described above how Fatma Aayache drew emotional strength from her traditional, gendered role as mother. After detention, Saharawis have developed specific ways of dealing with their trauma. Earlier in this section, I referred to the laconic episodes in women's stories of violence, where instances of rape are implied but not explicitly referred to. Nevertheless, an increasing number of Saharawi testimonies of rape are appearing in written and video formats on the internet. I argue here that Saharawis have begun to use testimony giving as a form of therapy and resistance.

Studies from various cultures illustrate that both male and female survivors of sexual torture face difficulties in revealing their stories.[143] Doing so can provoke feelings of shame and guilt and even intensify symptoms of posttraumatic stress disorder, and experience from psychotherapy with torture victims has illustrated that information about sexual torture is not usually disclosed until a late stage in therapy.[144] Indeed, psychotherapists have found that retelling traumatic stories of rape is not necessarily therapeutic. On the other hand, Dori Laub, a holocaust survivor and psychoanalyst, finds that giving a testimony of political violence is essential for the daily survival of those who have experienced such horrors. For Laub, giving testimony is a process through which the survivor reclaims her own life story by becoming the missing witness to the atrocities endured.[145] Other researchers have found that *reframing* a story of political and/or sexual violence has been shown to have therapeutic effects.[146] The testimony method is one such reframing method.

The testimony method is a form of psychological therapy for survivors of sexual torture. It was originally developed by psychologists A. J. Cienfuegos and C. Monelli with ex-political prisoners of the Chilean military dictatorship and was later modified by Inger Agger and Sóren Buus Jensen for use with political refugees more generally.[147] It has also been used with Bosniak women survivors of sexual torture and survivors of the civil war in Mozambique.[148] The testimony method sees victims constructing a narrative of their abuse in order to share their traumatic story with their therapist.[149] Through it, "private pain is transformed into political dignity," shame and guilt are reframed, and "evidence against repression" is created, which could be used by, for example, international organizations fighting for change.[150] Sharing testimonies becomes a political act as well as a therapeutic one.[151]

In the Occupied Territories, women have set up an organization that makes use of politicized therapies similar to the testimony method described above.

The Forum for the Future of Saharawi Women in the Occupied Territory (FAFESA) was founded in 2008 by ex-political prisoners, some of whom had survived sentences of up to sixteen years at Qal'at Mgouna and other secret detention centers, as well as younger activists such as El Haouasi and Hayat Rguibi who have endured several months in El Aaiún's Black Prison.[152] El Haouasi explains the purpose of the organization: "It supports the fight of Saharawi women. It carries the voices of these women to other organizations, to everyone. . . . We work to document the human rights violations that we have suffered. Also, each one of us tells the other women about what she has suffered. The idea is to make the burden communal, so that the suffering becomes shared."[153]

Women at FAFESA share their stories with one another as a form of therapy. Furthermore, they work to record each other's testimonies, written or via YouTube, and attempt to disseminate these as far as possible in order to break Morocco's media blockade on abuses in Western Sahara. By speaking out, the survivors nullify the attempts of the Moroccan torturers to destroy them. The approach also overlaps with the political aims of feminist therapy, which aims to challenge oppression in society, to empower the persons seeking therapy, and to see the voices of the oppressed and marginalized as a great source of knowledge and wisdom.[154] However, the founders and participants of FAFESA have developed their work organically—this is not a Western import influenced by Euroamerican psychological developments. The overlaps between FAFESA'S work, feminist therapy, and the testimony method are coincidental. Nevertheless, comparisons with these two strands of psychotherapy help us to envisage the political potential of FAFESA's methods. The organization's work can be read as a practical strategy for resisting the most heinous crimes of the Moroccan state.

Earlier in this section we discussed the gendered effects of surviving rape as a Saharawi woman. If she wishes to get married, which most—but not all—Saharawi women tend to, she can find difficulties in finding a husband because of the high importance of female chastity in Saharawi culture.[155] Nevertheless, many well-known women activists who have suffered such tortures remain single and, at least to a foreign public, voice their marital status as an active and political choice. "I don't even think about getting married until the Sahara becomes independent," says Soumaya Taher.[156] Like Lmdaimigh, the writer we met at the start of this chapter, Taher (at least to external onlookers) resists assuming Saharawi women's traditional role until the Moroccan occupation ends. Such women, in their *public* discourses, turn the sexual double standard that would prevent their fulfilment of women's traditional role on their head. Marriage and motherhood become not fates that are barred from them but fates that they refuse. Other Saharawi activists state that the discourse on single-by-choice is adopted through pride to hide such women's underlying disappointment at society's rejection of marriage prospects due to their perceived "nonvirgin" status.[157] In the following section, I further explore debates around society's gendered expectations in occupied Western Sahara.

### Feminism under Occupation?
### Challenging Gender Inequalities in the Occupied Territory

For most women activists in the Occupied Territory, the nationalist cause comes before everything. Although one can note a latent anger among less prominent women activists about sexism and a sense of deep frustration among some, there is no organized women's movement to challenge gender inequality within Saharawi society.[158] One interviewee, unusual in that she studied in Rabat (interviewees explained that it is mostly young men who study in Morocco, and the further north the university, the smaller the proportion of women), expressed some dissatisfaction at gender inequalities, but she did not elaborate: it was clear that she wished to focus our discussions on the "national cause." When I asked her if she considered herself a feminist, she responded, "Of course! I am proud that I am a woman and also that I am a Saharawi woman!"[159] With her statement, she highlights the extent to which women's rights are tied up with the wider Saharawi struggle. Her feminism could be described as feminist nationalist—for her, women's liberation cannot be achieved while the colonial oppression continues.[160]

As for the frustrations that other women voice, one can hear complaints, for example, about not having the freedom to dress as one would like. In the Occupied Territory, as in the camps, visitors will note that while most men will wear, with pride, their *derrāʿa* on occasions but are just as comfortable in jeans and a T-shirt, the majority of women almost always wear their *melhfa*. Most women are happy to do so, but others complain that they would like to wear other clothes but feel pressured not to. A quotation from a (male) informant shows the attitude such women face: "Women who wear short clothes show they respect neither themselves, nor society."[161] Another complaint, as one informant put it, is that "men repress [them]" by policing their movements.[162] This is bound up with compulsory feminine chastity, modesty, and honor. The inequalities bred of the importance of chastity manifest themselves in the ambiguous way that women survivors of torture such as Amidan are treated. Arguably, the voicing of her disappointment at the conduct of others toward her is in itself a form of resistance against the sexist social norms, given that she breaks the custom of maintaining the veneer of "Saharawi gender equality" before the eyes of a foreign observer.

According to Saharawi friends, however, women do find room to maneuver among the social norms that demand female chastity before marriage *if they want to*.[163] It is common for Saharawis to have (secret) romantic and sexual relationships before tying the knot and certain practices allow them to do so while maintaining the veneer of premarital sexual abstinence: some women insist on nonpenetrative sex with their partners, (illegal) abortions are not uncommon, and, interviewees told me, operations to insert a false hymen are increasingly becoming the norm for young women before the night of their first wedding. However, given the great expense (and, in the case of illegal abortions, the physical danger) of such operations, as well as the fact that these actions do not challenge the gendered power relations that enforce female but, crucially, not male chastity, I view the procurement of these operations as examples of resilience, that is, as ways of showing agency and "getting by" in the face of adversity rather than as resistance.

We should take into account here that Saharawis live under Moroccan administration, where abortion is only legal under restricted circumstances, and procuring an illegal abortion is often a highly traumatic, not to mention expensive, experience for women. Contraception is legal but sex education in schools and universities is limited to the biology of reproduction. Premarital sex is illegal and punishable by a prison sentence, and indeed, single, pregnant women are more easily criminalized in the sense that their condition is proof of the act.[164] The 2004 Moroccan reform of the Mudawanna (Family Law) extended some limited rights to women, such as placing the family under "the joint responsibility of both spouses" for the first time, establishing a minimum age for marriage (eighteen), and assigning custody rights to women as well as enshrining women's right to ask her husband for a divorce into law. However, this last right was already the norm in Saharawi society. Furthermore, as Paciello, Pepicelli, and Pioppi have pointed out, the law stopped short of regulating the unilaterally male rights to polygyny and repudiation.[165] Similarly, Katja Zvan Elliott has highlighted that the Mudawanna does little to protect unmarried women and makes no attempt to tackle the patriarchal attitudes that leave women vulnerable in the first place.[166]

As for the attitudes of young Saharawi men, friends explained the majority pursue premarital sex but would refuse to marry a woman whom they did not believe to be a "virgin." Women in the Occupied Territory falling pregnant before marriage also risk a legal punishment as they may, in the camps, and will, in most cases, face a period of ostracization from their families.

The importance of female chastity highlights the role of women as the vessel for transmitting national culture. In traditional Saharawi society, it was viewed badly for men and women to have premarital relations, in line with the community's Islamic beliefs. Although they should be approached with their colonial perspective in mind and with awareness of the nonhomogenous nature of Saharawi *qabā'el*, historic Spanish anthropological studies, however, suggest that women's sexuality was policed to a greater extent than men's, with harsh physical punishments for adulteress women and rituals celebrating the bride's, but not the groom's, virginity at weddings.[167] While, with regard to men, attitudes have changed and premarital sex is essential to proving the virility of his constructed (compulsory heterosexual) masculinity, this cannot be the case for women, who, in times of the nation's occupation, are charged with preserving Saharawi traditional culture. This is nothing unusual. Several researchers working on a variety of different national contexts have shown how nationalism places women in the role of cultural reproducers of the imagined community, especially in times of national humiliation.[168] To use Enloe's words, at times of national crisis, women become "the nation's most valuable possessions; the principal vehicles for transmitting the whole nation's values from one generation to the next; bearers of the community's future generations—crudely, nationalist wombs."[169]

The intersection of the occupation and gender subordination is well illustrated by the issue of coerced and forced marriage. Marriage and starting a family are key aspirations for Saharawi men and women, yet, because of the occupation and the subsequent high unemployment of Saharawis, few Saharawi male activists are in a position to fulfill their gendered role and provide for a wife and children. There is no space for an alternative to this strictly heteronormative family framework. "I'm single. If you don't have a house, you can't get married," Mahfood Hafdala, who lost his job as a fisherman after campaigning against the EU-Morocco Fisheries Agreement, regretfully tells me in an interview.[170]

Saharawi parents are keen to make a good marriage for their daughter and, in some cases, see her future economic stability as more important than her romantic or other desires. Furthermore, in a context of poverty and violence, linking a daughter to a trusted family via marriage can ensure extended access to resources, strengthened reciprocal networks, and increased social capital.[171] This is especially the case given that few men are able to provide economic stability. Significantly, as Hafdala's case illustrates, Saharawi men risk losing their jobs (or never getting a job) if they are publicly politically active. Taking this point into account hand in hand with the difficulties women activists who have survived rape face in getting married, we could almost say that the Moroccan regime is playing on gender inequalities to "breed out" Saharawi nationalist activism.

When highlighting chastity and modesty and their disproportionate importance for Saharawi women owing to the latter's role in culturally reproducing the nation, we cannot forget the impact of another aspect of the occupation: what Saharawis call "moral decay."[172] Fruit of economic inopportunity and discrimination, increasing numbers of Saharawis are developing drug and alcohol addictions. Drugs and alcohol were unknown in traditional Saharawi society and are still taboo, and Saharawi nationalists are convinced that Moroccan authorities foster these habits in an attempt to "corrupt" Saharawi society. Another issue that Saharawis raise in that regard is prostitution.[173] The influx of Moroccan military personnel has created the demand necessary for the movement of prostitutes from Morocco, creating large red light districts in Western Sahara's cities.[174] Saharawis see this "moral decay" as directly caused by the Moroccan occupation and feel resentment. Indeed, vulnerable women in prostitution (Moroccan women in prostitution continue to be a source of contempt in some media outlets of the Saharawi diaspora) have been stoned by Saharawi activists. Prostitutes are seen to dishonor Saharawi society. As Cynthia Enloe has pointed out with reference to an Iraqi wartime context, when women turn to prostitution, some men turn to violence against women in an attempt to restore the gendered order.[175]

Linked to the "moral decay" of the explosion of sex establishments on the scene in Western Sahara is the practice of prostitution among a small proportion of Saharawi women. Almost all of these women live far from their families to avoid "scandal." Poverty—fruit, once again, of economic inopportunity and discrimination—is the primary factor referred to by informants in explaining why such women use their bodies as a resource. While practicing prostitution has allowed some women to continue university studies and illustrates their resilience to extremely tough economic conditions, it comes at a high price: they commonly suffer rape and beatings from their "clients." Of course, such women's situation is fruit of gendered, classed, and ethnic power imbalances that cannot be separated from the Moroccan regime. One Saharawi woman who practiced prostitution in Agadir said she turned to this because of economic need but only after suffering an extremely violent rape (of course, all rape is violent but in this case the sexual assault was accompanied by grievous bodily harm) and being unable to seek justice: the attack happened previous to the 2014 amendment of Article 475 of the Moroccan penal code, which "punished" rapists by marriage to their victims. The Saharawi woman identified this incident, coupled with poverty, as the driving factor behind her decision to sell sex. She managed to complete her degree, but her family found out about her work and coerced her quickly into a marriage that turned out to be abusive.[176]

Unlike in the camps or elsewhere in exile, there are no organized movements concerning gender equality in the Occupied Territories. Resentment at gender inequalities is (quietly) voiced at an individual level and—in the case of society's stigmatization of survivors of Moroccan rape especially—voices are occasionally magnified during debates on "the roofs." Indeed, since Morocco has effectively lowered a portcullis around public space for Saharawi nationalist events, the roofs of Saharawi family homes are today for Saharawi activists what the churches were for US civil rights activists: a womb for political strategizing, cultural events, and occasionally even sociopolitical debates. In general though, women get on with the nationalist struggle while showing resilience and agency in the face of sexism. For most women activists in the Occupied Territory, Saharawi feminism is feminist nationalism: independence is the goal and if there are challenges to gender norms, they are mounted to further the nationalist cause.

### The Future of the Struggle: Hospitality as Resistance

A middle-aged man tiredly limps across the road from the garage opposite. His ragged vest is smeared with car grease and doesn't quite bridge the hill of his protruding belly to meet the ample waistband below. A dead rat of a moustache sits on his upper lip. When he gets to the whitewashed wall of the house, he meets a younger man. This one is dressed in a well-tailored suit and reflective sunglasses, the expensive type, silver lenses, the type that reveal no hint of the eyes behind. He throws a cigarette on the floor and stamps at its fire. It sits, tip glowing, among what is now a hillock of stubs. The two men greet each other. The smarter one swaggers off, barking into his mobile. The garage worker nests down for the long haul, sitting where they always sit: in view of the front door and in earshot of the only ground floor window.

Little Tfarrah is on the roof, where grandma used to keep the goats.[177] She stands on tiptoes to take a peek at the man through a gap in the brick wall. She wonders why his mother gave him a haircut with a hole in the middle. How silly! She is angry with him because he won't go away. And because he won't go away, she and mum can't take their secret guest to the seaside. She asks mum to cook sardines on the barbecue tonight, out there on the roof, so at least the foreign visitor can taste the ocean, even if she won't see its waves.

Safia (Tfarrah's aunt) did not identify as an activist but resisted the occupation in her own way every day. Plain-clothes police and Moroccan informers watched the family home twenty-four hours a day. This house had produced several "dangerous," nonviolent activists who wielded that most awesome of weapons well: nationalist poetry. To make sure the last poet (Safia's youngest brother) living in the house did not get up to hosting any inflammatory recitals, and perhaps to punish said wordsmith for his past infringements, spies would attempt to listen at the ground floor window. One morning, while folding her children's blankets, through the steel grill over the open window my hostess's eyes met those of a spy, a profession that, she later told me, is frowned upon in Islam. While continuing to fold the blankets, she uttered loudly, for the benefit of the spy, a phrase from the Quran: "And We have put a bar in front of them and a bar behind them, and further, We have covered them up; so that they cannot see."[178]

The act by the sisters of the house of hosting a foreign visitor was in itself a form of resistance that made use of their gendered roles as homemakers (that is not to say that the sisters did not play roles outside of the domestic sphere, one of them being a secondary school Arabic teacher—another reason for ensuring her resistance focused more on fostering the hidden transcript than on the militant activism of her brothers). As well as feeding and sheltering me, the two eldest sisters, who had their own homes and husbands elsewhere in the Sahara, stayed in their late mother's home with their children for the duration of my stay. During this time, they strategically invited many "non-activist" female friends over for tea every day. This was, on the one hand, to ensure that the house was always full and noisy so that my presence would be less obvious, and on the other hand, constant visitors helped to obscure the visits of well-known activists.

Why do Saharawis take such risks to house a foreign researcher and activist? They know what Zunes and Mundy have argued: mobilizing international civil society around their cause is essential to the success of their current non-violent strategy.[179] Anyone who can potentially act as a witness to the ongoing atrocities in occupied Western Sahara should be welcomed, feel the activists.[180] As one young interviewee put it, "When young people in the Occupied Territories see someone who is blonde they think that their small demonstration has the power to make a difference."[181] The plain-clothes police pretending not to watch me, even as I sat on a plane departing Morocco, obviously felt the same way. International witnesses, if they can make themselves heard, risk undoing the work of genderwashing by exposing the true, horrific extent of the Moroccan state's violent abuse of women. In this context, hospitality is a form of resistance to the occupation.

Saharawi women are at the forefront of the nonviolent nationalist resistance movement in the Occupied Territory, just as they were under Spanish colonialism. Gendered roles derived from the patriarchal organization of society that emphasize women's role as mothers and men's as breadwinners but that also include space for political activism have helped fuel women's resistance. However, Morocco, too, takes advantage of constructions of gender when designing its oppressive violence. It employs notions of honor, chastity, and virginity when targeting the vulnerable, sexualized female body and draws on homophobic discourses for the sexual abuse of male activists.

The Moroccan regime, like the Obiang one, takes into account Western orientalist gendered discourses when deciding who to incarcerate officially. In chapter 4, using the case study of Equatorial Guinea, we saw how Western orientalist constructions of African gender norms inform and contribute to the maintenance of the oppressive Obiang regime. However, we also saw how these same imagined gender norms influence POLISARIO nationalist discourses. What I have highlighted in this chapter is the effects of these Western-imagined norms on the resistance of activists themselves, in terms of their actions as well as their punishments.

As for the relationship between women's resistance to colonialism and patriarchy explored in chapter 1, we can see now that the difference between the Spanish period and the Moroccan is illuminating. The antiracist, mostly intersectional, feminist demands during the Spanish era were key to mobilizing women politically for independence, yet under the terror of the occupation, specifically feminist demands have lost weight. In a context of Moroccan state brutality, women face the pressing responsibilities of enduring immeasurable trauma, searching for disappeared loved ones, and ensuring the survival of their families. And yet the Saharawi women highlighted in this chapter move beyond even these daunting tasks. They take on a political engagement that assumes the most horrific, violent consequences. Aminatou, Izana, Fatma, Embarka, Sultana, and so many others struggle for human dignity for their people, for sovereignty, for land rights, and for the preservation of Saharawi culture and ways of life. One consequence of their struggle is a challenge to the West's hypocritical and patronizing stereotyping of Arab, Muslim women. For some activists, embedded in their nationalist struggle on an individual level is also a struggle against Saharawi patriarchal attitudes. However, we should not be surprised that the additional discriminations faced by women, the fruit of patriarchal culture and traditions, are not a priority for all activists. At the same time, we cannot untangle sexisms faced by Saharawi women from the situation of occupation and the sexist, racist global geopolitics that undermine the Saharawis as a people—it is no one's prerogative to call Saharawi feminists unpatriotic. The wider relationship between gender and resistance is thick, profound, far reaching, and easily manipulated and influenced by internal and external, even global, actors.

But to what extent are these gendered dynamics of Saharawi resistance in the Occupied Territory generalizable to other situations of resistance to (colonial) dictatorships? To address this question, we next focus on the case of Equatoguinean women's resistance to postcolonial dictatorships.

# CHAPTER SIX

# Gendering *Ngueismo* and
# Gendered Resistance

I N MALABO, it is difficult to take a photograph without receiving a repri-
mand from a regime informer. For the latter, images of government buildings indicate that the photographer might be a spy, while photographs
of the shanty towns risk exposing to the world outside the vast poverty that
plagues the majority of the population. Citizens going about their daily lives
are loath to be photographed in case they are implicated in some antiregime
activity. As such, the album of photographs of my time in Equatorial Guinea
consists, with few useful exceptions, of interesting trees and plants, a bright
pink seed rumored to be a powerful aphrodisiac, and a beautiful beach. Even
these resulted in bother with an angry soldier. Pictures of the frail (but painted
in mood-lifting, bright pastel colors), family-built dwellings of corrugated
iron, wooden sticks, and the odd cement block next to open trenches of raw
sewage remain untaken. Photographs of the (evidently ignored) instructions
state employees painted on the walls of building and shacks ("paint this," "pull
this down") were deleted. Such instructions were graffitied on homes and
shops ahead of the 2014 African Union Summit: poverty had to be covered up,
demolished, before the dignitaries arrived.

A friend who used to serve as the SADR's representative to the African
Union (AU) told me of the time he visited Equatorial Guinea when the country hosted the AU Summit in 2011. He had visited many African countries
in his role and, while finding (as in Europe, and especially Britain, where he
also served) that there was a noticeable difference in wealth between the ruling class and the masses in the majority of the continent, he had never seen
such a blatant and open flashing of wealth in a context of extreme poverty
as he witnessed in Equatorial Guinea. A two-story villa was built for the representative of each AU member country, exclusively for the conference, he
recalled.[1] Each one had its own lift as well as its own team of Moroccan, not

local, servants. Indeed, a visitor can view all fifty-two of these impressive villas while passing the newly built town of Sipopo on the main road between Malabo and the town of Baney. My friend's observations match what the statistics say: Equatorial Guinea's GDP per capita is the highest in Africa and one of the highest in the world, yet the country also holds, by quite some distance, the depressing distinction of having the largest gap in the world between its per capita wealth and its human development score.[2]

Poorer Equatoguineans have paid a price for the urban development, such as wide avenues, plush homes, and a casino, that characterizes some areas of Malabo, not least the stretch between the airport and the city center. Since 2003 over a thousand families have been affected by housing demolitions, carried out without consultation, adequate notice, and in most cases, compensation or rehousing.[3] And yet, during the initial days of my own stay in Guinea when I mixed with a few European immigrants, an architect working on a government contract told me that it was Eurocentric and colonialist to criticize Equatorial Guinea's regime and poverty, words echoed by an Equatoguinean citizen close to the regime.[4] Do these men have a point, or does the silence of the world external to Equatorial Guinea and of the neocolonial actors within it entrench the misery of the Equatoguinean population and dampen the efforts of those who resist Obiang's power? I take the latter view, and in this chapter I focus mainly on Equatoguinean resistance to *ngueismo*.

The following section begins where chapter 2 left us: with the Spanish Women's Section. I ask questions about the gender norms promoted by the Guinean Women's Section, which grew from the seed that Spain planted. I say, "Ask questions," as the fullest answers are still, for the most part, buried in the memories of older Equatoguinean citizens who fear for the dangerous political implications of Macías-era history. Indeed I discuss the politics of memory to explain why I, and other researchers, have left so many voids in our writings. Also in the section on Macías, I look briefly at how the dictator was able to establish and hold on to power. This gives context to later discussions of gender and resistance. From Macías, I move to his Nguema family relative, Obiang, who stole power in 1979. First, I briefly analyze how Obiang has managed to retain his dictatorship for four decades, and in doing so I reveal the centrality of gender in the oppressive mechanisms of Equatorial Guinea. The legacy of the Spanish and the Macías eras also becomes clearer through this analysis.

Second, I look at the tools employed by Equatoguinean women to resist the regime. As Bahati Kuumba points out, "Because of the gendered divisions in many societies and movements, some of the resistance strategies engaged in by women as an outgrowth of their productive and reproductive labor are the very ones that are submerged."[5] Using, once again, Scott's theories of everyday resistance and hidden transcripts helps me to highlight some of these women's strategies. Analyzing these, I argue that while traditional gender norms serve to exclude women from some forms of resistance, they simultaneously facilitate other strategies that make use of caring and nurturing skills. Furthermore, we see once again that Equatoguinean women's resistance can be interpreted as intersectional. Finally, with regard to gender and resistance, I look to the future. Making use of brief comparisons with the Saharawi case and the work of one Equatoguinean woman activist, I argue that if open, organized resistance movements wish to see more women joining their ranks, a commitment to feminist demands may be a useful strategy.

## Macías's Gendered Presidency: Women Supporting Authoritarianism

Marina Alene, like other Equatoguinean women, had strategically maintained a public transcript of compliance until it became clear that independence was near. Only then did she wash off her colonial makeup. Until the second half of 1968, Alene had been the model Women's Section student and colleague, but to the dismay of the Spanish directors of the Section, in November Alene publicly announced her intention to seek support for a separate, Equatoguinean-run Women's Section. While Spanish Women's Section leader Carmen Obón concluded that Alene had "a split personality," Soledad de Santiago, who had met Alene in Spain and concluded that she was "one of the best students," was equally winded by what she saw as a sudden change in character.[6]

The Spanish women's distaste at Alene's initiative seems surprising initially, since as I stated above, the Women's Section arrived in Equatorial Guinea with the aim of creating a system that would eventually be handed to Equatoguinean women themselves. Nevertheless, the colonialists had expected to handpick pro-Spanish Guinean women. Obón was "frankly disgusted" that she and her colleagues had become "replaceable so quickly" by Alene's unexpected project.[7]

Despite having been trained and sponsored by the Falangists, Alene was not one for maintaining Spanish interests postindependence. In February 1969 she reportedly held an "anti-whites" meeting in her house, preaching to her guests of the need to "step on the whites and crush their heads and not stop until we manage it."[8] Alene was to become a member of the Central Committee of Macías Unique National Party of Workers (Comite Central del Partido Unico Nacional de Trabajadores, PUNT), representing it internationally on the women's rights stage.[9]

The Women's Section that Franco's Falangists had carefully assembled over four years was pulled down and rebuilt by a new engineer. Under Alene's initial leadership, the Equatoguinean Women's Section became the PUNT's Women's Section. As Nerín notes, it carried a new name, "Organization of Revolutionary Women," and still received some materials from central (Madrid-based) Women's Section until the latter was dissolved in 1977.[10] Its role was to co-opt women as pro-Macías propaganda tools and to foster women's entrance into politics as spies.

While the rest of the Spanish gradually fled, Women's Section staff were able to stay put until March 1969. This was because, as Alene's alternative was not yet fully up and running, Macías had sent his wife to attend one of Spanish Women's Section schools. This afforded the Falangist women some level of protection for a time, but the six-month period between independence and their final exit was one characterized by progressive violence. Unfortunately for Spain, the metropolis had underestimated the seemingly meek and loyal Macías.

In early March, Carmen Obón and her colleagues fled to the barracks of the Spanish Civil Guard when scores of the newly constituted paramilitary group Youth Marching with Macías (Juventudes en Marcha con Macías, JMCM) stormed the school brandishing machetes and sticks. Thinking of his wife's training, the dictator personally visited the Spanish Falangistas at the barracks to attempt to persuade them to stay. In a report sent back to her colleague in Madrid, Obón describes how Macías calmly responded to her questions about what had happened to foreign affairs minister Atanasio Ndongo and representative of Equatorial Guinea to the UN Saturnino Ibongo, who both had died in unclear circumstances after having been accused of leading a failed coup d'état on 5 March. According to Macías, Ndongo had thrown himself out the window of the dictator's office, while Ibongo was forced to drink the "poison" that the "UN" had sent back with him destined for Macías.[11]

In her March 1969 report, Obón complained that the majority of the Section's pupils had "gone to hide in the forest."[12] Most were daughters or wives of government ministers and civil servants, a male demographic increasingly at risk of capture or slaughter. With few women and girls left to teach, and fearing for their own safety, the Spanish staff of the Women's Section left Equatorial Guinea by the start of April 1969.

The Spanish Women's Section staff had witnessed the beginnings of Macías's gradual elimination of all potential political opponents. He began with those communities expected of having voted for the other electoral candidates but soon proceeded to incarcerate or assassinate other figures of influence who could possibly rival him as president. Macías's success in tracking down even the quietest of critics was thanks to his system of surveillance. Those with political ambitions—women as well as men—could achieve power if they were prepared to report those individuals who had voiced any sign of discontent with Macías's rule.[13]

This is where the PUNT's Women's Section came into its own. Macías, arguably, was the first leader to advocate the political mobilization of Equatoguinean women. The PUNT Women's Section was his channel for making this policy practice, although "political mobilization" in the Macías era was synonymous with surveillance, informing, and violence. The grandmother of María Angeles Adugu Mba was a member of the Falangist Women's Section and later the Guinean one established under Macías. She passed on her memories to her granddaughter, who recounted them as follows: "Macías started to raise awareness about women's equality. Why? Because he said that all that about women being weak and unable to serve in the army or take up arms was untrue. Women can be as brave as men and can join the army like men. . . . It was a way to make sure that women weren't under men's thumbs, but it was also Macías's way to turn everyone into an informer. Women watched their husbands, and when they had the sensation that their husbands were doing something against Macías, they'd go and they'd tell on them. And a woman's testimony was valued just as much as a man's would have been."[14]

This comment by Adugu Mba suggests that Macías used the language of feminism in a way that may have empowered a few individual women but oppressed most and, more generally, mobilized women as tools of oppression. On one occasion in 1975, the dictator reportedly rushed back from neighboring Cameroon upon hearing that an ex–vice president had torn his picture, which had been pinned up on all front doors. Upon his arrival back in Equatorial Guinea, Macías's first action was to call a meeting with the Women's Section, where he gave a violent speech and asked attendees their advice for the punishment of the guilty ex-minister. Said a witness, "The women shouted, 'Kill him.'" Macías responded with the promise that, should the women ever have problems with their husbands, he would "receive" them.[15]

The Equatoguinean Women's Section leaders also enjoyed more direct forms of political power. According to Robert Klinteberg's descriptions, the mechanisms that governed life during the Macías era operated brutally, effectively, and mercilessly at a local district and village level. Each village, which would previously have been governed by (male) counselors who held spiritual authority, kinship loyalty, and the respect of other villagers was taken over by a Macías-appointed Comité de Base, responsible for "national security" and surveillance. These Base Committees also existed at district level and were composed of the same key members everywhere: the local PUNT president, the Youth Section president, and, the third prong of the trident, the Women's Section president.[16] The Spanish Falangists had not only advocated an ideology (submission to an authoritarian patriarch as head of state) that benefited Macías but had also put in place a molecular, structured, well-organized system ready for mobilization. Macías shrewdly realized this. PUNT Women's Section allowed an opportunity for women to play a formidably powerful, political role in public life, yet with "official" central government politics still understood as an exclusively masculine arena, women constituted less of a threat to the paranoid Macías than did his male allies. Memories of the mother of Epifania Avomo Bicó (today an opposition party leader and women's rights activist) and of Victorino Pancho Ripeu, an Equatoguinean historian living in exile in Spain, concord with Adugu Mba's view: The newborn PUNT Women's Section, the foster child of the Spanish Falange organization of the same name, was used as a platform to incorporate women into Macías's brand of rule by terror.[17] And its leading members were placed right in the control room of the nationwide surveillance system.

The gender roles promoted by the PUNT's Section deserve far more research, as does the possibility that women influenced by Macías's Women's Section put their relative "empowerment" to different uses, ones that Macías may not have approved. Unfortunately, for reasons discussed below regarding the dangerous politics of history in Equatorial Guinea, I am not able to address such research questions. The interviewees I have cited here are known opponents of government. Facing, as they do, the oppression of the Obiang regime, addressing the Macías-era taboo is a relatively lesser risk. Yet they are still unusual in confronting this forbidden history at all.

There are few sources that document life during the Macías era. While the Macías regime burned many colonial archives that remained in the country, the current government has dumped archives from the Macías era in the street.[18] Seventy-year-old Cristina confirmed this. I approached Cristina as she worked at a school named after a late Equatoguinean woman who features heavily in the Women's Section archives. I was looking for the latter's descendants, former neighbors, or any documentation that could tell me more about her. "You're best going to her village. As for documentation, you won't find much. The history of a whole people can be found in the rubbish piles around town, or in the hands of market women wrapping food," Cristina lamented.[19]

Eighty-nine-year-old Enrique worked as a civil servant under Macías. I visited him at his home in Malabo. "I lived the whole terror through my own flesh and blood," Enrique told me, but he was reluctant to recall much else. He nodded toward a sepia pile of papers resting on the garden table with his reading glasses beside them: "They're all documents I kept from my old job in that time. I'm just going through them. I'm glad I kept them because they're part of our history."[20] He picked up a small booklet from the top of the papers, a 1971 decree from Macías, with articles outlining the political crimes for which death would be the punishment. I asked Enrique if I might take photographs of the texts, in order to digitalize this small part of a lost archive, but he was not keen: "I'm not sure if it's forbidden for me to possess such documents."[21] It is common knowledge in Guinea that much of the inner circle of the current regime was also implicated in the Macías terror. In such circumstances memory becomes dangerous. For many older people talking of their life stories, 1968 to 1979 becomes "the dark period," and their voiced memories thus become choked and scarce. It is not easy to collect oral histories of the Macías era.

Approximately one hundred thousand Equatoguineans, or one-third of the country's population, were murdered or fled to exile during Macías's rule. The JMCM, whose attack on a school had been the last straw for the Spanish Women's Section staff, was the frontline of Macías's apparatus of terror. Public executions, tortures, and rapes at the hands of the JMCM were common.[22] Avomo Bicó recalls her school days in the town of Niefang, when government delegates, the so-called *grandes señores*, would abduct large groups of girls to abuse, imprisoning or killing anyone who attempted to confront them.[23] As María Nsué Angüe, whose father was executed by Macías, puts it, "They were gray days and terror reigned so completely that children were born with their hair on end."[24]

As if aware of the falling legitimacy of his own regime due to the never-ending cycle of violent oppression, as the years went on Macías became more and more fearful of his own population. After five years in power he began to wall himself away. The first step was securing the presidential palace in Malabo. In 1974 a huge security barrier was erected where residential houses used to stand. Later though, the wall was not enough for the increasingly paranoid Macías. He moved to continental Bata and then, in 1976, to his home village of Mongomo (he still occasionally made visits abroad, but was less keen to travel within Equatorial Guinea), leaving the daily running of the country in the hands of his nephew Obiang.[25]

As well as all-encompassing terror, the Macías era was characterized by the general economic collapse of the country. In 1972 Nigerian laborers launched street riots against bad working conditions. Some twenty thousand Nigerians left in the subsequent wave of government aggressions against their kin. A few years later, as conditions in the country worsened, the Nigerian military assisted its remaining citizens in Equatorial Guinea to escape (along with several thousand Equatoguineans posing as Nigerians).[26] The cocoa economy, which had relied on Nigerian labor since colonial times, was by now dwindling.[27] Other sectors were failing too—dozens of thousands of Equatoguineans had fled abroad and there were few workers. Macías's answer in 1976 was to make agricultural work compulsory for some twenty thousand Equatoguineans.[28] The Anti-Slavery Society in London accused Macías of reinstating the forced labor practiced formerly under Spanish rule.[29]

Conditions became progressively worse. Macías had the director of the central bank publicly executed in 1976, then moved the money to his own house.[30] Television and radio disappeared, as there were no technicians left to work and no investment in maintaining lines. In 1978 the electricity failed, submerging Malabo into darkness.[31]

Upon Obiang's 1979 coup, foreign journalists found a "dispirited people and a seriously dislocated society, most of whose institutions were badly damaged and barely functioning; the country had ceased to possess an 'economy' or government 'administration' in the ordinary meaning of these words."[32] How was Macías able to act as he did and retain power? Equatorial Guinea, as I argued in the previous chapter, had been left, upon Spain's exit, without a clear sense of national identity and unity. Furthermore, we saw how Spain had fostered divisions by ethnicity. Macías was, as Anne Foot has argued, able to further foster such divisions by enacting a system of patrimonialism along ethnic and clan lines.[33] While some (especially but not exclusively Fangs from Macías's Mongomo clan) were rewarded for their loyalty, the long-reaching hands of Macías's oppressive machine kept the majority of the population in check. And the little that we know about the PUNT Women's Section suggests that newly imagined gender norms fostered by Macías, ones that "empowered" loyal women to play a political role, allowed oppression to be practiced within families. Macías's machine of fear reached into the narrowest capillaries of society.

Foreign allies also supported the regime. Spain did not get the favored trading and political position that it had hoped for. The Soviet Union, which had negotiated rights over fisheries, equipped the army and police, while North Korea provided instruction at the mass gymnasiums where Women's Section members, among others, trained. China and Cuba also provided technical assistance.[34]

In explaining how Macías was able to cling to power, we should also go back to Spain once more. Foot argues that Spain left Equatorial Guinea with poor institutions and without having established meaningful arrangements for self-rule. Indeed, as First has pointed out, European colonialism in Africa in general terms was based on authoritarian command. "Government was run not only without, but despite, the people," and was therefore incompatible with any preparation for self-government.[35] Spain's envisaged decolonization of Equatorial Guinea amounted to what Frantz Fanon called false decolonization. Spain planned to gradually transfer power from the colonial bureaucracy to Equato-guinean elite auxiliaries, the latter of which were handpicked for their perceived loyalty to the metropolis. In this way, Spain would keep its fingers on the wal-let of the Equatoguinean coffee, cocoa, and logging economy.

In chapter 2 I argued that provincialization and the autonomous govern-ments were just ploys by Spain to avoid decolonization. False decolonization combined with a lack of national identity (fostered by Spain, which promoted ethnic divisions) and Macías's brand of patrimonialism and (gendered) oppres-sive mechanisms served to keep the dictator in power. In the following section, which opens with the political views of Dolores Molubela (whom we met in chapter 3), I move to the next chapter of Equatorial Guinea's history. Charting how *ngueismo* continued after Macías's death, I focus on the gendered dynam-ics of the Obiang regime and how gender comes into play when resisting it.

### The Obiang Regime: The Masculinization of Politics and the Strategic Use of Violence against Women

When I meet Dolores Molubela, we are alone. When she later tells me her opinion of the regime and its oil money in an interview, we are also alone, but she does not fearfully whisper her views. What would happen if she were to voice her views publicly, I ask her. "In other countries, you can speak about things like that, but here . . . they tie up your wrists and they throw you in prison."[36] And yet she speaks. This is not a woman who is content with the socioeconomic status quo, and if resigned to it, she is barely so.

Barrie Wharton blames the reticence of Obiang on the "unfortunate leg-acy" of the Second Republic's treatment of Equatoguineans.[37] Says Wharton, "It is this nostalgia and distaste in many ways for the democracy of the Sec-ond Republic which brought Obiang to power in 1979 and has maintained him there since, despite repeated opposition attempts to overthrow him, many with foreign help. Many of these attempts have foundered due to the lack of mass opposition or real interest in establishing democracy."[38]

While Wharton provides an illuminating picture of how regime changes in Spain affected the lives of Equatoguineans under colonial rule, I dispute his explanation for the Obiang regime's longevity and for Obiang's ascension to the presidency. Obiang became president through his own violence. Know-ing he could not rely on his people to support him, he turned to Morocco for assistance. Hassan II sent hundreds of mercenaries ahead of the coup. In return, Obiang renounced Equatorial Guinea's support for POLISARIO.[39]

It is also questionable that there have been many attempts to overthrow Obiang. According to Amnesty International, Obiang has invented the major-ity of the so-called attempted coups to justify the oppression of the very real prodemocracy opposition.[40] Indeed, I hope to dispel the popular myth, supported by Wharton, that there is no interest among Equatoguineans of ridding their country of *ngueismo* and establishing a fairer form of rule. Obiang's patronage networks may be extensive. But there are potentially also thousands of Dolores Molubelas.

This section focuses on Equatoguinean resistance since Obiang came to power. We have already seen, in chapter 3, how foreign allies and genderwashing have helped to keep Obiang in place, just as they maintain the Moroccan occupation of Western Sahara. Here, I begin with an analysis of Obiang's other self-preservation tools. These are, I argue below, patrimonialism; the construction of open, political resistance as a type of family betrayal; the masculine gendering of organized politics; the failure to construct a unifying Equatoguinean identity in the preindependence era; and the fear of (gendered) sanctions. Second, I look at resistance to the regime and how tactics are affected by gender.

Just as it was for Macías and the Spanish administration before him, patrimonialism is one tool that helps to ensure Obiang's rule. Individuals must display loyalty to Obiang for any wealth at all. It is hard to find employment if one is not a member of the PDGE, and thus the majority of the population is signed up to the ruling party. The extensive clientelist networks are funded first and foremost by oil money. Therefore, as Okenve has argued, the moment resources run out or Obiang loses control over them, loyalty is likely to rapidly evaporate.[41] As is the case in Western Sahara, the importance of resistance demands concerning natural resources (and most especially oil) cannot, therefore, be overstated.[42]

The *possibility* of reward is as important as reward itself. Just as Gene Sharp argues that it is not the sanctions themselves that prevent resistance but the *fear* of them, Okenve argues that even families who are not part of Obiang's clientelist network are still publicly loyal to him in the hope that, one day, a family member might be rewarded with a job.[43] As Okenve eloquently puts it, this has resulted in "electoral campaigns [becoming] a grotesque spectacle in which the electorate makes promises to the leader of the PDGE, rather than the other way around."[44]

Family obligations weigh on Equatoguineans. We have seen that during the Macías regime women were encouraged to spy on their family members. As if still tender from the blows of familial political betrayals, those who oppose the Obiang regime sometimes face anger from their relatives. As Okenve argues, the term *oppositionist* (*opositor*) carries negative connotations thanks to "an almost moral definition" of what is not politically acceptable.[45] This is, Okenve explains, further illustrated by the common Fang expression *wa kobo abe, wa kobo politik* (you're bad-mouthing, you're talking politics). Whether or not one is a good or bad citizen depends on whether or not one supports the established political order, and if one is an oppositionist, she is likely to bring misfortune not only on herself but also on her extended family.[46] This is particularly true for women, who are especially encouraged to be apolitical as a result of their gender.

The construction of politics and political spaces as male only, reinforced by Spanish colonialism, has still not been seriously challenged in Equatorial Guinea. The case of Clara Nsegue Eyi (also known as Lola), the first female president of a political opposition party, provides a strong example of this dynamic. She was imprisoned in 2013 for her prodemocracy political activities, and although she was released a few months later thanks to international pressure, she was not allowed back to the family home, nor even to seek shelter in the homes of extended family, so strong was many of her relatives' anger at what they see as her betrayal.[47] On the subject of Nsegue Eyi's case, Tutu Alicante, an activist living in the United States and director of the NGO EG Justice, makes the following illuminating comments: "Undoubtedly, young women still face more backlash from their families. . . . First of all, your family will be the first one to remind you that, you know, 'you're a woman, you should be having kids.' Your mother, aunts, sisters would remind you of the still prevalent archaic traditional expectations. Thus, most women are very hesitant to get into any type of politics because their families are the first ones discouraging them."[48]

Avomo Bicó and Adugu Mba similarly emphasize, in my interviews with them, that organized politics is seen, in hegemonic discourse, as outside the norms of femininity, and they attribute this to the persistent sexism inherited from past regimes.[49]

Hegemonic history for Saharawi people is one of politically active women. Politics, and now protest and open resistance, is "naturally" feminine, and it has "always been" that way. Adugu Mba, Avomo Bicó, and Alicante have here suggested that the opposite is true for Equatoguinean women. The hegemonic history (constructed with political aims in mind and never objective, as Hayden White has powerfully argued) of Equatorial Guinea tells us that women have always been excluded from the political sphere.[50] This history was not reimagined or reinterpreted by the proindependence movements, and it has yet to be reimagined by today's political opposition movements. This directly favors Obiang.

Family ties are knotted tightly in Equatorial Guinea. They extend beyond blood to marriage and the long-term obligations of the bridewealth. Deciding to openly oppose the regime, then, carries the weight of implicating a significant number of relatives and in-laws. Obiang knows how to foster this fear.

Arresting the family members of resistance activists is a common practice in Equatorial Guinea. On occasions, arrests go beyond relatives and become almost farcical. For example, in March 2002, when leader of the Republican Democratic Force party (Fuerza Demócrata Republicana, FDR) Felipe Ondó Obiang was among the wave of more than 150 Equatoguineans arrested on the perplexing accusation of "murdering the Head of State," not only were several members of his extended family detained but so, too, were people who had previously invited him to a wedding, drove him in a taxi, and greeted him in the street. One unfortunate detainee had merely once retrieved his escaped ducks from a garden opposite a house that Ondó's wife happened to be visiting at the time.[51]

Male relatives of opposition activists are targeted just as much as female ones, but the arrests of women have gendered implications. In Equatorial Guinea, it is not unusual for authorities to rape or sexually assault the wives, mothers, and other female relatives of presumed male political activists, sometimes in front of the latter.[52] This has parallels with the cases of Ali Salem Tamek, one of the current unofficial leaders of the Saharawi resistance movement, whose wife, Aicha Chafia, was gang raped in 2003 in the presence of the couple's infant daughter, and Mohamed Salem Buamud, whose mother and sister were raped in front of him in the family home during the 2005 intifada.[53] Victoria Rodriguez Rescia highlights that the torture of women often has the intended effect of "weakening the morale of husbands or partners."[54] The extent of this weakened morale is evident in the following comment by ex-disappeared Brahim Dahane. I use an example from Western Sahara, first, because meaningful comparisons with Equatorial Guinea can be drawn, and second, because I have been unable to interview an Equatoguinean survivor of this family-punishment policy. Dahane recalls the effect of hearing women being mauled by dogs (a torture method used in the eighties and nineties in the Mobile Intervention Unit [Poste de Commandement—Companie Mobile d'Intervention], secret detention cells of El Aaiún): "What hurt me was hearing women screaming because of the dogs. You can't imagine the pain, the scorn that you feel, the injustice and the desperation that you can feel and the hope or the desire that you will die there. I think if suicide weren't forbidden by religion, I would have done it there. If I had had weapons I would have used them to kill or to commit suicide."[55]

The overall aim of such gendered oppression in both Equatorial Guinea and Western Sahara is to dissuade men from political, antiregime activism. Temma Kaplan has researched the cases of men forced to watch the rape of wives, sisters, and daughters after capture by Pinochet regime officials. She finds that forcing male activists to remain passive in the face of the sexual torture of a (loved) woman diminishes the feelings of authority that help structure masculine identity in patriarchal cultures.[56] Indeed, although M. Bahati Kuumba rightly argues that traditional constructions of masculinity (such as man as protector) can benefit resistance movements, oppressive forces can harness these same constructions.[57] While Dahane has never stopped his activism, his comment reveals how strongly the regime's gendered weapon hit. In Equatorial Guinea, where the added dimension of family betrayal is in play, we can only imagine the terror felt by (potential) male activists.

The limits of the anticolonial national movements in Equatorial Guinea still have echoes today. Although there was resistance to the Spanish at all levels of society, we have seen that organized politics remained dominated by a small and divided elite. This contrasts with the Saharawi example, where the POLISARIO managed to make hegemonic a vision of nationalism that incorporated the demands of all levels of Saharawi society and therefore mobilized even the most harshly oppressed members of their community. The society-wide culture of participation in organized politics that exists in Western Sahara was not able to develop in Equatorial Guinea, then, before Macías took a rag to smother a culture of civic engagement. In Obiang's Guinea, political pluralism is a myth and civil society still struggles. His brand of nationalism is personal, as we saw in chapter 3, and his rule is painted as inevitable, as destiny, which helps to make resistance seem all the more futile.

The fear of sanctions is one of Obiang's most powerful tools. Talking to a shopkeeper from Chad while in Malabo, I mentioned that I had been to Western Sahara and had many Saharawi friends. "Saharawis?" he laughed, "Western Sahara? We don't recognize that country. . . . We don't talk about that country here."[58] When Obiang came to power in 1979, eight hundred Moroccan security officers were seconded to his country under a bilateral agreement with the Kingdom of Morocco.[59] During the eighties (and to a lesser extent in the early nineties) these Moroccan nationals, which were "crucial" to Obiang's ability to maintain his regime for at least its first decade, were actively involved in human rights violations.[60] Indeed, Moroccan security officers have imported some of their sadistic torture methods from Western Sahara, such as suspending detainees in contorted positions from poles to beat them, the beating of the soles of prisoners' feet (known as *falāqa* in Morocco and Western Sahara), and forcing prisoners to drink urine.[61] In summer 1993 the majority of Moroccan officers were finally withdrawn (only around thirty remained) thanks to international pressure.[62] Then France, Morocco's ex-colonial power and key partner in ensuring the latter's impunity in committing human rights violations against the Saharawis, stepped in to support the Obiang regime with a new team of thugs.

For France, Equatorial Guinea presents an opportunity to extend its sphere of influence in West Africa. Equatorial Guinea was the first non-Francophone country to enjoy a fixed exchange rate to the franc, and France was the first European power to set up a cultural center in Obiang's Guinea.[63] French military personnel attached to the French embassy in Malabo trained up a paramilitary unit, created in 1992, known as the Antorchas (Torches). When the Moroccan Guard left, the Antorchas took over the role of bodyguards to the ruling powers and spearheads of oppression.[64] Much like the Nazi Brownshirts, the group's nickname among the civilian population reflects its uniform: they are known as "Ninjas" because of their all-black attire.

Nowadays, Israel rivals Morocco for the number-one spot in terms of providing Obiang with arms and training to "secure" the country. This forms part of Israel's wider arms sales drive in Africa, where it has made inroads over recent years. Several Israeli military companies have won major, multimillion-dollar contracts in Equatorial Guinea, and Obiang's presidential guard has been trained by Israeli security companies.[65] We have already seen, in chapter 3, that the United States has played a role securing the maritime zones around Equatoguinean oil fields. These countries, much as France, the United States, and Saudi Arabia (among others) have in Western Sahara, help to oppress the prodemocracy opposition in Equatorial Guinea in order to maintain their own interests.

Walking around Malabo today, one can see several bars named after the Antorchas. In addition to this armed group are the police and military, all bodies used to protect the regime first and foremost. Government delegates at village level help to enforce social control in the most rural and inaccessible areas. There is also Seguridad (security).[66] The Equatoguinean Seguridad shares an important facet with the oppressive apparatus of the Moroccan regime. Like Morocco's network of informers and spies in civilian clothes, Seguridad members do not wear uniforms. Saharawis, Moroccans, and Equatoguineans must always question who can be trusted thanks to such plain-clothes spies. Meanwhile, the heart of the system is the close, militarized circle that surrounds Obiang.

Gender is used by the regime to increase the fear of sanctions. As well as the aforementioned forms of torture imported from Morocco, other methods include whipping, slicing ears with razor blades, confinements to tiny spaces (including, allegedly, cupboards of less than seventy by fifty centimeters in volume) for several weeks, and the breaking of hands, legs, and feet. Such violence is suffered by both women and men.

However, as mentioned above, sexual torture also exists and is applied differently according to the gender of the detainee. Reviewing relevant literature,

I have found but one example of the sexual torture of an Equatoguinean man.[67] The lack of examples may indicate that sexual torture is used on Equatoguinean men to a much lesser extent than on activists in Western Sahara, but not necessarily so. As we have seen, disclosures of sexual abuse, and especially rape, while in Moroccan police custody is a relatively new phenomenon among Saharawi activists. Similarly, Equatoguinean men perhaps face several barriers to disclosure, fruit of the constructions of masculinity hegemonic in Equatorial Guinea. Common barriers identified in other contexts include the belief that men should be "strong," "capable of defending themselves," and "able to cope," which prevents them from sharing their experience for fear of ridicule or blame, and in countries (such as Equatorial Guinea) where homophobia is particularly rife, fear of being labeled a homosexual is also a factor.[68] Sexual torture of women has been reported widely in Equatorial Guinea. Reports were particularly prevalent following a January 1998 Bubi uprising. Indeed, a deeper look at the suppression of this uprising serves as a case study that shows Obiang's full toolbox of gendered punishment.

Before the sun rose on 21 January 1998, groups of around thirty-five to forty Bubis, some of whom carried machetes and guns, attacked several military barracks on Bioko Island. Three soldiers and several civilians were killed. The regime, which blamed the Movement for the Self-determination of Bioko Island (MAIB), an outgrowth of the Bubi Union party founded during the Spanish colonial period, responded with systematic violence against the Bubi population. Over the remaining days of January, security forces hunted down Bubis in the villages that break up the forest, along the alleyways of the capital's markets, and at the many checkpoints that pepper the island's road network. In Rebola, a Bubi-dominated town on a hill a short drive from Malabo, the violence was particularly intense. The town is rumored to house the secret headquarters of the MAIB. There, over 80 percent of homes were reportedly destroyed.[69]

In the days that followed, Bubi women were prevented from drawing water from the wells, which they rely on for cooking, cleaning, and caring for their families. Bubi women trading at Malabo's main market had their wares destroyed. Said one market-goer, "The soldiers threw the food on the ground. They trampled on the ripe bananas and chopped up the green bananas with machetes."[70] Market trade of the food grown on their smallholdings forms the subsistence of the poorest Equatoguinean women and their children. In Bubi villages, soldiers allegedly threw rubbish in the cooking pots of women. All these sanctions seem directly designed to prevent women from carrying out their gendered roles. Representatives of the regime robbed women of their right and ability to provide for and nurture their communities according to gendered divisions of labor.[71]

While pregnant and nursing Saharawi women have been targeted by security forces systematically and *precisely because they were mothers* at certain moments of the Moroccan occupation, there does not seem to be a similar pattern in Equatorial Guinea. Nevertheless, if a wanted woman happens to be pregnant or has an infant, this is used by the regime to add further terror to its sanctions.[72] For example, the wife (Francisca Bisoco Biñe) of another alleged instigator of the January 1998 attack was arrested at her home in the town of Sampaca and taken to the Malabo police station. At the time, she was eight months pregnant. Despite this, she was whipped at the station and severely beaten. Her baby was stillborn a few weeks later.[73]

As well as Bisoco Biñe, eleven other women were among the five hundred Bubis detained in the days following 21 January. Most were held as hostages and sexually abused to force their husbands to come forward.[74] Outside the station walls, the sexual assault of Bubi women was more systematic. Women were raped in their homes by soldiers and Fang civilians close to the regime. Victorino Pancho Ripeu, a Bubi historian living in exile in Spain, claims many such women became pregnant.[75] In the streets, and especially in the villages far from the eyes of Western immigrants working in Malabo, security forces stood and watched as mobs of Fang PDGE supporters beat and raped Bubi women.[76]

The aim of this systematic sexual violence was to destroy women's dignity by reducing them to objects of penetration while simultaneously leaving Bubi men unable to prove their conformity with hegemonic notions of masculinity by protecting the victims. The intersection of gender and ethnicity is also significant. By encouraging targeted and mass rape (and alleged impregnation) of Bubi women by Fang men as a collective punishment for the uprising, the Obiang regime moved close to the widely researched and discussed use of "rape as a weapon of war."[77] As Bülent Diken and Carsten Bagge Lausten point out when discussing this concept, the sexual abuse of women belonging to the "enemy" community in a conflict is considered to be the ultimate humiliation and a symbol of total conquest.[78] The mass use of rape by regime forces and civilians loyal to the regime was dressed in ethnic terms, positioning Bubis as the enemy of the Fangs, and vice versa. A divided population not only strengthens Obiang's position in general terms, but the Fang versus Bubi dynamic also reinforces his patrimonial system in which Fangs are favored above other ethnicities.

In summary, gender norms are wielded by the regime not only to preclude women's participation in open, organized political resistance but also, through sexual torture, to increase the terror surrounding the threat of sanctions and to foster ethnic divisions. Gender is central to how Obiang maintains power, just as it is for comprehending how Macías ruled and how the Moroccan occupation attempts to suppress Saharawi nationalism. In short, these cases support the thesis of Alicia Decker's assessment of Idi Amin's Uganda: scholars focusing on authoritarian regimes have seriously underestimated the extent to which dictators use gendered discourse to consolidate power.[79]

I should clarify that, here, I have used "power" in a shallow way to refer to Obiang's hold over the economic and governmental levers of the country. The dictator's recourse to violent oppression to control his population indicates that he has very little "power" indeed if we were to use the word in the sense given to it by Foucault or Hannah Arendt, or to a lesser extent by Gramsci (hegemony) or Sharp. For Sharp, the more violent and cruel the oppression of resistance, the weaker and more fearful the regime is of those who resist.[80] As is the case for the Moroccan king, Obiang is in a permanent state of uneasiness. If he enjoyed hegemony over his population (or "power" in the Foucauldian sense) he would have no need to resort to violence. His (gendered) techniques of oppression reveal the inherent weakness of his regime and, therefore, also make evident the potential success that the (nonviolent) resistance of the Equatoguinean people could have. I wrote earlier that there are potentially thousands of angry Dolores Molubelas in Equatorial Guinea. What I should add now is that Obiang knows and fears that.

In the next section, I look at how gender shapes resistance to the Obiang regime. We have already seen that Obiang constructs organized politics as an "unfeminine" activity, with very real effects for political party leaders such as Clara Nsegue Eyi. I ask, then, how do women resist *ngueismo*?

### Women's Resistance to the Regime:
### Solidarity, Songs, Speaking Out, and the Semu Market Annex

On 15 December 2007 Brígida Asongsua Elo visited her husband, Guillermo Nguema, a prisoner of conscience, at the Black Beach prison. The following day, she was arrested as she left morning mass at Malabo cathedral. She was subsequently held in the Malabo central police station in a cell until 25 April 2008.[81] On several occasions while in detention she was ordered to sweep the floor of the secretary of state's office. She repeatedly refused to do so, even when assaulted.[82]

As discussed above, being an "oppositionist" often means implicating one's family in a reputation of "bad citizenship." In spite of this, Brígida Asongua Elo is not alone. Like Khadijatou, the friend of nationalist leader Bassiri whose story I told in chapter 1, there are numerous examples of female relatives standing by and supporting male political prisoners by visiting them, advocating on their behalf, taking them medicine or clothes, or pushing the love of a home-cooked meal through the prison bars. Others have tried to help their "wanted" partners or relatives to hide or escape.[83]

Bearing in mind the harassment that relatives of (alleged) political activists commonly suffer, the aforementioned seemingly simple acts equate to knowingly entering the lion's den. Prison visits and other shows of solidarity through material or spiritual support should therefore be read as forms of resistance.[84] In a regime where political opposition is treated as if it were a contagious disease, touching all those close to the oppositionist, women who pursue their gendered role as carers for their menfolk are challenging the regime. By continuing their support despite harassment, violence, or worse, these women let themselves become politically "infected" and thereby defy Obiang's wish to turn families against the politically active "black sheep."

As well as showing active solidarity with male political prisoners, some women offer logistical support to opposition party activists. Such was the case of Pilar Mañana, an owner of a bar in Malabo until a forbidden newspaper written by the Convergence for Social Democracy (CPDS) was found on her premises leading to her arrest. Although Mañana was not herself a member of any opposition party, her bar was known to be a meeting place for opposition activists.[85] Mañana's offering of a safe space for activists is reminiscent of Anita Awaho's actions and the secret back room of her bar in colonial Santa Isabel. We see, then, a continuation in women's strategies of resistance. Excluded from organized, formal politics because of constructions of gender that have changed little since colonial times, women find their own ways of offering support to a struggle that they believe in.

Fostering a popular culture of resistance is arguably another women-dominated practice that has its roots long before Obiang or Macías came to power. In September 1997 six women members of the CPDS were detained, stripped, and severely beaten in Akurenam after having been caught preparing to welcome CPDS leaders with songs.[86] We know that this was not the first time that Equatoguinean women, "who stand out for their ability to enchant with dances, tell folk stories and lead games," have employed popular culture as a form of resistance: I explained the role that women's dances and songs played in colonial times in chapter 2.[87] Neither was this 1997 event the last time such a form of resistance was used. Although not always the authors of songs, women are the key transmitters of an oral culture that is sometimes used to challenge the regime.[88] Take, for example, the following extract of the popular Bubi song "Baney Wept" ("Baney lloró"):

Tears fall from the eyes of the people of Baney
For not having any authority within the Government
Over so many years gone by.[89]

Baney is a Bubi town on Bioko Island. It is not clear if the singers would mean to attack the Obiang regime as a whole or, rather, just the dominance of Fangs within it, but either way, the lyrics denounce the political status quo. The same can be said of the following song, collected in 1999 by Ángel Antonio López Ortega when he encountered a Fang woman from Añisok in neighboring Gabon:

> I took the basket toward the village
> Halfway there
> I came across a soldier
> He told me to give him the fish
> I told him
> I had no fish
> The soldier hit me
> with his truncheon and his belt
> I fell to the floor
> He told me to get up
> I told him that I would not get up.[90]

As López Ortega insightfully notes, the lyrics, while showcasing aspects of a Fang woman's traditional life and role, also defiantly tell the listener that the harassed woman will not submit to the soldier. The song decries the military intimidation and abuse suffered by the poorest women daily. Furthermore, it would traditionally include an all-women chorus call, itself a show of feminine solidarity.[91] As Marcelle C. Dawson points out, the role of music in resistance is well researched, and through their repetition of ideas and their ability to be recited by many, songs are more powerful in raising consciousness than the more passive act of listening to political speeches.[92]

As a final example of oral tradition as resistance, let us turn to the Annobonese song "For Annobón" ("Por Ambô"). It was written in memory of three Annobonese men killed during an Annobón-wide "rebellion" that exploded following decades of acute poverty and oppression:[93]

> All the little birds of Awala
> Come and see, come and see . . .
>
> . . .
> The three islets of Mábana send you a message
> Palá Liku Mébana sends you a message
> Jobômbô Mébana sends you a message
> They tell you to protect the house

For Annobón he took lashes

For Annobón Simplicio died on the land
for Annobón Súmenè died in the sea
Malia died too.

With its title and repetition of the phrase "for Annobón" throughout, the song suggests that the youths were martyrs dying for the imagined community rather than just victims of violent oppression. Amnesty International, in its report on the violent suppression of the rebellion, finds that Simplicio Llorente was actually a bystander. In this folksong, itself a sign of a hidden transcript, he becomes a martyr of resistance to the regime.[94]

An Annobonese housemaid working in Malabo gave me an insight into another women's resistance tactic: the act of "speaking out." She told me, in the voice of someone who does not seem used to being listened to, that Equatorial Guinea "was not [her] country." She complained of the harsh socioeconomic inequalities of Malabo and concluded that "Annobón was [her] country."[95] This political observation was in response to a very general question about the woman's provenance. The fact that she replied with complaints about the socio-economic situation, and hinted that her national identity was not as Obiang would like, is in itself an act of resistance given that, as Okenve points out, even mild and indirect criticisms can be considered attacks on the government or even on Obiang.[96] Indeed, Amnesty International has recorded cases of women detained and imprisoned after their complaints against the government, made in private conversations in their own homes, were overheard by informers listening from the street.[97]

Although I spent just a short time in Malabo, daily interactions with members of the less well-off strata of Equatoguinean society, including immigrants, revealed a host of grievances regarding security force briberies and fines, the lack of employment opportunities and subsequent desire to migrate, the ill distribution of wealth, the *machista* culture, and so on.[98] Many women, responding to questions that were not designed to seek comment on the current political regime, spoke at length of the corruption, political violence, and terror that they and their families had suffered.[99] Such women challenge the current social order and the legitimacy of the regime with their words, and when done in a context where speech is policed, their boldness becomes all the more apparent.

Other women went further, speaking out not to a lone British researcher but to the regime itself. Raising grievances, that is, making formal or informal complaints before an organizational system, is a well-recognized and relatively well-researched form of resistance.[100] Following the systematic rape of Bubi women in January 1998, some survivors attempted to denounce their experiences before government. They went directly to the Ministry of the Interior to complain but found they were charged money to leave a statement.[101] While the reaction of the complaints office is obviously hugely unsatisfactory, by daring to go forth and denounce those who attacked them, these women showed public resistance to the regime and its misogyny. This is also true of the numerous women who dared to give testimonies to Amnesty International researchers. Revealing the gendered nature of political violence to external onlookers was (and is) in itself a political act. Just as it is for Saharawi women and men, the testimony of sexual torture becomes a form of resistance in the act of telling. Not only do the Equatoguinean tellers denounce the torturers but they also deny the dehumanization, humiliation, and shame that the latter have attempted to inflict on them.[102] There is a crossover here with feminist resistance. Some women survivors of domestic violence have been known to go to the Ministry of Social Affairs and the Promotion of Women and demand assistance.[103]

Other women fight with their harassers face to face: "A poor woman selling snails and arguing with a policeman who is trying to tax her is fighting too—joining a party isn't the only way to fight." This was the retort of an Equatoguinean feminist to a male opposition figure who aggressively decried his countrywomen for their "apathy" in the face of the regime (she was attempting to air her views on how to overcome sexism in her society when the opposition figure intervened with a "mansplaination").[104] Her point, and her reference to the street seller, brings us to a telling rumor concerning the unofficial alternative to Malabo's Semu market.

So the story goes, late one night, cloaked by the darkness of a moonless sky, dozens of women smallholders gathered as quietly as possible on the outskirts of Semu market, Malabo.[105] Each had brought what she could: pieces of wood, poles, rope, or corrugated tin. Unable and unwilling to pay the heavy subletting fees for shops in the new market built by the first lady, and yet in need of an outlet to sell their agricultural produce, these poor women would build their own solution. By morning, the wooden and scrap metal unofficial extension to Semu market was ready for business, and the local mayor did not dare force the mass of fierce women to pull it down.

Semu market, in its form today of concrete floors, high and sturdy roofs, and spacious lanes between the rows of benches for displaying goods, was built with funding officially (but, informers tell me, doubtfully) from the first lady's personal purse in 2011.[106] Mangue did well to package the market as a gift to her people: one must be gracious for a gift, say "thank you." One shouldn't

Women in Semu market, Malabo, 2012. Photo by Guillaume Darribau/Fractures Collective.

complain. This packaging of Semu market as a gift makes the defiant actions of the poor market vendors all the more brazenly subversive. Around the new, high-spec Semu market sprawls a much larger network of stalls built upon the muddy, stony land with wooden polls, pieces of rusty corrugated tin, and beds of tarpaulin on which to display wares.[107] I put the rumor as I had first heard it (as described above) to several interviewees. None could confirm on which date the related events happened, if they did, indeed, happen on one single night at all (the weight of the materials needed and the attention such an ambitious project of construction could draw would make this very difficult), but neither could anyone completely discount the story. Most interviewees responded with an anecdote of their own about the market women, which always revealed the latter's ways of resistance. However, they also sometimes highlighted the question of what is being resisted. This is well illustrated by the following quotation of Alba Engonga, a feminist working for state media: "If there is someone walking around the market who they don't particularly like, who strikes them as pretentious, . . . a foreign woman turning her nose up, for example, [the market women will] sing a song that mocks her. There's a lot of solidarity between them. It's the same if a soldier tries to extort one of them. They'll club together to try to get rid of him."[108]

With reference to Engonga's first example, it would be reasonable to conclude that the market women are showing a form of everyday resistance to racism, neocolonialism, and possibly classism. Regarding the second example though, are the women consciously resisting the Obiang regime as a whole or the power of the military to extort? Like many of the examples included in this chapter, especially those involving the poorest women, resistance is not specifically anti-Obiang. It does, however, almost always challenge the daily hardships caused by the way the state is run. The resistance of women like the market sellers challenges the poverty bred of the sociopolitical situation in the country, the racism and neocolonialism of foreign (white) migrants, and the misogynistic tendencies of Obiang's agents of oppression.

Like their foremothers under Spanish rule, we can interpret the resistance of today's poorest Equatoguinean women as intersectional. It is also everyday. Women make use of what Scott calls "the weapons of the weak," which, as we have seen in earlier chapters, is usual in situations of extreme domination. But excluded from "organized politics," these women do not take recourse to mass demonstrations.

Epifania Avomo Bicó highlights the lack of poor-women-led demonstrations with an example from August 2015. She tells me of a group of women who had been selling their wares on the street, far from the market. The women had not been able to afford to sublet a stall in one of the official markets. Subsequently, Malabo Council officials stole all their stock on the grounds that the women were selling "without permission." Avomo Bicó wondered, she tells me, if the market women would demonstrate following this incident. When they did not, she concluded that "they aren't able to."[109] Avomo Bicó nods toward a "missed opportunity" with regard to the market women. They resist in their own ways, but their exclusion from politics, in the traditional sense of the word, hinders their capabilities for collective, mass protest. In the next section, we look in more detail at such "missed opportunity," which, I argue, is created when antiauthoritarianism does not allow a space for feminism. To do so, I begin by summarizing the current context of open, public resistance to the Obiang regime in today's Equatorial Guinea, which has gained pace since 2015.

## Antiauthoritarianism and Feminism:
## A Pending Opportunity?

In February 2015 Equatorial Guinea made a rare appearance in the British press. The world had just watched the semifinal of the African Cup of Nations (CAN), as had Obiang from behind the glass of the stadium's VIP box. The match was undoubtedly an embarrassment for the dictator, and not only because the home team lost. First, a terribly inhospitable Equatoguinean audience had pelted the Ghanaian team with bottles, and second, Equatoguinean authorities had driven a police helicopter within thirty feet of the audience then dropped smoke bombs. After the match, riots broke out around Malabo.[110] But interpreting the violence against Ghana and ensuing disturbances at face value, as meaningless but embarrassingly bad behavior, is short sighted. Curiously, the worries of English monarch Edward II surrounding the earliest recorded instances of football hooliganism—that violence surrounding football would develop into social unrest and treason—are perhaps close to the sentiments of Obiang during CAN 2015.[111]

Before considering what happened in the stadium on the night of the Ghana match (5 February), we must go back to the days and weeks preceding the start of the tournament. Obiang offered to host the CAN at the last minute, after his friend Morocco dropped out because of fears over Ebola. Obiang faced immediate criticisms from political opposition groups for his decision. In early January the CPDS—which Obiang, taking advantage of the football stadium violence for his own purposes, blamed for inciting the violence—began to distribute leaflets denouncing the tournament and demanding a boycott on the basis that it would cost the country millions to host it, with few visible benefits for the population.[112]

Perhaps nervous that the CPDS-backed boycott of the tournament would be successful, the regime handed over match tickets to various businesses and ordered the population to fill the stadiums. Offices, businesses, and schools shut early throughout the tournament so that no one would have an excuse not to attend the matches.[113] In light of this, some opposition activists and foreign analysts read the on-pitch violence followed by the riots as unusual but meaningful, collective public displays of discontent.[114] Political graffiti adorning a square in Malabo (e.g., "No to CAN, yes to housing!") and the targeting, by window-smashing rioters, of the PDGE's Malabo office and the office of the Equatoguinean Football Federation, indicate that the interpretation of such activists and analysts is accurate.[115] In Scott's terms, the violence and civil disobedience surrounding CAN was a rare and spontaneous storming of the public transcript.

Graffiti against Equatorial Guinea's hosting of the African Cup of Nations (CAN), Malabo, 2015. Photo by Joanna Allan.

There have been other public protests since independence. As well as the protests of 1993 in Annobón mentioned earlier in the chapter, there have been well-documented demonstrations in 1992; strikes in 1981, 1993, and 1994; and demonstrations and sit-ins in 2013. This is nowhere near an exhaustive list: the difficulties that both Equatoguinean and external human rights organizations and journalists face in monitoring freedom of expression in Equatorial Guinea should not be underestimated. Nevertheless, a review of well-documented protests indicates that few have been quite so large and involved such acts of civil disobedience as those surrounding the CAN.[116] Most worrying for Obiang and his party, the CAN riots were just the first in a series of street protests that took place over the course of 2015 and have continued in small but threateningly choppy waves into 2017. These have varied from protests over the canceling of scholarships and other perceived educational inequalities that escalated in March 2015 into explicitly anti-Obiang demands involving students (in their dozens at first and later in their hundreds); the shutting down of the much-loved Rebola Cultural Center and detention of its cherished volunteer director Benjamín Choni in August 2015 over an allegedly antigovernment lyric included in a song by a cultural center pupil; and a general strike, the largest seen in Obiang's times, by taxi drivers that began in March 2017 over a new government administrative charge to be waged on them.[117] True, protests and strikes involving protesters in their hundreds are small in a country with a population of some eight hundred thousand. But every fruit begins as a bud. Furthermore, Obiang is aging. His most likely heir, playboy son Teodorín, is even more despised than Obiang himself. This, coupled with the ever-falling income (as the oil wells dry) for the ruling family and their patronage networks, could ripen into a political opportunity for those Equatoguineans tired of *ngueismo*. Will women step in to seize it?

In Equatorial Guinea at the time of writing, the only party that openly opposes the dictator and has managed to register (there are others that oppose the PDGE but fall short of criticizing Obiang himself) is the CPDS. Although it is impossible to break down the demographics of the CPDS and the other (unregistered and numerous) parties and movements by gender since many members and supporters are anonymous, it is also fair to say that the vast majority are male led.[118] As Ávila Laurel puts it, "Politics, as well as being dangerous, is power, and power belongs to men."[119]

Whereas for the nationalists of Western Sahara hegemonic discourse paints public politics as a "natural" part of Saharawi femininity, for Equatoguinean women, participating publicly in opposition to the regime means breaking with long-established gender norms. Furthermore, although the POLISARIO's current level of commitment to women's rights is debatable, their professed commitment to the same upon the emergence of the nationalist movement in the early seventies helped to mobilize Saharawi women.[120] In Equatorial Guinea, in order to change the gendered face of organized oppositional political movements, a commitment to feminist demands and to changing gender norms to allow a space for women is crucial. Some political activists, such as Epifania Avomo Bicó, are bringing their prodemocracy and feminist demands together by fostering women's groups within political parties.

Avomo Bicó is one of five women who make up the twenty-eight members of the National Executive Committee of the CPDS party. She acts as secretary for gender and the position of women. As well as this, Avomo Bicó is president of the CPDS's Women's Association. On top of attempting to engage women with the party, the association plays a feminist role. Avomo Bicó explains: "Today, what my association tries to do is to support women to play more roles. . . . We fight against discrimination in the field of employment and against gender inequalities more generally."[121]

This is where a comment by writer Mitoha Ondo'o Ayekaba is most pertinent: "The government's failure to take serious actions to resolve [gender inequalities] is perhaps due to the perception that to improve the lot of women would be counter-productive to maintaining tight control of the society and political process."[122] Perhaps Avomo Bicó attempts to address discriminations suffered by women precisely because women, doves of fire, present a potential largely untapped by the organized anti-Obiang opposition.

Several Equatoguinean feminists are not, at least publicly, linked to any organized anti-Obiang movement (anymore). Feminist interviewees rhetorically asked me why they would join such a movement when the latter are just as misogynist as the PDGE and have no project whatsoever to address sexism. The writings of Obono Ntutumu are particularly brave and scathing on this point. As well as highlighting the misogyny of the PDGE, she accuses opposition parties not only of profound sexism but also of tolerating gender-based violence, and she extends her criticisms in this regard to anti-Obiang civil society movements in the diaspora.[123]

Some prominent Equatoguinean feminists, especially those who are civil servants, prefer to work within the limits of the regime. They use their relatively privileged positions to (carefully) fight for women's rights. For example, one is using connections to the first lady to lobby for funding for educational projects for women and girl survivors of violence and sexual exploitation. Another uses her influence in state communications' channels to broadcast television and radio programs that shine a subtle light on sex discrimination. Others publish opinion pages with a feminist slant and propagate feminist lessons through their teaching positions. One interviewee explained her efforts to persuade her male relatives, who hold high positions in the PDGE, to change their views and adapt their policies. Uday Chandra and others have called such practices in which claims are made *within* the system "rightful resistance," recognizing the structures of domination within society but exploiting cracks in state sociopolitical arrangements to push forward subaltern agendas.[124]

If some women use advocacy to advance the rights of women, others use, once again, cultural means. For example, José Francisco Eteo Soriso has documented popular Bubi women's songs denouncing men who impregnate women and leave the latter without support, encouraging women to search for men who will provide for them properly, and asserting women's right to be considered the "head of the family." He has documented as well Ndowe women's songs that criticize male infidelity and Fang women's songs that express disgust at discrimination against women.[125] Fang women interviewees also highlight traditional songs that denounce polygyny and that criticize sexual double standards.[126] Eteo also highlights that, at times, a woman will design a song to specifically denounce a particular man who has wronged her.[127] As interviewees explained to me, female friends join the resistant woman in chorus, singing when the man, or men, in question are present.[128] Curiously, Deubel has noted that Saharawi women use song and a woman-only genre of poetry (*tabr'a*) in much the same way: to mock and deride men, with fellow women backing up the singer/composer in a call-and-response pattern.[129]

Significantly, one (Fang) Equatoguinean feminist tells me that it was precisely because of such songs that she has grown up as a feminist. She explains: "Demanding women's rights is the daily bread of Fang girls! Fang girls are brought up clutching the skirts of their mothers, they go everywhere with them. When their mothers go to work the land with other women, they talk about the problems they face as women. When they go to church (they're all believers), or when there's a birth or a wedding, they are there singing . . . and, listening to these songs, girls learn what equality means. . . . We live with our mothers' feminism from childhood."[130]

The comments of this woman, Trinidad Mba, raise once again the question asked over and over again by African feminists: why do we presume that feminism is a white woman's invention? Indeed, the vast majority of feminist interviewees felt frustrated that their feminism is interpreted as "imported ideas" by Equatoguinean society. They concord with feminist theorists writing on other African cases such as Peggy Gabo Ntseana and Minna Salami, who highlight the difficulties African feminists face in criticizing norms that are harmful to women.[131] Amid calls to return to "authentic precolonial culture" (which in any case is impossible since cultures are dynamic and ever-changing, not fossils), such feminists are accused of doing the West's bidding. Equatoguinean feminists' views on this issue also overlap with the indignation of younger Saharawi women (those who have participated in the #I'mNot LessSaharawi campaign discussed in chapter 3) upon accusations of being brainwashed by the West when they demand a new, feminist social order in Saharawi society. These Saharawi women are profoundly offended by the suggestion that their feminism is a "Western influence" rather than organic and/or inspired by their Saharawi, Arab, African, and/or Muslim foremothers.[132] In Equatorial Guinea, the accusation of "imported ideas" resembles the charges of "racism," "colonialism," and "enemies of the state" that, as Stephanie Wolters of the Institute for Security Studies points out, are launched at any organization that criticizes aspects of Obiang's rule.[133] These accusations are meant to sew mouths shut. And yet they are strengthened by the genderwashing collaboration between Obiang and his Western partners—the (false) picture of efforts for gender equality is imposed from outside. The most salient problem for Mba is that, when it comes to labeling feminist efforts as "imported ideas," opposition activists are just as guilty as regime members. In contrast, for Equatoguinean feminists, feminism is something organic to women of their own ethnicities, since the latter all have long traditions of fighting against patriarchal norms. As Obono Ntutumu puts it, "Guinean women of all ethnicities have always been feminists. . . . What young women are saying today has been said [by Equatoguinean women] for centuries."[134]

The key point that I wish to make in this brief section on feminist resistance is that, while often women's resistance can be interpreted as intersectional, fighting several oppressions at once, there are also feminist activists in Equatorial Guinea who have little link to the anti-Obiang movements. Indeed, many feminists express their rejection of what they see as profound sexism among the antiregime parties and groups. In other words, we cannot assume a direct, linear relationship between antiauthoritarian movements and increased challenges to sexism. The story of women's resistance told here indicates that an effort to join the two would be worthwhile for the antiregime, prodemocracy elements of Equatorial Guinea. The pain, anger, and knowledge of the Dolores Molubelas, the Annobonese housemaid, and the robbed market women is energy waiting to burst.

# Final Remarks

S TORIES OF WOMEN LIKE Tawfa and Silka, Dolores and Ana, Sultana and Aminatou teach us that authoritarianism, and resistance to it, are drenched in gendered implications. These incredible women's stories also force us to reconsider history. A gender-aware focus on the Spanish colonial period reveals that Saharawi women were resisting sexism and racism *before*, not just because of, the emergence of the nationalist movements, while Equatoguinean women, whose nationalist movements never seriously took them into account, resisted *in spite of* their country's proindependence organizations. From a theoretical point of view, listening to the stories of women like Tawfa or Silka, Helena or Ana indicates the need not only to make a gendered reading of the subaltern but also to gender subaltern studies itself. Otherwise we risk implying that reforms to tackle racism and sexism, such as those of the POLISARIO, were exclusively the brainchild of progressive male leaders, not the hard-fought-for accomplishments of "ordinary" women and enslaved peoples.

In Spanish Guinea, women like Helena, with her secondhand clothes, or Anita, with her hidden room behind the bar, were not encouraged to play public roles in the nationalist struggles, since politics was considered (and continues to be considered) a male-only arena. Despite this though, Helena, Anita, and doubtless thousands more unnamed women carved out a space for themselves in the battle for independence. Their simultaneous challenges to brutal and pernicious racism, to the most violent manifestations of sexism imaginable, to enforced Hispanicization, religious brainwashing, and to all the other oppressions that colonialism brought can be interpreted, like those of Saharawi women, as *intersectional* resistance. But because Guinean women's role in anticolonialism was largely behind the scenes and has been (made) almost completely invisible in histories of the country, Ana's label for such activists as "silent political women" is apt. They will remain silent until we start listening to them.

The stories of today's Equatoguinean women, struggling under *ngueismo*, are also actively silenced. Maria Angeles Adugu Mba, a feminist and CPDS activist, leans across the desk and looks me firmly in the eye when she describes the current situation in her country: "It's a white-washed sepulcher rotting on the inside."[1] Her Bible-borrowed metaphor works well to describe, more specifically, the image promoted by her government of gender equality compared with the reality of Equatoguinean women's continued experiences of sexism. The internal function of the Equatoguinean regime's discourses on gender and so-called gender equality is to preserve Obiang's rule. The scant commitment to addressing heterosexism, and the continued hegemony of heterosexist norms in nationalist discourses, dampen women's open participation in organized resistance movements.

We should also listen carefully when women choose to be silent. While researching this book, women told me stories filled with pauses, gaps, ellipses, . . . silences that spoke of unspeakable gendered torture. These stories, with all their silences, convince me that, in Equatorial Guinea and occupied Western Sahara, gendered brutality is not a mere unfortunate consequence of letting policemen and paramilitaries loose with free rein. Rather, this is purposeful, strategic, planned violence. Gendered brutality is state policy.

In the Saharawi case, wider taboos in Saharawi society surrounding female sexuality outside of marriage further cement one desired outcome of Morocco's strategy of gendered torture: preventing the reproduction of the Saharawi nation. Discrimination in the labor market and educational institutions is also important here. If Saharawi male activists face extra barriers to study and are unable to get a paid job, and if Saharawi female activists find it difficult to get married after having been detained (and therefore, society often rightly presumes, raped), it is the most nationalist Saharawis who are least likely to be able to start a family. Furthermore, if Saharawi men in hegemonic nationalist discourses are, as my previous research has argued, the protectors of the feminized nation and, at the family level, protectors of women, then the imprisonment and torture of Saharawi women and girls makes realizing their gendered masculine role impossible. Moroccan oppression makes the performance of hegemonic Saharawi masculinity and Saharawi femininity almost impossible for activists. Indeed, in both occupied Western Sahara and Equatorial Guinea, we have seen how authorities strategically and purposefully torture women and girls in front of their male kin. Oppression directly targets the gendered self.

Obiang and Mohammed VI will be able to sustain their regimes of gendered brutality as long as the world looks the other way. However, in the Saharawi case, the stories of Aminatou and Tekbar have shown that it is possible for women to *temporarily* break the ubiquitous Western media silence. In chapter 3 we saw how Tekbar and her supporters used orientalism strategically during her Canaries-based hunger strike to put Western Sahara on the front pages of Spanish newspapers. Having observed the Western media's emotionally provocative, if orientalist, depiction of Aminatou's earlier struggle, Tekbar's campaign deliberately and cleverly made use of orientalist stereotypes to foster all-important media attention. In other words, Western orientalist gender norms impact directly on the dynamics of the Saharawi nationalist struggle. In this example, we saw Tekbar and her sisters-in-arms struggling against the genderwashing of the Moroccan occupation by shrewdly appropriating genderwashing's very own weapons. But the fact that she had to choose public starvation, consciously use Spanish (not Saharawi) soil as her stage, and entertain Western gendered, racist fantasies while doing so speaks volumes of the tremendous sacrifices required of Saharawi women who wish to break the international silence on their situation just for a few fleeting moments.

Genderwashing is, in essence, a silencing tool. It is a silencing tool that keeps authoritarian regimes in power, a silencing tool designed to meet Western natural resource greed, a silencing tool that puts women in their place. Chapter 4 charted how the Obiang regime uses its own construction of Equatoguinean society as one of gender equality to appease allies in the West (just as the POLISARIO does, albeit in a position of resistance rather than of an authoritarian oppressive regime). Indeed, its allies such as the United States fund these PR efforts to maintain their own self-images as international leaders in women's rights. In other words, the construction of gender equality in the nationalist discourses of the regime, which are promoted (and partly funded) abroad, are vital for keeping Obiang in power. Meanwhile, Obiang's Western allies, France, Israel, Morocco, and the United States among others, provide heavy hands to help quell domestic prodemocracy opposition, thereby maintaining their own economic and political interests. Obiang and his corporate and state allies are collaborating in genderwashing. They co-opt the language of feminism to market their self-serving activities, which actually undermine, rather than promote, gender equality.

Western corporations and governments partnering with Obiang use his rhetorical (but empty) support for gender equality as a PR tool to shield themselves from criticism. The current vogue for "women's empowerment" in Western governments' "development" agendas also has a direct effect on who resists in what way, and how activists are punished, in occupied Western Sahara. The West's genderwashing promotes the cover-up of women's excruciating stories of torture. Western hegemonic constructions of Arab, Muslim women as

submissive victims and of Arab men as "terrorists" add further weight to the
consequences. Morocco, enjoying its status as the West's main ally in the North
Africa region, is all too aware of these discourses and thus seeks to minimize
coverage of its state-sponsored torture of Saharawi women activists by avoiding trials and official imprisonments of the latter, instead detaining them in
secret torture cells for short periods. The Saharawi (Arab or black Muslim) male
activists, on the other hand, are far more "imprisonable," given their status in
Western discourse as "undeserving victims." This leads women to dominate
public protest, knowing they are much less likely to face long sentences, while
the illegal imprisonment of "just another" male Arab, Muslim "troublemaker"
is not a story worth telling for Western media.

So much silence.

From a table in the uncomfortably quiet reading room of the Alcalá de
Henares archives, the blemishes and untidy scrawl left by a tired and nervous
hand transport me to Women's Section office, El Aaiún, October 1975, where
a typewriter clacks and spins and exudes its sooty scent for the last time. As
Spanish women frantically recorded their parting actions, and cleared their
desks, did documents get mixed up, left in the wrong place? I presume that is
what happened, for among the cardboard boxes of typed pages, newspaper
clippings, and the occasional handwritten note is a small envelope of personal
photographs. A white bungalow with potted plants on the veranda . . . a summer barbeque . . . family members . . . young Saharawi friends on the beach,
smiling. A Spanish woman's life in El Aaiún, and her dear ones from that time,
are left here in this archive. I wonder what the owner of this envelope felt
when she left. Did Saharawi women inspire her to question Falangist gender
norms? Was she ashamed and horrified at the manner of Spain's withdrawal?
And what of her own role? Was she embarrassed or proud of, or just indifferent
to, her doings in the Sahara? What of her colleagues in Guinea? And then I
realize I should be thinking of my own part. Genderwashing, as I have described
it in this book, connects me to how women like Sultana Khaya, whose eye was
beaten out of her head, are treated by authoritarian governments. Western
states and corporates genderwash with authoritarian regimes in order to access
natural resources. If I were to carry on paying British Gas to heat my home, or
keep buying particular brands of cherry tomatoes, tinned tuna, and fish oil at
my local supermarket, I would be investing in stolen Saharawi and Equatoguinean resources. I would indirectly, in some small way, be supporting genderwashing, supporting the silencing of women like Clara Nsegue Eyi and her
party. And, still in a small way but much more directly, I would be undermining
the life's work of Sultana, who dedicates her skills to the fight against resource
exploitation and pays such an unfathomable price for doing so. It is not just

the previous colonists and current regimes that are responsible for the fates of Equatoguinean and Saharawi women. The globalized mechanisms by which genderwashing works mean that I, too, am implicated.

The reach of Western, gendered orientalist discourses is far and sinister. Gender (equality) is essential to the international geopolitics that allow the continuation of the Obiang regime and the Moroccan occupation. Western current "prioritization" of "women's empowerment" in "developing countries" is used to bolster certain countries' support of Obiang and affects Morocco's treatment of Saharawis down to the level of who it punishes and how. Western state rhetorical support of "gender equality" is nothing but hypocritical while Western countries continue to bolster the Moroccan occupation and the Obiang regime economically and politically. Adugu Mba might be right that her country is a whitewashed sepulcher rotting on the inside, but it is the West providing the paint.

If we are to understand the relationship between gender and resistance, we must focus on the idiosyncrasies of local gender constructions but also other constructions that are hegemonic at a global level. Through genderwashing, authoritarian regimes on the one hand and their Western corporate and state partners on the other draw on orientalist discourses about Arab, African societies, in the first instance, to prolong their rule and, in the second instance, to exploit natural resources. In other words, the interplay of the internationally influential Western orientalist gender constructions and the particular constructions of gender in Western Sahara and Equatorial Guinea is inextricably linked to the protests of Malabo's market women, to the length of prison sentences handed down to Saharawi men in Moroccan courts, and to even the smallest weekly women's demonstration on Smara Street, El Aaiún.

# Archives Consulted

For this book I used the *Revista de la Guinea Española*, a media publication by the Claretian missionaries in Equatorial Guinea (all issues 1903–69), available online at http://www.bioko.net/guineaespanola/laguies.htm (accessed 1 February 2014); works written by Spaniards living in, or visiting, the African colonies during the colonial period held at the Spanish national library in Madrid; all available documents of the Women's Section of the Falange in Guinea and the Sahara, held at the Archive of the General Administration (AGA), in Alcalá de Henares; documents photocopied by Francesco Correale and passed to me by Enrique Bengochea from the personal archive of Luís Rodrigez de Viguri y Gil (the last secretary general of Spanish Sahara), known as the Fondo Documental del Sahara; further documents from the AGA, including papers of the Spanish Patronato, which was responsible for justice for the "natives" and letters from Equatoguineans to the governor general (Enrique Martino has usefully digitalized these documents and uploaded them to his website, www.opensourceguinea.org [accessed 25 May 2016]); documents from the British consul in Santa Isabel (capital of Spanish Guinea) from the United Kingdom National Archive (TNA) (digitalized on www.opensourceguinea.org); documents of the General Government of the Sahara Province and the Territorial Police, which are annexed to the PhD dissertation of Claudia Barona Castañeda, "Sahara Al-Garbia (1958–1976): Estudio sobre la identidad nacional saharaui" (Autonomous University of Madrid, 1998); articles on Spanish Sahara and Spanish Guinea published between 1948 and 1957 in the *Cuaderno de Estudios Africanos* (African Studies Journal) of the Instituto de Estudios Políticos (Political Studies Institute), a public agency founded in 1939 and linked to the Falangist faction of the Franco regime (available online at http://www.cepc.gob.es/publicaciones/revistas/fondo-historico [accessed 16 May 2016]); and documents from the Saharawi Arab Democratic Republic (SADR) national archives in Rabuni, Algeria (digitalized and passed to me by Pablo San Martin), including *El Pueblo* (issue number 1, 1974), *La opinión de las masas* (issues 1 to 13 and two specials from 1976 and one unnumbered issue from 1977), *20 de Mayo* (issues 6 to 14 from 1974, issue 23 from 1975, issues 40 and 42 from 1977, the March, May, and August issues from 1980, and the March issue from 1981), and *Sahara Libre* (issues 1 and 2 from 1975, issues 5 to 24 from 1976, issues 29 to 45 from 1977, issues 48 to 67 from 1978, issues 115 to 122 from 1981, issues 146 to 190 and two specials from 1983, issues 232 to 262 from 1985, issues 315 to 330 from 1988, and issues 333 to 352 from 1989).

# Glossary

*abóm*: Fang mechanism, often controversially translated as "kidnap," by which a woman could avoid an unwanted marriage by eloping on her wedding night with another lover.

Antorchas: Equatoguinean paramilitaries trained by French military personnel and used by Obiang to discipline the population.

*ādrārī*: plural form of *derrā'a*.

*āḥīām*: plural form of *ḥaīma*.

*āmlāḥaf*: plural form of *melḥfa*.

*bādīa*: the countryside of Western Sahara.

*daira*: Saharawi municipality.

*dawāir*: plural of *daira*.

*derrā'a*: the tunic worn by Saharawi men, in sky blue or white with gold trim around the neck.

Djemaa: a Spanish orchestrated puppet "autonomous government" set up in 1962. The term was borrowed and appropriated by Spanish colonists from a Saharawi term that denoted the leading decision-making assembly within a *qabīla*.

Falangista: member or supporter of the Spanish Falange.

*frigān*: collective of *āḥīām*.

*ḥaīma*: traditional Saharawi tent.

Harakat Tahrir: Vanguard Organization for the Liberation of the Sahara.

*ḥishma*: traditional Saharawi social codes of modesty.

*mahr*: Saharawi bridewealth.

*melhfa*: a single piece of cloth worn by women that covers the whole body, traditionally in black but today in multicolors.

*mu'alaqa*: a "hanging" woman, who is separated from her husband, yet unable to remarry as she has not been granted a divorce.

*mu'alaqat*: plural form of *mu'alaqa*.

Mudawanna: Moroccan state's Family Law, reformed in 2004.

*mugṭāḍa*: the official state of anger of a Saharawi woman who wishes to seek some form of redress from the husband with whom she is angry.

*nafaqa*: financial maintenance a Muslim husband is obliged to provide for his wife and children and for children after divorce from their mother.

*ngueismo*: the authoritarian form of rule adopted by Francisco Macías Nguema and his successor Teodoro Obiang Nguema.

Patronato: short form of Patronato de Indígenas (Native Law), which was created by the Spanish colonists in Guinea in 1906, ostensibly as a justice body to defend Guineans from exploitation by planters.

*qabīla*: a traditional Saharawi form of social organization, often simplistically and problematically translated into English as "tribe."

*qabā'el*: plural form of *qabīla*.

*rhīl*: the marriage gift a Saharawi bride receives from her own family.

*sayba*: used to refer to Saharawi girls who leave the family home without a specific purpose, or too often, or who do not wear the *melhfa*.

Seguridad: plain-clothes informers of the Obiang regime.

*tía*: aunty. This is a term used by Equatoguineans for describing and addressing respected older women, as is *mama*.

*wilāya*: Saharawi province.

*wilāyāt*: plural of *wilāya*.

# Notes

## Introduction

1. There is, however, a university in POLISARIO-controlled Western Sahara. The University of Tifariti hosted its first research seminar in March 2016.

2. Sultana Khaya, personal interview, Zaragoza, 26 November 2014.

3. Translated from Castilian. All translations from documents are mine, and from Castilian, unless otherwise stated. Luis Ondo Ayang, Anacleto Bokesa Camó, and Max Liniger-Goumaz, *Nguemismo: 33 años de auto-golpes y torturas, corrupción nacional e internacional* (La Chaux, Switzerland: Editorial Tiempos Próximos, 2002), 8.

4. Espacios Europeos, "La activista guineana Clara Nsegue Eyi, Lola, continua todavía en Mongomo (Guinea Ecuatorial)," 14 October 2013, http://espacioseuropeos .com/la-activista-guineana-clara-nsegue-eyi-lola-continua-todavia-en-mongomo-guinea -ecuatorial/?utm_source=twitterfeed&utm_medium=twitter.

5. Alex Vines, "Well Oiled: Oil and Human Rights in Equatorial Guinea," Human Rights Watch, 9 July 2009, 11, https://www.hrw.org/sites/default/files/reports/bhr0709 web_0.pdf.

6. Justo Bolekia Boleká, *Aproximación a la historia de Guinea Ecuatorial* (Salamanca: Amarú Ediciones, 2003), 70–71.

7. James C. Scott, *Domination and the Arts of Resistance: Hidden Transcripts* (New Haven, CT: Yale University Press, 1990).

8. Ernesto Laclau and Chantal Mouffe, *Hegemonía y estrategia socialista: Hacía una radicalización de la democracia* (Madrid: España Editores, 1987), 172.

9. Both of these theories share similarities with Steven Lukes's "third dimension of power" and Pierre Bourdieu's "habitus" in their concern for how subalterns are persuaded that their subordination is natural. Likewise, there are similarities between Gramscian hegemony and Michel Foucault's conceptualization of power as ubiquitous and diffuse and, at its strongest, creating individuals and gestures and impulses within them. I have elected to use Laclau and Mouffe's theory over these other similar ones since Laclau and Mouffe's shows clearly the potential for resistance created through the deployment of counterhegemonic discourse (the idea of which perhaps overlaps with Foucault's conception of resistance as something that must be creative, productive,

and seeking of power). Also, their logic of equivalence is interesting to cases of multiple oppression and, therefore, multiple resistance, as is the case of Saharawi and Equato-guinean women. Pierre Bourdieu, *Outline of a Theory of Practice*, trans. Richard Nice (Cambridge: Cambridge University Press, 1977); Michel Foucault, "The Subject and Power," *Critical Inquiry* 8, no. 4 (1982); Steven Lukes, *Power: A Radical View*, 2nd ed. (Hampshire: Palgrave Macmillan, 2005).

10. Frantz Fanon, *The Wretched of the Earth* (London: Penguin Classics, 2001), 32–33.

11. Albert Memmi has powerfully analyzed the terrible psychological impact of colo-nization on the colonized. Albert Memmi, *The Colonizer and the Colonized* (London: Earthscan Publications, 2003).

12. K. W. Crenshaw, "Demarginalizing the Intersection of Race and Sex: A Black Feminist Critique of Antidiscrimination Doctrine, Feminist Theory and Antiracist Pol-itics," in *The Politics of Law: A Progressive Critique*, ed. D. Kairys (New York: Pantheon, 1990).

13. Joanna Allan, "Imagining Saharawi Women: The Question of Gender in POLISARIO Discourse," *Journal of North African Studies* 15, no. 2 (2010); Elena Fiddian-Qasmiyeh, *The Ideal Refugees: Gender, Islam, and the Sahrawi Politics of Survival* (Syra-cuse, NY: Syracuse University Press, 2013).

14. Joyce M. Chadya, "Mother Politics: Anti-colonial Nationalism and the Women Question in Africa," *Journal of Women's History* 15, no. 3 (2003).

15. Cherifa Bouatta, "Feminine Militancy: Moujahidates During and After the Civil War," in *Gender and National Identity: Women and Politics in Muslim Societies*, ed. Val-entine Moghadam (London: Zed Books, 1994).

16. Sherna Berger Gluck, "Palestine: Shifting Sands. The Feminist-Nationalist Con-nection in the Palestinian Movement," in *Feminist Nationalism*, ed. Lois A. West (Lon-don: Routledge, 1997), 105; Andrea Khalil, "Tunisia's Women: Partners in Revolution," *Journal of North African Studies* 19, no. 2 (2014): 187.

17. Aili Marie Tripp, *Women and Power in Postconflict Africa* (Cambridge: Cambridge University Press, 2015).

18. Alicia C. Decker, *In Idi Amin's Shadow: Women, Gender, and Militarism in Uganda* (Athens: Ohio University Press, 2014).

19. Madawi Al-Rasheed, *A Most Masculine State: Gender, Politics, and Religion in Saudi Arabia* (Cambridge: Cambridge University Press, 2013), 171.

20. See especially Jasmin Lorch and Bettina Bunk, "Gender Politics, Authoritarian Regime Resilience, and the Role of Civil Society in Algeria and Mozambique," *GIGA Working Papers*, no. 292 (2016).

21. Khalil, "Tunisia's Women," 192; Amina Mama, "Khaki in the Family: Gender Discourses and Militarism in Nigeria," *African Studies Review* 41, no. 2 (1998).

22. Samia Errazzouki and Maryam Al-Khawaja, "Beware of the Middle East's Fake Feminists," *Foreign Policy*, 22 October 2013.

23. See, for example, Nadje Al-Ali and Nicola Pratt, *What Kind of Liberation? Women and the Occupation in Iraq* (Berkeley: University of California Press, 2009); Cynthia Enloe, *Bananas, Beaches and Bases: Making Feminist Sense of International Politics* (Lon-don: Pandora, 1989); Cynthia Enloe, *Nimo's War, Emma's War* (Berkeley: University of California Press, 2010); Corinne L. Mason, "Global Violence against Women as a

National Security 'Emergency,'" *Feminist Formations* 25, no. 2 (2013); Melanie Richter-Montpetit, "Empire, Desire and Violence: A Queer Transnational Feminist Reading of the Prisoner 'Abuse' in Abu Ghraib and the Question of 'Gender Equality,'" *International Feminist Journal of Politics* 9, no. 1 (2007); Laura J. Shepherd, "Veiled References: Constructions of Gender in the Bush Administration Discourse on the Attacks on Afghanisation Post-9/11," *International Feminist Journal of Politics* 8, no. 1 (2006).

24. Mason, "Global Violence."

25. I realize "Western" is a contested concept, but it is useful to describe, in general terms, the political and economic power divide between North America, Europe, and others, on the one hand, and Africa, Latin American, and parts of Asia on the other.

26. Leif Wenar, *Blood Oil: Tyrants, Violence and the Rules that Run the World* (Oxford: Oxford University Press, 2016), 68.

27. International Monetary Fund (IMF), "Republic of Equatorial Guinea: IMF Country Report No. 15/260," September 2015.

28. Tony Hodges, *Western Sahara: The Roots of a Desert War* (Westport, CT: Lawrence Hill, 1983), chapter 17.

29. Classic works on this issue include Joanna Liddle and Shirin Rai, "Feminism, Imperialism and Orientalism: The Challenge of the 'Indian Woman,'" *Women's History Review* 7, no. 4 (1998); Chandra Mohanty Talpade, Ann Russo, and Lourdes Torres, eds., *Third World Women and the Politics of Feminism* (Bloomington: Indiana University Press, 1991); Gayatri Chakravorty Spivak, "Can the Subaltern Speak?," in *Colonial Discourse and Post Colonial Theory*, ed. Patrick Williams and Laura Chrisman (New York: Columbia University Press, 1994).

30. Hodges, *Desert War*, 256.

31. Pablo San Martín, and Joanna Allan, "The Largest Prison in the World: Landmines, UXOs and the Role of the UN in the Western Sahara," Spanish Strategic Studies Group (GEES), Madrid, 2007.

32. International Court of Justice (ICJ), "Western Sahara: Advisory Opinion of 16 October 1975," https://www.icj-cij.org/files/case-related/61/6197.pdf.

33. Tara Flynn Deubel, "Between Homeland and Exile: Poetry, Memory, and Identity in Sahrawi Communities" (PhD diss., University of Arizona, 2010), 79.

34. Both Alice Wilson and Konstantina Isidoros highlight the problematics of labeling Saharawi precolonial social structures as tribes. Konstantina Isidoros, "The Silencing of Unifying Tribes: The Colonial Construction of Tribe and Its 'Extraordinary Leap' to Nascent Nation-State Formation in Western Sahara," *Journal of the Anthropological Society of Oxford* 7, no. 2 (2015); Alice Wilson, *Sovereignty in Exile: A Saharan Liberation Movement Governs* (Philadelphia: University of Pennsylvania Press, 2016).

35. Hodges, *Desert War*, 26.

36. Pazzanita cited in Deubel, "Homeland and Exile," 80.

37. Harry T. Norris, *The Arab Conquest of Western Sahara* (Beirut: Longman and Librairie du Liban, 1986), 135–39.

38. Hodges, *Desert War*, 149–50.

39. Deubel, "Homeland and Exile," 87.

40. Hodges, *Desert War*; Jacob Mundy, "Performing the Nation, Prefiguring the State: The Western Saharan Refugees, Thirty Years Later," *Journal of North African*

*Studies* 45, no. 2 (2007); Pablo San Martín, *Western Sahara: The Refugee Nation* (Cardiff: University of Wales Press, 2010).

41. Hamza Lakhal, personal interview, El Aaiún, 21 August 2014.

42. For more on the role of the UN in the conflict, see San Martín and Allan, "The Largest Prison"; Andreu Sola-Martin, *Peacekeeping and Conflict Resolution in Western Sahara* (Ceredigion: Edwin Mellen Press, 2006); Andreu Sola-Martin, "Lessons from MINURSO: A Contribution to New Thinking on Peacekeeping," *International Peacekeeping Journal* 13, no. 3 (2006).

43. These are Spain's North African possessions, which Morocco claims.

44. US Embassy to Morocco, "Wikileaks Cable: Moroccan Relations with Sub-Saharan African Countries—A Survey," Rabat, 3 June 2008.

45. Jon Lunn, "Equatorial Guinea: A Quick Introduction," ed. UK Parliament (London: House of Commons Library, 2011), 2.

46. Trinidad Morgades Besari, "Antígona," *Arizona Journal of Hispanic Cultural Studies* 8, no. 1 (2004): 244.

47. Trifonia Melibea Obono Ntutumu, "Acerca de la mujer guineana: Un largo camino por recorrer," ASODEGUE, http://www.asodegue.org/marzo0809.htm, 8 March 2009 (accessed 23 May 2016).

48. For more, see Human Rights Watch, "Well Oiled."

49. Clifford Geertz, "What Is a State if It Is Not Sovereign?," *Politics in Complicated Places* 4, no. 5 (2004): 579.

50. Stellan Vinthagen, "Political Undergrounds: Can Raging Riots and Everyday Theft Become Politics of Normality?" (unpublished working paper, 2006), 5.

51. Pazzanita cited in Deubel, "Homeland and Exile," 80.

52. Nadje Al-Ali, "Gendering the Arab Spring," *Middle East Journal of Culture and Communication* 5 (2012).

53. Samia Al Nagar and Liv Tønessen, "Women's Rights and the Women's Movement in Sudan (1952–2014)," in *Women's Activism in Africa*, ed. Balghis Badri and Aili Mari Tripp (London: Zed Books, 2017), 137–38.

54. Jo Fisher, *Mothers of the Disappeared* (London: Zed Books, 1989); Marguerite Guzman Bouvard, *Revolutionizing Motherhood: The Mothers of the Plaza de Mayo* (Lanham, MD: SR Books, 1994).

55. So says his poem "Mitología," available at http://literaturasaharaui.blogspot .co.uk/2008/04/los-versos-de-la-madera-limam-boicha.html (accessed 30 April 2016).

56. Limam Boicha, personal interview, Madrid, 6 February 2008.

57. Paul Thompson, *The Voice of the Past: Oral History* (Oxford: Oxford University Press, 1978).

58. On top of this, power relations exist between interviewer and interviewee. Although, following the spirit of feminist scholarship, I attempted to mitigate these, I am doubtful mitigation is fully possible when a white, middle-class European is interviewing a woman in a still-colonized country or a Western-backed authoritarian dictatorship.

59. For more on this, see chapter 5 of Thompson, *Oral History*.

60. See the introduction of Decker, *Idi Amin's Shadow*.

61. Joanna Allan, "Activist Ethics: The Need for a Nuanced Approach to Resistance Studies Field Research," *Journal of Resistance Studies* 3, no. 2 (2017).

62. Ibid. It took me eighteen months to secure only a three-week visa, hence the need for an interdisciplinary methodology that does not rely solely on participant observation.

63. Antonio Gramsci, *Selections from the Prison Notebooks*, ed. and trans. Quentin Hoare and Geoffrey Nowell Smith (London: Lawrence and Wishart, 1971).

64. Meriel Bloor and Thomas Bloor, *The Practice of Critical Discourse Analysis: An Introduction* (London: Hodder Arnold, 2007); Norman Fairclough, *Critical Discourse Analysis: The Critical Study of Language* (London: Longman Group, 1995); David Howarth, *Discourse: Concepts in the Social Sciences* (Philadelphia, PA: Open University Press, 2000), 3; Teun A. Van Dijk, "Contextual Knowledge Management in Discourse Production, a CDA Perspective," in *A New Agenda in (Critical) Discourse Analysis: Theory, Method and Interdisciplinarity*, ed. Ruth Wodak and Paul Chilton (Amsterdam: John Benjamins, 2005); Ruth Wodak, Rudolf de Cillia, Martin Reisigl, and Karin Liebhart, *The Discursive Construction of National Identity* (Edinburgh: Edinburgh University Press, 1999), 8; Ruth Wodak and Paul Chilton, eds. *A New Agenda in (Critical) Discourse Analysis: Theory, Method and Interdisciplinarity* (Amsterdam: John Benjamins, 2005). On the necessity of allying oneself with those who most suffer from domination and inequality, see Teun A. Van Dijk, "Principle of Critical Discourse Analysis," *Discourse and Society* 4, no. 2 (1993): 252.

65. Stanley R. Barrett, *Anthropology: A Student's Guide to Theory and Method* (Toronto: University of Toronto Press, 1996); Peggy Gabo Ntseane, "Culturally Sensitive Transformational Learning: Incorporating the Afrocentric Paradigm and African Feminism," *Adult Education Quarterly* 61, no. 4 (2011): 313; Patricia Hill Collins, *Black Feminist Thought: Knowledge, Consciousness, and the Politics of Empowerment* (New York: Routledge, 2000); Ama Mazama, "The Afrocentric Paradigm: Contours and Definitions," *Journal of Black Studies* 31, no. 4 (2001).

66. Howarth, *Discourse: Concepts*; Laclau, *Hegemonía*.

67. bell hooks, *Ain't I a Woman: Black Women and Feminism* (London: Pluto, 1982); Mohanty Talpade, Russo, and Torres, *Third World Women*.

68. Ranjoo Seodu Herr, "Reclaiming Third World Feminism: Or Why Transnational Feminism Needs Third World Feminism," *Meridians: Feminism, Race, Transnationalism* 12, no. 1 (2014): 8.

69. Laura Zahra McDonald, "Islamic Feminism," *Feminist Theory* 9, no. 3 (2008).

70. Deniz Kandiyoti, "The Politics of Gender and Reconstruction in Afghanistan: Old Dilemmas or New Challenges," in *Gendered Peace: Women's Struggles for Post-War Justice and Reconciliation*, ed. Donna Pankhurst (London: Routledge, 2008), 155.

71. Lehdia Dafa, personal interview, Madrid, 28 November 2014.

72. Sherry B. Ortner, "Resistance and the Problem of Ethnographic Refusal," *Comparative Studies in Society and History* 37, no. 1 (1995).

73. Ibid.

74. Nana Darkoa Sekyiamah, "Standing on African Feminist Land: Personal Reflections on the 4th African Feminist Forum," AWID, 25 April 2016, https://www.awid.org/news-and-analysis/standing-african-feminist-land.

75. Judith Butler, *Gender Trouble: Feminism and the Subversion of Identity* (London: Routledge, 2006), 5–6 and 47–48.

76. I found that Equatoguinean feminists, in particular, made great use of the concept when explaining the gender dynamics of their societies to me in interviews. See also, for example, Al-Rasheed, *Most Masculine State*; Kola Eke, "Responses to Patriarchy in African Women's Poetry," *Matatu*, no. 41 (2013); Anindita Ghosh, ed., *Behind the Veil: Resistance, Women and the Everyday in Colonial South Asia* (Basingstoke, UK: Palgrave Macmillan, 2008); Valentine Moghadam, *From Patriarchy to Empowerment* (Syracuse, NY: Syracuse University Press, 2007); Sisonke Msimang, "African Feminisms II: Reflections on Politics Made Personal," *Agenda* 17, no. 54 (2002); Minna Salami, "7 Key Issues in African Feminist Thought," in *Ms Afropolitan* (16 August 2012).

77. Suad Joseph and Susan Slyomovics, "Introduction," in *Women and Power in the Middle East*, ed. Suad Joseph and Susan Slyomovics (Philadelphia: Pennsylvania Press, 2001), 10.

78. Ifi Amadiume, *Male Daughters, Female Husbands: Gender and Sex in an African Society* (London: Zed Books, 1987).

79. Donna Haraway, *Simians, Cyborgs, and Women: The Reinvention of Nature* (New York: Routledge, 1991); A. Styhre and U. Eriksson-Zetterquist, "Thinking the Multiple in Gender and Diversity Studies: Examining the Concept of Intersectionality," *Gender in Management* 23, no. 8 (2008).

80. K. W. Crenshaw, "Mapping the Margins: Intersectionality, Identity Politics, and Violence against Women of Color," in *The Public Nature of Private Violence*, ed. Martha Albertson Fineman and Roxanne Mykitiuk (New York: Routledge, 1994).

81. Ibid.; Crenshaw, "Race and Sex."; Styhre, "Thinking the Multiple."

82. By "activism" I mean extraordinary action to bring about social, cultural, and/ or political change.

83. For the equality versus difference debate, see Jill Vickers, "Bringing Nations In: Some Methodological and Conceptual Issues in Connecting Feminisms with Nationhood and Nationalisms," *International Feminist Journal of Politics* 8, no. 1 (2006): 101. For Eurocentric equality, see Samuel Huntington, "A Clash of Civilisations?," *Foreign Affairs*, Summer (1993).

84. P. San Martín, *Refugee Nation*.

85. John Mercer, *Spanish Sahara* (London: George Allen & Unwin, 1976), 231.

86. Deubel, "Homeland and Exile," 139–42.

87. Ibid.

88. P. San Martín, *Refugee Nation*. See also Isidoros, "Silencing of Unifying Tribes," for a nuanced reading of the "banning" of tribes.

89. Wilson, *Sovereignty in Exile*.

90. Sébastien Boulay, "'Returnees' and Political Poetry in Western Sahara: Defamation, Deterrance and Mobilisation on the Web and Mobile Phones," *Journal of North African Studies* 21, no. 4 (2016): 668.

91. Matthew Porges and Christian Leuprecht, "The Puzzle of Nonviolence in Western Sahara," *Democracy and Security* 12, no. 2 (2016): 66.

92. P. San Martín, *Refugee Nation*, 10.

93. Eugene Kontorovich, "Economic Dealings with Occupied Territories," *Columbia Journal of Transnational Law* 53, no. 3 (2015): 611–12.

94. Stephen Zunes, "Western Sahara, Resources, and International Accountability," *Global Change, Peace and Security* 27, no. 3 (2015): 290.

95. *Middle East Eye*, "Ban Ki-Moon Demands Western Sahara Mission Be Fully Restored," Middle East Eye, 19 April 2016, http://www.middleeasteye.net/news/ban-ki -moon-demands-western-sahara-mission-be-fully-restored-1606934184.

96. Zunes, "Western Sahara, Resources," 290.

97. Court of Justice of the European Union, "Appeal—Agreement between the European Union and the Kingdom of Morocco concerning liberalisation measures on agricultural and fishery products," in *Case C-104/16 P*, ed. Court of Justice of the European Union, InfoCuria, 21 December 2016, curia.europa.eu/juris.

98. Freedom House, "Freedom in the World 2016: Anxious Dictators, Wavering Democracies," January 27, 2016, https://freedomhouse.org/article/new-report-freedom -world-2016-anxious-dictators-wavering-democracies.

Chapter 1. Spanish Sahara, Falangistas, and Gendering Subaltern Studies

1. Tawfa Saleh, personal interview, Auserd camp, 11 December 2015; Silka Bilaal, personal interview, Auserd camp, 11 December 2015.

2. Spanish and French states, "Convenio entre España y Francia (Africa Occidental—Costa del Sahara, Golfo de Guinea), 27 March 1900" (Paris: Gaceta de Madrid, 30 March 1900).

3. For more on the expeditions of Spaniards to what was to become Spanish Sahara, see the introduction of Hermenegildo Tabernero Chacobo, *Legislación de A.O.E.: Recopilación Legislativa, por orden cronológico, de África Occidental Española (Territorios de Ifni y Sahara)* (Madrid: Selecciones Gráficas, 1947).

4. Diego Saavedra y Magdalena, *España en el Africa Occidental (Río de Oro y Guinea)* (Madrid: Imprenta Artística Española, 1910), xxxiii.

5. Tabernero Chacobo suggests 1934 was the year the Spanish finally took possession of Ifni, while Emilio Sola suggests 1942 for Western Sahara. Tabernero Chacobo, *Legislación*; Emilio Sola, *Sahara Occidental: Viaje al país de la esperanza* (Madrid: Editorial Molinos de Agua, 1981).

6. Enslaved North Americans and Europeans cited in Christine E. Sears, *American Slaves and African Masters: Algiers and the Western Sahara, 1776–1820* (New York: Palgrave Macmillan, 2012), 113.

7. Ibid.

8. Saavedra y Magdalena, *España*, 5.

9. Cervera was undertaking an exploratory mission to the Sahara. Julio Cervera, "Viaje de exploración por el Sahara Occidental: Estudios Geográficos" (paper presented at the La reunión ordinaria de 2 de Noviembre de 1886, de Boletín Sociedad Geográfica de Madrid, Tomo XXII, Primer semestre de 1887, Madrid, 1886), 10. For more on Saharawi resistance led by the legendary Malainin and later by his son, El Hiba, see Belkacem Hacene-Djaballah, "Conflict in Western Sahara: A Study of POLISARIO as an Insurgency Movement" (PhD diss., Catholic University of America, 1985).

10. For more on how Spain gradually colonized the Sahara, see chapter 7 of Mercer, *Spanish Sahara*.

11. Francisco del Río Joan, *África occidental española (Sáhara y Guinea): Memoria elevada al Excmo. señor Ministro de Estado por el comandante de ingenieros D. Francisco del Río Joan* (Madrid: Ministerio de Estado, Sección Colonial, 1915).

12. Río Joan, *África occidental*, 258. On "penetration" as a masculine sexual metaphor used by European colonialists, see Anne McClintock, *Imperial Leather: Race, Gender and Sexuality in the Colonial Contest* (New York: Routledge, 1995).

13. Saavedra y Magdalena, *España*, 41; Bartolomé Soler, "Cien Días en el Sahara Español," archives of the Institute of African Studies (Madrid National Library), Madrid, 14 January 1953, 44.

14. Saavedra y Magdalena, *España*, 55. If the colonialist writers saw Saharawi resistance as masculine, their views on the relative empowerment of Saharawi women vary. Saavedra y Magdalena observes that the Saharawi woman "enjoys much freedom and works little" (*España*, 50). Cervera agrees, observing that Saharawi women do as they please, unburdened with domestic tasks or other types of work thanks to their "black slaves" ("Viaje de exploración," 10). An ethnography undertaken with Saharawi nomads finds that women "enjoy great freedom" (see Attilio Gaudio, "Apuntes para un estudio sobre los aspectos etnológicos del Sáhara Occidental: Su constitución básica," *Cuaderno de Estudios Africanos*, no. 19 [July–September 1952]: 62). Yet Soler depicts a different view: "[Saharawi women's life] is interminably passive, constantly absent, reduced, if you like, to a relic, hidden, shut up in a tent" (Cien Días en el Sahara Español," 56.) A full analysis of Spanish constructions of gender equality and how the state used them to justify their colonial project are outside the scope of this thesis, but the cursory look here reminds us of their significance in Western Sahara's history. For more on the various possible readings of the Sahara's pre-Spanish history in gender terms, see Joanna Allan, "Gender Equality and the Politics of Representation in the Western Sahara" (BA Hons, University of Leeds, 2006).

15. Sola, *Sahara Occidental*, 25. On the caution taken by the colonialists to avoid interfering in Saharawi political structures as well as religion, see also Río Joan, *África occidental*, 276.

16. Igor Cusack, "Being Away from 'Home,'" *Journal of Contemporary African Studies* 17, no. 1 (1999): 30; General Government of the Sahara Province, "Censo Escolar," El Aaiún, 1975, 2.

17. We should bear in mind that forced labor of the indigenous population characterized Spanish Guinea. Enrique Martino, "Touts and Despots: Recruiting Assemblages of Contract Labour in Fernando Pó and the Gulf of Guinea, 1858–1979 (PhD diss., Humboldt University of Berlin, 2016).

18. This is the story as recounted to Ana Tortajada in the refugee camps. *Hijas de la arena: Cartas desde los campamentos saharauis* (Barcelona: Debolsillo, 2004), 162–65.

19. Enrique Martino, "Nsoa ('dote'), dinero, deuda y peonaje: Cómo el parentesco fang tejió y destejió la economía colonial de la Guinea española," *Endoxa: Revista Universitaria de Filosofía* 37 (2016): 346.

20. Hodges, *Desert War*, 20.

21. Larosi Haidar, "Prólogo," in *La esclavitud en el Sáhara Occidental*, ed. Pablo Ignacio de Dalmases (Barcelona Ediciones Carena, 2012), 11–12.

22. Pablo Ignacio de Dalmases, *La esclavitud en el Sáhara Occidental* (Barcelona: Ediciones Carena, 2012), 157.

23. Caratini quoted in ibid., 50.

24. Mercer, *Spanish Sahara*, 130.

25. Dalmases, *Esclavitud*, 62. Mercer's review concords with this. He finds that slaves were used to performing menial tasks and that women were preferred as they could be used to produce children. This contrasts with the treatment of white slaves in earlier decades. According to Christine Sears, although sexual exploitation of boy enslaved sailors was an issue, North American and European slaves were generally not heavily used for labor but, rather, maintained with minimum rations until they could be sold at an urban center. Mercer, *Spanish Sahara*, 130; Sears, *American Slaves*, chapter 6.

26. Dalmases, *Esclavitud*, 68–69.

27. In *Esclavitud*, his study of contemporary sources comprised of testimonials and writings by Spanish residents of the Sahara and research by European anthropologists, Dalmases finds that some would-be escapees were tortured or killed and that Saharawi slave owners attempted to justify the enslavement of black people by stating that it was permitted by the Prophet and Allah. He also cites myths and folktales recorded by Sophie Caratini that attempt to assert the naturalness of slavery and are sometimes mixed with religion. Writs by religious leaders were also used to attempt to defend the practice. The Spanish authorities saw slavery as part of Saharawi "politico-religious" and "legal-religious" customs that should not be interfered with. However, Julio Caro Baroja finds cases of colonial authorities sanctioning Saharawis for trading in, and "robbing," slaves. He also lists cases involving enslaved people and notes cases of slaves being found dead in mysterious circumstances. Julio Caro Baroja, *Estudios Saharianos* (1955; repr., Madrid: Calamar ediciones, 2008), 188.

28. Mercer, *Spanish Sahara*, 130.

29. Caratini, quoted in Dalmases, *Esclavitud*, 124.

30. Caro Baroja, *Estudios Saharianos*, 271. Some such men were driven to cooking their own food, in case a meal made by a slave or woman was laced with a curse.

31. Dalmases gives two examples of such cases. See Dalmases, *Esclavitud*, 121–22.

32. Charco-Villaseñor, quoted in ibid., 150.

33. Caratini, quoted in ibid., 153.

34. Ibid., 122, 132.

35. Ibid., 73.

36. Ibid., 72, 147–48.

37. Allan, "Imagining Saharawi Women."

38. McClintock, *Imperial Leather*.

39. See, for example, Nupur Chaudhuri and Margaret Strobel, eds., *Western Women and Imperialism: Complicity and Resistance* (Bloomington: Indiana University Press, 1992); Reina Lewis, *Gendering Orientalism: Race, Femininity and Representation* (London: Routledge, 1996); McClintock, *Imperial Leather*.

40. Andreas Stucki, "The Hard Side of Soft Power: Spanish Rhetorics of Empire from the 1950s to the 1970s" (paper presented at the conference Rhetoric of Empire: Imperial Discourse and the Language of Colonial Conflict, Exeter University's Center for War, State and Society, 2014), 9.

41. Women's Section, "Informe que presenta la delegada provincial de la Sección Femenina, de los hechos ocurridos en el Taller Escuela a este Gobierno General de Sahara," El Aaiún, January 1974, 1; Concha Mateo, "Primer plan previo de enseñanzas y actividades," El Aaiún April 1964.

42. For more on colonial constraints that inhibited traditional solutions to drought, see Isidoros, "Silencing of Unifying Tribes."

43. The 8,000 included 5,465 unskilled laborers, 345 industrial workers, 707 drivers, 190 office employees, 141 teachers, and 1,341 soldiers and policemen. See Hodges, *Desert War*, 130. In 1970–72, the national mining company Fosbucraa created blocks of housing for its Saharawi employees. However, even Spanish architects described the housing as "poor." See Juan Luís Dalda, Carles Martí Ares, and Lluís Pau Coromines, "Dossier forming part of the exposition, 'Aaiun 1939–73, formación de una ciudad española en el Sahara Occidental,' study carried out in El Aaiún," Girona, 1977.

44. Isidoros, "Silencing of Unifying Tribes," 173–74.

45. Concha Mateo, "Informe de la labor realizada en la escuela de hogar para nativas: 18 Mayo–18 Julio 1964," El Aaiún, 1964.

46. What requires more research is how ex-slaves coped with newfound freedom. There is no record in the Women's Section archives of any support being accorded to ex-slaves. Indeed, Mercer finds that, while Spain claims to have freed two thousand slaves and given them subsequent "protection," some former enslaved peoples, left out of work, decided to enter into contracts with their former enslavers. Mercer, *Spanish Sahara*, 130.

47. Mateo, "Primer plan previo de enseñanzas y actividades."

48. Elisa Monreal and Maria Jesus Curto, "Informe general de la labor realizada en la promoción de la mujer saharaui durante el primer semestre de 1973," Unknown (Western Sahara), 1973, AGA (3) 51.19 Caja 237.

49. Gustau Nerín, *La Sección Femenina de la Falange en la Guinea Española (1964–1969)* (Valencia: CEIBA, 2006), 8. Benita Sampedro is currently researching the "boys" of Spanish Guinea. While imagining domestic chores as women's work, even the staff of the Women's Section itself employed "boys." Nigerian men cleaned the schools of the Women's Section and the homes of its female Spanish staff as well as cooked the meals of the latter. Not forgetting that, according to Scott's framework, robbery is a sign of subaltern resistance, one of the "boys" got revenge on his Women's Section employees. As Otilia Soto wrote in a letter to Madrid: "The other day we were met with the surprise that someone had forced open one of our windows and come in to rob us. It was the boy they had before I got here, and who had robbed them before." Otilia Soto, Letter to Soledad de Santiago, Santa Isabel, 30 November 1965.

50. Concha Mateo, "Notas para la conferencia de Teresa: Situación de la mujer saharaui," El Aaiún, 1966.

51. Teresa Loring, "Notas para la presentación en el Instituto de Estudios Africanos," Madrid, 1967, 5.

52. Concha Mateo, "Informe correspondiente al curso 1964–65, Escuela Hogar de Nativas," El Aaiún, 1965, 1.

53. Of course, their personal views may be different from what the archives imply.

54. Mateo, "Notas para la conferencia." Her statement seems to be based on the practice of the husband-to-be giving a bridewealth to the father of the girl to be wed.

55. Enrique Bengochea Tirado, "Las mujeres saharauis a través de la Sección Femenina, un sujeto colonizado," *Arenal* 19, no. 1 (2012): 152.

56. Leila Ahmed, using the case study of British-controlled Egypt, shows how women's rights were used as an excuse for colonialism. Leila Ahmed, *Women and Gender in Islam* (New Haven, CT: Yale University Press, 1992).

57. Reports and communications of the Women's Section repeatedly draw attention to the staff's difficulties in engaging with teenage women, since most were married (and in many cases, therefore, not able to go to school, although there is a report of one married and heavily pregnant thirteen-year-old attending class, and Silka, too, was married when she attended class) aged twelve or thirteen. See, for example, Concha Mateo, Letter to María Nieves Sunyer in Madrid, El Aaiún, 16 March 1966; Concha Mateo, Letter to Soledad de Santiago in Madrid, El Aaiún, 17 March 1966; Provincial Director of the Training and Youth Participation Department, "Cuestionario de actividades de los círculos de juventudes," El Aaiún, 27 September 1974; Provincial Director of the Training and Youth Participation Department, "Actividades para la juventud del Sahara, Curso 1974–75, Trimestre Primero," El Aaiún, October 1974. On the scarcity of girls in "normal" (non–Women's Section) schools and the Spanish perceived reasons behind this, see Mateo, Letter to Soledad de Santiago in Madrid, 17 March 1966; Maria Angeles Mozaz, "Actas de reuniones celebradas recientemente con mujeres nativas, ex alumnas de los centros de Sección Femenina," El Aaiún, 24 October 1974. On custody rights after divorce, see Mateo, "Notas para la conferencia," 1.

58. Sophie Caratini, "La prisión del tiempo: Los cambios sociales en los campamentos de refugiados saharauis," *Cuadernos Bakeaz* 77 (2006): 7.

59. Ibid.

60. James C. Scott, *Weapons of the Weak: Everyday Forms of Peasant Resistance* (New Haven, CT: Yale University Press, 1985).

61. Anonymous Social Worker, "Informe del primer semestre de 1974," 30 July 1974.

62. Claudia Barona Castañeda's comprehensive PhD dissertation covers how the Spanish instilled political and legal control in Spanish Sahara. Claudia Barona Castañeda, "Sahara Al Garbia (1958–1976)" (PhD diss., Autonomous University of Madrid, 1998).

63. Alice Wilson, personal communications, December 2015.

64. Majhula Cheikh el Mami, personal interview, Auserd camp, 12 December 2015.

65. Corinne Fortier, "The Right to Divorce for Women (*khul*) in Islam: Comparative Practices in Mauritania and Egypt," *Droits et Cultures* 59, no. 1 (2010).

66. Caro Baroja, *Estudios Saharianos*, 188.

67. Sophie Caratini, *La République des sables: Anthropologie d'une révolution* (Paris: L'Harmattan, 2003), 101.

68. For example, an anonymous woman cited by Nicoletta Gandolfi tells such a story of her best friend (a Saharawi woman forced into marriage but who fell in love with a cousin). Nicoletta Gandolfi, "A propósito del Sáhara Occidental: Testimonios de los Canarios que allí residieron durante el periodo colonial," *Oriente Moderno*, nos. 7–12 (1989), http://www.arso.org/canariosita.htm.

69. This is an excerpt from the song "Ya lali, old man," the lyrics of which appear in the booklet accompanying the CD. Various, *Starry Nights in Western Sahara* (Cambridge, MA: Rounder Records, 2003).

70. Alfonso Lafarga, "Mariem Hassan, la voz que cantó la lucha del pueblo saharaui por el mundo," *Por un sahara libre* (blog), 24 August 2015, http://porunsaharali bre.org/2015/08/mariem-hassan-la-voz-que-canto-la-lucha-de-pueblo-saharaui-por-el -mundo/. Caro Baroja found in the 1950s that husbands were usually at least ten years older than their spouses. However, he also found exceptional cases of wives older than

their husbands, as well as husbands as much as four decades older than their wives. *Estudios Saharianos*, 164–70.

71. Caro Baroja, *Estudios Saharianos*, 164–70.

72. Lila Abu-Lughod, "The Romance of Resistance: Tracing Transformations of Power through Bedouin Women," *American Ethnologist* 17, no. 1 (1990).

73. Parental authority was and is important in Saharawi culture, for both women and men.

74. Abu-Lughod, "Romance of Resistance."

75. Caro Baroja, *Estudios Saharianos*, 234.

76. Commonly known as *tuiza*. See ibid., 124–25.

77. Wilson, *Sovereignty in Exile*, 71.

78. Wilson, personal communications, December 2015; Germaine Tillion, *The Republic of Cousins: Women's Oppression in Mediterranean Society* (London: Al Saqi Books, 1983), 28–29.

79. Khadijatou Mokhtar, personal interview, Auserd camp, 13 December 2015.

80. Saleh, 11 December 2015.

81. Ibid.

82. Sophie Caratini, *Hijos de las nubes* (Madrid: Ediciones del Oriente y del Mediterráneo, 2008), 129.

83. Mercer, *Spanish Sahara*, 202.

84. See Mateo, "Informe de la labor," 1; Mateo, "Informe correspondiente," 1, 2. Mateo explains that the Spanish teachers have learned how to tell when the natives "are taking the mick. At least we realize it and know where to attack."

85. Mateo, "Informe de la labor," 4.

86. Women's Section, "Informe e evaluación de actividades," Villa Cisneros, October 1972; Women's Section, "Informe e evaluación curso 1972–1973," Villa Cisneros, 8 June 1973; Women's Section, "Junta quincenal de directoras de departamento," El Aaiún, 20 March 1975.

87. The 1972 report from Villa Cisneros, for example, describes that it was difficult to run the jersey-sewing classes, and so literacy classes were favored, in response to the request of the students. Women's Section, "Informe e evaluación de actividades."

88. Concha Mateo, "Proyecto de nuevo edificio para escuela de primera enseñanza de patronato de Sección Femenina," El Aaiún, 4 May 1971, 1.

89. Headmistress Smara Domestic School, "Informe de las actividades realizadas durante el curso 73/74 en la Escuela Hogar de patronato de Seccion Femenina de Sahara," Smara, 30 June 1974.

90. As Aurora Morcillo has pointed out in her study of Catholic womanhood under Franco, by the sixties Women's Section discourse in Spain had incorporated the idea of a professional woman, but women were nevertheless expected to leave their jobs once a husband or child arrived. Aurora G. Morcillo, *True Catholic Womanhood: Gender Ideology in Franco's Spain* (Dekalb: Northern Illnois University Press, 2000), 104; Heliodoro Manuel Pérez Moreno, "La Sección Femenina de la España de Franco (1939–1975) y sus Contradicciones entre "Perfil de Mujer" y Medios Educativos," *Cadernos de História da Educação*, no. 7 (January/December 2008): 84.

91. General Government of the Sahara Province, "Actitud alumnas Sección Femenina," Villa Cisneros, 24 January 1975.

92. Arabic language was also taught, along with Islamic art and history, the history of Arab Spain, and Saharawi dance and music. See Headmistress, "Informe de las actividades."

93. Pérez Moreno, "Sección Femenina."

94. Enrique Bengochea Tirado, "Políticas imperiales y género: La Sección Femenina en la provincia de Sahara (1961–1975)" (PhD diss., University of Valencia, 2016).

95. Spain borrowed the term "Djemaa" from a Saharawi term that denoted the leading decision-making assembly within a tribe. In 1974 some of its members became part of an all-male puppet political party set up by the Spanish, known as the Partido de Unión Nacional Saharaui (PUNS). We can see parallels between Spanish colonial policy (with regard to co-opting some Saharawis through the Djemaa as well as tolerance of Islam) with Portuguese colonial policy in Guinea Bissau and Mozambique. See Mário Machaqueiro, "Ambiguities of Seduction: Photography and the 'Islamic' Policy of Portuguese Colonialism," *Anthropological Quarterly* 88, no. 1 (2015).

96. Lehdia Dafa, "En el Día de la Mujer, recuerdo y homenaje a las pioneras de la sanidad saharaui," *Democracia Saharaui* (blog), 7 March 2015, http://lehdiamohamed dafa.blogspot.com/2015/03/en-el-dia-de-la-mujer-recuerdo-y.html.

97. Maria Angeles Mozaz, "Actas de reuniones celebradas recientemente con mujeres nativas, ex alumnas de los centros de Sección Femenina," El Aaiún, 9 October 1974, 1.

98. Mozaz, "Actas de reuniones," 24 October 1974.

99. Saleh, 11 December 2015.

100. Ibid.

101. Women's Section, "Informe general, Catedra de Smara, 13 Enero a 13 Junio," Smara, no date, 2; Women's Section, "Informe general de la Escuela Hogar de Villa Cisneros, curso 1973–1974," Villa Cisneros, 1974, 1; Mateo, "Proyecto de nuevo edificio"; Women's Section, "Nota Informativa sobre las actividades que la Sección Femenina realiza en el Sahara," El Aaiún, December 1974.

102. Monreal, "Informe general," 2.

103. Maria Angeles Mozaz, Letter to Soledad de Santiago in Madrid, El Aaiún, 17 May 1975. Indeed, Mozaz wanted the government's actions to be recorded in the archives. In the letter she writes, "As I already explained on the telephone it's very important that these documents are archived in our National Archive."

104. Maria Angeles Mozaz, "Liquidación que se presenta a gobierno del taller-escuela 'Confecciones Sahara,'" El Aaiún, 15 April 1975.

105. See also Women's Section, "Informe general, catedra de Smara," 2; Maria Angeles Mozaz, "Informe motivado de los cursos que ésta delegación provincial de Sección Femenina de Sahara imparte a la mujer nativa con cargo al Fondo Nacional de Protección al Trabajo," El Aaiún, estimated 1974. See also Women's Section, "Informe general, Catedra de Smara."

106. Anonymous Social Worker, "Informe del primer semestre de 1974," 3.

107. Although some women further down the ranks were married to Spanish soldiers, most of the leaders were single.

108. Morcillo, *True Catholic Womanhood*, 108.

109. Enrique Bengochea Tirado, "Mujeres, nacionalismo y políticas coloniales en la provincia de Sáhara (1958–1975)," *Noticias del Sáhara* (blog), July 2014, http://dias porasaharaui-es.blogspot.co.uk/2014/07/mujeres-nacionalismo-y-politicas.html.

110. Ibid.

111. Bengochea Tirado, "Las mujeres saharauis a través de la Sección Femenina"; Bengochea Tirado, "Mujeres, nacionalismo y políticas coloniales"; Amalia Morales Villena and Soledad Vieitez Cerdeño, "La Sección Femenina en la 'llamada de África': Saharauis y guineanas en el declive del colonialismo español," *Vegueta: Anuario de la Facultad de Geografía e Historia (Universidad de Granada)* 14 (2014); Stucki, "Hard Side of Soft Power."

112. Gayatri Chakravorty Spivak, "The New Subaltern: A Silent Interview," in *Mapping Subaltern Studies and the Postcolonial,* ed. Vinayak Chaturvedi (London: Verso, 2000).

113. Sumit Sarkar, "Orientalism Revisited: Saidian Frameworks in the Writing of Modern Indian History," in *Mapping Subaltern Studies and the Postcolonial,* ed. Vinayak Chaturvedi (London: Verso, 2000). Women's studies and other disciplines have arguably made more headway in this respect. For example, Suad Joseph and Susan Slyomovics point out that patriarchy oppressed women across the Middle East and North Africa before the arrival of European colonialism. Now, precolonial and postcolonial patriarchies intersect in the nation-building projects of the region. Suad Joseph and Susan Slymovics, eds., *Women and Power in the Middle East* (Philadelphia: University of Philadelphia Press, 2001).

114. Sarkar, "Orientalism Revisited."

115. Enloe, *Nimo's War, Emma's War,* 25.

116. Sahara Section of the General Government of the Canaries, "Motivos de descontento en el Barrio llamado 'Casas de Piedra,'" El Aaiún, 14 January 1975, 1.

117. Alejandro García Llinás quoted in Dalmases, *Esclavitud,* 75.

118. Monreal, "Informe general," 2.

119. Concha Mateo, "Informe sobre la actitud política de la mujer saharaui," El Aaiún, October 1974, 13.

120. (First name unknown) Murillo, paper letterheaded with the Falange logo, "Informe sobre la situación actual de Sahara," El Aaiún, 7 June 1974, 8.

121. Anonymous man cited in Gandolfi, "A propósito del Sáhara Occidental." It should be noted that not all Saharawis felt discrimination. Khadijatou Mokhtar, for example, says she never felt any sense of this at all (13 December 2015). On the other hand, Susan Martin-Márquez has made a strong argument concerning the astute construction by Saharawi nationalists of a fraternal and historical friendly relationship between the Spanish and the Saharawis. See Susan Martin-Márquez, "Brothers and Others: Fraternal Rhetoric and the Negotiation of Spanish and Saharawi Identity," *Journal of Spanish Cultural Studies* 7, no. 3 (2006).

122. Khadijatou Mokhtar, personal interview, Madrid, 28 November 2014.

123. Allan, "Imagining Saharawi Women," 198.

124. The war began as a joint effort of some Saharawi tribes and Moroccan Berbers to liberate their lands from colonialists (although Morocco was officially "decolonized" by this point, it was still occupied by French forces). However, after a series of betrayals, the episode turned into the first step on the road to Morocco's colonization of Saharawi lands and ended in violent clashes between Saharawis and Moroccans in Tarfaya. For a full description of the war and its consequences, see San Martín, *Refugee Nation,* 66–73. For an analysis of Spanish military perspectives on the war, see Francesco Correale, "La

'última guerra colonial' de España y la literatura militar entre memoria y conocimiento" (paper presented at the Seventh African Studies Congress, Lisbon, 2010).

125. Ahmed Baba Miské, *Front Polisario: L'âme d'un peuple* (Paris: Editions rupture, 1978), 116.

126. General Government of the Sahara Province, "Recopilación de informes y documentos de interés relacionados con el O.A.L.S. y los incidentes del 17 de Junio de 1970," El Aaiún, 22 October 1970, 3.

127. San Martín, *Refugee Nation.*

128. Isidoros has argued that Saharawi nationalists did not reject "tribalism" (indeed she rightly questions the use of the term "tribe") but, rather, the Spanish-imposed repressive model of the "tribe." For me, official POLISARIO discourses of the seventies call loudly for a social revolution that would see the traditional forms of social organization completely reimagined. Nevertheless, bearing Isidoros's insights in mind, perhaps there was an official, public perspective and a simultaneous "behind the scenes" effort to work with traditional tribal leaders. Isidoros, "Silencing of Unifying Tribes."

129. Caro Baroja, *Estudios Saharianos*, 33.

130. San Martín, *Refugee Nation*, 27; Sola, *Sahara Occidental.*

131. Bilaal, 11 December 2015; Saleh, 11 December 2015. Khadijatou Mokhtar has similar memories, 13 December 2015.

132. This is a quote from the Spanish colonial government report on *Harakat Tahrir*, written shortly before the Zemla protest. General Government of the Sahara Province, "Informe sobre el partido saharaui clandestino denominado 'Organización Avanzada para la Liberación de la Saguia el Hamra y Rio de Oro,'" El Aaiún, 12 June 1970, 9.

133. Baba Miské, *Front Polisario*, 126.

134. Isidoros, analyzing the conciliatory tone of a letter sent by Bassiri to the Spanish governor in early June, concludes that Bassiri's movement, at this stage, desired only autonomy and a redefined system of Saharawi political representation still under Spanish rule. However, such a tone is, as we have seen, common among subaltern peoples, and Alicia Campos's work on the "double language" of the Equatoguinean proindependence activists (discussed in more detail in chapter 7) is illuminating in this regard. It is my view that Bassiri was maintaining a polite public transcript in his attempted negotiations with the Spanish. Indeed, the testimonies of Bassiri's comrades collected by Juan Carlos Gimeno Martín and Juan Ignacio Robles Picón illustrate that independence was an aim from the outset. Isidoros, "Silencing of Unifying Tribes," 177; Juan Carlos Gimeno Martín and Juan Ignacio Robles Picón, "Ambivalencia y orden colonial español en el Sahara Occidental (1969–1973)," *Antropología* 5 (September 2013).

135. Saleh, 11 December 2015.

136. General Government of the Sahara Province, "Informe sobre el partido saharaui clandestino," 8.

137. Tomás Bárbulo, *La historia prohibida del Sáhara Español* (Barcelona: Ediciones Destino S.A., 2002), 66–68.

138. San Martín, *Refugee Nation*, 81.

139. This story was recounted to me by Tawfa Saleh and Silka Bilaal. Majhoula Cheikh el Mami also confirmed that Bassiri was kidnapped from Khadijatou's house. Saleh, 11 December 2015; Bilaal, 11 December 2015; Cheikh el Mami, 12 December 2015.

140. San Martín, *Refugee Nation.*

141. Enrique Bengochea Tirado, "La movilización nacionalista saharaui y las mujeres durante el último periodo colonial español," *Revista Historia Autónoma* 3 (2013): 119.

142. Baba Miské, *Front Polisario*, 129.

143. Mateo, "Informe sobre la actitud política," 8.

144. Saleh, 11 December 2015. See also Tara Flynn Deubel, "Poetics of Diaspora: Sahrawi Poets and Postcolonial Transformations of a Trans-Saharan Genre in Northwest Africa," *Journal of North African Studies* 17, no. 2 (2012): 307; Violeta Ruano Posada and Vivian Solana Moreno, "The Strategy of Style: Music, Struggle, and the Aesthetics of Sahrawi Nationalism in Exile," *Transmodernity: Journal of Peripheral Cultural Production of the Luso-Hispanic World* 5, no. 3 (2015): 44.

145. Lafarga, "Mariam Hassan."

146. Vivian Solana Moreno, "'No somos costosas. Somos valiosas': La lucha de las mujeres saharauis 40 años después," in *Sahara Occidental: 40 años después*, ed. Isaías Barreñada and Raquel Ojeda (Madrid: Catarata, 2016), 83.

147. Saleh, 11 December 2015.

148. Allan, "Imagining Saharawi Women," 198.

149. Women's Section, "Informe que presenta la delegada provincial de la Sección Femenina, de los hechos ocurridos en el Taller Escuela a este Gobierno General de Sahara," 2.

150. Women's Section, "Informe sobre situación en el Taller-Escuela 'Confecciones Sahara,'" El Aaiún, 6 February 1974.

151. Anonymous Social Worker, "Informe del primer semestre de 1974," 3.

152. Saleh, 11 December 2015.

153. Concha Mateo, Letter from Concha Mateo to Soledad de Santiago in Madrid, El Aaiún, 22 October 1974.

154. Esteban Carvallo de Cora y Romero, Territorial Police, "Informando sobre disturbios ocurridos en el día de hoy," El Aaiún, 20 November 1974.

155. Anne Lippert, "Sahrawi Women in the Liberation Struggle of the Sahrawi People," *Signs* 17, no. 3 (1992): 640.

156. Mateo, "Informe sobre la actitud política," 5. The "people" of the Liberation Front is translated from the original "los chicos," which I assume refers to both women and men.

157. Dafa and Bouzeid argue in this vein in written publications, but several Sahrawi women (and men) also debate this on social media.

158. Bengochea Tirado, "Políticas imperiales."

159. Indeed, in 1976 POLISARIO was to discourage marriage before the age of sixteen. Allan, "Imagining Saharawi Women," 191.

160. Dalmases, *Esclavitud*, 15–16.

161. Saleh, 11 December 2015.

162. Bilaal, 11 December 2015; Saleh, 11 December 2015.

163. Leila Sidi Mahmoud, personal interview, Auserd camp, 12 December 2015.

164. Bilaal, 11 December 2015; Saleh, 11 December 2015.

165. Women's Section, "Informe correspondiente a la labor realizada por el departamento de promoción el 1er semestre de 1975," El Aaiún, June 1975.

166. Spanish Administration, "Nota informativa al Gobierno General de Sahara," El Aaiún, 7 July 1975.

167. United Nations General Assembly (UNGA), "'Report of the United Nations Visiting Mission to Spanish Sahara, 1975' in The Report of the Special Committee on the Situation with Regard to the Implementation of the Declaration on the Granting of Independence to Colonial Countries and Peoples," 1975, 59.

168. Mateo cited in Joanna Allan, "Natural Resources and Intifada: Oil, Phosphates and Resistance to Colonialism in Western Sahara," *Journal of North African Studies* 21, no. 4 (2016): 649.

169. Mateo, "Informe sobre la actitud política," 9.

170. Carvallo de Cora y Romero, Esteban, Territorial Police, "Informe sobre reunion con estudiantes," El Aaiún, 30 January 1975.

171. Spanish Administration, "Nota informativa al Gobierno general de Sahara."

172. Ibid.

173. On 18 January 1975, for example, thirteen young Saharawi women appeared at the government office of Villa Cisneros with complaints concerning the quality and scope of Women's Section courses and the disrespect shown to them by the Spanish teachers. Spanish Government South Delegation, "Nota informativa a delegación gubernativa sur," Villa Cisneros, 24 January 1975; Saharawi Women, Document addressed to the Spanish colonial government signed "Mujeres Saharauis," El Aaiún, 12 October 1975. See also Saharawi Women, Document addressed to the Spanish colonial government signed "Mujeres Saharauis," El Aaiún, 12 October 1975.

174. Spanish Government South Delegation, "Nota informativa a delegación gubernativa sur."

175. Using gender identities to mobilize resistance among women (and men) is not unusual in nationalist movements. As Nadje al-Ali and Nicola Pratt point out, the actions of politicians and armed groups are dependent on their ability to mobilize citizens using nationalist or religious identities that draw on gender in specific ways. Nadje Al-Ali and Nicola Pratt, "Between Nationalism and Women's Rights: The Kurdish Women's Movement in Iraq," *Middle East Journal of Culture and Communication* 4, no. 3 (2011): 338.

176. Interviewees recall individual cases of Spaniards acting to support the Saharawi nationalist struggle that range from reporting to Saharawis on the secret Tripartite Agreements, writing pro-Saharawi editorials (Tawfa claims that a Spanish colleague of hers was imprisoned for such an "offense"), joining in nationalist protests, refusing to treat members of the PUNS who had been beaten by Saharawi nationalists, raising the Saharawi flag, and defecting to the POLISARIO. As for the Women's Section, interviewees say that those in the organization remained fervently pro-Spanish colonialism. Nevertheless, Khadijatou Mokhtar, now leader of the UNMS's external engagement, has come across some of the former Women's Section Spanish teachers at UNMS conferences held in Spain. Reportedly, these formerly Francoist women have told her that they are now supportive of Saharawi independence.

177. Mateo, "Informe sobre la actitud política," 14.

178. Moroccan forces had in fact already invaded the northeast corner of Western Sahara, ahead of the Green March. See Jacob Mundy, "How the US and Morocco Seized the Spanish Sahara," *Le Monde Diplomatique*, January 2006.

179. Baba Miské, *Front Polisario*, 196–97. The Spanish state continued to receive royalties from the phosphate mines until 2006.

180. Women's Section, "Informe que presenta la Delegación Nacional de la Sección Femenina sobre las actividades con especial relieve," Madrid, July 1975. Even if Spain had not given the Sahara to Morocco, the government did not react well to Saharawi staff suggested by Women's Section, since all were seen as pro-POLISARIO.

181. Women's Section, no title [handwritten notes on plain paper], El Aaiún, 23 October 1975.

182. The Provincial Delegate, "Communication regarding the closure of the Women's Section," El Aaiún, 29 October 1975.

183. Montse Escorbe (also known by the name Hurria, given to her by Saharawis as an honor), Gurutze Irizar (aka Fatimetu), and Ana Gaspar, for example, joined the Saharawis in their struggle. For their testimonies, see Carlos Martín Beristain and Eloísa González Hidalgo, *El oasis de la memoria: Memoria histórica y violaciones de Derechos Humanos en el Sáhara Occidental*, vol. 1 (Bilbao: Hegoa, 2012).

184. The Spanish colonization of Equatorial Guinea was a cultural one to an infinitely greater extent than that of Western Sahara.

Chapter 2. Women's Resistance and Gender in Spanish Guinea

1. Walter Rodney, *How Europe Underdeveloped Africa* (Washington, DC: Howard University Press, 1982), 274.

2. Eugenio Nkogo Ondó, "La Guinea Ecuatorial: Reminiscencia histórica, experiencia de las luces y de las sombras de un proyecto político" (paper presented at the conference Between Three Continents: Rethinking Equatorial Guinea on the Fortieth Anniversary of Its Independence from Spain, Hofstra University, 2009); Gustau Nerín, *La última selva de España: Antropódagos, misioneros y guardias civiles* (Madrid: Catarata, 2010); Donato Ndongo-Bidyogo, *Historia y Tragedia de Guinea Ecuatorial* (Madrid: Cambio 16, 1977); Enrique Okenve, "Equatorial Guinea 1927–1979: A New African Tradition" (PhD diss., School of Oriental and African Studies [SOAS], University of London, 2007); Ibrahim Sundiata, *From Slaving to Neoslavery: The Bight of Biafra and Fernando Po in the Era of Abolition, 1827–1930* (Madison: University of Wisconsin Press, 1996); Cristina Dyombe Dyangani, *Identidad Cultural Ndowe* (New York: Ndowe International Press, 2008) (pages 41 to 45 of this book look at the contributions of Ndowe men to the fight for independence); Adolfo Obiang Biko, *Equatorial Guinea: From Spanish Colonialism to the Discovery of Oil* (New York: O. Writers, 2010); Alicia Campos Serrano, "The Decolonization of Equatorial Guinea: The Relevance of the International Factor," *Journal of African History* 44 (2003); Enrique Martino, "Clandestine Recruitment Networks in the Bight of Biafra: Fernando Pó's Answer to the Labour Question, 1926–1945," *Internationaal Instituut voor Sociale Geschiedenis (IRSH)* 57, special issue (2012).

3. Cécile Stephanie Stehrenberger, "Folklore, Nation, and Gender in a Colonial Encounter: Coros y Danzas of the Sección Femenina of the Falange in Equatorial Guinea," *Afro-Hispanic Review* 28, no. 2 (2009): 238–39; Rosa Medina-Doménech, "Scientific Technologies of National Identity as Colonial Legacies: Extracting the Spanish Nation from Equatorial Guinea," *Social Studies of Science* 39, no. 1 (2009): 96; see also Sampedro Vizcaya and Baltasar Fra-Molinero's edition of Raquel Ilombe's poetry,

*Ceiba II (Poesía Inédita)* (Madrid: Verbum, 2015), and Sipi Mey's publishing house Editorial Mey, which features Equatoguinean women's writing.

4. Veronica Mayo (pseudonym), personal conversations, Malabo, 29 June 2015.

5. Trinidad Mba (pseudonym), personal interview, Malabo, 16 June 2015.

6. Francisca Sale (pseudonym), personal communication, 28 May 2015.

7. Spivak, "Can the Subaltern Speak?," 82–83. On the domination of the lives and deeds of white men in history, see also Sheila Rowbotham, *Hidden from History: 300 Years of Women's Oppression and the Fight against It* (London: Pluto Press, 1975); Padma Anagol, *The Emergence of Feminism in India, 1850–1920* (Burlington, VT: Ashgate Publishing, 2005).

8. Liddle, "Feminism, Imperialism and Orientalism," 512.

9. For colonial accounts of Guinean societies see, for example, Julio Arija Martinez de Espinosa, *La Guinea española y sus riquezas* (Buenos Aires: Espasa-Calpe, 1930); Antonio Aymemí, *Los Bubis en Fernando Poo: Colección de los artículos publicados en la revista colonial "La Guinea Española"* (Madrid: Galo Sáez, 1942). On women's subordinate status, see, for example, Fernando Ballano Gonzalo, *Aquel Negrito de África Tropical: El Colonialismo en Guinea (1778–1968)* (Madrid: Sial Ediciones, 2014). Ballano's very well researched historiography of the colonial period paints a grim picture of the lives of Equatoguinean women but draws little attention to how they resisted discrimination. Similarly, Nerín's groundbreaking work on gender relations during the colonial period highlights the extremely negative (and long-lasting) impact of colonialism on Equatoguinean women's lives, but their agency receives relatively little attention. Gustau Nerín, *Guinea Ecuatorial, historia en blanco y negro* (Barcelona: Ediciones Península, 1998).

10. Mayka De Castro, "El Colonialismo franquista en Guinea Ecuatorial: Una lectura crítica en clave decolonial" (master's thesis, University of Granada, September 2013); Medina-Doménech, "Scientific Technologies"; Nerín, *Guinea Ecuatorial.*

11. Pseudonym.

12. Francisca Sale (pseudonym), personal conversations, Malabo, 25 June 2015.

13. Sale (pseudonym), 25 June 2015.

14. The Catholic Claretians dominated the missionary scene in Equatorial Guinea from the 1850s until the Spanish exit. By the time of World War I, they had a post in Annobón, five along Rio Muni's coast, and seven in Fernando Po. The Claretians were hostile to the (mostly British) Protestants who had preceded them. The English Baptists left in 1958. In 1920 there was one American Presbyterian station in Rio Muni, five English Methodist posts on Fernando Po, and one French Roman Catholic mission in Bata on the continent. Foreign Office of the British Government, "Spanish Guinea," *Peace Handbooks* 20, no. 125 (1920); William G. Clarence-Smith, "Spanish Equatorial Guinea, 1898–1940," in *The Cambridge History of Africa: From 1905 to 1940*, ed. Arthur D. Roberts (Cambridge: Cambridge University Press, 1986).

15. Banapá Mission of Claretians, *La Revista de la Guinea Española*, 12 January 1904.

16. Igor Cusack, "Equatorial Guinea: The Inculcation and Maintenance of Hispanic Culture," Bristol, 1997, 15.

17. Ndongo quoted in ibid.

18. David Aworawo, "Decisive Thaw: The Changing Pattern of Relations between Nigeria and Equatorial Guinea, 1980–2005," *Journal of International and Global Studies* 1, no. 2 (2010): 92.

19. Martino, "Clandestine Recruitment," 40.

20. René Pélissier, *Los territorios españoles de Africa* (Madrid: Consejo Superior de Investigaciones Científicas, 1964).

21. See, for example, Lola Martins, "Journey to Hell's Island: How It All Started," *Express*, Lagos, 21 February 1962; Peter Pan, "The Brutal Island," *Sunday Times*, Lagos, 18 February 1962; Isaac Pepple, "Free Ticket to Hell," *Drum*, Lagos, April 1957.

22. An observation from the British vice-consulate in Fernando Po helps to underline that robbery specifically opposed the Spanish plantation owners, since laborers did not tend to rob each other. In a letter back to the commissioner of labor in Lagos, the vice-consulate said, "It seems that the saying that there is honour among thieves is very apt in this case, for whereas all labourers seem to consider robbing their employers as all in a day's work, they do not rob each other with the same monotonous regularity." W. M. Bradley, "Labour Report to the Honourable Commissioner of Labour, Lagos, No. 3 for the Period 1st of October to the 31st December 1949," Santa Isabel, 11 January 1950. The British vice-consulate reported cases of Nigerian laborers cutting themselves to encourage the consulate to take action against Spanish plantation owners. See, for example, W. M. Bradley, "Labour Report to the Honourable Commissioner of Labour, Lagos, No. 1 for the Period 1st January to 31st March 1950, British Vice Consulate," Santa Isabel, 31 March 1950. See also Martino, "Clandestine Recruitment," 56.

23. Saheed Aderinto's research into Nigerian migrant sex workers/prostitutes in colonial British West Africa is illuminating, from the spectrum of agency at one end to outright trafficking of girl children for sexual exploitation at the other. Saheed Aderinto, "Journey to Work: Transnational Prostitution in Colonial British West Africa," *Journal of the History of Sexuality* 24, no. 1 (2015).

24. Bradley, "Labour Report to the Honourable Commissioner of Labour, Lagos, No. 3."

25. Bradley, "Labour Report to the Honourable Commissioner of Labour, Lagos, No. 1."

26. Women have a history of taking recourse to the colonial apparatus in various colonial contexts. British India is a famous example. See Padma Anagol, "From the Symbolic to the Open: Women's Resistance in Colonial Maharashtra," in *Behind the Veil: Resistance, Women, and the Everyday in Colonial South Asia*, ed. Ghosh Anindita (London: Palgrave Macmillan, 2008).

27. Aymemí, *Los Bubis*, 49. Although this case is fascinating, we should approach it with wariness: Aymemí states that the woman's crime was unfaithfulness. However, the death penalty for disloyalty to one's husband was very unusual in Bubi culture. Perhaps Aymemí had exaggerated the story to fuel the genderwashing of colonial pursuits. On the other hand, it was indeed common for missionaries to take in women escaping abuse and coerced marriage.

28. As Nugent has highlighted, although they would not admit it, many colonial regimes settled for less than their envisaged "civilizing mission" as they were loath to invest resources in curbing the "native" dissent that could be provoked. We saw this dynamic strongly in Spanish Sahara, but, to a lesser extent, it was present in Spanish

Guinea. Paul Nugent, "States and Social Contracts in Africa," *New Left Review* 63 (2010): 44.

29. Illegible signature, Letter to the Governor General of the Spanish Territories of the Gulf of Guinea, En Mikomeseng, 15 May 1945.

30. Okenve, "Equatorial Guinea 1927–1979," 126.

31. Okenve finds that divorce was difficult for Fang women. However, Edouard Trezenem, a French ethnographer who wrote of Fangs living in Gabon in 1936, tells a different story. He finds that there were some incidents where women could obtain a divorce. Here, I privilege in the main text the Equatoguinean historian over the ethnography from colonial times and do so throughout this chapter, but for Trezenem's perspective, see Edouard Trezenem, "Notes Ethnographiques sur les Tribus Fan du Moyen Ogooué (Gabon)," *Journal de la Société des Africanistes* 6, no. 1 (1936): 89–90.

32. Okenve, "Equatorial Guinea 1927–1979," 220.

33. See chapter 18 of Günther Tessmann, *Los Pamues (Los Fang): Monografía etnológica de una rama de las tribus negras del Africa Occidental* (1913; repr., Alcalá de Henares: Universidad de Alcalá, 2003).

34. Okenve, "Equatorial Guinea 1927–1979," 220.

35. Ibid., 76.

36. James W. Fernandez, *Bwiti: An Ethnography of the Religious Imagination in Africa* (Princeton, NJ: Princeton University Press, 1982), 147; Robert Klinteberg, *Equatorial Guinea, Macías Country: The Forgotten Refugees* (Geneva: International University Exchange Fund [IUEF], 1978), 7.

37. Sundiata, *From Slaving to Neoslavery*, 163–64.

38. University of Granada Media, video of Remei Sipi Mayo in conversation with Benita Sampedro, 20 June 2016, http://www.asodeguesegundaetapa.org/la-huella-de -la-colonizacion-espanola-en-las-mujeres-de-guinea-ecuatorial-remei-sipi-y-benita -sampedro-ugrmedia/.

39. Ana Alogo Mikue (pseudonym), telephone interview, 22 August 2016.

40. Aymemí, *Los Bubis*, 69.

41. 20 Chiefs of Rio Benito, Letter to the General Governor of the Spanish Territories in the Gulf of Guinea, Bata, Rio Muni (continental Guinea), 9 June 1942.

42. Some men still practice this form of hyperhospitality, offering wives, concubines, or female relatives in order to strengthen economic or political alliances. See Nerín, *Guinea Ecuatorial*.

43. Ibid.

44. Ballano Gonzalo, *Aquel Negrito*, 188.

45. Medina-Doménech, "Scientific Technologies," 88.

46. Ballano Gonzalo, *Aquel Negrito*, 188–90.

47. Ayakaba Nzue, Request from Ayakaba Nzue to the President of the Native Patronato for Separation from Her Husband, Santa Isabel, Fernando Po, 12 May 1937.

48. Secretary of the Patronato, "Comparencia," Santa Isabel, Fernando Po, 8 June 1937.

49. Secretary of the Patronato, "Comparencia," Santa Isabel, Fernando Po, 9 June 1937.

50. Secretary of the Patronato, "Comparencia," Santa Isabel, Fernando Po, 23 June 1937.

51. Another case a month earlier, that of Mangue Emba, who wrote to the Patronato begging for help and fearing for her life at the hands of her brutal husband, is very similar to that of Nchama Nsono's. Mangue Emba, Request Sent to the President of Patronato, 13 May 1937.

52. There appeared to be a gap between law and practice. The Spanish prohibited the marriage of "native" girl children before puberty by decree in 1928, according to Ballano Gonzalo, *Aquel Negrito*, 356. This decree, however, did not take into account Fang cultural norms that sought to protect girls from sexual abuse, at least before puberty: although, as in many societies, children were given in marriage to other families (and unborn children were promised), it was taboo to have sex with one's wife before she had her first period. Nevertheless, the girls suffered trauma, as Okenve notes. Okenve, "Equatorial Guinea 1927–1979," 126. For more on Fang customs in marriage and sexuality, see Fernandez, *Bwiti*.

53. Pseudonym.

54. Pilar Nyangi (pseudonym), personal interview, Malabo, 21 June 2015.

55. Baltasar Fra-Molinero, "De libros: CEIBA II. Regreso al país natal," *Atanga*, 2015.

56. Martino, "Nsoa ('dote')."

57. Joanna Allan, "El colonialismo y el patriarcado en la literatura afrohispana: Los escritos de resistencia de Lehdia Dafa y María Nsue Angüe," in *Trans-afrohispanos: Puentes culturales críticos entre África, Latinoamérica y España*, ed. Dorothy Odartey-Wellington (Leiden: Brill, 2018), 137–51.

58. Baltasar Fra-Molinero, "El deber de contar y la pasión de escribir: Entrevista a María Nsue Angüe," 10 June 2010.

59. María Nsue Angüe, *Ekomo* (Madrid: UNED, 1985), 164.

60. Okenve, "Equatorial Guinea 1927–1979," 127. Similarly, James W. Fernandez found that it was the "control of men over women that Fang felt to have been most disturbed by colonial contact." He goes on: "A constant complaint of village life was the escape of women from fathers' and husbands' supervision." Fernandez, *Bwiti*, 147.

61. Okenve, "Equatorial Guinea 1927–1979," 127.

62. Pseudonym.

63. The people of northeast Rio Muni were under curfew at this time. Ana Alogo Mikue (pseudonym), telephone interview, 22 August 2016.

64. Mba (pseudonym), 16 June 2015. However, Mba is keen to emphasize that although Fang women had this space to claim rights as a *wife* or *mother*, there was no such space to claim their rights *as women*.

65. The Fang *abáá*, the Bubi *wedjaa*, and the Annobonese *vidjil* were the respective seats of political power in each village. One commonality between the three was the infrequence of inviting women to participate in discussions there. However, I do not presume to suggest that women did not have other, less formal channels of political influence.

66. For more on how the Spanish violently attacked Rio Muni, and the forced labor subsequently practiced there, see Nerín, *Guinea Ecuatorial*, 55.

67. For Bubi resistance to missionaries and the colonials more generally, see chapter 9 of Sundiata, *From Slaving to Neoslavery*.

68. Banapá Mission of Claretians, *La Revista de la Guinea Española*, 28 March 1904, 2–3.

69. Yolanda Aixelà Cabré, "Africanas en el mundo contemporáneo: Las mujeres de Guinea Ecuatorial," in *Introducción a Los Estudios Africanos*, ed. Y. Aixelà, L. L. Mallart, and J. Martí (Barcelona: CEIBA, 2009). For further examples of Bubi resistance to the missionaries, see Aymemí, *Los Bubis*.

70. Nerín, *Guinea Ecuatorial*, 57.

71. Ibid.

72. Ibid.; José Francisco Eteo Soriso, *Cancionero Tradicional de Bioko* (Barcelona: Ceiba Ediciones, 2008), 100.

73. Justo Bolekia Boleká, personal communication, 13 April 2017; Justo Bolekia Boleká, *Recuerdos del abuelo Bayebé y otros relatos bubis* (Madrid: Sial Ediciones, 2014), 149.

74. This was how Ignacio Nsue Enhate (pseudonym) described the dance to me in our interview on 1 April 2014. This is the "official," current regime view of the dance, as also told in the government-endorsed history of Equatorial Guinea: Rosendo-Ela Nsue Mibui, *Historia de la Guinea Ecuatorial: Periodo Pre-Colonial* (Madrid: Gráficas Algoran, 2005), 133. Anthropologist James W. Fernandez has a different take on this dance, however, and does not necessarily attach it to anticolonialism. For more on this, and other Fang dance traditions, see Fernandez, *Bwiti*, 141–45. Enènge A'Bodjedi offers yet another interpretation of the dance, finding that the dancers mocked colonial men, specifically religious figures who wore "women's dress" (long white robes). See Enènge A'Bodjedi, "El sexo y la violencia: El caso de Masié Nguema Biyogo," *Oráfrica, revista de oralidad africana* 6 (2010).

75. Remei Sipi Mayo recalls the tradition of grandmothers and mothers passing on folktales and has begun to document modern women's short stories. See, for example, Remei Sipi Mayo, "Ribocho: Identidad y encuentro," in *Baiso: Ellas y sus relatos*, ed. Remei Sipi Mayo (Barcelona: Editorial Mey, 2015).

76. Nsue Angüe, *Ekomo*; Maria Luisa Iriarte, "Informe del curso 1967–1968," Santa Isabel, 25 May 1968.

77. Donato Ndongo-Bidyogo, "El Gobernador Faustino Ruiz González y el nacionalismo en Guinea Ecuatorial" (paper presented at the Seminario Internacional Actores coloniales españoles y espacios africanos SS, 19–20, University of Alcalá, 2–3 December 2010), 7.

78. Ibid., 1.

79. Although I know little of her backstory, the mother of the late writer María Nsué Angüe, Alfonsina Mangue, was in prison in 1948 for such "crimes." See Joanna Allan, "María Nsue Angüe," in *The Literary Encyclopedia*, vol. 8.2.2., ed. Helen Rachel Cousins, accessed 19 April 2017, http://www.litencyc.com/php/speople.php?rec=true& UID=138772017.

80. Nkogo Ondó, "Guinea Ecuatorial," 2.

81. Campos Serrano, "Decolonization of Equatorial Guinea," 101.

82. Ibid., 97.

83. Campos argues that it was *the* key reason. Ibid., 114.

84. Historian Agustín Nze Nfumu has looked at the effect of other African independence revolutions on Equatoguineans. Agustín Nze Nfumu, *Macías, verdugo o víctima* (Madrid: Herrero y Asociados, 2004), 18.

85. Suzanne Cronjé, *Equatorial Guinea: The Forgotten Dictatorship* (London: Anti-Slavery Society, 1976), 9–10.

86. Nkogo Ondó, "Guinea Ecuatorial," 2; Rosa Pardo Sanz, "La herencia de la descolonización del África española," in *Europe face à son passé colonial*, ed. Olivier Dard and Daniel Lefeuvre (Paris: Riveneuve Editions, 2008), 181.

87. Nze Nfumu, *Macías*, 18; ibid., 19.

88. Nkogo Ondó, "Guinea Ecuatorial," 3.

89. Ibid.

90. Cronjé, *Forgotten Dictatorship*, 11.

91. Alogo Mikue (pseudonym), 22 August 2016.

92. Obiang Biko, *Equatorial Guinea*, 79; Nkogo Ondó, "Guinea Ecuatorial," 6.

93. Maria Jesus Ntutumu (pseudonym), personal interview, Malabo, 16 June 2015; Remei Sipi Mayo, "Introducción," in *Voces femeninas de Guinea Ecuatorial: Una antología*, ed. Remei Sipi Mayo (Barcelona: Ediciones Mey, 2015), 10.

94. Constancia Balboa (pseudonym), personal interview, Malabo, 22 June 2015.

95. Sipi Mayo, "Introducción," 10; Sale (pseudonym), 25 June 2015.

96. Frantz Fanon's analysis of women's role in the Algerian revolution, facilitated, in some ways, because of French sexist and racist attitudes that saw Algerian women as backward, submissive, and incapable of political activity, has inspired similar studies in a whole range of contexts. Frantz Fanon, *A Dying Colonialism* (New York: Grove, 1967).

97. Alogo Mikue (pseudonym), 22 August 2016.

98. Anne Laurence, *Women in England, 1500–1760: A Social History* (London: Phoenix Press, 2002), 248.

99. Alicia Campos Serrano, "Nacionalismo Anticolonial en Guinea Ecuatorial: De Españoles a Guineanos," *Araucaria* 5, no. 9 (2003): 4.

100. Salvador López de la Torre, "El referéndum de Guinea Ecuatorial ha sido un verdadero ejemplo para todos los pueblos de Africa," *ABC*, Madrid, 17 December 1963.

101. Ballano Gonzalo, *Aquel Negrito*, 576.

102. Nkogo Ondó, "Guinea Ecuatorial," 7.

103. MUNGE, "Movimiento de Unión Nacional de la Guinea Ecuatorial (MUNGE), Declaración de principios," Madrid, 18 January 1964. For an example of Spain's positive lauding of the MUNGE, see Jose Salas Guirior, "Viaje a las Sombras de España," *ABC*, Madrid, 7 March 1976.

104. MUNGE, "Declaración," 5.

105. Campos Serrano, "Decolonization of Equatorial Guinea," 102.

106. María Nieves Sunyer, "Informe de la inspección a Fernando Poo realizada por la Regidora Central de Juventudes del 4 al 8 de Marzo de 1965," Santa Isabel de Fernando Po, 17 March 1965, 2.

107. Ibid., 4.

108. Okenve, "Equatorial Guinea 1927–1979," 285.

109. Ballano Gonzalo, *Aquel Negrito*, 590.

110. The strike dates were 21–23 April 1966. Campos Serrano, "Decolonization of Equatorial Guinea," 105.

111. Carmen Obón, Letter to Soledad de Santiago, Bata, 1 February 1968.

112. Campos Serrano, "Decolonization of Equatorial Guinea," 111.

113. Juan María Calvo, "Guinea Ecuatorial: La ocasión perdida," Asociación para la solidaridad democrática con Guinea Ecuatorial (ASODEGUE), 1989, http://www .asodegue.org/hdojmc.htm; Nze Nfumu, *Macías*, 18.

114. Nkogo Ondó, "Guinea Ecuatorial."

115. Murray Steele quoted in Anne Foot, "A Policy of Plunder: The Development and Normalisation of Neo-Patrimonialism in Equatorial Guinea" (master's thesis, Stellenbosch University, 2014), 49.

116. Campos Serrano, "Decolonization of Equatorial Guinea," 102.

117. Nze Nfumu, *Macías*, 130.

118. Ndongo-Bidyogo, "Gobernador Faustino," 15.

119. Edmundo Bosio Dioco and Ricardo Bolopá, Letter, Madrid, 20 June 1968.

120. The extent to which this history was imagined or "real" is not the main question here but, rather, the POLISARIO's ability to make hegemonic its own vision of the nation's history. It seems undeniable, though, that the Saharawi tribes enjoyed several political, cultural, religious, and linguistic commonalities that the various ethnicities of Equatorial Guinea did not.

121. An ethnic group is usefully defined by Anthony Smith as "a type of cultural collectivity, one that emphasizes the role of myths of descent and historical memories, and that is recognized by one or more cultural differences like religion, customs, language, or institutions." Anthony Smith, *National Identity* (Reno: University of Nevada Press, 1991), 20.

122. Nze Nfumu, *Macías*.

123. Cusack, "Being Away from 'Home.'" Indeed, Obiang studied at the infamous Military Academy of Zaragoza.

124. Nze Nfumu, *Macías*, 21–26.

125. Enrique Gori Molubela, Letter to Teresa Loring, Santa Isabel de Fernando Po, 22 September 1964. As Cécile Stephanie Stehrenberger has highlighted, Women's Section dance groups had visited Equatorial Guinea before this date to perform for "natives" and "Europeans" alike. Stehrenberger, "Folklore, Nation, and Gender."

126. Teresa Loring (Sub-delegada Nacional de la Sección Femenina), Letter to Antonio Trujillo, Madrid, 27 April 1964; Dolores Bermúdez Cañete, "Informe del viaje de la Regidora Central de S.E.U. a la isla de Fernando Poo y Rio Muni," May 1964, 2.

127. Women's Section, "Sección Femenina," Santa Isabel, March 1967, 2.

128. See, for example, Iriarte, "Informe del curso 1967–1968"; Women's Section, "Proyecto de curso en regimen de internado para muchachas o señoras casadas, nativas de las provincias africanas," Madrid, December 1964.

129. Iriarte, "Informe del curso 1967–1968," 4.

130. University of Granada Media, video of Remei Sipi Mayo in conversation with Benita Sampedro.

131. Nerín, *Guinea Ecuatorial*, 115.

132. Purita García Morales, Letter to Soledad de Santiago, Bata, 4 April 1965.

133. When deciding which girls would go to Spain for the 1964/65 school year, Angeles Mallado precluded girls who had had abortions and who were rumored to be sexually active from the selection process. See Angeles Mallado, Letter to Dolores Bermudez Cañete, Santa Isabel, 22 June 1964.

134. María Nieves Sunyer, "Informe de la inspección a Rio Muni realizada por la Regidora Central de Juventudes del 4 al 8 de Marzo de 1965," Bata, 8 March 1965, 2.

135. Foot, "Policy of Plunder."

136. On study grants, see Soledad de Santiago, Letter to "Mina" ("Auxiliar Central de Juventudes"), Madrid, 27 May 1967; Rafael M. Matala, Letter to Soledad de Santiago, Santa Isabel, 20 April 1967; Teresa Loring, Letter to Federico Ngomo Nandongo, Madrid, 10 May 1965; Soledad de Santiago, Letter to Carmen Obón, Madrid, 22 March 1967; Soledad de Santiago, Letter to Carmen Obón, Madrid, 17 June 1967; Soledad de Santiago, Letter to Carmen Obón, Madrid, 15 July 1967; Soledad de Santiago, Letter to Carmen Obón, Bata, 29 February 1968. There are no such similar examples from the archives of the Women's Section in the Sahara. On recruiting "native" teachers, see Dolores Bermúdez Cañete, Letter to Soledad de Santiago, Bata, 8 July 1964.

137. Women's Section, Letter to Soledad de Santiago, Santa Isabel, 11 March 1968.

138. Stucki, "Hard Side of Soft Power," 13.

139. Women's Section, "School report of Adela Ntang Nbeng, 1966–67," Castellón, 1967; Women's Section, "School report of Carmen Eyenga Mba-Oyana, 1966–67," Castellón, 1967.

140. Pilar Ozores, "School report of Angela Nefiri Bacale Usuru," Madrid, 5 April 1968; Women's Section, "School report of Florentina Ntutumu Nchama," Las Navas del Marques School, Avila, 11 April 1968; Women's Section, "School report of Rosario Tomos Coffi," Heroinas de los Sitios School, Gerona, 4 March 1967.

141. Daniel A. McFarland, "Student Resistance: How the Formal and Informal Organization of Classrooms Facilitate Everyday Forms of Student Defiance," *American Journal of Sociology* 107, no. 3 (2001).

142. Ibid.

143. Maria Jesus Ntutumu (pseudonym), personal conversation, Malabo, 19 June 2015.

144. See, for example, the complaints of one Women's Section employee about disobedience among Equatoguinean students in Madrid, sneaking out, ignoring curfews, etc.: María Inés Pineda Barrantes, Letter to Soledad de Santiago, Aranjuez, 28 May 1968.

145. Maria Luisa Iriarte, Letter to Soledad de Santiago, Santa Isabel, 6 November 1967; Obón, Letter to Soledad de Santiago, 1 February 1968.

146. Carmen Obón, Letter to Soledad de Santiago (1), Bata, 22 February 1969.

147. Tentor described women as "not very grateful" for the classes (Letter to Soledad de Santiago, Santa Isabel, 17 April 1967.) A report on activities in Rio Muni from September 1965 states, "The women . . . were arriving late for class, an hour late, and for any (small, from our point of view) reason, they would not turn up for class at all." Carmen Obón, "Informe de las cátedras realizadas en la provincia de Rio Muni por los equipos de la Delegación Nacional de la Sección Femenina," Bata, September 1965, 2.

148. Carmen Obón, Letter to Soledad de Santiago, Santa Isabel, 8 August 1967.

149. Concha Tentor, Letter to Soledad de Santiago, Santa Isabel, 26 February 1966.

150. Women's Section, Letter to Soledad de Santiago, 11 March 1968.

151. See Alba Valenciano-Mañé, "Vestido, identidad y folklore: La invención de un vestido nacional de Guinea Ecuatorial," *Revista de Dialectología y Tradiciones Populares* 67, no. 1 (2012): 280.

152. Soledad de Santiago, "Guión para la visita de la delegación nacional a las provincias de Africa," Madrid, 23 January 1967.

153. Mallado, Letter to Dolores Bermudez Cañete, 22 June 1964.

## Chapter 3. Saharawi Women's Resistance in the Diaspora

1. Sidi Mahmoud, 12 December 2015.

2. Martín Beristain and González Hidalgo, *El oasis*, vol. 1, 127.

3. Ibid., 137.

4. Sidi Mahmoud, 12 December 2015. Several other eye witnesses make the same observation in Martín Beristain and González Hidalgo, *El Oasis*, vol. 1.

5. This point is argued more forcefully by Martín Beristain and González Hidalgo, *El Oasis*, vol. 1, 102.

6. Lbjuali quoted in San Martín, *Refugee Nation*, 108.

7. Bilaal, 11 December 2015; Saleh, 11 December 2015.

8. Alejandro García, Historias del Sahara: El Mejor y el Peor de los Mundos (Madrid: Catarata, 2001), 240.

9. Gisela Kaplan, "Feminism and Nationalism: The European Case," in *Feminist Nationalism*, ed. Lois A. West (New York: Routledge, 1997), 3. Jelena Batinic has explored Western discourses on the Yugoslav conflicts in this vein. Jelena Batinic, "Feminism, Nationalism, and War: The 'Yugoslav Case' in Feminist Texts," *Journal of International Women's Studies* 3, no. 1 (2001).

10. Lois A. West, ed., *Feminist Nationalism* (London: Routledge, 1997); Seodu Herr, "Reclaiming Third World Feminism."

11. Al-Ali and Pratt, "Between Nationalism and Women's Rights."

12. Limam Boicha, 'Galb,' translated by Ed Atkins (original in Spanish). The poem is reproduced here with the kind permission of Limam Boicha.

13. This section is derived in part from Allan, "Imagining Saharawi Women."

14. Benedict Anderson, *Imagined Communities: Reflections on the Origin and Spread of Nationalism* (London: Verso, 2006.)

15. Howarth, *Discourse: Concepts*, 3.

16. Gramsci, *Prison Notebooks*.

17. Pablo San Martín, "Nationalism, Identity and Citizenship in the Western Sahara," *Journal of North African Studies* 10, no. 3/4 (2005): 569.

18. García, *Historias del Sahara*, 135.

19. Ernesto Laclau, "Ideology and Post-Marxism," *Journal of Political Ideologies* 11, no. 2 (2006).

20. Gillian Hart, "Changing Concepts of Articulation: Political Stakes in South Africa Today," *Review of African Political Economy* 34, no. 111 (2007): 91.

21. Pablo San Martín, "Is Nationalism an Ideology? A Critical Exploration from the Asturian Case," 2007 (unpublished paper in author's possession).

22. POLISARIO, "La opinión de las masas: *Boletín* Especial 20 de Mayo" (1976), 4.

23. POLISARIO, "El Pueblo: *Boletín* 1" (1974), 4; POLISARIO, "La opinión de las masas: *Boletín* Especial 20 de Mayo," 4.

24. J. R. Diego Aguirre, *Guerra en el Sáhara* (Madrid: Ediciones ISTMO, 1991); POLISARIO, "SADR Constitution," 1999, SADR National Archive, accessed 14 May 2008, www.arso.org/03-const.99.htm.

25. Michael Freeden's concept of decontestation stems from the idea that political concepts (such as justice, freedom, or democracy) have no fixed and definite meaning but are constructed concepts. The task of any ideological operation is, therefore, to partially "fix" the meaning of such concepts in order to make them appear definite and inherent and, thereby, encourage a particular way of seeing society. Michael Freeden, *Ideologies and Political Theory: A Conceptual Approach* (Oxford: Oxford University Press, 1996).

26. See, for example, POLISARIO, "Sahara Libre," no. 178 (1983), 4.

27. POLISARIO, "El Pueblo," *Boletín* 1, 3.

28. Ibid., 8.

29. POLISARIO, "La opinión de las masas: *Boletín* Especial 20 de Mayo," 6; POLISARIO, "La opinión de las masas: *Boletín* no. 7" (1976), 3; POLISARIO, "La opinión de las masas: *Boletín* Especial 20 de Mayo," 3.

30. POLISARIO, "La opinión de las masas: Boletín no. 8" (1976), 5.

31. UNMS cited in POLISARIO, "Sahara Libre," nos. 240–241 (1985), 4.

32. The "success story," a supposed achievement that is exaggerated, mythified, and elevated to the position of a perfect example, or indisputable piece of evidence, is often employed by politicians to justify certain policies or decisions and to "sell" a policy or model to other societies. In this case, the POLISARIO's gender policies are presented as an example of "good practice" for other Muslim, Arabic, and African countries to follow.

33. For more on metonymical slidings, see Jacob Torfing, *New Theories of Discourse: Laclau, Mouffe and Žižek* (Oxford: Blackwell, 1999), 112.

34. See Richter-Montpetit, "Empire, Desire and Violence."

35. POLISARIO, "La opinión de las masas: *Boletín* Especial 20 de Mayo," 5.

36. Frantz Fanon, *Black Skin, White Masks* (London: Pluto, 2008).

37. Edward Said, *Orientalism* (London: Penguin, 1995.)

38. Joanna Allan, "Representations of Gender in Saharawi Nationalist Discourse(s)" (master's by research, University of Leeds, 2008); Allan, "Imagining Saharawi Women."

39. Fiddian-Qasmiyeh, *The Ideal Refugees.*

40. I. Szeman, *Zones of Instability: Literature, Postcolonialism, and the Nation* (Baltimore: Johns Hopkins University Press, 2003), 13. See also Eric Hobsbawm and Terence Ranger, eds., *The Invention of Tradition* (Cambridge: Cambridge University Press, 1992).

41. Hayden White, *The Content of Form: Narrative Discourse and Historical Representation* (London: Johns Hopkins University Press, 1989), ix.

42. Baida Embarek Rahal, "Decolonization and Gender Equality" (paper presented at the International Women's Conference on the Western Sahara Women's Rights for Resistance, Windhoek, Namibia, 4 November 2015).

43. Bouatta, "Feminine Militancy," 24.

44. Wilson has highlighted that positive discrimination along racial lines has so far been omitted from the quota system. See Wilson, *Sovereignty in Exile*, chapter 7, for more on the quota systems introduced since 2008, and on the democratic systems of the SADR.

45. Fatma Mehdi, personal interview, Windhoek, Namibia, 4 November 2015.

46. Allan, "Imagining Saharawi Women."

47. Ibid.

48. Allan, "Representations of Gender," 54.

49. Mehdi, 4 November 2015.

50. Ibid.

51. For more on the construction of motherhood in Saharawi nationalist discourses, see Allan, "Representations of Gender," 38–56.

52. Personal communications with Vivian Solana Moreno, 2–8 May 2017.

53. Fatimetou Zrug Yomani, personal interview, Algiers, 5 April 2008. Similar observations are made in the film *Tebraa*, which covers the stories of illiterate girls unable to go to school since their mothers depend on their help at home, and by psychologists Carlos Martín Beristain and Itziar Lozano Urbieta, who suggest that the heavy domestic burden of women is carried at the cost of their physical and mental health (both cited in Allan, "Representations of Gender," pages 41 and 28, respectively).

54. Maimona Sayed, personal interview, Smara camp, 29 March 2008.

55. For more on demographic policies in the camps, see Allan, "Representations of Gender."

56. Butler, *Gender Trouble: Feminism and the Subversion of Identity*; R. W. Connell, *Masculinities* (Cambridge: Polity Press, 2005); Anne Fausto-Sterling, "The Five Sexes: Why Male and Female Are Not Enough," *The Sciences* 20, no. 4 (1992).

57. Arlie Russell Machung and Anne Hochschild, *The Second Shift: Working Families and the Revolution at Home* (New York: Viking Penguin, 1989.)

58. Remei Sipi Mayo quote in Joanna Allan, field notes, Malabo, June–July 2015. On UNMS statements, see Mokhtar, 28 November 2014. These slogans were a past campaign. The walls of the UNMS headquarters in Boujdour camp are now adorned with a colorful mural in tribute to the late revolutionary singer Mariam Hassan.

59. Allan, "Representations of Gender," 57.

60. Agaila Abba, "Who I Admire the Most and Why?," *Zeina: The Rise of Young Saharawi Women Writers*, 8 January 2008, http://saharawiyazeina.blogspot.com/2008/01/who-i-admire-most-and-why.html.

61. Asria Taleb Mohammed, Facebook post, 15 November 2015.

62. Asria Taleb Mohammed, personal communication, 10 December 2015.

63. Alice Wilson, "Household and the Production of Public and Private Domains: Revolutionary Changes in Western Sahara's Liberation Movement," *Paideuma* 58 (2012): 32.

64. See Wilson, *Sovereignty in Exile*, chapter 6, for a deeper look at how the market economy has provided both challenges and opportunities for gender, racial and tribal (in)equalities.

65. Allan, "Representations of Gender," 54.

66. Fatma El-Mehdi, "La resistencia saharaui: Una mirada histórica desde las perspectivas de las mujeres saharauis," in *Mujeres saharauis: Tres tuizas para la memoria de la resistencia*, ed. Rocío Medina Martín (Seville: Aconcagua Libros, 2016), 26.

67. United Nations High Commission for Refugees (UNHCR), "2015 UNHCR country operations profile—Algeria," 2015, http://www.unhcr.org/pages/49e485e16.html.

68. Habibulah Mohamed Lamin, "Amid Decreasing Aid, Sahrawis Seek Self-Determination," *Al-Monitor*, 25 May 2016, http://www.al-monitor.com/pulse/originals/2016/05/western-sahara-sahrawi-melhfa-civil-society.html.

69. Solana Moreno, "'No somos costosas,'" 85.

70. Aminetou Errer Bouzeid, personal communication, 19 December 2015. I look at the feminine sphere of childbirth and midwifery in Allan, "Representations of Gender," 44.

71. Some women are put off from working in Rabouni because of the threat of sexual harassment or damages to their reputation (working in Rabouni involves regularly sleeping away from home for many women). See Allan, "Representations of Gender." See also Wilson, *Sovereignty in Exile*, 198–99; Fiddian-Qasmiyeh, *The Ideal Refugees*.

72. Al-Ali and Pratt, "Between Nationalism and Women's Rights"; Frances Hasso, "The 'Women's Front': Nationalism, Feminism, and Modernity in Palestine," *Gender and Society* 12, no. 4 (1998).

73. Joanna Allan, field notes, Smara and Rabuni camps, April 2008.

74. I explored the issue of "kidnapped" women in 2008, at which time such cases only, at best, made local media in Spain. See Allan, "Representations of Gender." Caratini observed a similar case, involving a Saharawi woman studying in Cuba who married and had children with a (non-Muslim) Cuban. She was allegedly forced to leave her family and return to the camps. Caratini, "Prisión del tiempo," 10–11.

75. La Vanguardia, "Denuncia el secuestro de joven saharaui de acogida por su familia biológica," October 1, 2014, http://www.lavanguardia.com/local/valencia /20141001/54416527123/denuncia-el-secuestro-de-joven-saharaui-de-acogida-por-su -familia-biologica.html. Much of the so-called "kidnapping" cases occur when women have just completed their studies. This is the moment when their families feel they should be coming back to the camps to make a life.

76. The distressed Spanish sister of Mayuba commented on Facebook on 18 October 2014 that it had been impossible to hold discussions with any POLISARIO representative in Spain, who, she said, had neglected to speak to them on the telephone during the preceding three months.

77. Queralt Castillo Cerezuela, "Mayuba Mohamed, retenida en Tinduf por su familia biológica: 'Quiero salir de aquí,'" *Público*, October 21, 2014, http://www.publico .es/actualidad/551500/mayuba-mohamed-retenida-en-tinduf-por-su-familia-biologica -quiero-salir-de-aqui.

78. Zahra Ramdán Ahmed, Facebook status update, 20 October 2014.

79. Khadijatou Mokhtar, "La mujer saharaui en los campamentos de refugiados" (paper presented at the Jornadas de sensibilización sobre la cuestión del Sahara Occidental, University of Granada, 18 November 2014).

80. Dafa, 28 November 2014; Aminetou Errer Bouzeid, "Sexismo en la sociedad saharaui actual: Un acercamiento a la sociedad saharaui desde el trato a sus mujeres. Propuesta de intervención" (master's thesis, University of Zaragoza, 2015), 7.

81. Human Rights Watch, "Western Sahara/Algeria: Refugees Face Curbs on Rights," 18 October 2014.

82. Paco Cerdà, "'Lo de Mayuba es chantaje; no creo que los saharauis pidan más ayudas a la diputación,'" *Levante*, October 17, 2014, https://www.levante-emv.com/ comunitat-valenciana/2014/10/17/mayuba-chantaje-creo-saharauis-pidan/1175626 .html.

83. Shaya Deh, comment on a Facebook post by Lehdía Mohamed Dafa concerning the Hamdidaf case, 23 October 2014.

84. Hurria Salama, comment on the Facebook page of Lehdia Mohammed Dafa, 17 October 2014.

85. One indicator of this is acute malnutrition, which reaches 9.1 percent in children aged between six and fifty-nine months, while 29 percent of children in the camps suffer from stunted growth. Carlos S. Grijalva-Eternod et al., "The Double Burden of Obesity and Malnutrition in a Protracted Emergency Setting: A Cross-Sectional Study of Western Sahara Refugees," *PLOS Medicine* 9, no. 10 (2012).

86. For more on these campaigns, see Silvia Almenara Niebla, "Diásporas digitales: Una aproximación feminista al estudio de las minorías online; El caso de la diáspora saharaui," in *Ciberpolítica: Gobierno abierto, redes, deliberación, democracia*, ed. Ramón Cotarelo and Javier Gil (Madrid: Instituto Nacional de Administración Pública, 2017).

87. The sociolinguistical concept of *sayba* is used to refer to girls who leave the family home without a specific purpose, or too often, or who do not wear the *melḥfa*. Errer Bouzeid, "Sexismo en la sociedad saharaui," 53–57. With this campaign, we have seen young Saharawi women reclaiming a word that usually has negative connotations.

88. This is how Saharawi participants in the campaign described its aims.

89. "Slut," "whore," and so on.

90. Nira Yuval-Davis, *Gender and Nation* (London: SAGE, 1997).

91. In March 2017, a young Saharawi woman complained (in Hassania) via social media about the pressure on victims of sexual harassment and assault to remain silent about their experiences for fear of damaging their own reputations. She later posted about the vitriolic, misogynist responses she had received for daring to raise the issue publicly.

92. I looked in previous research at how the POLISARIO has discursively reprimanded women, but not men, who have liaisons before marriage. Allan, "Imagining Saharawi Women."

93. Silvia Almenara Niebla, "Beyond Online Comments and Gossip. Collective Identity and New Subjectivities in the Sahrawi Case," 2017 (unpublished paper in author's possession).

94. Joanna Allan, "Privilege, Marginalization and Solidarity: Women's Voices Online in Western Sahara's Struggle for Independence," *Feminist Media Studies* 14, no. 4 (2014).

95. "Soumaya" is a psuedonym.

96. Susan Martin-Márquez rightly criticizes how some women writers on the Saharawi case equate Saharawi women's struggles with gender-based injustices with their own in order to create a misleading narrative of "shared sisterhood." My intention in drawing a parallel between Saharawi and British norms on chastity is not to imply a unified struggle between the women of the two nations but rather to emphasize that, although I am critical of the fact that unmarried women may face a prison sentence if they fall pregnant, I do not deem to suggest in any way that my own cultural background is superior to the Saharawi one. Much the same norms on women's sexuality purvey gender relations in the United Kingdom, with heinous effects such as sexual violence, hence the need for movements such as "Slutwalk." Susan Martin-Marquéz, *Disorientations: Spanish Colonialism in Africa and the Performance of Identity* (New Haven, CT: Yale University Press, 2008), chapter 6.

97. Moghadam quoted in Allan, "Imagining Saharawi Women," 193.

98. Nira Yuval-Davis reinforces this perception. She states that "a figure of a woman . . . symbolizes in many cultures the spirit of the collectivity." Yuval-Davis quoted in ibid. See also the work of Partha Chaterjee, who shows how nationalist Indians created a "new patriarchy" in which Indian women were tasked with representing the new modern nation, blending aspects of traditional Indian and Western conceptions of womanhood. Partha Chatterjee, "Colonialism, Nationalism, and the Colonized Women: The Contest in India," *American Ethnologist* 16, no. 4 (1989).

99. Errer Bouzeid, "Sexismo en la sociedad saharaui," 84.

100. Wilson, *Sovereignty in Exile*, 164.

101. Dafa, 28 November 2014.

102. Deniz Kandiyoti, "Islam and Patriarchy: A Comparative Perspective," in *Feminist Approaches to Theory and Methodology: An Interdisciplinary Reader*, ed. Sharlene Hesse-Biber, Christine Gilmartin, and Robin Lydenberg (New York: Oxford University Press, 1999), 230.

103. Alice Wilson, personal communications, December 2015. See also Fortier, "Right to Divorce."

104. Marcelino Obono Alogo (pseudonym), personal interview, Granada, 18 July 2014.

105. For further discussion of this subject, see Solana Moreno, "'No somos costosas,'" 88–89.

106. Wilson, *Sovereignty in Exile*, 96.

107. On demand for higher bridewealths, see Dafa, 28 November 2014; on marriage contracts, see Wilson, *Sovereignty in Exile*, 95 and 107.

108. Solana Moreno, "'No somos costosas,'" 88.

109. Wilson, *Sovereignty in Exile*, 96–99.

110. Pascale Harter, "Sahara Women Relish Their Rights," *BBC News Africa*, 30 October 2003, http://news.bbc.co.uk/1/hi/world/africa/3227997.stm; Hamza Lakhal, personal conversations, Norway, April 2015.

111. Dafa, 28 November 2014.

112. Laura Limón Rivas, "La diversidad sexual en el Islam: El caso saharaui," *Perspectiva: Revista Trabajo Social* 18 (2008).

113. This is most apparent on some Saharawi blogs that have launched character assassinations of European solidarity activists who are openly, or suspected of being, gay and of those who are suspected of being pro–gay rights in their own countries.

114. Pramod Kumar Srivastava, "Resistance and Repression in India: The Hunger Strike at the Andaman Cellular Jail in 1933," *Crime, History and Societies* 7, no. 2 (2003).

115. Mokhtar, 28 November 2014. As my observations in chapter 4 suggest, other interviewees and informants point to the (hidden) existence of abortion in Saharawi society. The reason for the anomaly could be explained in two ways. First, my subject position as a white, Western researcher interested in women's rights may understandably persuade a government representative to give the best picture possible of Saharawi society. Second, the UNMS, as the women's wing of a nationalist movement, must pursue a pronatalist policy in which having many children is encouraged "for the cause," and thus abortion and contraception cannot be encouraged.

116. We could ask what "tolerated" means in practice for those who are gay. Unfortunately, I can only imagine an answer since I have never met a Saharawi prepared to

identify him- or herself as such. Brian Whitaker, referring to "tolerance" of gay practices in the Middle East and North Africa region more generally, suggests the term means a life of secrecy, enduring homophobia to the levels of hate speech, no justice if discrimination on the basis of sexuality is suffered, possible unwanted marriages, no state-sponsored advice on sexual health or sexuality more generally, and an inability—for some—to reconcile their faith with their sexuality. Brian Whitaker, *Unspeakable Love: Gay and Lesbian Life in the Middle East* (London: Saqi Books, 2006).

117. Trifonia Melibea Obono Ntutumu, *La hija de una soltera fang*.

118. See, for example, Whitaker, *Unspeakable Love*; Scott Siraj al-Haqq Kugle, "Sexuality, Diversity, and Ethics in the Agenda of Progressive Muslims," in *Progressive Muslims*, ed. Safi Omid (Oxford: Oneworld, 2003).

119. Whitaker, *Unspeakable Love*, 14.

120. Melanie Richter-Montpetit, "Beyond the Erotics of Orientalism: Lawfare, Torture and the Racial-Sexual Grammars of Legitimate Suffering," *Security Dialogue* 45, no. 1 (2014). She also, importantly, undoes this myth of Western states "leading the fight" for LGBT rights globally by using the example of the United States' performance of torture along a homophobic and transphobic script in Abu Ghraib.

121. POLISARIO "licentious" quote in Allan, "Imagining Saharawi Women," 193.

122. Ibid.; Fiddian-Qasmiyeh, *The Ideal Refugees*.

123. Amnesty International, "Urgent Action: Allow Human Rights Defender to Return Home," https://www.amnesty.org/download/Documents/48000/mde290142009 en.pdf, AI Index MDE 29/014/2009, 4 December 2009.

124. Conxi Moya, *Las 32 Batallas de Aminatu Haidar* (Madrid: Bubok, 2010), 31.

125. Blog quoted in Vivian Solana Moreno, "'A Woman Is Stronger Than Our State': Performing Sovereignty on the Margins of the State," *Explorations in Anthropology* 11, no. 1 (2011): 66.

126. See the large collection of Spanish news articles in Conxi Moya's excellent work *32 batallas*. For British ones, see, for example, Xan Rice, "Western Sahara Activist on Hunger Strike at Lanzarote Airport," *The Guardian*, 17 November 2009.

127. See, for example, Tomás Bárbulo, "La Voluntad y la Fuerza," in *Las treinta y dos batallas de Aminetu Haidar*, ed. Conxi Moya (Madrid: Bubok, 2010); Dani Pozo and Susana Hidalgo, "Lo más duro es cuando escucho llorar a mi hijo," in *Las treinta y dos batallas de Aminetu Haidar*, ed. Conxi Moya (Madrid: Bubok, 2010); Tomás Bárbulo, "Nunca pensé que el Gobierno la haría un favor tan sucio a Marruecos," in *Las treinta y dos batallas de Aminetu Haidar*, ed. Conxi Moya (Madrid: Bubok, 2010).

128. Her open letter, issued during her hunger strike, mentions her children only in the penultimate paragraph. Aminatou Haidar, "Carta abierta de Aminetu Haidar a la sociedad española en el Día Internacional de los Derechos Humanos," in *Las treinta y dos batallas de Aminetu Haidar*, ed. Conxi Moya (Madrid: Bubok, 2010), 76. See also the following exchange (my translation from Spanish) between Bárbulo and Haidar: "Q. You have two young children. Have you thought about what would happen to them if you died? A. I have two children, but I also have my dignity, and that comes before my children. . . . They'll live without a mother, but with dignity." Bárbulo, "Nunca pensé," 91. See also the exchange between Haidar, Poso, and Hidalgo (my translation): "Q. If you win in the end, what will be the first thing you do when you board the plane? Will you telephone your children? A. The first thing I will do is thank

all the people who have been with me since the first day of the strike. I will also thank the journalists, who have played a fundamental role in communicating the reality. The last time I phoned my relatives from the plane [she refers to the flight stopped in El Aaiún last 4 December], and in the end the journey was impossible. Now I'll demand a total guarantee that I am able to return home, and that is when I will call my children." Pozo and Hidalgo, "Lo más duro," 94.

129. Ignacio Cembrero, "Si cedo, expulsarán a muchos saharauis igual que a mi," in *Las treinta y dos batallas de Aminetu Haidar*, ed. Conxi Moya (Madrid: Bubok, 2010), 108.

130. Lorraine Bayard de Volo, "A Revolution in the Binary? Gender and the Oxymoron of Revolutionary War in Cuba and Nicaragua," *Signs* 37, no. 2 (2012): 424; Said, *Orientalism*; Shepherd, "Veiled References"; Al-Ali and Pratt, *What Kind of Liberation?*

131. For more on the hegemony of Western models of activism online and how Saharawi women have adapted to this, see Almenara Niebla, "Diásporas digitales."

132. These mothers and grandmothers became famous for their silent marches in Plaza de Mayo, Buenos Aires, in protest at the state terrorism that had seen their children and grandchildren forcibly disappeared. See Guzman Bouvard, *Revolutionizing Motherhood*. They wore white scarves, symbolizing their children's nappies (and, therefore, motherhood) as well as peace.

133. This holds parallels with the Palestinian case. See Julie M. Peteet, "Icons and Militants: Mothering in the Danger Zone," in *Gender, Politics and Islam*, ed. T. Saliba, C. Allen, and J. A. Howard (Chicago: University of Chicago Press, 2002).

134. See, for example, Kerry Kennedy, "Morocco Has Pressured UN to Ignore Western Sahara," *The Guardian*, 23 July 2015.

135. Stephen Zunes and Jacob Mundy, *Western Sahara: War, Nationalism, and Conflict Irresolution* (Syracuse, NY: Syracuse University Press, 2010).

136. Haddi held her hunger strike for thirty-six days, when she was hospitalized. She agreed to pass her hunger strike to internationals, who began a "hunger strike chain," ongoing at the time of writing, each person striking for twenty-four hours before passing the baton to the next in line.

### Chapter 4. Constructions of Gender in the Nationalist Discourses of the Obiang Regime

1. Dolores Molubela (pseudonym), personal interview, Malabo, 21 June 2015.

2. Allan, "Imagining Saharawi Women."

3. Alejandro Artucio, *The Trial of Macías in Equatorial Guinea. The Story of a Dictatorship* (Geneva: International Commission of Jurists and International University Exchange Fund, 1979).

4. Scared by Macías's alleged powers of witchcraft, no Equatoguinean dared to fire the shot.

5. On heading Black Beach prison, see Global Investment Center, *Equatorial Guinea: Company Laws and Regulations Handbook*, vol. 1, *Strategic Information and Regulations* (Washington, DC: Global Investment Center, 2013), 73; on former torturers as ministers in Obiang's government, see Robert Klitgaard, *Tropical Gangsters: One Man's Experience with Development and Decadence in Deepest Africa* (New York: Basic Books, 1990), 21.

6. Igor Cusack, "'Equatorial Guinea's National Cuisine Is Simple and Tasty': Cuisine and the Making of National Culture," *Arizona Journal of Hispanic Cultural Studies* 8 (2004): 132.

7. Equatoguinean state radio quoted in BBC News, "Equatorial Guinea's 'God,'" 6 July 2003, http://news.bbc.co.uk/1/hi/world/africa/3098007.stm; Government of Equatorial Guinea's Information and Press Office, "Title Page," n.d., http://www.guineaecuatorialpress.com. This is the slogan of the government's official website.

8. "Nation-Builders at Work: The Equatoguinean 'Myth' of Bantu Unity," *Nationalism and Ethnic Politics* 7, no. 3 (2001).

9. Ballano Gonzalo, *Aquel Negrito*, 51; Oscar Scafidi, *Equatorial Guinea* (Chalfont St. Peter: Brandt, 2015).

10. Cusack, "Nation-Builders"; Cusack, "Cuisine."

11. Cusack, "Nation-Builders," 83.

12. Gene Sharp, *The Politics of Nonviolent Action: Parts 1–3* (Boston: Porter Sargent, 1973).

13. For more on the use of the personality cult in articulating national identities, see Victoria Clement, "Articulating National Identity in Turkmenistan: Inventing Tradition through Myth, Cult and Language," *Nations and Nationalism* 20, no. 3 (2014).

14. Allan, field notes, June–July 2015.

15. Freedom House, "Freedom in the World: Equatorial Guinea," 2014, http://www.freedomhouse.org/report/freedom-world/2014/equatorial-guinea-0#.UXWLdzfhgo.

16. Correct at time of writing (5 August 2016).

17. Stephanie Wolters, "Equatorial Guinea's Web of Wealth and Repression," Institute for Security Studies, 15 July 2014, https://issafrica.org/about-us/press-releases/equatorial-guineas-web-of-wealth-and-repression.

18. Central Intelligence Agency (CIA), "The World Fact Book: Equatorial Guinea," 29 April 2014, https://www.cia.gov/library/publications/the-world-factbook/geos/ek.html; Government of Equatorial Guinea's Information and Press Office, "The Government of Equatorial Guinea," 2014, http://www.guineaecuatorialpress.com/noticia.php?id=126.

19. For some of the issues with the "elections," see EG Justice, "Opposition Party Boycotts Presidential Elections," 18 April 2016, http://www.egjustice.org/post/opposition-party-boycotts-presidential-elections.

20. (CIA), "World Fact Book."

21. Freedom House, "Equatorial Guinea."

22. EG Justice, "Human Rights Annual Report of Equatorial Guinea," 2015, 3, http://egjustice.org/sites/default/files/Human%20Rights%20Report%20Equatorial%20Guinea%20%202015.pdf.

23. Reporters without Borders, "Facebook and Opposition Websites Blocked Ahead of Elections," 14 May 2013, http://en.rsf.org/guinee-equatoriale-facebook-and-opposition-websites-14-05-2013,44618.html; EG Justice, "Equatorial Guinea: Ensure Media Freedom," 12 April 2016, http://www.egjustice.org/post/equatorial-guinea-ensure-media-freedom.

24. EG Justice, "Presidential Elections 2016 to Entrench Dictatorship," 18 March 2016, http://www.egjustice.org/post/presidential-elections-2016-entrench-dictatorship;

EG Justice, "Severe Crackdown on Opposition and Media," 20 April 2016, http://www
.egjustice.org/post/severe-crackdown-opposition-and-media-0; EG Justice, "Democracy Held Hostage," 25 April 2016, http://www.egjustice.org/post/democracy-held
-hostage; *New Vision*, "Africa's Longest-Serving Leader Re-elected," 28 April 2016,
http://www.newvision.co.ug/new_vision/news/1423403/africas-serving-leader-elected
-94-vote.

25. As Paul Nugent said of Macías's Equatorial Guinea and other states where fear
is key to state rule: "The primary objective of citizens [is] to avoid being noticed by
representatives of the state at all. Participating in public veneration of the leader when
required to do so [is] the minimum price that [has] to be paid." Nugent, "States and
Social Contracts," 56. On Equatoguinean citizens' choice of clothing, see Allan, field
notes, June–July 2015. For more on the history of politicized dress in Equatorial
Guinea, see Valenciano-Mañé, "Vestido, identidad y folklore."

26. Mama, "Khaki in the Family."

27. Ibid., 12.

28. Dzodzi Tsikata, "Women's Organizing in Ghana since the 1990s: From Individual Organizations to Three Coalitions," *Development* 52, no. 2 (2009): 187.

29. Sarilusi Tarifa King, "Equatorial Guinea Women Make Progress in All Sectors,"
Government of Equatorial Guinea's Information and Press Office, 3 August 2011,
http://www.guineaecuatorialpress.com/noticia.php?id=1802.

30. Eulalia Envo Bela quoted in Clemente Ela Ondo Onguene, "The Chinese
Embassy Offers a Special Reception for the International Day of Women," Government of Equatorial Guinea's Office for Information and Press, 12 March 2011, http://
www.guineaecuatorialpress.com/noticia.php?id=1400.

31. Nsue Enhate (pseudonym), 1 April 2014.

32. Tarifa King, "Women Make Progress."

33. Government of Equatorial Guinea, "Consideration of Reports Submitted by
States Parties under Article 18 of the Convention on the Elimination of All Forms of
Discrimination against Women. Second and Third Periodic Reports of States Parties:
Equatorial Guinea," Committee on the Elimination of Discrimination against Women
(CEDAW), 27 September 1995, 3.

34. Maria Jesus Nsang Nguema, "Meeting for Women in the Equatorial Guinean
Embassy in Spain," Government of Equatorial Guinea's Information and Press Office,
15 March 2013, http://www.guineaecuatorialpress.com/noticia.php?id=3607.

35. Valenciano-Mañé, "Vestido, identidad y folklore," 278; Mba (pseudonym), 16
June 2015; Balboa (pseudonym), 22 June 2015.

36. Committee on the Elimination of All Forms of Discrimination against Women
(CEDAW), "CEDAW 31st Session. Summary record of the 652nd meeting," 2004, 8,
https://documents-dds-ny.un.org/doc/UNDOC/GEN/N04/416/90/PDF/N0441690
.pdf?OpenElement.

37. Ntutumu (pseudonym), 16 June 2015; Mba (pseudonym), 16 June 2015; Balboa
(pseudonym), 22 June 2015; Alba Engonga (pseudonym), personal interview, Malabo,
25 June 2015; Maria Angeles Adugu Mba (pseudonym), personal interview, Malabo, 30
June 2015.

38. Mba (pseudonym), 16 June 2015.

39. Ricardo Soriso Sipi, personal communication, 15 January 2015.

40. Also indicative of the inequality is the mean number of years of schooling: 4 for girls compared with 7.2 for boys. United Nations Development Program, "Human Development Report 2016: Human Development for Everyone. Table 4: Gender Development Index," 2016, http://hdr.undp.org/sites/default/files/2016_human_devel opment_report.pdf.

41. To ensure the individual's safety, I cannot give further details.

42. Maria Jesus Nsang Nguema, "Speech by the First Lady at the 5th Congress of the PDGE," Government of Equatorial Guinea's Information and Press Office, 21 April 2012, http://guineaecuatorialpress.com/noticia.php?id=2578&lang=en.

43. Ibid.

44. See Envo Bela quoted in Sarilusi Tarifa King, "End of the Fifth Summit of Women, Gender and Development," Government of Equatorial Guinea's Information and Press Office, 25 June 2011, http://www.guineaecuatorialpress.com/noticia.php?id =1693.

45. Obiang cited in bold and italics in the top corner of the homepage of Ministry of Social Affairs and Promotion of Women, "Homepage," accessed December 2015, https://www.minasige.com/.

46. Committee on the Elimination of All Forms of Discrimination against Women (CEDAW), "CEDAW 31st Session," 2.

47. Ibid., 6.

48. Government of Equatorial Guinea, "Responses to the List of Issues and Questions for Consideration of the Combined Second, Third, Fourth and Fifth Periodic Reports: Equatorial Guinea," Committee on the Elimination of Discrimination against Women (CEDAW), 2004, 6.

49. Ibid.

50. Sarilusi Tarifa King, "Celebration of the World Day of Rural Women," Government of Equatorial Guinea's Information and Press Office, 18 October 2011, http:// www.guineaecuatorialpress.com/noticia.php?id=1989.

51. Nsang Nguema, "Speech by the First Lady."

52. Sarilusi Tarifa King, "Meeting of the Wives of Government Members," Government of Equatorial Guinea's Information and Press Office, 15 May 2013, http:// www.guineaecuatorialpress.com/noticia.php?id=3795.

53. Sarilusi Tarifa King, "Celebration of International Women's Day in Malabo," Government of Equatorial Guinea's Information and Press Office, 11 March 2014, http://www.guineaecuatorialpress.com/noticia.php?id=4907.

54. See, for example, the state television news report, uploaded on the *Diario Rombe* website, of the taxi driver who speaks with indignation after finding the girl prostitute whom he has solicited is actually a boy. As *Diario Rombe* observes, an effort is made to block out the face of the taxi driver, but not that of the prostituted child. Discursively, the taxi driver is an everyday man, and his infidelity and solicitation of sex with a minor are made banal while the child is the guilty party. State television report uploaded to *Diario Rombe* website, "La policía detiene a un 'homosexual' y taxista y los exhiben en la TVA," 7 April 2014, http://www.diariorombe.es/la-policia-detiene -un-homosexual-y-taxista-y-los-exhiben-en-la-tva/. The 2002 draft law is an initiative of the Ministry of Social Affairs and Advancement of Women (MINASPROM) and, as they have lamented in reports to the CEDAW Committee quoted below, it has not

yet been passed. It would outlaw the current practice of imprisoning women who are unable to return the bridewealth upon divorce. *Diario Rombe*, "Descarga los proyectos de ley que regulan el Matrimonio Tradicional en Guinea Ecuatorial," 27 March 2014, http://www.diariorombe.es/descarga-los-proyectos-de-ley-que-regulan-el-matrimonio -tradicional-en-guinea-ecuatorial/.

55. Espacios Europeos, "La policía de Guinea Ecuatorial detiene a un homosexual y el gobierno lo exhibe en la televisión como si fuera un trofeo," 14 April 2014, http:// espacioseuropeos.com/54707/la-policia-de-guinea-ecuatorial-detiene-a-un-homosexual -y-el-gobierno-lo-exhibe-en-la-television-como-si-fuera-un-trofeo/.

56. *Diario Rombe*, "La policía detiene a un 'homosexual.'"

57. Equatoguinean state radio quoted in BBC News, "Equatorial Guinea's 'God.'"

58. Sharp, *Nonviolent Action*.

59. Government of Equatorial Guinea, "Consideration of Reports Submitted by States Parties under Article 18 of the Convention on the Elimination of All Forms of Discrimination against Women, Combined Fourth and Fifth Periodic Reports," Committee on the Elimination of All Forms of Discrimination against Women (CEDAW), 2004, 10–11. I should highlight here that one woman who contributed to CEDAW submissions is also involved in the work of a pro-equality NGO.

60. Ibid., 11.

61. Government of Equatorial Guinea, "Consideration of Reports Submitted by States Parties under Article 18 of the Convention on the Elimination of All Forms of Discrimination against Women. Sixth Periodic Reports of States Parties: Equatorial Guinea," 2011, 31.

62. Scott, *Weapons*, 33.

63. Cindi Katz breaks up previously wide understandings of resistance such as Scott's into three levels: *resistance* is consciously oppositional and open and aims for emancipatory change, *reworking* alters the organization of power relations to benefit the weak but does not challenge the overall polarization of power relations, and forms of *resilience* enable subalterns to survive without altering the circumstances in which they must struggle to cope with. Cindi Katz, *Growing Up Global: Economic Restructuring and Children's Everyday Lives* (Minneapolis: University of Minnesota Press, 2004).

64. Evelyn Accad, "Sexuality and Sexual Politics: Conflicts and Contradictions for Contemporary Women in the Middle East," in *Gender and National Identity: Women and Politics in Muslim Societies*, ed. Valentine Moghadam (London: Zed Books, 1994); Al-Rasheed, *Most Masculine State*; Bouatta, "Feminine Militancy"; Doria Cherifati-Merabtine, "Algeria at a Crossroads: National Liberation, Islamization and Women," in *Gender and National Identity: Women and Politics in Muslim Societies*, ed. Valentine Moghadam (London: Zed Books, 1994); Valentine N. Moghadam, "Nationalist Agendas and Women's Rights," in *Feminist Nationalism*, ed. Lois A. West (London: Routledge, 1997); Julie M. Peteet, "Women and the Palestinian Movement: No Going Back?," in *Women and Power in the Middle East*, ed. Suad Joseph and Susan Slymovics (Philadelphia: University of Pennsylvania Press, 2001); Pauline L. Rankin, "Gender and Nation Branding in 'The True North Strong and Free,'" *Place Branding and Public Diplomacy* 8, no. 4 (2012); Nayereh Tohidi, "Modernity, Islamization and Women in Iran," in *Gender and National Identity: Women and Politics in Muslim Societies*, ed. Valentine Moghadam (London: Zed Books, 1994).

65. Sharp, *Nonviolent Action*.

66. I have since fruitlessly attempted to confirm the prize giver, yet the ironic laughter displayed by all at the event was telling enough.

67. See especially Wolters, "Equatorial Guinea's Web"; Hannah Appel, "Walls and White Elephants: Oil Extraction, Responsibility, and Infrastructural Violence in Equatorial Guinea," *Ethnography* 13, no. 4 (2012). As Appel notes, the "prestige projects" extend to high-rises that may look imposing but often lack electricity or water, or indeed any inhabitants. She reads these as a type of infrastructural violence built, as they are, while Equatorial Guinea has minimal basic infrastructure (decent roads, schools, hospitals, and so on).

68. Simon Anholt, "Should Place Brands Be Simple?," *Place Branding and Public Diplomacy* 5, no. 2 (2009): 95.

69. It is important to recognize, as Balghis Badri and Aili Mari Tripp do, that African women have played a large role in pressuring international organizations to put women's rights at the forefront of development agendas. Balghis Badri and Aili Mari Tripp, "African Influences on Global Women's Rights: An Overview," in *Women's Activism in Africa*, ed. Balghis Badri and Aili Mari Tripp (London: Zed Books, 2017).

70. Reem Mohamed, "Women and the Arab Spring: Tough Choices to Make," *Open Democracy*, 25 October 2013, http://www.opendemocracy.net/arab-awakening/reem-mohamed/women-and-the-arab-spring-tough-choices-to-make.

71. Mason, "Global Violence."

72. Mason, "Global Violence," 63. See also Lila Abu-Lughod, "Do Muslim Women Really Need Saving? Anthropological Reflections on Cultural Relativism and Its Others," *American Anthropologist* 104, no. 3 (2002).

73. Justine Greening, "Investing in Growth: How DfID Works in New and Emerging Markets," 11 March 2013, https://www.gov.uk/government/speeches/investing-in-growth-how-dfid-works-in-new-and-emerging-markets.

74. José María Larrú, "Foreign Aid in Equatorial Guinea: Macroeconomic Feature and Future Challenges," Munich Personal RePEc Archive paper no. 25001, 2010, 16, https://mpra.ub.uni-muenchen.de/25001/1/MPRA_paper_25001.pdf.

75. The Organization for Economic Cooperation and Development (OECD), "Development Aid at a Glance: Statistics by Region," 2015, 8.

76. Larrú, "Foreign Aid," 16.

77. Ibid., 9.

78. Ibid., 31.

79. Ibid., 21.

80. Ibid., 31.

81. Ibid., 9.

82. Mario Esteban, "The Chinese *Amigo*: Implications for the Development of Equatorial Guinea," *China Quarterly* 199 (2009): 679. For the reopening of the US embassy in Malabo, see Sandra T. Barnes, "Global Flows: Terror, Oil, and Strategic Philanthropy," *African Studies Review* 48, no. 1 (2005): 5.

83. See, for example, Ignacio Fariza, "El Instituto Cervantes y la UNED invitan en Bruselas al dictador Obiang," *El País*, 19 March 2014; *La Vanguardia*, "Críticas al Gobierno por la invitación del Instituto Cervantes y la UNED al dictador Obiang," 20 March 2014, http://www.lavanguardia.com/contacto/index.html; *El Mundo*, "Teodoro Obiang

agradece al Rey su influencia para participar en un acto en el Cervantes en Bruselas," 1 April 2014, http://www.elmundo.es/espana/2014/04/01/533a997522601dcf748b4572 .html. Regarding the football match, human rights organizations and Spanish autonomous governments criticized the team. See, for example, Raphael Minder, "Spanish Soccer Team under Fire for Game in Equatorial Guinea," *New York Times*, 14 November 2013.

84. For more on soft power, see Joseph S. Nye, *The Future of Power* (New York: Public Affairs, 2011).

85. Email from adelaide.schwartz@stratfor.com to africa@stratfor.com (Wikileaks, the GI Files), 7 December 2011, https://wikileaks.org/gifiles/docs/28/2867601_re-africa -equatorial-guinea-uk-energy-ct-ukaccuses-eq.html.

86. Human Rights Watch, "Well Oiled," 23. For more on the Riggs Bank scandal, see Leif Wenar, "Clean Trade in Natural Resources," *Ethics and International Affairs* 25, no. 1 (2011); Cecily Rose, "The Application of Human Rights Law to Private Sector Complicity in Governmental Corruption," *Leiden Journal of International Law* 24 (2011).

87. Ines Ortega, "The First Lady Receives the Title of Doctor Honoris Causa," Government of Equatorial Guinea's Information and Press Office, 27 November 2013, http://www.guineaecuatorialpress.com/noticia.php?id=4529.

88. Maria Jesus Nsang Nguema and Reina Ngomo Avomo, "Return of Constancia Mangue de Obiang," Government of Equatorial Guinea's Information and Press Office, 20 June 2013, http://www.guineaecuatorialpress.com/noticia.php?id=3919.

89. Whether or not she has *succeeded* in increasing her legitimacy is a different question not addressed here, although I suspect not.

90. Lawrence Jackson, "President Barack Obama and First Lady Michelle Obama pose for a photo during a reception at the Metropolitan Museum in New York with Teodoro Obiang Nguema Mbasogo, President of the Republic of Equatorial Guinea, and his wife, First Lady Constancia Mangue de Obiang" (White House, Washington, DC, 2009); William Sands, "Equatorial Guinea: Legitimizing Obiang," Pulitzer Center on Crisis Reporting, 24 April 2012, http://pulitzercenter.org/reporting/equatorial-guinea -president-teodoro-obiang-legitimization-corruption-oil-unesco-eiti-dodd-frank.

91. International Monetary Fund (IMF), "Republic of Equatorial Guinea," 7.

92. Global Investment Center, *Equatorial Guinea: Company Laws and Regulations Handbook*, vol. 1, *Strategic Information and Regulations* (Washington, DC: Global Investment Center, 2012), 30.

93. Smith (first name unknown) (US Embassy to Equatorial Guinea), "Wikileaks Cable 09MALABO48_a: Equatorial Guinea Raw, Paper 6: Refining our Approach," Malabo, 21 May 2009.

94. For OPIC funding, see Global Investment Center, *Equatorial Guinea* (2012), 49. For MPRI's development of a coastguard, see Esteban, "The Chinese *Amigo*," 673.

95. Barnes, "Global Flows."

96. Ibid., 11.

97. Smith (US Embassy to Equatorial Guinea), "Equatorial Guinea Raw."

98. Esteban, "The Chinese *Amigo*," 673.

99. David Wallechinsky, "Dictator of the Month: Teodoro Obiang Nguema of Equatorial Guinea," 25 July 2011, http://www.allgov.com/news/us-and-the-world/dic tator-of-the-month-teodoro-obiang-nguema-of-equatorial-guinea?news=843015.

100. Esteban, "The Chinese *Amigo*," 673.

101. Government of Equatorial Guinea's Information and Press Office, "The President of the Spanish Government Will Attend the AU Summit in Equatorial Guinea," 16 June 2014, http://www.guineaecuatorialpress.com/noticia.php?id=5290.

102. Government of Equatorial Guinea, 2011, "Consideration of Reports," 9.

103. Up until 2012 at least, almost one-third of the Social Development Fund has been ring-fenced for MINASPROM. Ibid.

104. Smith (US Embassy to Equatorial Guinea), "Equatorial Guinea Raw."

105. Ibid.

106. Government of Equatorial Guinea, 2011, "Consideration of Reports," 11.

107. Ibid., 29.

108. Allan, field notes, June–July 2015; Government of Equatorial Guinea, 2011, "Consideration of Reports," 12.

109. Obiang and Mangue's son Teodorín, embroiled in several international money laundering scandals, is also a client of Qorvis. Ken Silverstein, "Obiang's American Enablers," *100 Reporters*, 14 December 2011, http://100r.org/2011/12/obiangs-american-enablers/.

110. For Qorvis's original press release, see Qorvis Communications LLC, "Equatorial Guinea Reports Progress on Gender Equality, Elimination of Violence against Women," 14 March 2013, http://equatorialguineainfo.blogspot.co.uk/2013/03/equatorial-guinea-reports-progress-on.html.

111. For a discussion of how gender equality is used in Canada's nation branding strategy, see Rankin, "Gender and Nation." For an exploration of the use of constructions of gender by US authorities upon their invasion of Afghanistan, see Shepherd, "Veiled References."

112. Bruno De Cordier, "On the Thin Line Between Good Intentions and Creating Tensions: A View on Gender Programmes in Muslim Contexts and the (Potential) Position of Islamic Aid Organizations," *European Journal of Development Research* 22, no. 2 (2010): 236.

113. Michael L. Ross, "Oil, Islam, and Women," *American Political Science Review* 102, no. 1 (2008).

114. Appel, "Walls and White Elephants"; Hannah Appel, "Offshore Work: Oil, Modularity, and the How of Capitalism in Equatorial Guinea," *American Ethnologist* 39, no. 4 (2012).

115. Obono Alogo (pseudonym), 18 July 2014; Ntutumu (pseudonym), 16 June 2015; Balboa (pseudonym), 22 June 2015. See also Alicia Campos Serrano, "Extraction Offshore, Politics Inshore, and the Role of the State in Equatorial Guinea," *Journal of the International African Institute* 83, no. 2 (2013): 319.

116. US Department of State, "Trafficking in Persons Report: Equatorial Guinea," 2015.

117. Ibid.

118. Allan, field notes, June–July 2015.

119. Soriso Sipi, 15 January 2015.

120. Obono Alogo (pseudonym), 18 July 2014.

121. Indeed, although not as extensive as was the case in Spanish Guinea, John Mercer has highlighted that sexual transactions occurred between Saharawi women

and the relatively rich colonial soldiers of Spanish Sahara. Mercer, *Spanish Sahara*, 176.

122. For similar examples on women's rights and oil, the cases of Uganda and the Democratic Republic of Congo are discussed in Global Rights Alert, "Towards Balancing Gender: Women's Participation in Uganda's Oil Sector; Case of Rural Women in Four Sub Counties of Hoima and Buliisa Districts," 2013.

123. Lucía Zamora Nsang (pseudonym), personal communication, 16 January 2015; Campos Serrano, "Extraction Offshore," 319. The figure comes from Larrú, "Foreign Aid," 7.

124. The issue of ethnicity is salient here. Polygyny is common among Fangs but not among Bubis and Annobonese. Zamora Nsang (pseudonym), 16 January 2015.

125. Engonga (pseudonym), 25 June 2015.

126. Campos Serrano, "Extraction Offshore," 319.

127. Buscant Llavors, "Tontines: La soberanía financiera de las mujeres africanas," June 2015, http://www.buscantllavors.org/tontines-la-soberania-financiera-de-las -mujeres-africanas/.

128. Aixelà Cabré, "Africanas en el mundo"; Buscant llavors, "Tontines."

129. Human Rights Watch reported that in 2004 around one thousand African migrants were deported, several after having been raped. Amnesty International has reported that security forces often raid the homes of West Africans, beating and fining them and stealing their property. Human Rights Watch, "Well Oiled," 81; Amnesty International, "Continued Institutional and Key Human Rights Concerns in Equatorial Guinea: Submission to the UN Universal Periodic Review, May 2014," October 2013, 7. See also Campos Serrano, "Extraction Offshore," 320.

130. Carmen Campanet (pseudonym), personal interview, Malabo, 28 June 2015.

## Chapter 5. Women, Gender, and Resistance in Moroccan-Occupied Western Sahara

1. The Moroccan state has a history of using forced disappearance as a political tool. See Susan Slyomovics, *The Performance of Human Rights in Morocco* (Philadelphia: University of Pennsylvania Press, 2005). The story of Fatima Ghalia Leili's abduction was recounted to me by Soukaina Yaya during an interview in El Aaiún, 22 August 2014.

2. Soukaina Yaya, personal interview, El Aaiún, 22 August 2014.

3. Apparently even infants were a threat to the invading Moroccans, as the case of Embarka Mitmaila and her week-old baby illustrates. Both were disappeared in Tan Tan in the lead-up to the Black March in 1975. Ibid.

4. Ten members of the family were taken to a secret detention center in Agadir, but were later moved to Agdz fort and finally Qal'at M'Gouna. Martín Beristain and González Hidalgo, *El oasis*, vol. 2, 500; Arso, "Weekly News," 5 November 1995, http:// www.arso.org/01-e-44.htm.

5. Yaya, 22 August 2014.

6. Ibid.

7. Allan, "Representations of Gender."

8. Pseudonym.

9. Mokhtar, 13 December 2015.

10. Jordi Negre Rigol, "Sahara: España arria su bandera," *Diario de Barcelona*, 20 December 1975.

11. Tomás Bárbulo quoted in Moya, *32 batallas*, 100.

12. Amnesty International, "Amnesty International Briefing: Morocco," 1977, 10. See also Amnesty International, "Report of an Amnesty International Mission to the Kingdom of Morocco," 1982.

13. The International Federation for Human Rights quoted in Hacene-Djaballah, "Conflict in Western Sahara," 186.

14. Lippert, "Sahrawi Women," 642.

15. Radiotelevisión de Sahara via Radio Argel, "La Voz del Sahara Libre," Algeria, 15 January 1976.

16. Dafa, "En el Día de la Mujer, recuerdo y homenaje a las pioneras de la sanidad saharaui."

17. Lahbib quoted in Martín Beristain and González Hidalgo, *El oasis*, vol. 1, 203.

18. Lahbib quoted in ibid., 197.

19. The ceremony was in Bir Lehlu, in POLISARIO-controlled Western Sahara.

20. France Liberté Foundation and French Association of Friendship and Solidarity with the Peoples of Africa (AFASPA), "International Mission of Investigation in Western Sahara," 2003, 12.

21. See also a list of women who reportedly miscarried in Moroccan prisons during the year 1976: POLISARIO, "La opinión de las masas," *Boletín* 4 (1976), 11.

22. France Liberté Foundation and French Association of Friendship and Solidarity with the Peoples of Africa (AFASPA), "International Mission," 11.

23. Women were blindfolded, beaten, and tortured, and several watched their babies die in the cells. Amnesty International cited in Jacob Mundy, "The Dynamics of Repression and Resistance: Sahrawi Nationalist Activism in the Moroccan Occupied Western Sahara" (paper presented at the annual meeting of the International Studies Association, San Francisco, 2011), 6.

24. For example, see the case of Ghalia Ment Baba Ould Sidi, who, while in prison, was breastfeeding her baby son when a policeman pulled him from her breast and bashed him against the wall. The baby died a month later. See France Liberté Foundation and French Association of Friendship and Solidarity with the Peoples of Africa (AFASPA), "International Mission," 11. T. M. Linda Scholz has also highlighted the gender-based nature of such forms of abuse. See "The Rhetorical Power of *Testimonio* and *Ocupación*: Creating a Conceptual Framework for Analyzing Subaltern Rhetorical Agency" (PhD diss., University of Colorado, 2007). For further examples of the torture of children in front of their mothers as a gendered form of torture, see Margaret Power, "Dictatorship and Single-Party States," in *The Oxford Encyclopedia of Women in World History*, ed. Bonnie G. Smith (Oxford: Oxford University Press, 2008), 56.

25. Mahfood Dahou, personal interview, El Aaiún, 29 August 2014.

26. Mohammed Mayara, personal interview, El Aaiún, 27 August 2014.

27. Amnesty International, "Morocco: Breaking the Wall of Silence: The 'Disappeared' in Morocco," 13 April 1993, 64–66. Saharawi disappeareds have been held at Qal'at Mgouna, an ancient fort in the picturesque valley of Wadi Dades, popular with

tourists; in the ancient fort of Agdz town, southern Morocco; and at remote forts in the mountain triangle between Er-Rachidia, Ouarzazate, and Agadir, including Qal'at al-Qaid Abdellah, Qsar Ait Chair, Oued el-Male, and Oued Ounil.

28. Allan, "Representations of Gender."

29. Lonely Planet, "Introducing Agdz," 2015.

30. Testimony of Mohammed Nadrani, arrested in April 1976, released on 31 December 1984, quoted in Amnesty International, "Morocco: Breaking the Wall of Silence," 44–58.

31. Allan, "Imagining Saharawi Women."

32. Libby Tata Arcel, "Torture, Cruel, Inhuman and Degrading Treatment of Women. Psychological Consquences," *Psyke & Logos* 22 (2001).

33. For advantages of invisible detention centers for other world powers, especially the United States, Britain, Israel, and France, see Laleh Khalili, *Time in the Shadows: Confinement in Counterinsurgencies* (Stanford, CA: Stanford University Press, 2013), 127–37.

34. Yaya, 22 August 2014; Hamza Lakhal, 21 August 2014.

35. Dahou, 29 August 2014.

36. Scott, *Domination*, 4.

37. Ibid., 86.

38. Khaya, 26 November 2014.

39. Malainin Lakhal, personal communication, 13 May 2014.

40. Scott, *Domination*, 197.

41. Ibid., 3.

42. Doug McAdam, Sidney Tarrow, and Charles Tilly, *Dynamics of Contention* (Cambridge: Cambridge University Press, 2001), 5.

43. Charles Tilly and Sidney Tarrow, *Contentious Politics* (London: Paradigm Publishers, 2007), 49.

44. Fernando Orgambides, "La misión de la ONU llega hoy al Sáhara," *El País*, 20 November 1987.

45. Mundy, "Dynamics of Repression," 8; France Liberté Foundation and French Association of Friendship and Solidarity with the Peoples of Africa (AFASPA), "International Mission," 10.

46. Aminatou Haidar, "Testimony of Human Rights Violations against Saharawis" (paper presented at the Conference on Multilateralism and International Law with Western Sahara as a Case Study, Pretoria, South Africa, 4–5 December 2008), 266–67.

47. Fatma Aayache, "Death Was Better than Being Raped!!!," Union of Saharawi Writers and Journalists, 23 June 2007, http://www.upes.org/bodyarticulos_eng.asp?field =articulos_eng&id=259.

48. Ibid.

49. Ibid.

50. Ibid.

51. Ibid.

52. Ibid.

53. For more on the concept of "revolutionary motherhood," see Fisher, *Mothers of the Disappeared*; Guzman Bouvard, *Revolutionizing Motherhood*.

54. Aayache, "Death."

55. Malainin Lakhal, personal conversations, Algiers, 5 April 2008.

56. Many cultural feminists highlight the cultural significance of motherhood. Carol Gilligan argues that we have become accustomed "to seeing life through men's eyes" and that women's experiences are systematically side-lined. See Carol Gilligan, *In a Different Voice: Psychological Theory and Women's Development* (London: Harvard University Press, 1998), 6. Cultural feminists therefore argue for a reevaluation of the attributes socially constructed as associated with the female. See Maggie Humm, *The Dictionary of Feminist Theory* (Hemel Hempstead, Hertfordshire: Harvester Wheatsheaf, 1989), 66; Catherine King, "The Politics of Representation: A Democracy of the Gaze," in *Imagining Women: Cultural Representations and Gender*, ed. Frances Bonner, Lizbeth Goodman, Richard Allen, Linda Jones, and Catherine King (Cambridge: Polity Press, 1992), 137; Alicia Ostriker, "A Wild Surmise: Motherhood and Poetry," in *Imagining Women: Cultural Representations and Gender*, ed. Frances Bonner, Lizbeth Goodman, Richard Allen, Linda Jones, and Catherine King (Cambridge: Polity Press, 1992), 106.

57. Caron E. Gentry, "Twisted Maternalism: From Peace to Violence," *International Feminist Journal of Politics* 11, no. 2 (2009): 237–38.

58. For more on the relationship between maternalism and politics, see Marian van der Klein, Rebecca Jo Plant, Nichole Sanders, and Lori R. Weintrob, eds., *Maternalism Reconsidered: Motherhood, Welfare and Social Policy in the Twentieth Century* (New York: Berghahn Books, 2012). See also Temma Kaplan, "Female Consciousness and Collective Action: The Case of Barcelona, 1910–1918," *Signs* 7, no. 3 (1982). Other examples of Saharawi women who cite their status as mothers as the primary reason for their politicization are the mothers of the "Oxford Six," who led protests after their children were kidnapped and disappeared before traveling to a conflict resolution workshop in Oxford in August 2009. I do not mean here to suggest that discrimination on the basis of national identity and ethnicity and economic inequalities are separable from one's identity as mother and mother of discriminated children. Rather, I mean to highlight that Saharawi women activists who are also mothers tend to emphasize their radicalization *because they are Saharawi* rather than *because they are mothers*.

59. For a discussion of this, see Cathy A. Rakowskis, "Women as Political Actors: The Move from Maternalism to Citizenship Rights and Power," *Latin American Research Review* 38, no. 2 (2003).

60. Aayache, "Death."

61. Nicolien Zuijdgeest, "Aminatou Haidar: The Sahrawi Gandhi," blog, 15 March 2013, http://nicolien.com/aminatou-haidar-the-sahrawi-gandhi/.

62. This is just a fraction of the total disappeared. As the US Department of State has highlighted, international human rights organizations estimate the total number of forced disappearances is closer to fifteen hundred. US Department of State, "Country Reports on Human Rights Practices: Western Sahara 1999," Washington, DC, 2000; US Department of State, "Country Reports on Human Rights Practices: Western Sahara 2001," Washington, DC, 2002; US Department of State, "Country Reports on Human Rights Practices: Western Sahara 2002," Washington, DC, 2003.

63. France Liberté Foundation and French Association of Friendship and Solidarity with the Peoples of Africa (AFASPA), "International Mission," 3.

64. Aayache, "Death."

65. Salka Barca and Stephen Zunes, "Nonviolent Struggle in Western Sahara," in *Civilian Jihad: Nonviolent Struggle, Democratization, and Governance in the Middle East*, ed. Maria J. Stephan (New York: Palgrave Macmillan, 2009), 159.

66. Lakhal, 13 May 2014.

67. For example, 1995 saw the brutal repression of pro-POLISARIO protests (see Amnesty International, "Morocco and Western Sahara. Fear of Torture/unfair Trial: Ahmed El Kouri, Nebt Ramdane Bouchraya, Arbi Brahim Baba, Cheykhatou Bouh, M'Rabih Rabou Neysan, Abdelhay Lekhal, Mahfoud Brahim Dahou, Salama Ahmed Lembarki, all male, aged 18–20," 5 July 1995). In February 1998 in Lemseyed, Saharawi protestors burned Moroccan flags and photographs of the king before setting a public building on fire. Amnesty International, "Morocco/Western Sahara. 'Turning the Page': Achievements and Obstacles," 3 August 1999, 17. For analysis of the 1992 Intifada of Three Cities, see Claudia Barona Castañeda, "Memorias de una resistencia: La otra historia del Sahara Occidental," 1 January 2015, http://emam.revues.org/859.

68. Amnesty International, "Morocco/Western Sahara: Kelthoum Ahmed Labid El-Ouanat Prisoner of Conscience," March 1996, AI Index MDE 29/03/96. El Ouanat went to prison in 1992 and was released in May 1996.

69. For more on the reasons behind the 1999 intifada, see Toby Shelley, *Endgame in the Western Sahara* (London: Zed Books, 2004).

70. US Department of State, "Western Sahara 1999."

71. Malainin Lakhal, personal communications, June 2008.

72. Malainin Lakhal, personal communications, 2 March 2015. Saharawis identify *āḥīām* as a quintessential and national emblem of their nomadism, that is, as a border marker between Saharawi and Moroccan culture.

73. US Department of State, "Country Reports on Human Rights Practices: Western Sahara 2000," Washington, DC, 2001.

74. Maria J. Stephan and Jacob Mundy, "A Battlefield Transformed: From Guerrilla Resistance to Mass Non-Violent Struggle in Western Sahara," *Journal of Military and Strategic Studies* 8, no. 3 (2006): 12.

75. Lakhal, 13 May 2014.

76. Lakhal, June 2008.

77. Embarka Hassan is a pseudonym.

78. RASD is the Spanish acronym for the Saharawi Arab Democratic Republic.

79. Embarka Hassan, personal interview, Madrid, 26 October 2014.

80. Mundy, "Dynamics of Repression," 3.

81. Ahmed Baba, personal interview, Rabat, 28 April 2014.

82. Hassan, 26 October 2014. Prisoners are expected to provide for these themselves. Amnesty International, "Western Sahara/Morocco: Torture of Detainees Must End," 24 June 2004.

83. Stephan and Mundy, "A Battlefield Transformed," 13–14.

84. Jacob Mundy, "Autonomy & Intifada: New Horizons in Western Saharan Nationalisms," *Review of African Political Economy* 108 (2006). See Zunes, *War, Nationalism and Conflict Irresolution*.

85. For more on the 2005 intifada, see Stephan and Mundy, "A Battlefield Transformed." One important point concerning this intifada was the use of cameras, telephones, and the internet by citizens to communicate the protests (and their oppression)

to the outside world. For more on the use of the internet for communicating the Saharawi struggle, see Tara Flynn Deubel, "Mediascapes of Human Rights: Emergent Forms of Digital Activism for the Western Sahara," *Transmodernity: Journal of Peripheral Cultural Production of the Luso-Hispanic World* 5, no. 3 (2015).

86. Elliana Bisgaard-Church, "Sahrawis Campaign for Independence in the Second Intifada, Western Sahara, 2005–2008," Global Nonviolent Action Database, 27 November 2011, http://nvdatabase.swarthmore.edu/content/sahrawis-campaign-independence-second-intifada-western-sahara-2005<HY>2008.

87. The other of the two cases highlighted by Zunes is Aminatou Haidar's 2008 securing of the Robert F. Kennedy Foundation's Human Rights Award. Stephen Zunes, "Upsurge in Repression Challenges Nonviolent Resistance in Western Sahara," *Open Democracy*, 17 November 2010.

88. Gómez Martín, "Gdeim Izik," 10.

89. Hamza Lakhal, personal conversations, London, March 2016.

90. For more, see Allan, "Natural Resources and Intifada."

91. Sidi Breika, personal interview, London, 31 March 2014.

92. UN population estimate cited in Alice Wilson, "On the Margins of the Arab Spring," *Social Analysis* 57, no. 2 (2013): 91.

93. Ibid., 82.

94. Democracy Now!, "'The Genie Is Out of the Bottle': Assessing a Changing Arab World with Noam Chomsky and Al Jazeera's Marwan Bishara," 17 February 2011, http://www.democracynow.org/2011/2/17/the_genies_are_out_of_the.

95. Wilson, "On the Margins of the Arab Spring."

96. Nguia El Haouasi, personal interview, Zaragoza, 26 November 2014. Smara Street holds historical importance for Saharawis. Built by the Spanish, it once led to Zemla Square (now built over to form Maatalla, the center of Saharawi resistance), the site of Bassiri's protest.

97. Hassana Aalia, personal interview, Zaragoza, 26 November 2014.

98. Izana Amidan, personal interview, El Aaiún, 22 August 2014.

99. Hayat Rguibi, personal interview, Zaragoza, 26 November 2014.

100. This is not to say that she always is. For occasions when Muslim women are not "worthy victims," see Yasmin Jiwani, "Trapped in the Carceral Net: Race, Gender, and the 'War on Terror,'" *Global Media Journal—Canadian Edition* 4, no. 2 (2011). On the other hand, on the white feminization of victimhood, and how the state uses this, see Cecilia Åse, "Crisis Narratives and Masculinist Protection: Gendering the Original Stockholm Syndrome," *International Feminist Journal of Politics* 17, no. 4 (2015). See also Abu-Lughod, "Do Muslim Women Really Need Saving?"

101. Maria Cristina Paciello, Renata Pepicelli, and Daniela Pioppi, "Public Action towards Youth in Neo-Liberal Morocco: Fostering and Controlling the Unequal Inclusion of the New Generation," *Power2Youth Papers*, no. 5 (February 2016), 13, https://unora.unior.it/retrieve/handle/11574/165777/19842/p2y_05.pdf.

102. Ibid., 8.

103. Ibid., 20–21.

104. See, for example, European Commission, "Gender Equality: Encouraging First Results of EU Gender Action Plan in Developing Countries," 15 December 2011, http://europa.eu/rapid/press-release_IP-11<HY>1557_en.htm.

105. European External Action Service, "L'Union européenne appuie l'égalité des genres au Maroc," 3 July 2012, http://eeas.europa.eu/delegations/morocco/press_cor ner/all_news/news/2012/20120703_fr.htm.

106. European Commission, "European Neighbourhood Policy and Enlargement Negotiations," 23 June 2016, http://ec.europa.eu/enlargement/neighbourhood/coun tries/morocco/index_en.htm; European External Action Service, "L'Union européenne appuie l'égalité des genres au Maroc."

107. United Nations Women and International Development Cooperation of Spain, "Advancing Gender Equality: Promising Practices," 2013.

108. At the time of writing, said agreements are the subject of two legal actions by the POLISARIO and one by Western Sahara Campaign UK.

109. Connell, *Masculinities*.

110. Samia Errazzouki, "Working-Class Women Revolt: Gendered Political Economy in Morocco," *Journal of North African Studies* 19, no. 2 (2014).

111. Dhiraj Murthy, " Muslim Punk' Music Online: Piety and Protest in the Digital Age," in *Music, Culture and Identity in the Muslim World*, ed. Kamal Salhi (Abingdon, UK: Taylor and Francis, 2013), 161; Michelle Aguayo, "Representation of Muslim Bodies in 'The Kingdom': Deconstructing Discourses in Hollywood," *Global Media Journal* 2, no. 2 (2009); Peter Gottschalk, and Gabriel Greenberg, *Islamophobia: Making Muslims the Enemy* (Lanham, MD: Rowman & Littlefield, 2008); Edward Said, *Covering Islam: How the Media and the Experts Determine How We See the World* (New York: Vintage Books, 1997); Jiwani, "Trapped in the Carceral Net."

112. Aguayo, "Representation of Muslim Bodies."

113. Salaam quoted in Nick Jubber, "Salaam's Story," *Sandblast*, 4 July 2012, http://sandblast-arts.blogspot.co.uk/2012/07/salaams-story-by-nick-jubber.html.

114. El Ghalia Djimi quoted in Loveday Morris, "Women on Frontline in Struggle for Western Sahara," *The Guardian*, 16 July 2013.

115. Ibid.

116. El Ghalia Djimi quoted in Loveday Morris, "In Western Sahara, Women Play Large Role in Forgotten Struggle for Independence," *Washington Post*, 7 July 2013.

117. Khaya, 26 November 2014.

118. Rguibi, 26 November 2014.

119. Dafa, 28 November 2014.

120. Joanna Allan, field notes, Algeria, December 2015.

121. When a Saharawi woman shares a photograph of wounds on her buttocks on social media, for example, some activists will support her by sharing her picture as widely as possible (this is her intention—the horror of such an image immediately grabs attention, thus leading external audiences to discover more about the conflict). Yet others leave comments calling her to delete the picture immediately, stating that it is *harām*. Usually there are similar numbers of "sharers" as unsupportive "commenters."

122. Mahfouda Lefkir quoted in Joanna Allan and Hamza Lakhal, "Acting with Impunity: Morocco's Human Rights Violations in Western Sahara and the Silence of the International Community," SAIH (Studentenes og Akademikernes Internasjonale Hjelpefond), April 2015, 15, https://saih.no/assets/docs/Acting-With-Impunity-Western -Sahara-report.pdf.

123. Yaya, 22 August 2014.

124. Lahweij Rguibano quoted in Allan and Lakhal, "Acting with Impunity," 14.

125. Mohammed Khar, Khaled Errohi, Aali Saadouni, Hamza Ahl Filali, Nour Eddine Elarkoubi, and Emrabih Esaaydi quoted in ibid., 20.

126. For more on why state officials use rape as a method of torture and a weapon of war, see Tata Arcel, "Psychological Consquences." Susan Brownmiller argues that rape supports the maintenance of patriarchal society. Susan Brownmiller, *Against Our Will—Men, Women and Rape* (New York: Ballatine Books, 1975).

127. Here I quote Tata Arcel, who describes the purpose of states employing rape as a tool against populations more generally. "Psychological Consquences," 328.

128. Amidan, 22 August 2014. Comment in italics from Hamza Lakhal.

129. Martín Beristain and González Hidalgo, *El oasis*, vol. 1, 380.

130. Mohammed Laabied, quoted in ibid., 379.

131. Martín Beristain and González Hidalgo, *El oasis*, vol. 2, 115.

132. Sarah Graham-Brown, "Women's Activism in the Middle East: A Historical Perspective," in *Women and Power in the Middle East*, ed. Suad Joseph and Susan Slymovics (Philadelphia: University of Pennsylvania Press, 2001), 28.

133. Amidan, 22 August 2014; Hamza Lakhal, personal conversations, El Aaiún, August to September 2014; Joanna Allan, field notes, El Aaiún, August–September 2014. Important exceptions to this are many male ex-political prisoners who have married female ex-political prisoners. I am aware that virginity is a constructed concept.

134. Work by Nayanika Mookherjee is a valuable exception. Nayanika Mookherjee, "The Absent Piece of Skin: Gendered, Racialized and Territorial Inscriptions of Sexual Violence during the Bangladesh War," *Modern Asian Studies* 46, no. 6 (2011).

135. Sandesh Sivakuman, "Sexual Violence against Men in Armed Conflict," *European Journal of International Law* 18, no. 2 (2007).

136. Inger Agger, "Sexual Torture of Prisoners: An Overview," *Journal of Traumatic Stress* 2, no. 3 (1989): 313. See also Tata Arcel, "Psychological Consquences," 342. Agger explains that beating the genitals of prisoners (as security officers do with both men and women, not just in prison but also in the street) is designed to bring the prisoner to associate pain and panic with sexuality. Tata Arcel, whose study focuses on women, describes how survivors of sexual torture often come to fear sex with their long-term, trusted partners.

137. Agger, "Sexual Torture," 308.

138. On forced miscarriages in detention, a recent case in point at the time of writing is that of Lalla Al Mosawi, who was five months pregnant when she was kidnapped on 15 February 2015. After ten hours of torture, she miscarried. Allan, "Acting with Impunity." On the politics of reproduction, see Allan, "Representations of Gender."

139. See, for example, Don Couturier, "The Rape of Men: Eschewing Myths of Sexual Violence in War," *On Politics* 6, no. 2 (2012).

140. Amnesty International, "Morocco/Western Sahara: Moroccan Authorities Must Respect Freedom of Assembly," 3 April 2013, 2; Tata Arcel, "Psychological Consquences," 342. One case in point is that of El Ghalia Djimi, who can no longer grow hair on her head owing to the damage caused by water boarding with chemicals. Her face is also scarred by dog bites. See Prisca Borrel, "El Ghalia Djimi, militante sahraouie en territoire occupé," Haut Courant, 8 January 2009, http://www.hautcourant.com/El-Ghalia-Djimi-militante.

141. Tata Arcel, "Psychological Consquences," 342.

142. Sébastien Boulay, "Corps, mouvement et création sur le Web: Incarnations numériques de la lutte pacifique au Sahara Occidental," in *La question (irrésolue) du Sahara Occidental*, ed. Francesco Correale and Sébastien Boulay (Tours: François Rabelais University Press, forthcoming).

143. Agger, "Sexual Torture"; Beth Goldblatt and Shiela Meintjes, "Gender and the Truth and Reconciliation Commission: A Submission to the Truth and Reconciliation Commission," Department of Justice and Constitutional Development, Republic of South Africa, May 1996, http://www.justice.gov.za/trc//hrvtrans/submit/gender.htm.

144. Agger, "Sexual Torture," 312.

145. Dori Laub, "Truth and Testimony: The Process and the Struggle," in *Trauma: Explorations in Memory*, ed. Cathy Caruth (Baltimore: Johns Hopkins University Press, 1995).

146. Ibid., 314.

147. A. J. Cienfuegos and C. Monelli, "The Testimony of Political Repression as a Therapeutic Instrument," *American Journal of Orthopsychiatry* 53, no. 1 (1983). The written recording of testimonies of brutality has been also been used for solely political and feminist purposes elsewhere in Latin America. See Maureen E. Shea, "Latin American Women and the Oral Tradition: Giving Voice to the Voiceless," *Critique* 34, no. 3 (1993); Inger Agger and Sóren Buus Jensen, "Testimony as Ritual and Evidence in Psychotherapy for Political Refugees," *Journal of Traumatic Stress* 3, no. 1 (1990).

148. Mladen Lončar, Vesna Medved, Nikolina Jovanović, and Ljubomir Hotujac, "Psychological Consequences of Rape in 1991–1995 War in Croatia and Bosnia and Herzegovina," *Croation Medical Journal* 47, no. 1 (2006); Victor Igreja, Wim C. Kleijn, Bas J. N. Schreuder, Janie A. Van Dijk, and Margot Verschuur, "Testimony Method to Ameliorate Post-Traumatic Stress Symptoms: Community-Based Intervention Study with Mozambican Civil War Survivors," *British Journal of Psychiatry* 184 (2004).

149. Holly L. Guthrey, *Victim Healing and Truth Commissions: Transforming Pain through Voice in the Solomon Islands and Timor-Leste* (New York: Springer, 2015), 38.

150. Agger, "Testimony as Ritual and Evidence in Psychotherapy for Political Refugees," 115, 315.

151. See also Annie Pohlman, "Testimonio and Telling Women's Narratives of Genocide, Torture and Political Imprisonment in Post-Suharto Indonesia," *Life Writing* 5, no. 1 (2008).

152. As is the case with most Saharawi-led organizations, Morocco has not granted it permission to officially register.

153. El Haouasi, 26 November 2014.

154. Laura S. Brown, *Feminist Therapy* (Washington, DC: American Psychological Association, 2010).

155. When I asked interviewees if they hoped to get married and have children in the future, their responses included an element of surprise that I would bother asking a question with such an obvious answer. As I have argued in previous research, marriage and motherhood are seen as women's proper function and women's desires are shaped around these institutions. Allan, "Representations of Gender."

156. Pseudonym, personal interview, Madrid, 21 October 2014.

157. Allan, field notes, August–September 2014. Another view (but not one raised by research participants) is that, because of sexual violence, such women's desire for an affectionate and sexual relationship is diminished.

158. The interviews I undertook in Western Sahara and Morocco were largely unstructured: I encouraged participants to focus on what they found important, and the issue of gender inequality was not one raised by the more prominent women activists. I found that less prominent activists studying in Morocco (the women I interviewed there were not part of any organization, only occasionally joined protests, and played no leadership role in the latter) were more inclined to raise the issue of gender inequalities within Saharawi society. Nevertheless, constant harassment and interference from Moroccan police limited the time and depth of interviews. Unfortunately, then, I am unable to draw meaningful conclusions on the existence of a relationship between the depth of nationalist activism and the perception of being repressed along gendered lines. Nevertheless, I suspect that the most prominent activists in the Occupied Territories are, like the POLISARIO, keen to promote an image of gender equality to further the Saharawi cause externally. My subject position as a white, European researcher is important here: I am precisely the target of the externally promoted image.

159. Tag Sayed (pseudonym), personal interview, Rabat, 26 April 2014.

160. For more on feminist nationalism, see West, *Feminist Nationalism*.

161. Allan, field notes, August–September 2014.

162. Allan, field notes, August–September 2014.

163. I am not suggesting that sexual relations are necessarily a form of "liberation" for women. I merely highlight that women who wish to have sex have found ways to do so while simultaneously avoiding society's disapproval.

164. Kai Kreutzberger, "Single Mothers and Children Born out of Wedlock in the Kingdom of Morocco," *Yearbook of Islamic and Middle Eastern Law* 14 (2008–2009); Ida Sophie Winter, "Many Moroccan Students Pursue Sex but Few Get Sex Education," *Al-Fanar Media*, 17 August 2015, http://www.al-fanarmedia.org/2015/08/many-moroccan-students-pursue-sex-but-few-get-sex-education/.

165. Paciello, Pepicelli, and Pioppi, "Public Action," 13.

166. Katja Zvan Elliott, *Modernizing Patriarchy: The Politics of Women's Rights in Morocco* (Austin: University of Texas Press, 2015).

167. Angel Doménech Lafuente, "Sahara Español. Del vivir nómada de las tribus," *Cuaderno de Estudios Africanos*, no. 21 (January–March 1953): 35; Gaudio, "Apuntes." Gaudio (59) states that "in the case of adultery, the husband can beat a woman, shut her for up to three days inside or refuse to live with her. A woman discovered committing the flagrant crime of adultery can be stoned publicly by the tribe."

168. Yuval-Davis, *Gender and Nation*; Accad, "Sexuality and Sexual Politics"; West, *Feminist Nationalism*; Vickers, "Bringing Nations In."

169. Enloe, *Bananas*, 54. For more on the intertwining of sexual reproduction, nationalism, and resistance, see Rhoda Ann Kanaaneh, *Birthing the Nation: Strategies of Palestinian Women in Israel* (Berkeley: University of California Press, 2002).

170. Mahfood Hafdala (pseudonym), personal interview, El Aaiún, 23 August 2014.

171. Although their research focuses on early marriage rather than coerced marriage of adult women, see work by Jane E. M. Callaghan, Yaganama Gambo, and

Lisa C. Fellin, "Hearing the Silences: Adult Nigerian Women's Accounts of 'Early Marriages,'" *Feminism and Psychology* 25, no. 4 (2015).

172. Lakhal, August to September 2014.

173. I have used "prostitution" and "sex work" depending on the term interviewees and informants themselves use. Although in this paragraph the agency or otherwise of the women concerned was not the consideration of the informants, generally, I found that they used "prostitution" rather than "sex work" when they wished to highlight exploitation and coercion and "sex work" where they wished to highlight women's agency, as was the case with some women from Equatorial Guinea but none from Western Sahara.

174. According to Stephen Zunes and Jacob Mundy, the influx of Moroccan military personnel is significant, with no less than one-third of the Moroccan population in Western Sahara consisting of soldiers, and on top of this, they point out, are unknown numbers of police, gendarmes, Interior Ministry agents, royal secret services, plain-clothes agents, and civilian informers. Zunes and Mundy, *War, Nationalism and Conflict Irresolution*, 158.

175. Enloe, *Nimo's War, Emma's War*, 38.

176. Allan, field notes, August–September 2014.

177. Tfarrah is a pseudonym.

178. From the ninth verse of chapter 36, "Surat Ya Sin," in the Quran.

179. Zunes and Mundy, *War, Nationalism and Conflict Irresolution*.

180. With this welcome comes an ethical imperative to fulfill one's potential as a witness, I argue elsewhere. See Allan, "Activist Ethics."

181. Mahdi Mayara, personal interview, Rabat, 28 April 2014.

## Chapter 6. Gendering *Ngueismo* and Gendered Resistance

1. See also David Smith, "Equatorial Guinea Builds Luxury Resort for Week-Long Summit," *The Guardian*, 7 June 2011; Human Rights Watch, "Equatorial Guinea: Abuses Ahead of AU Summit," 22 June 2011.

2. Human Rights Watch, *World Report 2015: Events of 2014* (New York: Seven Stories Press, 2015).

3. For more information, see Amnesty International, "Los desalojos forzosos violan los derechos humanos," 20 June 2007; Amnesty International, "Equatorial Guinea: Fear of Forced Evictions/Fear of Excessive Force," 14 November 2006.

4. The interviewee was married to one of the more powerful of the government ministers and was a close friend of one of Obiang's ("legitimate") sons. Gaspar Nsue Adaha (pseudonym), personal interview, London (location altered to protect anonymity), 18 February 2014.

5. M. Bahati Kuumba, *Gender and Social Movements* (Walnut Creek, CA: AltaMira Press, 2001), 107.

6. Carmen Obón, Letter to Soledad de Santiago, Bata, 4 February 1969; Soledad de Santiago, Letter to Carmen Obón, Madrid, 21 November 1968.

7. Carmen Obón, Letter to Soledad de Santiago, Bata, 4 December 1968.

8. Carmen Obón, Letter to Soledad de Santiago (3), Bata, 22 February 1969.

9. For example, she contributed to the UN's 1974 International Forum on the Role of Women in Population and Development in Warrenton, Virginia. United Nations, "International Forum on the Role of Women in Population and Development,"

Warrenton, VA, 1974, document number ST/ESA/SER.B/4. With regard to the PUNT, in February 1972 all other political parties were suspended by Macías and all Equato-guinean citizens over the age of seven were forced to become members.

10. Nerín, *La Sección Femenina*, 22.

11. Carmen Obón, "Situación de la Sección Femenina desde Octubre de 1968," Bata, March 1969. The 1969 coup by MONALIGE leaders concerned by Macías's increasingly despotic behavior was planned in Madrid with the knowledge of the Spanish Ministry of Foreign Affairs. Pardo Sanz, "La herencia de la descolonización," 177.

12. Obón, "Situación de la Sección Femenina."

13. Macias quoted in Nze Nfumu, *Macías*, 62; Klinteberg, *Macías Country*, 19.

14. Adugu Mba (pseudonym), 30 June 2015. Agustín Nze Nfumu, historian and survivor of Macías's Black Beach prison, recalls the death from torture of at least one fellow inmate who had been informed on by his wife. He also recalls how Women's Section members had to sing songs praising Macías over national radio for as long as the latter worked. Nze Nfumu, *Macías*, 70 and 110.

15. This anecdote is told in Klinteberg, *Macías Country*, 48.

16. Ibid., 19.

17. Epifania Avomo Bicó, telephone interview, 28 August 2015; Victorino (pseud-onym) Pancho Ripeu, personal communication, 28 September 2015.

18. Enrique Martino, "Maoist China and Macias' Equatorial Guinea—write up of some of the notes of from [*sic*] fragmentary conversation with a secret and sort of expensive informant. Malabo, July 2013," 15 September 2013, http://www.opensource guinea.org/2013/09/maoist-china-and-macias-equatorial.html. For a thorough, if out-dated, map of the surviving archives, see Constantino Ocha'a Mve, *Fuentes archivísti-cas y bibliotecarias de Guinea Ecuatorial: Guía general del administrativo, del investigador y del estudiante* (Madrid: Anzos, 1985).

19. Cristina Boleká (pseudonym), personal interview, Malabo, 24 June 2015.

20. Enrique Momo (pseudonym), personal interview, Malabo, 24 June 2015.

21. Ibid.

22. Nyangi (pseudonym), 21 June 2015.

23. Avomo Bicó, 28 August 2015.

24. María Nsué Angüe, *Relatos* (Malabo: Centro Cultural Hispano-Guineano, 1999).

25. Robert H. Jackson and Carl G. Rosberg, *Personal Rule in Black Africa: Prince, Autocrat, Prophet, Tyrant* (Berkeley: University of California Press, 1982), 248.

26. This was in 1976. Ballano Gonzalo, *Aquel Negrito*, 601; Martino, "Economies of Forced and Contract Labour."

27. Production at independence was 40,000 tons annually. Commercial sources put the 1975 figure at 2,340 tons. UK Foreign and Commonwealth Office, "Equatorial Guinea: Current Conditions," 1979, 3.

28. Ibid., 2.

29. Jackson and Roseberg, *Personal Rule*, 251.

30. On execution of the director of the central bank, see Foot, "Policy of Plunder," 48. On transfer of money, see Nze Nfumu, *Macías*, 14.

31. Ibid., 48.

32. Jackson and Roseberg, *Personal Rule*, 251.

33. Foot, "Policy of Plunder." For an excellent analysis of how patrimonial systems work and of the conditions necessary for their overthrow, see Francesca Comunello and Giuseppe Anzera, "Will the Revolution Be Tweeted? A Conceptual Framework for Understanding the Social Media and the Arab Spring," *Islam and Christian-Muslim Relations* 23, no. 4 (2012).

34. UK Foreign and Commonwealth Office, "Equatorial Guinea: Current Conditions."

35. Ruth First, *The Barrel of a Gun: Political Power in Africa and the Coup d'État* (London: Penguin, 1970), 40.

36. Molubela (pseudonym), 21 June 2015.

37. Barrie Wharton, "Masters and Servants: The Spanish Civil War in Equatorial Guinea," *International Journal of the Canadian Institute for Mediterranean Studies* 26, no. 1 (2005): 50.

38. Ibid.

39. Morocco and Equatorial Guinea continue to enjoy a strong relationship. For more on the history of how Morocco has propped up Obiang, see Max Liniger-Goumaz, *Guinea Ecuatorial: Memorándum; Medio siglo de terror y saqueo* (Madrid: Sial Ediciones, 2013).

40. Amnesty International states that the alleged numerous foreign-backed plots for coup d'états surrounding the 1993 elections were never proved to have existed but were a convenient excuse to expel Spanish nationals living in Equatorial Guinea who were known to be friends of opposition activists. Amnesty International, "Equatorial Guinea: A Missed Opportunity to Restore Respect for Human Rights," 1 February 1994, 6. Similarly, the NGO argues that accusations of a plot led by a group of returnees from Gabon to overthrow the government were based on no evidence whatsoever. The "grossly unfair" trial of the fifteen alleged coup organizers resulted in torture and long sentences, including a twelve-year sentence for one woman, María Teresa Akumu. The alleged leader, Antonio Ndong Nve, was murdered by security forces. Amnesty International, "Equatorial Guinea: A Dismal Record of Broken Promises," July 1995, 12. Later, in 2002, three members of the Democratic Republican Force (Fuerza Demócrata Republicana [FDR]) were arrested on what Amnesty International alleges was a false allegation of attempting to organize a coup. See Amnesty International, "Equatorial Guinea: No Free Flow of Information," 5 June 2000, 2. See also Amnesty International, "Key Human Rights Concerns."

41. Enrique Okenve, "'Wa kobo abe, wa kobo politik': Three Decades of Social Paralysis and Political Immobility in Equatorial Guinea" (paper presented at the conference Between Three Continents: Rethinking Equatorial Guinea on the Fortieth Anniversary of Its Independence from Spain, Hofstra University, 2009), 5.

42. While resistance to Obiang led from abroad (without wishing to deny that this is almost always realized with the collaboration of in-country contacts) is not within the scope of this thesis, I would direct readers to the work of the Washington-based NGO EG Justice on this issue.

43. Sharp, *Nonviolent Action*, 25.

44. Okenve, "Three Decades of Social Paralysis," 4.

45. Ibid., 7.

46. Ibid.

47. Tutu Alicante, Skype interview, 28 May 2015.

48. Ibid.

49. Avomo Bicó, 28 August 2015; Adugu Mba (pseudonym), 30 June 2015.

50. White, *The Content of Form*.

51. Amnesty International, "Equatorial Guinea: A Parody of a Trial in Order to Crush the Opposition," 30 June 2002, 6.

52. See, for example, Amnesty International, "Equatorial Guinea: A Country Subject to Terror and Harassment," 1 January 1999, 6; Amnesty International, "Equatorial Guinea: A Parody of a Trial in Order to Crush the Opposition," 5; Amnesty International, "Morocco/Western Sahara: Justice Must Begin with Torture Enquiries," 22 June 2005, 5.

53. Tamek's testimony was published by Amnesty International, "Morocco/Western Sahara: The Grueling Experience of One Sahrawi HRD," 18 April 2007. Indeed, Amnesty International has reported the rape and threat of rape of female relatives as a common form of torture for male Saharawi political prisoners. See, for example, Amnesty International, "Western Sahara/Morocco: Torture of Detainees Must End"; Amnesty International, "Morocco/Western Sahara: Briefing to the Committee against Torture," 11 November 2003, 5. Buamad recounts his episode in Martín Beristain and González Hidalgo, *El oasis*, vol. 2, 116.

54. Victor Rodriguez Rescia, "Torture as a Form of Gendered Violence," *Essex Human Rights Review* 6, no. 2 (2010): 139.

55. Dahane quoted in Martín Beristain and González Hidalgo, *El oasis*, vol. 1, 285.

56. Temma Kaplan, "Acts of Testimony: Reversing the Shame and Gendering the Memory," *Signs* 28, no. 1 (2002).

57. Bahati Kuumba, *Gender and Social Movements*, 90–91.

58. Allan, field notes, June–July 2015.

59. Pardo Sanz, "La herencia de la descolonización," 182. Morocco to this day offers education and training programs for Equatoguineans in Morocco, while Morocco holds substantial business interests in Equatorial Guinea. For example, the Moroccan construction company SOMAGEC has won major contracts across Equatorial Guinea. See SOMAGEC Morocco, "Homepage," accessed December 2015, http://www.somagec.ma/e_acceuil.asp; SOMAGEC Equatorial Guinea, "Homepage," accessed December 2015, http://www.somagecge.com/. The Obiang family owns several luxury residential properties in Morocco.

60. Amnesty International, "A Missed Opportunity." On Moroccan nationals and Obiang's regime during its first decade, see Marisé Castro, "Equatorial Guinea," in *Africa South of the Sahara*, 33rd ed., ed. Katherine Murison (London: Europa Publications, 2004), 377. See also Afrol News, "Moroccan Life Guard to Leave Equatorial Guinea," 10 January 2000, http://www.afrol.com/News2001/eqg001_moroccan_guard.htm.

61. For example, Celestino Bacale and other detained teachers reported receiving fifty blows to the sole of each foot: see Amnesty International, "Equatorial Guinea. Torture and Legal Concern: Over 100 people including Celestino Bacale, Pedro Esono, Maximio Miko, Arsenio Moro, Angel Obama," 22 December 1992. For further examples of *falāqa*, see Amnesty International, "A Missed Opportunity"; Amnesty International,

"Equatorial Guinea: An Opportunity to Put an End to Impunity," 30 June 1997, 3; Amnesty International, "Equatorial Guinea: A Country Subject to Terror"; Amnesty International, "Equatorial Guinea: Arrests of Pro-Democracy Activists—A Changing Pattern of Human Rights Violations," 1 November 1991; 6. Amnesty International, "Key Human Rights Concerns," 5.

62. Amnesty International, "A Missed Opportunity," 12.

63. Neil Hughes, "Democracy and Imperial Rivalry in Equatorial Guinea," *Review of African Political Economy* 23, no. 69 (1996): 445.

64. Amnesty International, "A Missed Opportunity," 3; Ana Camacho, "Los 'ninjas' toman posiciones en Guinea Ecuatorial," *El País*, 15 August 1993.

65. See, for example, United Press International, "Israeli Arms Companies Target Third World," 8 April 2011, http://www.upi.com/Business_News/Security-Indus try/2011/04/08/Israeli-arms-companies-target-Third-World/29731302286121/. See also Agustín Velloso, "Israel starts business in Equatorial Guinea: Disaster Closes in Obiang Nguema's Regime," CSCAweb, 27 June 2005, https://www.nodo50.org/csca/agenda 05/palestina/velloso_20-06-05.html.

66. Okenve, "Three Decades of Social Paralysis."

67. Lino Lisoha, arrested for "knowing the whereabouts of fugitives," was the victim. Amnesty International, "Equatorial Guinea: A Country Subject to Terror," 6.

68. For more on the barriers faced by male survivors of sexual violence, see Thema Bryant-Davis, *Surviving Sexual Violence: A Guide to Recovery and Empowerment* (Lanham, MD: Rowman & Littlefield, 2011), 307; Nina Burrows and Tessa Horvath, "The Rape and Sexual Assault of Men—A Review of the Literature," Survivors UK, 2013.

69. Amnesty International, "Equatorial Guinea: A Country Subject to Terror."

70. Eyewitness quoted in ibid., 5.

71. Temma Kaplan argues that the state's robbing of, or inability to ensure, this right is often cause for the development of what she describes as a "female consciousness": a sense of community that emerges among women when their gendered role as providers of life is threatened. Kaplan, "Female Conciousness."

72. There are reports of women being taken to forced labor camps while their infants are interned in military camps. Amnesty International, "Equatorial Guinea: A Country Subject to Terror," 28.

73. Ibid., 12.

74. Ibid., 10–11.

75. Pancho Ripeu, 28 September 2015.

76. Amnesty International, "Equatorial Guinea: A Country Subject to Terror," 6.

77. We should use this concept carefully. It has been employed by the West to justify military interventions. For further discussion see Kerry F. Crawford, Amelia Hoover Green, and Sarah E. Parkinson, "Wartime Sexual Violence Is Not Just a 'Weapon of War,'" *Washington Post*, 24 September 2014.

78. Bülent Diken and Carsten Bagge Lausten, "Becoming Abject: Rape as a Weapon of War," *Body and Society* 11, no. 1 (2005): 118.

79. Decker, *Idi Amin's Shadow*.

80. Sharp, *Nonviolent Action*, 471.

81. Human Rights Watch, "Well Oiled," 69; Amnesty International, "Equatorial Guinea: Woman Held in Prison Cell with Up to 100 Male Detainees," 14 February 2008.

82. Amnesty International, "Equatorial Guinea: Further Information on Detention without Charge or Trial/Harsh Detention Conditions, Brígida Asongsua Elo," 30 April 2008.

83. See, for example, the case of Domiciana Bisobe Robe in Amnesty International, "Equatorial Guinea: A Country Subject to Terror," 20.

84. Bahati Kuumba has pointed out that strategies of resistance employed by women in oppressive situations, including providing food and shelter, promoting liberation education, or the very maintenance of a particular "way of life" (in the face of colonial domination, for example) are, erroneously, not considered forms of resistance. Bahati Kuumba, *Gender and Social Movements*, 108–12.

85. Amnesty International, "Equatorial Guinea: Arrest of a Possible Prisoner of Conscience/Fear of Ill-Treatment Pilar Mañana," 14 June 1992.

86. Amnesty International, "Equatorial Guinea: A Country Subject to Terror," 27.

87. Eteo Soriso, *Cancionero*, 11.

88. Ibid.; Francisca Sale (pseudonym), personal interview, Barcelona, 25 February 2015; Ángel Antonio López Ortega, *La poesía oral de los pueblos de Guinea Ecuatorial: Géneros y funciones* (Barcelona: Ceiba Ediciones, 2008), 142.

89. Full song lyrics in Eteo Soriso, *Cancionero*, 314.

90. López Ortega, *La poesía oral*, 105–6.

91. Ibid., 106.

92. Marcelle C. Dawson, "Protest, Performance and Politics: The Use of 'Nano-Media' in Social Movement Activism in South Africa," *Research in Drama Education: The Journal of Applied Theatre and Performance* 17, no. 3 (2012): 332.

93. Amnesty International, "Equatorial Guinea: A Missed Opportunity." For a fictional representation of the story of suffering of the Annobonese people, see Juan Tomás Avila Laurel, *By Night the Mountain Burns*, trans. Jethro Soutar (London: And Other Stories, 2014).

94. Amnesty International, "Equatorial Guinea: A Missed Opportunity."

95. Campanet (pseudonym), 28 June 2015. For more on Annobonese nationalism, see Iñaki Gorozpe, "Reivindicación Política y Particularismo en Annobón," *Lusotopie* 2 (1995).

96. Okenve, "Three Decades of Social Paralysis," 6.

97. Amnesty International, "Equatorial Guinea: A Country Subject to Terror," 28.

98. Allan, field notes, June–July 2015.

99. I limited myself to posing such questions to members of parties who openly oppose the regime.

100. See, for example, Pamela Lutgen-Sandvik, "Take This Job and . . . : Quitting and Other Forms of Resistance to Workplace Bullying," *Communication Monographs* 73, no. 4 (2006): 417; Victoria Law, *Resistance Behind Bars: The Struggles of Incarcerated Women* (Oakland, CA: PM Press, 2009), 111–26.

101. Amnesty International, "Equatorial Guinea: A Country Subject to Terror," 28.

102. See also the work of Temma Kaplan on the gendered memory and testimony-giving of Chilean survivor of sexual torture Nieves Ayress. Kaplan, "Acts of Testimony."

103. Ntutumu (pseudonym), 16 June 2015.

104. Allan, field notes, June–July 2015.

105. As told to me by a local friend on my first visit to the market and repeated, slightly differently each time, by other informants.

106. Josimar Oyono Eseng, personal communication, 28 July 2015.

107. Who is able to rent the sought-after stalls in the new market and who is relegated to the homemade sprawling market? *Diario Rombe* and several informers have claimed nepotism. See, for example, *Diario Rombe*, "La Alcadesa se hace dueña del nuevo mercado de Malabo," 6 August 2013, http://www.diariorombe.es/la-alcaldesa-se-hace-duena-del-nuevo-mercado-de-malabo/.

108. Engonga (pseudonym), 25 June 2015.

109. Avomo Bicó, 28 August 2015.

110. Nick Ames, "Ghana Players, Fans Pelted with Missiles in Win over Equatorial Guinea," *The Guardian*, 5 February 2015.

111. Sean Ingle and Mark Hodgkinson, "When Did Football Hooliganism Start?," *The Guardian*, 13 December 2001.

112. Adugu Mba (pseudonym), 30 June 2015.

113. Ibid.; Juan Tomás Ávila Laurel, personal communication, 13 January 2015. I witnessed such graffiti during my field trip to Malabo.

114. For example, see *Diario Rombe*, "El PDGE convoca una reunión urgente en Malabo," 6 February 2015, http://www.diariorombe.es/ultima-hora-el-pdge-convoca-una-reunion-urgente-en-malabo/; Ames, "Ghana Players, Fans Pelted with Missiles in Win over Equatorial Guinea." Tutu Alicante also interpreted the events in this way. Alicante, 28 May 2015.

115. *Diario Rombe*, "El PDGE convoca una reunión urgente en Malabo."

116. On 24 November 1992, forty-one students took part in a demonstration (the precise demand of which is unknown). Amnesty International, "Equatorial Guinea: Fear of Extrajudicial Execution/Torture: Alfredo Bijuan and 40 Students," 27 November 1992. A few weeks later, Celestino Bacale, a CPDS member and then a teacher at the Rey Malabo school, was imprisoned and tortured. On 17 December 1992 in Malabo, more than one hundred people, mostly Bacale's school colleagues and students but also a handful of opposition party members and some priests, demonstrated publicly for his release. See Amnesty International, "Equatorial Guinea. Torture and Legal Concern: Over 100 people including Celestino Bacale, Pedro Esono, Maximio Miko, Arsenio Moro, Angel Obama." As Campos Serrano and Micó Abogo have reported, there have been several attempts to set up trade unions since Obiang came to power, although few of these have been legalized. Some of the underground unions have supported strikes over the years, including a (successful) forty-eight-hour strike in 1991 by Equatoguinean UN Development Program workers for a salary increase, a two-month strike by secondary school teachers in Malabo (which ended in tortures, imprisonments, and the dismissal of twenty-seven strikers), (unsuccessful) strikes by teachers demanding pay increases in September 1993 and March 1994, and an (unsuccessful) strike by 111 Equatoguinean workers employed by the Spanish government's development agency for equal pay between Equatoguinean and Spanish workers. Alicia Campos Serrano and Plácido Micó Abogo, "Labour and Trade Union Freedom in Equatorial Guinea" (Fundación Paz y Solidaridad "Serafín Aliaga"—CCOO and International Confederation of Free Trade Unions [ICFTU], Madrid, 2006), 71–75. In February 1981, there was also a students' strike sparked by anger at the lack of jobs. See

Liniger-Goumaz, *Guinea Ecuatorial*, 60. In May 2013 ahead of the elections, the newly founded Popular Protest Movement (created by members of the MAIB, the UP, and Clara Nsegue Ayi's party, the Democratic Party of Social Justice) called for a demonstration against the "antidemocratic ruling system." Espacios Europeos, "Agradecimiento de la plataforma Movimiento de Protesta Popular," 5 June 2013, https://espacioseu ropeos.com/2013/06/agradecimiento-de-la-plataforma-movimiento-de-protesta-pop ular-de-guinea-ecuatorial/. Clara Nsegue Ayi and others who had been coordinating the demonstration were arrested and imprisoned. Similarly, after the elections, the CPDS was prevented from holding a march demanding the recount of votes. Nevertheless, fifty to one hundred CPDS members did manage to hold a sit-in outside their own office in Malabo on 26 June (the adjacent streets were cordoned off as military personnel surrounded them). Amnesty International, "Equatorial Guinea: The Authorities Must Allow Freedom of Expression and Peaceful Demonstrations to Take Place," 1 July 2013. In August 2013 *Diario Rombe* reported on the case of thirty ex-workers of the National Library of Equatorial Guinea who had allegedly been dismissed by the minister of culture, Guillermina Mekuy, without reasonable grounds and without pay for previous months' work. The thirty women and men staged a sit-in outside the library on two consecutive days, demanding the pay they were due, before being moved on by police. *Diario Rombe*, "Guillermina Mekuy Mba Ministra Delegada de Cultura," 1 August 2013, http://www.diariorombe.es/guillermina-mekuy-mba-ministra-delegada -de-cultura/.

117. See *Diario Rombe*, "Huelga de taxistas en Guinea Ecuatorial," 4 May 2017, http://www.africafundacion.org/spip.php?article27431.

118. Alicia Campos Serrano and Plácido Micó Abogo have also highlighted that opposition parties, as well as the PDGE, are dominated by men. Campos Serrano and Micó Abogo, "Labour and Trade Union Freedom," 24–25.

119. Ávila Laurel, 13 January 2015.

120. For more on the debate over POLISARIO's commitment to women's rights, see Allan, "Representations of Gender"; Errer Bouzeid, "Sexismo en la sociedad saharaui"; Fiddian-Qasmiyeh, *The Ideal Refugees*.

121. Avomo Bicó, 28 August 2015.

122. Mitoha Ondo'o Ayekaba, "The Politics of Gender Parity in Equatorial Guinea: Toward a more Sustained Political and Social Civility in the Twenty First Century" (paper presented at the conference Between Three Continents: Rethinking Equatorial Guinea on the Fortieth Anniversary of Its Independence from Spain, Hofstra University, New York, 2009), 7.

123. See especially Trifonia Melibea Obono Ntutumu, "Guinea Ecuatorial: Misoginia en los partidos políticos," *Tiempos Canallas*, 8 March 2013.

124. Uday Chandra provides a useful review of the literature on rightful resistance in "Rethinking Subaltern Resistance," *Journal of Contemporary Asia* 45, no. 4 (2015): 566.

125. Eteo Soriso, *Cancionero*.

126. Mba (pseudonym), 16 June 2015; Engonga (pseudonym), 25 June 2015.

127. Eteo Soriso, *Cancionero*, 163.

128. Engonga (pseudonym), 25 June 2015; Mba (pseudonym), 16 June 2015.

129. Deubel, "Homeland and Exile," 126–30.

130. Mba (pseudonym), 16 June 2015.

131. Gabo Ntseane, "Culturally Sensitive Transformational Learning: Incorporating the Afrocentric Paradigm and African Feminism," 315; Salami, "7 Key Issues in African Feminist Thought." See also M. Bahati Kuumba, "African Women, Resistance Cultures and Cultural Resistances," *Agenda: Empowering Women for Gender Equity* 20, no. 68 (2006): 191.

132. So they explain via public Facebook posts and during informal conversations. See also Asria Taleb Mohammed, "'Influenciado por Occidente,' una acusación que funciona: Y seis lecciones que debemos aprender de Occidente," *Democracia Saharaui* (blog), 2 April 2017, http://lehdiamohameddafa.blogspot.co.uk/2017/04/influenciado -por-occidente-una.html.

133. Wolters, "Equatorial Guinea's Web."

134. Ana Henríquez Pérez, "Entrevista a la escritora y activista Trifonia Melibea Obono: 'Las guineanas siempre han sido feministas,'" 6 June 2017, http://www.africaye .org/guineanas-feministas-melibea-obono/.

## Final Remarks

1. Adugu Mba (pseudonym), 30 June 2015.

# Bibliography

Interviews with Saharawis

Senia Abdurahman, personal communication, 20 March 2006

Agaila Abba, personal communication, 2 May 2006

Embarka Hamoudi, personal communication, 7 July 2006

Sidi Omar (ex-POLISARIO Representative to the UK, and also to the African Union), personal communication, 12 July 2006

Larosi Haidar, personal interview, Granada (Spain), 20 November 2007

Limam Boicha, personal interview, Madrid (Spain), 6 February 2008

Bahia Awah, personal interview, Madrid, 7 February 2008

Zahra Ramdan (president of the Association of Saharawi Women in Spain), personal interview, Madrid, 7 February 2008

Mohammed Selma (lawyer who previously worked in Saharawi courts), personal interview, Granada (Spain), 20 February 2008

Castro (nickname), personal interview, Smara camp (Algeria), 29 March 2008

Maimona Said, personal interview, Smara camp, 29 March 2008

Sid Ahmed Abdulramdan, personal interview, Smara camp, 31 March 2008

Fanna Nafe, personal interview, Smara camp, 2 April 2008

Bashir Mustapha Sayed (one of the POLISARIO founders and minister), personal interview, Rabuni camp (Algeria), 2 April 2008

Embarka Abdusalem (pseudonym), personal interview, Algiers (Algeria), 5 April 2008

Malainin Lakhal, personal conversation, Algiers, 5 April 2008

Fatimetou Zrug Yomani (then member of parliament for the Youth Union), personal interview, Algiers, 5 April 2008

Agaila Abba, personal communication, 27 April 2008

Limam Mohammed Ali (current POLISARIO representative to the United Kingdom), personal communication, 28 April 2008

Limam Khalil, personal interview, Leeds (United Kingdom), 5 May 2008

Malainin Lakhal, personal communications, June 2008

Sidi Breika (ex-POLISARIO representative to the United Kingdom), personal interview, London, 31 March 2014

Fatan Abaali, personal interview, Agadir (Morocco), 22 April 2014

Bachir Ismaili, personal interview, Agadir, 22 April 2014

Discussion group with seven male Saharawi students, Agadir, 22 April 2014

Discussion group with six male Saharawi students, Marrakech (Morocco), 23 April 2015

Shaykh Alhala, personal interview, Rabat (Morocco), 26 April 2014

Tag Sayed, personal interview, Rabat, 26 April 2014

Ahmed Baba, personal interview, Rabat, 28 April 2014

Khawla Khaya, personal interview, Rabat, 28 April 2014

Khairo Mayara, personal interview, Rabat, 28 April 2014

Mahdi Mayara, personal interview, Rabat, 28 April 2014

Malainin Lakhal, personal communication, 13 May 2014

Saharawi host family (anonymous), personal conversations, El Aaiún (occupied Western Sahara), August 2014

Hamza Lakhal, personal conversations, El Aaiún, August to September 2014

Hamza Lakhal, personal interview, El Aaiún, 21 August 2014

Izana Amidan, personal interview, El Aaiún, 22 August 2014

Mahfooda Lefkir, personal interview, El Aaiún, 22 August 2014

Soukaina Yaya, personal interview, El Aaiún, 22 August 2014

Mohammed El Baikam, personal interview, El Aaiún, 23 August 2014

Mahfood Hafdala (pseudonym), personal interview, El Aaiún, 23 August 2014

Mohammed Brahim (pseudonym), personal interview, El Aaiún, 25 August 2014

Mohammed Mayara, personal interview, El Aaiún, 27 August 2014

Mahfoud Dahou, personal interview, El Aaiún, 29 August 2014

Soumaya Taher (pseudonym), personal interview, Madrid (Spain), 21 October 2014

Embarka Hassan (pseudonym), personal interview, Madrid, 26 October 2014

Hassana Aalia, personal interview, Zaragoza (Spain), 26 November 2014

Nguia El Haouasi, personal interview, Zaragoza, 26 November 2014

Sultana Khaya, personal interview, Zaragoza, 26 November 2014

Hayat Rguibi, personal interview, Zaragoza, 26 November 2014

Lehdia Dafa, personal interview, Madrid, 28 November 2014

Khadijatou Mokhtar (UNMS director of external affairs), personal interview, Madrid, 28 November 2014

Lahcen Dalil (acting president of Support Committee for the Protection of Natural Resources [CSPRON]), personal communication, 18 December 2014

Malainin Lakhal, personal communication, 2 March 2015

Hamza Lakhal, personal conversations, Norway, April 2015

Fatma Mehdi (secretary general of the UNMS), Windhoek (Namibia), 4 November 2015

Mohammed Saleh, personal conversations, Auserd camp, 8–15 December 2015

Asria Taleb Mohammed, personal communication, 10 December 2015

Nahjiba Saleh (pseudonym), personal conversation, Boujdour camp (Algeria), 10 December 2015

Silka Bilaal, personal interview, Auserd camp (Algeria), 11 December 2015

Tawfa Saleh, personal interview, Auserd camp, 11 December 2015

Salek Baba Hassana (governor of Auserd camp), personal conversation, Auserd camp, 11 December 2015

Majhula Cheikh el Mami, personal interview, Auserd camp, 12 December 2015
Leila Sidi Mahmoud, personal interview, Auserd camp, 12 December 2015
Khadijatou Mokhtar, personal interview, Auserd camp, 13 December 2015
Ali Salem Tamek, personal conversation, Auserd camp, 13 December 2015
Aminatou Errer Bouzeid, personal communication, 19 December 2015
Hamza Lakhal, personal conversations, London, March 2016

### Interviews with Equatoguineans

Ismael Abuy (pseudonym), personal interview, Jaen (Spain), 13 October 2013
Gaspar Nsue Adaha (pseudonym), personal interview, London (location altered to
    protect anonymity), 18 February 2014
Ignacio Nsue Enhate (pseudonym), personal interview, Brussels (Belgium), 1 April 2014
Marcelino Obono Alogo (pseudonym), personal interview, Granada, 18 July 2014
Juan Tomás Ávila Laurel, personal communication, 13 January 2015
Ricardo Soriso Sipi (pseudonym), personal communication, 15 January 2015
Lucia Zamora Nsang (pseudonym), personal communication, 16 January 2015
Francisca Sale (pseudonym), personal interview, Barcelona (Spain), 25 February 2015
Tutu Alicante, Skype interview, 28 May 2015
Francisca Sale (pseudonym), personal communication, 28 May 2015
Maria Jesus Ntutumu (pseudonym), personal interview, Malabo (Equatorial Guinea),
    16 June 2015
Trinidad Mba (pseudonym), personal interview, Malabo, 16 June 2015
Alicia Watson (pseudonym), personal interview, Malabo, 17 June 2015
Maria Jesus Ntutumu (pseudonym), personal conversations, 19 June 2015
Dolores Molubela (pseudonym), personal interview, Malabo, 21 June 2015
Pilar Nyangi (pseudonym), personal interview, Malabo, 21 June 2015
Constancia Balboa (pseudonym), personal interview, Malabo, 22 June 2015
Cristina Boleká (pseudonym), personal interview, Malabo, 24 June 2015
Enrique Momo (pseudonym), personal interview, Malabo, 24 June 2015
Alba Engonga (pseudonym), personal interview, Malabo, 25 June 2015
Miguel Nze (pseudonym), personal interview, Malabo, 25 June 2015
Francisca Sale (pseudonym), personal conversations, Malabo, 25 June 2015
Carmen Campanet (pseudonym), personal interview, Malabo, 28 June 2015
Claudette Kendo (pseudonym), personal interview, Malabo, 29 June 2015
Veronica Mayo (pseudonym), personal conversations, Malabo, 29 June 2015
Maria Angeles Adugu Mba (pseudonym), personal interview, Malabo, 30 June 2015
Patricio Nvuar (pseudonym), personal interview, Malabo 30 June 2015
Josimar Oyono Eseng, personal communication, 28 July 2015
Epifania Avomo Bicó, telephone interview, 28 August 2015
Victorino Pancho Ripeu (pseudonym), personal communication, 28 September 2015
Ana Alogo Mikue (pseudonym), telephone interview, 22 August 2016
Justo Bolekia Boleká, personal communication, 13 April 2017

### Other Interviews and Field Notes

Field notes. Smara camp and 'liberated' Western Sahara, February-March 2006.
Field notes. Smara and Rabuni camps, April 2008.

Field notes. El Aaiún, August–September 2014.

Field notes. Malabo, June–July 2015.

Field notes. Boujdour and Auserd camps, December 2015.

Alice Wilson, personal communications, December 2015.

Primary Archival Sources

20 Chiefs of Rio Benito. Letter to the General Governor of the Spanish Territories in the Gulf of Guinea, Bata, Rio Muni (continental Guinea), 9 June 1942, AGA 81/08182.

Anonymous Social Worker. "Informe del primer semestre de 1974." 30 July 1974, AGA (3) 51.19 Caja 237.

Ayakaba Nzue. Request from Ayakaba Nzue to the President of the Patronato for Separation from her Husband, Santa Isabel, 12 May 1937, AGA 81/08527.

Banapá Mission of Claretians. *La revista de la Guinea Española*, 28 March 1904, 1–4.

———. *La revista de la Guinea Española*, 12 January 1904, 1–4.

———. "El Problema de los Braceros." *La revista de la Guinea Española*, 1903, 1–4.

Bermúdez Cañete, Dolores. "Informe del viaje de la Regidora Central de S.E.U. a la isla de Fernando Poo y Rio Muni." May 1964, AGA (3) 51.19 Caja 244.

———. Letter to Soledad de Santiago, Bata, 8 July 1964, AGA (3) 51.19 Caja 248.

Bosio Dioco, Edmundo, and Ricardo Bolopá. Letter, Madrid, 20 June 1968, AGA (3) 51.19 Caja 251.

Bradley, W. M. "Labour Report to the Honourable Commissioner of Labour, Lagos, No. 3 for the Period 1st of October to the 31st December 1949." Santa Isabel, 11 January 1950, TNA, CO 554/169/1.

———. "Labour Report to the Honourable Commissioner of Labour, Lagos, no. 1 for the Period 1st January to 31st March 1950, British Vice Consulate." Santa Isabel, 31 March 1950, TNA CO 554/169/2.

Carvallo de Cora y Romero, Esteban, Territorial Police. "Informando sobre disturbios ocurridos en el día de hoy." El Aaiún, 20 November 1974. Document available as an appendix to the doctoral dissertation of Claudia Barona Castañeda, "Sahara Al-Garbia (1958–1976): Estudio Sobre la Identidad Nacional Saharaui," Autonomous University of Madrid, 1998.

———. "Informe sobre reunión con estudiantes." El Aaiún, 30 January 1975. Document available as an appendix to Barona, 1998.

Dalda, Juan Luís, Carles Martí Ares, and Lluís Pau Coromines. "Dossier Forming Part of the Exposition, 'Aaiun 1939–73, Formación de una Ciudad Española en el Sahara Occidental,' Study Carried out in El Aaiún." Col.legi Oficial d'Aparelladors i Arquitectes Tècnics de Girona, 1977.

De Santiago, Soledad. "Guión para la visita de la Delegación Nacional a las provincias de Africa." Madrid, 23 January 1967, AGA (3) 51.19 Caja 244.

———. Letter to Carmen Obón, Madrid, 22 March 1967, AGA (3) 51.19 Caja 248.

———. Letter to "Mina" ("Auxiliar Central de Juventudes"), Madrid, 27 May 1967, AGA (3) 51.19 Caja 246.

———. Letter to Carmen Obón, Madrid, 17 June 1967, AGA (3) 51.19 Caja 248.

———. Letter to Carmen Obón, Madrid, 15 July 1967, AGA (3) 51.19 Caja 248.

———. Letter to Carmen Obón, Bata, 29 February 1968, AGA (3) 51.19 Caja 248.

———. Letter to Carmen Obón, Madrid, 21 November 1968, AGA (3) 51.19 Caja 251.

Emba, Mangue. Request Sent to the President of Patronato, 13 May 1937, AGA 81/08527.

García Morales, Purita. Letter to Soledad de Santiago, Bata, 4 April 1965, AGA (3) 51.19 Caja 248.

General Government of the Sahara Province. "Informe sobre el partido saharaui clandestino denominado 'Organización Avanzada para la Liberación de la Saguia el Hamra y Rio de Oro.'" El Aaiún, 12 June 1970. Document available as an appendix to Barona, 1998.

———. "Recopilación de informes y documentos de interés relacionados con el O.A.L.S. y los incidentes del 17 de Junio de 1970." El Aaiún, 22 October 1970. Document available as an appendix to Barona, 1998.

———. "Actitud alumnas Sección Femenina." Villa Cisneros, 24 January 1975. Document available as an appendix to Barona, 1998.

———. "Censo escolar." El Aaiún, 1975. Document available as an appendix to Barona, 1998.

Gori Molubela, Enrique. Letter to Teresa Loring, Santa Isabel de Fernando Po, 22 September 1964, AGA (3) 51.19 Caja 247.

Headmistress, Smara Domestic School. "Informe de las actividades realizadas durante el curso 73/74 en la Escuela Hogar de patronato de Sección Femenina de Sahara." Smara, 30 June 1974, AGA (3) 51.19 Caja 240.

Illegible signature. Letter to the Governor General of the Spanish Territories of the Gulf of Guinea. En Mikomeseng, 15 May 1945, AGA Caja 81/08214.

International Court of Justice (ICJ). "Western Sahara: Advisory Opinion of 16 October 1975." https://www.icj-cij.org/files/case-related/61/6197.pdf.

Iriarte, Maria Luisa. Letter to Soledad de Santiago, Santa Isabel, 6 November 1967, AGA (3) 51.19 Caja 246.

———. "Informe del curso 1967–1968." Santa Isabel, 25 May 1968, AGA (3) 51.19 Caja 247.

López de la Torre, Salvador. "El referéndum de Guinea Ecuatorial ha sido un verdadero ejemplo para todos los pueblos de Africa." *ABC*, Madrid, 17 December 1963.

Loring, Teresa. (Sub-delegada Nacional de la Sección Femenina). Letter to Antonio Trujillo, Madrid, 27 Abril 1964, AGA (3) 51.19 Caja 244.

———. Letter to Federico Ngomo Nandongo, Madrid, 10 May 1965, AGA (3) 51.19 Caja 248.

———. "Notas para la presentación en el Instituto de Estudios Africanos." Madrid, 1967, AGA (3) 51.19 Caja 242.

Mallado, Angeles. Letter to Dolores Bermudez Cañete, Santa Isabel, 22 June 1964, AGA (3) 51.19 Caja 246.

Matala, Rafael M. Letter to Soledad de Santiago, Santa Isabel, 20 April 1967, AGA (3) 51.19 Caja 246.

Mateo, Concha. "Cultura del plan general: Profesorado de la Escuela Hogar." El Aaiún, April 1964. AGA (3) 51.19 Caja 239.

———. "Informe de la labor realizada en la Escuela de Hogar para nativas: 18 Mayo–18 Julio 1964." El Aaiún, 1964, AGA (3) 51.19 Caja 239.

———. "Informe correspondiente al curso 1964–65, Escuela Hogar de nativas." El Aaiún, 1965, AGA (3) 51.19 Caja 239.

———. Letter to María Nieves Sunyer in Madrid, El Aaiún, 16 March 1966, AGA (3) 51.19 Caja 240.

———. Letter to Soledad de Santiago in Madrid, El Aaiún, 17 March 1966, AGA (3) 51.19 Caja 240.

———. "Notas para la conferencia de Teresa: Situación de la mujer saharaui." El Aaiún, 1966, AGA (3) 51.19 Caja 242.

———. "Primer plan previo de enseñanzas y actividades." El Aaiún, April 1964, AGA (3) 51.19 Caja 239.

———. "Proyecto de nuevo edificio para escuela de primera enseñanza de patronato de Sección Femenina." El Aaiún, 4 May 1971, AGA (3) 51.19 Caja 240.

———. "Informe sobre la actitud política de la mujer saharaui." El Aaiún, October 1974, AGA (3) 51.19 Caja 235.

———. Letter to Soledad de Santiago, El Aaiún, 22 October 1974, AGA (3) 51.19 Caja 235.

Martins, Lola. "Journey to Hell's Island: How It All Started." *Express*, Lagos, 21 February 1962.

Monreal, Elisa, and Maria Jesus Curto. "Informe general de la labor realizada en la promoción de la mujer saharaui durante el primer semestre de 1973." Unknown (Western Sahara), 1973, AGA (3) 51.19 Caja 237.

Mozaz, Maria Angeles. Letter to Soledad de Santiago, El Aaiún, 17 May 1975, AGA (3) 51.19 Caja 239.

———. "Actas de reuniones celebradas recientemente con mujeres nativas, ex alumnas de los centros de Sección Femenina." El Aaiún, 9 October 1974, AGA (3) 51.19 Caja 239.

———. "Actas de reuniones celebradas recientemente con mujeres nativas, ex alumnas de los centros de Sección Femenina." El Aaiún, 24 October 1974, AGA (3) 51.19 Caja 239.

———. "Informe motivado de los cursos que ésta delegación provincial de Sección Femenina de Sahara imparte a la mujer nativa con cargo al Fondo Nacional de Protección al Trabajo." El Aaiún, estimated 1974, AGA (3) 51.19 Caja 237.

———. "Liquidación que se presenta a gobierno del taller-escuela 'Confecciónes Sahara.'" El Aaiún, 15 April 1975, AGA (3) 51.19 Caja 239.

MUNGE. "Movimiento de Unión Nacional de la Guinea Ecuatorial (MUNGE), Declaración de principios." Madrid. 18 January 1964, AGA (3) 51.19 Caja 248.

Murillo, (first name unknown). Paper letterheaded with the Falange logo. "Informe sobre la situación actual de Sahara." El Aaiún, 7 June 1974. Document available as appendix to Barona, 1998.

Negre Rigol, Jordi. "Sahara: España arria su bandera." *Diario de Barcelona*. Barcelona, 20 December 1975.

Obón, Carmen. "Informe de las cátedras realizadas en la provincia de Rio Muni por los equipos de la Delegación Nacional de la Sección Femenina." Bata, September 1965, AGA (3) 51.19 Caja 249.

———. Letter to Soledad de Santiago, Santa Isabel, 8 August 1967, AGA (3) 51.19 Caja 248.

————. Letter to Soledad de Santiago, Bata, 1 February 1968, AGA (3) 51.19 Caja 248.

————. Letter to Soledad de Santiago, Bata, 4 December 1968, AGA (3) 51.19 Caja 251.

————. Letter to Soledad de Santiago, Bata, 4 February 1969, AGA (3) 51.19 Caja 251.

————. Letter to Soledad de Santiago (1), Bata, 22 February 1969, AGA (3) 51.19 Caja 251.

————. Letter to Soledad de Santiago (3), Bata, 22 February 1969, AGA (3) 51.19 Caja 251.

————. "Situación de la Sección Femenina desde Octubre de 1968." Bata, March 1969, AGA (3) 51.19 Caja 251.

Orgambides, Fernando. "La misión de la ONU llega hoy al Sáhara." *El País*, 20 November 1987.

Ozores, Pilar. "School Report of Angela Nefiri Bacale Usuru." Madrid, 5 April 1968, AGA (3) 51.19 Caja 246.

Pan, Peter. "The Brutal Island." *Sunday Times*, 18 February 1962.

Pepple, Isaac. "Free Ticket to Hell." *Drum*, April 1957.

Pineda Barrantes, María Inés. Letter to Soledad de Santiago, Aranjuez, 28 May 1968, AGA (3) 51.19 Caja 246.

POLISARIO. "El Pueblo." *Boletín* 1 (1974). SADR National Archive, Rabuni, Algeria.

————. "La opinión de las masas." *Boletín* 4 (1976). SADR National Archive.

————. "La opinión de las masas." *Boletín* 7 (1976). SADR National Archive.

————. "La opinión de las masas." *Boletín* 8 (1976). SADR National Archive.

————. "La opinión de las masas." *Boletín* Especial 20 de Mayo (1976). SADR National Archive.

————. "SADR Constitution." 1999. SADR National Archive. Accessed 14 May 2008. www.arso.org/03-const.99.htm.

————. "Sahara Libre." No. 178 (1983). SADR National Archive.

————. "Sahara Libre." No. 240–41 (1985). SADR National Archive.

Provincial Director of the Training and Youth Participation Department. "Cuestionario de actividades de los círculos de juventudes." El Aaiún, 27 September 1974, AGA (3) 51.19 Caja 237.

————. "Actividades para la juventud del Sahara, Curso 1974–75, Trimestre Primero." El Aaiún, October 1974, AGA (3) 51.19 Caja 237.

Radiotelevisión de Sahara via Radio Argel. "La Voz del Sahara Libre." Algeria, 15 January 1976.

Sahara Section of the General Government of the Canaries. "Motivos de descontento en el barrio llamado 'Casas de Piedra.'" El Aaiún, 14 January 1975. Document available as an attachment to Barona, 1998.

Saharawi Women, document addressed to the Spanish colonial government signed "Mujeres saharauis," El Aaiún, 12 October 1975. AGA, Fondo de Cultura, Caja 2877.

Secretary of the Patronato. "Comparencia." Santa Isabel, Fernando Po, 8 June 1937, AGA 81/08527.

————. "Comparencia." Santa Isabel, Fernando Po, 9 June 1937, AGA 81/08527.

————. "Comparencia." Santa Isabel, 23 June 1937, AGA 81/08527.

Soto, Otilia. Letter to Soledad de Santiago, Santa Isabel, 30 November 1965, AGA (3) 51.19 Caja 248.

Spanish Administration. "Nota informativa al Gobierno General de Sahara." El Aaiún 7 July 1975. Document from Fondo Documental del Sahara (Luís Rodrigez de Viguri y Gil), currently held at Fundación Sur.

Spanish and French states. "Convenio entre España y Francia (Africa Occidental—Costa del Sahara, Golfo de Guinea), 27 March 1900." Paris: Gaceta de Madrid, 30 March 1900.

Spanish Government South Delegation. "Nota informativa a delegación gubernativa sur." Villa Cisneros, 24 January 1975. Document from Fondo Documental del Sahara (Luís Rodrigez de Viguri y Gil), currently held at Fundación Sur.

Sunyer, María Nieves. "Informe de la inspección a Rio Muni realizada por la Regidora Central de Juventudes del 4 al 8 de Marzo de 1965." Bata, 8 March 1965, AGA (3) 51.19 Caja 244.

———. "Informe de la inspección a Fernando Poo realizada por la Regidora Central de Juventudes del 4 al 8 de Marzo de 1965." Santa Isabel, 17 March 1965, AGA (3) 51.19 Caja 244.

Tentor, Concha. Letter to Soledad de Santiago, Santa Isabel, 26 February 1966, AGA (3) 51.19 Caja 246.

———. Letter to Soledad de Santiago, Santa Isabel, 17 April 1967, AGA (3) 51.19 Caja 246.

The Provincial Delegate. Communication regarding the closure of the Women's Section. El Aaiún, 29 October 1975, AGA (3) 51.10 Caja 241.

United Nations General Assembly (UNGA). "'Report of the United Nations Visiting Mission to Spanish Sahara, 1975' in the Report of the Special Committee on the Situation with Regard to the Implementation of the Declaration on the Granting of Independence to Colonial Countries and Peoples." 1975.

Women's Section. "Informe general, Catedra de Smara, 13 January to 13 June." Smara, no date, AGA (3) 51.19 Caja 237.

———. "Proyecto de curso en regimen de internado para muchachas o señoras casadas, nativas de las provincias africanas." Madrid, December 1964, AGA (3) 51.19 Caja 244.

———. "Informe Escolar de Adela Ntang Nbeng, 1966–67." Castellón, 1967, AGA (3) 51.19 Caja 246.

———. "Informe Escolar de Carmen Eyenga Mba-Oyana, 1966–67." Castellón, 1967, AGA (3) 51.19 Caja 246.

———. "Sección Femenina." Santa Isabel, March 1967, AGA (3) 51.19 Caja 246.

———. "Informe Escolar de Rosario Tomos Coffi." Heroinas de los Sitios School, Gerona, 4 March 1967, AGA (3) 51.19 Caja 246.

———. Letter to Soledad de Santiago, Santa Isabel, 11 March 1968, AGA (3) 51.19 Caja 246.

———. "Informe Escolar de Florentina Ntutumu Nchama." Las Navas del Marques School, Avila, 11 April 1968, AGA (3) 51.19 Caja 246.

———. "Informe e evaluación de actividades." Villa Cisneros, October 1972, AGA (3) 51.19 Caja 237.

———. "Informe e evaluación curso 1972–1973." Villa Cisneros, 8 June 1973, AGA (3) 51.19 Caja 237.

———. "Informe general de la Escuela Hogar de Villa Cisneros, Curso 1973–1974." Villa Cisneros, 1974, AGA (3) 51.19 Caja 237.

———. "Informe que presenta la delegada provincial de la Sección Femenina, de los hechos ocurridos en el Taller Escuela a este Gobierno General de Sahara." El Aaiún, January 1974, AGA (3) 51.19 Caja 239.

———. "Informe sobre situación en el Taller-Escuela 'Confecciones Sahara.'" El Aaiún, 6 February 1974, AGA (3) 51.19 Caja 239.

———. "Nota Informativa sobre las actividades que la Sección Femenina realiza en el Sahara." December 1974, AGA (3) 51.19 Caja 237.

———. "Junta quincenal de directoras de departamento." El Aaiún, 20 March 1975, AGA (3) 51.19 Caja 237.

———. "Informe correspondiente a la labor realizada por el departamento de promoción el 1er semestre de 1975," El Aaiún, June 1975, AGA, Fondo de Cultura, Caja 2877.

———. "Informe que presenta la Delegación Nacional de la Sección Femenina sobre las actividades con especial relieve." Madrid, July 1975, AGA (3) 51.19 Caja 236.

———. No title [handwritten notes on plain paper], El Aaiún, 23 October 1975, AGA (3) 51.19 Caja 241.

## Secondary Sources

A'Bodjedi, Enènge. "El sexo y la violencia: El caso de Masié Nguema Biyogo." *Oráfrica, revista de oralidad africana* 6 (2010): 129–52.

Aayache, Fatma. "Death Was Better than Being Raped!!!" Union of Saharawi Writers and Journalists, 23 June 2007. http://www.upes.org/bodyarticulos_eng.asp?field =articulos_eng&id=259.

Abba, Agaila. "Who I Admire the Most and Why?" *Zeina: The Rise of Young Saharawi Women Writers*, 8 January 2008. http://saharawiyazeina.blogspot.com/2008/01/who -i-admire-most-and-why.html.

Abu-Lughod, Lila. "Do Muslim Women Really Need Saving? Anthropological Reflections on Cultural Relativism and Its Others." *American Anthropologist* 104, no. 3 (2002): 783–90.

———. "The Romance of Resistance: Tracing Transformations of Power through Bedouin Women." *American Ethnologist* 17, no. 1 (1990): 1–55.

Accad, Evelyn. "Sexuality and Sexual Politics: Conflicts and Contradictions for Contemporary Women in the Middle East." In *Gender and National Identity: Women and Politics in Muslim Societies*, edited by Valentine Moghadam, 237–50. London: Zed Books, 1994.

Aderinto, Saheed. "Journey to Work: Transnational Prostitution in Colonial British West Africa." *Journal of the History of Sexuality* 24, no. 1 (2015): 99–124.

Afrol News. "Moroccan Life Guard to Leave Equatorial Guinea." 10 January 2000. http://www.afrol.com/News2001/eqg001_moroccan_guard.htm.

Agger, Inger. "Sexual Torture of Prisoners: An Overview." *Journal of Traumatic Stress* 2, no. 3 (1989): 305–18.

Agger, Inger, and Sóren Buus Jensen. "Testimony as Ritual and Evidence in Psychotherapy for Political Refugees." *Journal of Traumatic Stress* 3, no. 1 (1990): 115–30.

Aguayo, Michelle. "Representation of Muslim Bodies in 'The Kingdom': Deconstructing Discourses in Hollywood." *Global Media Journal* 2, no. 2 (2009): 41–56.

Ahmed, Leila. *Women and Gender in Islam*. New Haven, CT: Yale University Press, 1992.

Aixelà Cabré, Yolanda. "Africanas en el mundo contemporáneo: Las mujeres de Guinea Ecuatorial." In Introducción a Los Estudios Africanos, edited by Y. Aixelà, LL. Mallart y J. Martí, 51–64. Barcelona: CEIBA, 2009.

Al-Ali, Nadje. "Gendering the Arab Spring." *Middle East Journal of Culture and Communication* 5 (2012): 26–31.

Al-Ali, Nadje, and Nicola Pratt. "Between Nationalism and Women's Rights: The Kurdish Women's Movement in Iraq." *Middle East Journal of Culture and Communication* 4, no. 3 (2011): 339–55.

———. *What Kind of Liberation? Women and the Occupation in Iraq*. Berkeley: University of California Press, 2009.

Allan, Joanna. "Activist Ethics: The Need for a Nuanced Approach to Resistance Studies Field Research." *Journal of Resistance Studies* 3, no. 2 (2017): 89–121.

———. "El colonialismo y el patriarcado en la literatura afrohispana: Los escritos de resistencia de Lehdia Dafa y María Nsue Angüe." In *Trans-afrohispanos: Puentes culturales críticos entre África, Latinoamérica y España*, edited by Dorothy Odartey-Wellington, 137–51. Leiden: Brill, 2018.

———. "Gender Equality and the Politics of Representation in the Western Sahara." BA Hons., University of Leeds, 2006.

———. "Imagining Saharawi Women: The Question of Gender in POLISARIO Discourse." *Journal of North African Studies* 15, no. 2 (2010): 189–202. http://www.tandfonline.com/doi/abs/10.1080/13629380902861103?journalCode=fnas20.

———. "María Nsue Angüe." In *The Literary Encyclopedia*, vol. 8.2.2., edited by Helen Rachel Cousins. Accessed 19 April 2017. http://www.litencyc.com/php/speople.php?rec=true&UID=13877.

———. "Natural Resources and Intifada: Oil, Phosphates and Resistance to Colonialism in Western Sahara." *Journal of North African Studies* 21, no. 4 (2016): 645–66.

———. "Privilege, Marginalization and Solidarity: Women's Voices Online in Western Sahara's Struggle for Independence." *Feminist Media Studies* 14, no. 4 (2014): 704–8.

———. "Representations of Gender in Saharawi Nationalist Discourse(s)." Masters by research, University of Leeds, 2008.

Allan, Joanna, and Hamza Lakhal. "Acting with Impunity: Morocco's Human Rights Violations in Western Sahara and the Silence of the International Community." SAIH (Studentenes og Akademikernes Internasjonale Hjelpefond), April 2015. https://saih.no/assets/docs/Acting-With-Impunity-Western-Sahara-report.pdf.

Almenara Niebla, Silvia. "Beyond Online Comments and Gossip: Collective Identity and New Subjectivities in the Sahrawi Case." 2017. Unpublished paper in author's possession.

———. "Diásporas digitales: Una aproximación feminista al estudio de las minorías online; El caso de la diáspora saharaui." In *Ciberpolítica: Gobierno abierto, redes, deliberación, democracia*, edited by Ramón Cotarelo and Javier Gil, 341–62. Madrid: Instituto Nacional de Administración Pública, 2017.

Al Nagar, Samia, and Liv Tønessen. "Women's Rights and the Women's Movement in Sudan (1952–2014)." In *Women's Activism in Africa*, edited by Balghis Badri and Aili Mari Tripp, 121–55. London: Zed Books, 2017.

Al-Rasheed, Madawi. *A Most Masculine State: Gender, Politics, and Religion in Saudi Arabia*. Cambridge: Cambridge University Press, 2013.

Amadiume, Ifi. *Male Daughters, Female Husbands: Gender and Sex in an African Society*. London: Zed Books, 1987.

Ames, Nick. "Ghana Players, Fans Pelted with Missiles in Win over Equatorial Guinea." *The Guardian*, 5 February 2015.

Amnesty International. "Amnesty International Briefing: Morocco." AI Index PUB 78/00/77, 1977.

———. "Continued Institutional and Key Human Rights Concerns in Equatorial Guinea: Submission to the UN Universal Periodic Review, May 2014." AI Index AFR 24/013/2013, October 2013.

———. "Equatorial Guinea: A Country Subject to Terror and Harassment." AI Index AFR 24/01/99, 1 January 1999.

———. "Equatorial Guinea: A Dismal Record of Broken Promises." AI Index FR 24/09/95, July 1995.

———. "Equatorial Guinea: A Missed Opportunity to Restore Respect for Human Rights." AI Index AFR 24/01/94, 1 February 1994.

———. "Equatorial Guinea: A Parody of a Trial in Order to Crush the Opposition." AI Index AFR. 24/014/2002, 30 June 2002.

———. "Equatorial Guinea: An Opportunity to Put an End to Impunity." AI Index AFR 24/01/97, 30 June 1997.

———. "Equatorial Guinea. Arrest of a Possible Prisoner of Conscience/Fear of Ill-Treatment Pilar Mañana." AI Index AFR 24/008/1992, 14 June 1992.

———. "Equatorial Guinea: Arrests of Pro-Democracy Activists—A Changing Pattern of Human Rights Violations." AI Index AFR 24/04/91, 1 November 1991.

———. "Equatorial Guinea: Fear of Extrajudicial Execution/Torture: Alfredo Bijuan and 40 Students." AI Index AFR 24/013/1992, 27 November 1992.

———. "Equatorial Guinea: Fear of Forced Evictions/Fear of Excessive Force." AI Index AFR 24/ 012/2006, 14 November 2006.

———. "Equatorial Guinea: Further Information on Detention without Charge or Trial/Harsh Detention Conditions, Brígida Asongsua Elo." AI Index AFR 24/ 005/2008, 30 April 2008.

———. "Equatorial Guinea: No Free Flow of Information." AI Index AFR 24/004/ 2000, 5 June 2000.

———. "Equatorial Guinea: The Authorities Must Allow Freedom of Expression and Peaceful Demonstrations to Take Place." AI Index AFR 24/004/2013, 1 July 2013.

———. "Equatorial Guinea. Torture and Legal Concern: Over 100 people including Celestino Bacale, Pedro Esono, Maximio Miko, Arsenio Moro, Angel Obama." AI Index AFR 24/014/1992, 22 December 1992.

———. "Equatorial Guinea: Woman Held in Prison Cell with Up to 100 Male Detainees." Press release, 14 February 2008. https://www.amnesty.org.uk/press-releases/equatorial-guinea-woman-held-prison-cell-100-male-detainees.

———. "Los desalojos forzosos violan los derechos humanos." AI Index AFR 24/009/ 2007, 20 June 2007.

———. "Morocco and Western Sahara. Fear of Torture/Unfair Trial: Ahmed El Kouri, Nebt Ramdane Bouchraya, Arbi Brahim Baba, Cheykhatou Bouh, M'Rabih Rabou

Neysan, Abdelhay Lekhal, Mahfoud Brahim Dahou, Salama Ahmed Lembarki, all male, aged 18–20." AI Index MDE 29/004/1995, 5 July 1995.

———. "Morocco: Breaking the Wall of Silence: The 'Disappeared' in Morocco." AI Index MDE 29/001/1993, 13 April 1993.

———. "Morocco/Western Sahara: Briefing to the Committee against Torture." AI index MDE 29/011/2003, 11 November 2003.

———. "Morocco/Western Sahara: Justice Must Begin with Torture Enquiries." AI Index MDE 29/003/2005, 22 June 2005.

———. "Morocco/Western Sahara: Kelthoum Ahmed Labid El-Ouanat Prisoner of Conscience." AI Index MDE 29/03/96, March 1996.

———. "Morocco/Western Sahara: Moroccan Authorities Must Respect Freedom of Assembly." AI Index MDE 29/002/2013, 3 April 2013.

———. "Morocco/Western Sahara: The Grueling Experience of One Sahrawi HRD." AI Index MDE 29/007/2007, 18 April 2007.

———. "Morocco/Western Sahara. 'Turning the Page': Achievements and Obstacles." AI Index MDE 29/17/90, 3 August 1999.

———. "Report of an Amnesty International Mission to the Kingdom of Morocco." AI Index MDE 29/001/1982, 1982.

———. "Urgent Action: Allow Human Rights Defender to Return Home." AI Index MDE 29/014/2009, 4 December 2009.

———. "Western Sahara/Morocco: Torture of Detainees Must End." AI Index MDE 29/008/2004, 24 June 2004.

Anagol, Padma. *The Emergence of Feminism in India, 1850–1920.* Burlington, VT: Ashgate, 2005.

———. "From the Symbolic to the Open: Women's Resistance in Colonial Maharashtra." In *Behind the Veil: Resistance, Women, and the Everyday in Colonial South Asia,* edited by Ghosh Anindita, 21–57. London: Palgrave Macmillan, 2008.

Anderson, Benedict. *Imagined Communities: Reflections on the Origin and Spread of Nationalism.* London: Verso, 2006.

Anholt, Simon. "Should Place Brands Be Simple?" *Place Branding and Public Diplomacy* 5, no. 2 (2009): 91–96.

Appel, Hannah. "Offshore Work: Oil, Modularity, and the How of Capitalism in Equatorial Guinea." *American Ethnologist* 39, no. 4 (2012): 692–709.

———. "Walls and White Elephants: Oil Extraction, Responsibility, and Infrastructural Violence in Equatorial Guinea." *Ethnography* 13, no. 4 (2012): 439–65.

Arija Martinez de Espinosa, Julio. *La Guinea española y sus riquezas.* Buenos Aires: Espasa-Calpe, 1930.

Arso. "Weekly News." 5 November 1995. http://www.arso.org/01-e-44.htm.

Artucio, Alejandro. *The Trial of Macías in Equatorial Guinea: The Story of a Dictatorship.* Geneva: International Commission of Jurists and International University Exchange Fund, 1979.

Åse, Cecilia. "Crisis Narratives and Masculinist Protection: Gendering the Original Stockholm Syndrome." *International Feminist Journal of Politics* 17, no. 4 (2015): 595–610.

Ávila Laurel, Juan Tomás. *By Night the Mountain Burns.* Translated by Jethro Soutar. London: And Other Stories, 2014.

Aworawo, David. "Decisive Thaw: The Changing Pattern of Relations between Nigeria and Equatorial Guinea, 1980–2005." *Journal of International and Global Studies* 1, no. 2 (2010): 89–109.

Aymemí, Antonio. *Los bubis en Fernando Poo: Colección de los artículos publicados en la revista colonial "La Guinea Española."* Madrid: Galo Sáez, 1942.

Baba Miské, Ahmed. *Front Polisario: L'âme d'un peuple.* Paris: Editions rupture, 1978.

Badri, Balghis, and Aili Mari Tripp. "African Influences on Global Women's Rights: An Overview." In *Women's Activism in Africa*, edited by Balghis Badri and Aili Mari Tripp, 1–32. London: Zed Books, 2017.

Bahati Kuumba, M. "African Women, Resistance Cultures and Cultural Resistances." *Agenda: Empowering Women for Gender Equity* 20, no. 68 (2006): 112–21.

———. *Gender and Social Movements.* Walnut Creek, CA: AltaMira Press, 2001.

Ballano Gonzalo, Fernando. *Aquel Negrito de África Tropical: El Colonialismo en Guinea (1778–1968).* Madrid: Sial Ediciones, 2014.

Bárbulo, Tomás. *La historia prohibida del Sáhara Español.* Barcelona: Ediciones Destino S.A., 2002.

———. "La Voluntad y la Fuerza." In *Las treinta y dos batallas de Aminetu Haidar*, edited by Conxi Moya, 100–106. Madrid: Bubok, 2010.

———. "Nunca pensé que el Gobierno la haría un favor tan sucio a Marruecos." In *Las treinta y dos batallas de Aminetu Haidar*, edited by Conxi Moya, 89–91. Madrid: Bubok, 2010.

Barca, Salka, and Stephen Zunes. "Nonviolent Struggle in Western Sahara." In *Civilian Jihad: Nonviolent Struggle, Democratization, and Governance in the Middle East*, edited by Maria J. Stephan, 157–68. New York: Palgrave Macmillan, 2009.

Barnes, Sandra T. "Global Flows: Terror, Oil, and Strategic Philanthropy." *African Studies Review* 48, no. 1 (2005): 1–23.

Barona Castañeda, Claudia. "Memorias de una resistencia. La otra historia del Sahara Occidental." 1 January 2015. http://emam.revues.org/859.

———. "Sahara Al Garbia (1958–1976)." PhD diss., Autonomous University of Madrid, 1998.

Barrett, Stanley R. *Anthropology: A Student's Guide to Theory and Method.* Toronto: University of Toronto Press, 1996.

Batinic, Jelena. "Feminism, Nationalism, and War: The 'Yugoslav Case' in Feminist Texts." *Journal of International Women's Studies* 3, no. 1 (2001): 1–23.

Bayard de Volo, Lorraine. "A Revolution in the Binary? Gender and the Oxymoron of Revolutionary War in Cuba and Nicaragua." *Signs* 37, no. 2 (2012): 413–39.

BBC News. "Equatorial Guinea's 'God.'" 26 July 2003. http://news.bbc.co.uk/1/hi/world/africa/3098007.stm.

Bengochea Tirado, Enrique. "La movilización nacionalista saharaui y las mujeres durante el último periodo colonial español." *Revista Historia Autónoma* 3 (2013): 113–28.

———. "Las mujeres saharauis a través de la Sección Femenina, un sujeto colonizado." *Arenal* 19, no. 1 (2012): 143–59.

———. "Mujeres, nacionalismo y políticas coloniales en la provincia de Sáhara (1958–1975)." *Noticias del Sáhara* (blog), July 2014. http://diasporasaharaui-es.blogspot.co.uk/2014/07/mujeres-nacionalismo-y-politicas.html.

————. "Políticas imperiales y género: La Sección Femenina en la provincia de Sahara (1961–1975)." PhD diss., University of Valencia, June 2016.

Berger Gluck, Sherna. "Palestine: Shifting Sands. The Feminist-Nationalist Connection in the Palestinian Movement." In *Feminist Nationalism*, edited by Lois A. West, 101–29. London: Routledge, 1997.

Bisgaard-Church, Elliana. "Sahrawis Campaign for Independence in the Second Intifada, Western Sahara, 2005–2008." Global Nonviolent Action Database, 27 November 2011. http://nvdatabase.swarthmore.edu/content/sahrawis-campaign-independence-second-intifada-western-sahara-2005<HY>2008.

Bloor, Meriel, and Thomas Bloor. *The Practice of Critical Discourse Analysis: An Introduction*. London: Hodder Arnold, 2007.

Bolekia Boleká, Justo. *Aproximación a la historia de Guinea Ecuatorial*. Salamanca: Amarú Ediciones, 2003.

————. *Recuerdos del abuelo Bayebé y otros relatos bubis*. Madrid: Sial Ediciones, 2014.

Borrel, Prisca. "El Ghalia Djimi, militante sahraouie en territoire occupé." Haut Courant, http://www.hautcourant.com/El-Ghalia-Djimi-militante,599, 8 January 2009.

Bouatta, Cherifa. "Feminine Militancy: Moujahidates During and After the Civil War." In *Gender and National Identity: Women and Politics in Muslim Societies*, edited by Valentine Moghadam, 18–39. London: Zed Books, 1994.

Boulay, Sébastien. "Corps, mouvement et création sur le Web: Incarnations numériques de la lutte pacifique au Sahara Occidental." In *La question (irrésolue) du Sahara Occidental*, edited by Francesco Correale and Sébastien Boulay. Tours: François Rabelais University Press, forthcoming.

———— "'Returnees' and Political Poetry in Western Sahara: Defamation, Deterrance and Mobilisation on the Web and Mobile Phones." *Journal of North African Studies* 21, no. 4 (2016): 667–86.

Bourdieu, Pierre. *Outline of a Theory of Practice*. Translated by Richard Nice. Cambridge: Cambridge University Press, 1977.

Brown, Laura S. *Feminist Therapy*. Washington, DC: American Psychological Association, 2010.

Brownmiller, Susan. *Against Our Will—Men, Women and Rape*. New York: Ballatine Books, 1975.

Bryant-Davis, Thema. *Surviving Sexual Violence: A Guide to Recovery and Empowerment*. Lanham, MD: Rowman & Littlefield, 2011.

Burrows, Nina, and Tessa Horvath. "The Rape and Sexual Assault of Men—A Review of the Literature." Survivors UK, 2013.

Buscant Llavors. "Tontines: La soberanía financiera de las mujeres africanas." June 2015. http://www.buscantllavors.org/tontines-la-soberania-financiera-de-las-mujeres-africanas/.

Butler, Judith. *Gender Trouble: Feminism and the Subversion of Identity*. London: Routledge, 2006.

Callaghan, Jane E. M., Yaganama Gambo, and Lisa C. Fellin. "Hearing the Silences: Adult Nigerian Women's Accounts of 'Early Marriages.'" *Feminism and Psychology* 25, no. 4 (2015): 506–27.

Calvo, Juan María. "Guinea Ecuatorial: La ocasión perdida." Asociación para la solidaridad democrática con Guinea Ecuatorial (ASODEGUE), 1989. http://www.aso degue.org/hdojmc.htm.

Camacho, Ana. "Los 'ninjas' toman posiciones en Guinea Ecuatorial." *El País*, 15 August 1993.

Campos Serrano, Alicia. "The Decolonization of Equatorial Guinea: The Relevance of the International Factor." *Journal of African History* 44 (2003): 95–116.

———. "Extraction Offshore, Politics Inshore, and the Role of the State in Equatorial Guinea." *Journal of the International African Institute* 83, no. 2 (2013): 314–39.

———. "Nacionalismo Anticolonial en Guinea Ecuatorial: De Españoles a Guineanos." *Araucaria* 5, no. 9 (2003): 1–16.

Campos Serrano, Alicia, and Plácido Micó Abogo. "Labour and Trade Union Freedom in Equatorial Guinea." Fundación Paz y Solidaridad "Serafín Aliaga"—CCOO and International Confederation of Free Trade Unions (ICFTU), Madrid, 2006.

Caratini, Sophie. *Hijos de las nubes*. Madrid: Ediciones del Oriente y del Mediterráneo, 2008.

———. "La prisión del tiempo: Los cambios sociales en los campamentos de refugiados saharauis." *Cuadernos Bakeaz* 77 (2006): 1–21.

———. *La République des sables: Anthropologie d'une révolution*. Paris: L'Harmattan, 2003.

Caro Baroja, Julio. *Estudios Saharianos*. 1955. Reprint, Madrid: Calamar ediciones, 2008.

Castillo Cerezuela, Queralt. "Mayuba Mohamed, retenida en Tinduf por su familia biológica: 'Quiero salir de aquí.'" *Público*, October 21, 2014. http://www.publico.es /actualidad/551500/mayuba-mohamed-retenida-en-tinduf-por-su-familia-biologica -quiero-salir-de-aqui.

Castro, Marisé. "Equatorial Guinea." In *Africa South of the Sahara*, 33rd ed., edited by Katherine Murison, 373–86. London: Europa, 2004.

Cembrero, Ignacio. "Si cedo, expulsarán a muchos saharauis igual que a mi." In *Las treinta y dos batallas de Aminetu Haidar*, edited by Conxi Moya, 106–11. Madrid: Bubok, 2010.

Central Intelligence Agency (CIA). "The World Fact Book: Equatorial Guinea." Accessed 29 April 2014. https://www.cia.gov/library/publications/the-world-fact book/geos/ek.html.

Cerdà, Paco. "'Lo de Mayuba es chantaje; no creo que los saharauis pidan más ayudas a la diputación.'" *Levante*, October 17, 2014. https://www.levante-emv.com/comu nitat-valenciana/2014/10/17/mayuba-chantaje-creo-saharauis-pidan/1175626.html.

Cervera, Julio. "Viaje de exploración por el Sahara Occidental. Estudios geográficos." In *La reunión ordinaria de 2 de Noviembre de 1886, de Boletín Sociedad Geográfica de Madrid, Tomo XXII, primer semestre de 1887*. Madrid, 1886.

Chadya, Joyce M. "Mother Politics: Anti-colonial Nationalism and the Women Question in Africa." *Journal of Women's History* 15, no. 3 (2003): 153–57.

Chandra, Uday. "Rethinking Subaltern Resistance." *Journal of Contemporary Asia* 45, no. 4 (2015): 563–73.

Chatterjee, Partha. "Colonialism, Nationalism, and the Colonized Women: The Contest in India." *American Ethnologist* 16, no. 4 (1989): 622–33.

Chaudhuri, Nupur, and Margaret Strobel, eds. *Western Women and Imperialism: Complicity and Resistance*. Bloomington: Indiana University Press, 1992.

Cherifati-Merabtine, Doria. "Algeria at a Crossroads: National Liberation, Islamization and Women." In *Gender and National Identity: Women and Politics in Muslim Societies*, edited by Valentine Moghadam, 40–62. London: Zed Books, 1994.

Cienfuegos, A. J., and C. Monelli. "The Testimony of Political Repression as a Therapeutic Instrument." *American Journal of Orthopsychiatry* 53, no. 1 (1983): 43–51.

Clarence-Smith, William G. "Spanish Equatorial Guinea, 1898–1940." In *The Cambridge History of Africa: From 1905 to 1940*, edited by Arthur D. Roberts, 537–44. Cambridge: Cambridge University Press, 1986.

Clement, Victoria. "Articulating National Identity in Turkmenistan: Inventing Tradition through Myth, Cult and Language." *Nations and Nationalism* 20, no. 3 (2014): 546–62.

Committee on the Elimination of All Forms of Discrimination against Women (CEDAW). "CEDAW 31st Session. Summary record of the 652nd meeting." 2004. https://documents-dds-ny.un.org/doc/UNDOC/GEN/N04/416/90/PDF/N04416 90.pdf?OpenElement.

Comunello, Francesca, and Giuseppe Anzera. "Will the Revolution Be Tweeted? A Conceptual Framework for Understanding the Social Media and the Arab Spring." *Islam and Christian-Muslim Relations* 23, no. 4 (2012): 453–70.

Connell, R. W. *Masculinities*. Cambridge: Polity Press, 2005.

Correale, Francesco. "La 'última guerra colonial' de España y la literatura militar entre memoria y conocimiento." Paper presented at the Seventh African Studies Congress, Lisbon, 2010.

Court of Justice of the European Union. "Appeal—Agreement between the European Union and the Kingdom of Morocco concerning liberalisation measures on agricultural and fishery products." In *Case C-104/16 P*, edited by Court of Justice of the European Union. InfoCuria, 21 December 2016. curia.europa.eu/juris.

Couturier, Don. "The Rape of Men: Eschewing Myths of Sexual Violence in War." *On Politics* 6, no. 2 (2012): 1–15.

Crawford, Kerry F., Amelia Hoover Green, and Sarah E. Parkinson. "Wartime Sexual Violence Is Not Just a 'Weapon of War.'" *Washington Post*, 24 September 2014.

Crenshaw, K. W. "Demarginalizing the Intersection of Race and Sex: A Black Feminist Critique of Antidiscrimination Doctrine, Feminist Theory and Antiracist Politics." In *The Politics of Law: A Progressive Critique*, edited by D. Kairys, 195–217. New York: Pantheon, 1990.

———. "Mapping the Margins: Intersectionality, Identity Politics, and Violence against Women of Color." In *The Public Nature of Private Violence*, edited by Martha Albertson Fineman and Roxanne Mykitiuk, 93–118. New York: Routledge, 1994.

Cronjé, Suzanne. *Equatorial Guinea: The Forgotten Dictatorship*. London: Anti-Slavery Society, 1976.

Cusack, Igor. "Being Away from 'Home.'" *Journal of Contemporary African Studies* 17, no. 1 (1999): 29–48.

———. "Equatorial Guinea: The Inculcation and Maintenance of Hispanic Culture." University of Bristol Occasional Papers Series, 1997.

———. "'Equatorial Guinea's National Cuisine Is Simple and Tasty': Cuisine and the Making of National Culture." *Arizona Journal of Hispanic Cultural Studies* 8 (2004): 131–48.

———. "Nation-Builders at Work: The Equatoguinean 'Myth' of Bantu Unity." *Nationalism and Ethnic Politics* 7, no. 3 (2001): 77–97.

Dafa, Lehdia. "En el Día de la Mujer, recuerdo y homenaje a las pioneras de la sanidad saharaui." *Democracia Saharaui* (blog), 7 March 2015. http://lehdiamohameddafa.blogspot.com/2015/03/en-el-dia-de-la-mujer-recuerdo-y.html.

Dalmases, Pablo Ignacio de. *La esclavitud en el Sáhara Occidental.* Barcelona: Ediciones Carena, 2012.

Darkoa Sekyiamah, Nana. "Standing on African Feminist Land: Personal Reflections on the 4th African Feminist Forum." AWID, 25 April 2016. http://www.forum.awid.org/forum16/posts/standing-african-feminist-land.

Dawson, Marcelle C. "Protest, Performance and Politics: The Use of 'Nano-Media' in Social Movement Activism in South Africa." *Research in Drama Education: The Journal of Applied Theatre and Performance* 17, no. 3 (2012): 321–45.

De Castro, Mayka. "El Colonialismo franquista en Guinea Ecuatorial: Una lectura crítica en clave decolonial." Master's thesis, University of Granada, September 2013.

De Cordier, Bruno. "On the Thin Line Between Good Intentions and Creating Tensions: A View on Gender Programmes in Muslim Contexts and the (Potential) Position of Islamic Aid Organisations." *European Journal of Development Research* 22, no. 2 (2010): 234–51.

Decker, Alicia C. *In Idi Amin's Shadow: Women, Gender, and Militarism in Uganda.* Athens: Ohio University Press, 2014.

Democracy Now! "'The Genie Is Out of the Bottle': Assessing a Changing Arab World with Noam Chomsky and Al Jazeera's Marwan Bishara." 17 February 2011. http://www.democracynow.org/2011/2/17/the_genies_are_out_of_the.

Deubel, Tara Flynn. "Between Homeland and Exile: Poetry, Memory, and Identity in Sahrawi Communities." PhD diss., University of Arizona, 2010.

———. "Mediascapes of Human Rights: Emergent Forms of Digital Activism for the Western Sahara." *Transmodernity: Journal of Peripheral Cultural Production of the Luso-Hispanic World* 5, no. 3 (2015): 5–19.

———. "Poetics of Diaspora: Sahrawi Poets and Postcolonial Transformations of a Trans-Saharan Genre in Northwest Africa." *Journal of North African Studies* 17, no. 2 (2012): 295–314.

*Diario Rombe.* "Descarga los proyectos de ley que regulan el Matrimonio Tradicional en Guinea Ecuatorial." 27 March 2014. http://www.diariorombe.es/descarga-los-proyectos-de-ley-que-regulan-el-matrimonio-tradicional-en-guinea-ecuatorial/.

———. "El PDGE convoca una reunión urgente en Malabo." 6 February 2015. http://www.diariorombe.es/ultima-hora-el-pdge-convoca-una-reunion-urgente-en-malabo/.

———. "Guillermina Mekuy Mba Ministra Delegada de Cultura." 1 August 2013. http://www.diariorombe.es/guillermina-mekuy-mba-ministra-delegada-de-cultura/.

———. "Huelga de taxistas en Guinea Ecuatorial." 4 May 2017. http://www.africafundacion.org/spip.php?article27431.

———. "La Alcadesa se hace dueña del nuevo mercado de Malabo." 6 August 2013. http://www.diariorombe.es/la-alcaldesa-se-hace-duena-del-nuevo-mercado-de-malabo/.

————. "La policía detiene a un 'homosexual' y taxista y los exhiben en la TVA." 7 April 2014. http://www.diariorombe.es/la-policia-detiene-un-homosexual-y-taxista -y-los-exhiben-en-la-tva/.

Diego Aguirre, J. R. *Guerra en el Sáhara*. Madrid: Ediciones ISTMO, 1991.

Diken, Bülent, and Carsten Bagge Lausten. "Becoming Abject: Rape as a Weapon of War." *Body and Society* 11, no. 1 (2005): 111–28.

Doménech Lafuente, Angel. "Sahara Español. Del vivir nómada de las tribus." *Cuaderno de Estudios Africanos*, no. 21 (January–March 1953): 31–43.

Dyombe Dyangani, Cristina. *Identidad Cultural Ndowe*. New York: Ndowe International Press, 2008.

EG Justice. "Democracy Held Hostage." 25 April 2016. http://www.egjustice.org/post /democracy-held-hostage.

————. "Equatorial Guinea: Ensure Media Freedom." 12 April 2016. http://www .egjustice.org/post/equatorial-guinea-ensure-media-freedom.

————. "Human Rights Annual Report of Equatorial Guinea." 2015. http://egjustice .org/sites/default/files/Human%20Rights%20Report%20Equatorial%20Guinea%20 %202015.pdf.

————. "Opposition Party Boycotts Presidential Elections." 18 April 2016. http:// www.egjustice.org/post/opposition-party-boycotts-presidential-elections.

————. "Presidential Elections 2016 to Entrench Dictatorship." 18 March 2016. http://www.egjustice.org/post/presidential-elections-2016-entrench-dictatorship.

————. "Severe Crackdown on Opposition and Media." 20 April 2016. http://www .egjustice.org/post/severe-crackdown-opposition-and-media-0.

Eke, Kola. "Responses to Patriarchy in African Women's Poetry." *Matatu*, no. 41 (2013): 3–18.

*El Mundo*. "Teodoro Obiang agradece al Rey su influencia para participar en un acto en el Cervantes en Bruselas." 1 April 2014. http://www.elmundo.es/espana/2014/04 /01/533a997522601dcf748b4572.html.

El-Mehdi, Fatma. "La resistencia saharaui: Una mirada histórica desde las perspectivas de las mujeres saharauis." In *Mujeres saharauis: Tres tuizas para la memoria de la resistencia*, edited by Rocío Medina Martín, 23–28. Seville: Aconcagua Libros, 2016.

Ela Ondo Onguene, Clemente. "The Chinese Embassy Offers a Special Reception for the International Day of Women." Government of Equatorial Guinea's Office for Information and Press, 12 March 2011. http://www.guineaecuatorialpress.com/noti cia.php?id=1400.

Embarek Rahal, Baida. "Decolonization and Gender Equality." Paper presented at the International Women's Conference on the Western Sahara Women's Rights for Resistance, Windhoek, Namibia, 4 November 2015.

Enloe, Cynthia. *Bananas, Beaches and Bases: Making Feminist Sense of International Politics*. London: Pandora, 1989.

————. *Nimo's War, Emma's War*. Berkeley: University of California Press, 2010.

Errazzouki, Samia. "Working-Class Women Revolt: Gendered Political Economy in Morocco." *Journal of North African Studies* 19, no. 2 (2014): 259–67.

Errazzouki, Samia, and Maryam Al-Khawaja. "Beware of the Middle East's Fake Feminists." *Foreign Policy*, 22 October 2013.

Errer Bouzeid, Aminetou. "Sexismo en la sociedad saharaui actual: Un acercamiento a la sociedad saharaui desde el trato a sus mujeres. Propuesta de intervención." Master's thesis, University of Zaragoza, 2015.

Espacios Europeos. "La activista guineana Clara Nsegue Eyi, Lola, continua todavía en Mongomo (Guinea Ecuatorial)." 14 October 2013. http://espacioseuropeos.com/la-activista-guineana-clara-nsegue-eyi-lola-continua-todavia-en-mongomo-guinea-ecuatorial/?utm_source=twitterfeed&utm_medium=twitter.

———. "Agradecimiento de la plataforma Movimiento de Protesta Popular." 5 June 2013. https://espacioseuropeos.com/2013/06/agradecimiento-de-la-plataforma-movimiento-de-protesta-popular-de-guinea-ecuatorial/.

———. "La policía de Guinea Ecuatorial detiene a un homosexual y el gobierno lo exhibe en la televisión como si fuera un trofeo." 14 April 2014. http://espacioseuropeos.com/54707/la-policia-de-guinea-ecuatorial-detiene-a-un-homosexual-y-el-gobierno-lo-exhibe-en-la-television-como-si-fuera-un-trofeo/.

Esteban, Mario. "The Chinese *Amigo*: Implications for the Development of Equatorial Guinea." *China Quarterly* 199 (2009): 667–85.

Eteo Soriso, José Francisco. *Cancionero Tradicional de Bioko*. Barcelona: Ceiba Ediciones, 2008.

European Commission. "European Neighbourhood Policy and Enlargement Negotiations." 23 June 2016. http://ec.europa.eu/enlargement/neighbourhood/countries/morocco/index_en.htm.

———. "Gender Equality: Encouraging First Results of EU Gender Action Plan in Developing Countries." 15 December 2011. http://europa.eu/rapid/press-release_IP-11<HY>1557_en.htm.

European External Action Service. "L'Union européenne appuie l'égalité des genres au Maroc." 3 July 2012. http://eeas.europa.eu/delegations/morocco/press_corner/all_news/news/2012/20120703_fr.htm.

Fairclough, Norman. *Critical Discourse Analysis: The Critical Study of Language*. London: Longman Group, 1995.

Fanon, Frantz. *Black Skin, White Masks*. London: Pluto, 2008.

———. *A Dying Colonialism*. New York: Grove, 1967.

———. *The Wretched of the Earth*. London: Penguin Classics, 2001.

Fariza, Ignacio. "El Instituto Cervantes y la UNED invitan en Bruselas al dictador Obiang." *El País*, 19 March 2014.

Fausto-Sterling, Anne. "The Five Sexes: Why Male and Female Are Not Enough." *The Sciences* 20, no. 4 (1992): 20–25.

Fernandez, James W. *Bwiti: An Ethnography of the Religious Imagination in Africa*. Princeton, NJ: Princeton University Press, 1982.

Fiddian-Qasmiyeh, Elena. *The Ideal Refugees: Gender, Islam, and the Sahrawi Politics of Survival*. Syracuse, NY: Syracuse University Press, 2013.

First, Ruth. *The Barrel of a Gun: Political Power in Africa and the Coup d'État*. London: Penguin, 1970.

Fisher, Jo. *Mothers of the Disappeared*. London: Zed Books, 1989.

Foot, Anne. "A Policy of Plunder: The Development and Normalisation of Neo-Patrimonialism in Equatorial Guinea." Master's thesis, Stellenbosch University, 2014.

Foreign Office of the British Government. "Spanish Guinea." *Peace Handbooks* 20, no. 125 (1920): 1–60.

Fortier, Corinne. "The Right to Divorce for Women (khul') in Islam: Comparative Practices in Mauritania and Egypt." *Droits et Cultures* 59, no. 1 (2010): 59–83.

Foucault, Michel. "The Subject and Power." *Critical Inquiry* 8, no. 4 (1982): 777–95.

Fra-Molinero, Baltasar. "De libros: CEIBA II. Regreso al país natal." *Atanga*, 2015, 44–49.

———. "El deber de contar y la pasión de escribir: Entrevista a María Nsue Angüe." 10 June 2010. http://abacus.bates.edu/~bframoli/pagina/mariansue.htm.

France Liberté Foundation and French Association of Friendship and Solidarity with the Peoples of Africa (AFASPA). "International Mission of Investigation in Western Sahara." Bagnolet, France, 2003.

Freeden, Michael. *Ideologies and Political Theory: A Conceptual Approach.* Oxford: Oxford University Press, 1996.

Freedom House. "Freedom in the World: Equatorial Guinea." 2014. https://freedom house.org/report/freedom-world/2014/equatorial-guinea#.UXWLdzfhgo.

———. "Freedom in the World 2016: Anxious Dictators, Wavering Democracies." January 27, 2016. https://freedomhouse.org/article/new-report-freedom-world-2016 -anxious-dictators-wavering-democracies.

Gabo Ntseane, Peggy. "Culturally Sensitive Transformational Learning: Incorporating the Afrocentric Paradigm and African Feminism." *Adult Education Quarterly* 61, no. 4 (2011): 307–23.

Gandolfi, Nicoletta. "A propósito del Sáhara Occidental: Testimonios de los Canarios que allí residieron durante el periodo colonial." *Oriente Moderno*, nos.7–12 (1989). http://www.arso.org/canariosita.htm.

García, Alejandro. *Historias del Sahara: El mejor y el peor de los mundos.* Madrid: Catarata, 2001.

Gaudio, Attilio. "Apuntes para un estudio sobre los aspectos etnológicos del Sáhara Occidental. Su constitución básica." *Cuaderno de estudios africanos*, no. 19 (July–September 1952): 57–65.

Geertz, Clifford. "What Is a State if It Is Not Sovereign?" *Politics in Complicated Places* 4, no. 5 (2004): 577–93.

Gentry, Caron E. "Twisted Maternalism: From Peace to Violence." *International Feminist Journal of Politics* 11, no. 2 (2009): 235–52.

Ghosh, Anindita, ed. *Behind the Veil: Resistance, Women and the Everyday in Colonial South Asia.* Basingstoke, UK: Palgrave Macmillan, 2008.

Gilligan, Carol. *In a Different Voice: Psychological Theory and Women's Development.* London: Harvard University Press, 1998.

Gimeno Martín, Juan Carlos, and Juan Ignacio Robles Picón. "Ambivalencia y orden colonial español en el Sahara Occidental (1969–1973)." *Antropología* 5 (September 2013): 151–77.

Global Investment Center. *Equatorial Guinea: Company Laws and Regulations Handbook.* Vol. 1, *Strategic Information and Regulations.* Washington, DC: Global Investment Center, 2013.

———. *Equatorial Guinea: Company Laws and Regulations Handbook.* Vol. 1, *Strategic Information and Regulations.* Washington, DC: Global Investment Center, 2012.

Global Rights Alert. "Towards Balancing Gender: Women's Participation in Uganda's Oil Sector; Case of Rural Women in Four Sub Counties of Hoima and Buliisa Districts." 2013.

Goldblatt, Beth, and Shiela Meintjes. "Gender and the Truth and Reconciliation Commission: A Submission to the Truth and Reconciliation Commission." Department of Justice and Constitutional Development, Republic of South Africa, May 1996. http://www.justice.gov.za/trc//hrvtrans/submit/gender.htm.

Gómez Martín, Carmen. "Gdeim Izik: A Change in the Struggle Strategies of the Sahrawi Population." In *From Social to Political: New Forms of Mobilization and Democratization*, edited by B. Teferina, and I. Perugorría, 58–72. Bilbao: Servicio Editorial de la Universidad del País Vasco, 2012.

Gorozpe, Iñaki. "Reivindicación Política y Particularismo en Annobón." *Lusotopie* 2 (1995): 251–57.

Gottschalk, Peter, and Gabriel Greenberg. *Islamophobia: Making Muslims the Enemy*. Lanham, MD: Rowman & Littlefield, 2008.

Government of Equatorial Guinea. "Consideration of Reports Submitted by States Parties under Article 18 of the Convention on the Elimination of All Forms of Discrimination against Women, Combined Fourth and Fifth Periodic Reports." Committee on the Elimination of All Forms of Discrimination against Women (CEDAW), 2004.

———. "Consideration of Reports Submitted by States Parties under Article 18 of the Convention on the Elimination of All Forms of Discrimination against Women. Second and Third Periodic Reports of States Parties: Equatorial Guinea." CEDAW, 27 September 1995.

———. "Consideration of Reports Submitted by States Parties under Article 18 of the Convention on the Elimination of All Forms of Discrimination against Women. Sixth Periodic Reports of States Parties: Equatorial Guinea." CEDAW, 2011.

———. "Responses to the List of Issues and Questions for Consideration of the Combined Second, Third, Fourth and Fifth Periodic Reports: Equatorial Guinea." CEDAW, 2004.

Government of Equatorial Guinea's Information and Press Office. "The Government of Equatorial Guinea." 2014. http://www.guineaecuatorialpress.com/noticia.php?id=126.

———. "The President of the Spanish Government Will Attend the AU Summit in Equatorial Guinea." 16 June 2014. http://www.guineaecuatorialpress.com/noticia.php?id=5290.

———. "Title Page." n.d. http://www.guineaecuatorialpress.com.

Graham-Brown, Sarah. "Women's Activism in the Middle East: A Historical Perspective." In *Women and Power in the Middle East*, edited by Suad Joseph and Susan Slymovics, 23–33. Philadelphia: University of Pennsylvania Press, 2001.

Gramsci, Antonio. *Selections from the Prison Notebooks*. Edited and translated by Quentin Hoare and Geoffrey Nowell Smith. London: Lawrence and Wishart, 1971.

Greening, Justine. "Investing in Growth: How DfID Works in New and Emerging Markets." 11 March 2013. https://www.gov.uk/government/speeches/investing-in-growth-how-dfid-works-in-new-and-emerging-markets.

Grijalva-Eternod, Carlos S., Jonathan C. K. Wells, Mario Cortina-Borja, Nuria Salse-Ubach, Mélody C. Tondeur, Carmen Dolan, Chafik Meziani, Caroline Wilkinson,

Paul Spiegel, and Andrew J. Seal. "The Double Burden of Obesity and Malnutrition in a Protracted Emergency Setting: A Cross-Sectional Study of Western Sahara Refugees." *PLOS Medicine* 9, no. 10 (2012): 1–12.

Guthrey, Holly L. *Victim Healing and Truth Commissions: Transforming Pain through Voice in the Solomon Islands and Timor-Leste*. New York: Springer, 2015.

Guzman Bouvard, Marguerite. *Revolutionizing Motherhood: The Mothers of the Plaza de Mayo*. Lanham, MD: SR Books, 1994.

Hacene-Djaballah, Belkacem. "Conflict in Western Sahara: A Study of POLISARIO as an Insurgency Movement." PhD diss., Catholic University of America, 1985.

Haidar, Aminatou. "Carta abierta de Aminetu Haidar a la sociedad española en el Día Internacional de los Derechos Humanos." In *Las treinta y dos batallas de Aminetu Haidar*, edited by Conxi Moya, 75–76. Madrid: Bubok, 2010.

———. "Testimony of Human Rights Violations against Saharawis." Paper presented at the Conference on Multilateralism and International Law with Western Sahara as a Case Study, Pretoria, South Africa, 4–5 December 2008.

Haidar, Larosi. "Prólogo." In *La esclavitud en el Sáhara Occidental*, edited by Pablo Ignacio de Dalmases, 7–13. Barcelona: Ediciones Carena, 2012.

Haraway, Donna. *Simians, Cyborgs, and Women: The Reinvention of Nature*. New York: Routledge, 1991.

Hart, Gillian. "Changing Concepts of Articulation: Political Stakes in South Africa Today." *Review of African Political Economy* 34, no. 111 (2007): 85–101.

Harter, Pascale. "Sahara Women Relish their Rights." *BBC News Africa*, 30 October 2003. http://news.bbc.co.uk/1/hi/world/africa/3227997.stm.

Hasso, Frances. "The 'Women's Front': Nationalism, Feminism, and Modernity in Palestine." *Gender and Society* 12, no. 4 (1998): 441–65.

Henríquez Pérez, Ana. "Entrevista a la escritora y activista Trifonia Melibea Obono: 'Las guineanas siempre han sido feministas.'" *Africaye.org*, 6 June 2017. http://www.africaye.org/guineanas-feministas-melibea-obono/.

Hill Collins, Patricia. *Black Feminist Thought: Knowledge, Consciousness, and the Politics of Empowerment*. New York: Routledge, 2000.

Hobsbawm, Eric, and Terence Ranger, eds. *The Invention of Tradition*. Cambridge: Cambridge University Press, 1992.

Hochschild, Arlie Russell, and Anne Machung. *The Second Shift: Working Families and the Revolution at Home*. New York: Viking Penguin, 1989.

Hodges, Tony. *Western Sahara: The Roots of a Desert War*. Westport, CT: Lawrence Hill, 1983.

hooks, bell. *Ain't I a Woman: Black Women and Feminism*. London: Pluto, 1982.

Howarth, David. *Discourse: Concepts in the Social Sciences*. Philadelphia, PA: Open University Press, 2000.

Hughes, Neil. "Democracy and Imperial Rivalry in Equatorial Guinea." *Review of African Political Economy* 23, no. 69 (1996): 442–45.

Human Rights Watch. "Equatorial Guinea: Abuses Ahead of AU Summit." 22 June 2011. https://www.hrw.org/news/2011/06/22/equatorial-guinea-abuses-ahead-au-summit.

———. "Western Sahara/Algeria: Refugees Face Curbs on Rights." 18 October 2014. https://www.hrw.org/news/2014/10/18/western-sahara/algeria-refugees-face-curbs-rights.

————. *World Report 2015: Events of 2014*. New York: Seven Stories Press, 2015.

Humm, Maggie. *The Dictionary of Feminist Theory*. Hemel Hempstead, Hertfordshire: Harvester Wheatsheaf, 1989.

Huntington, Samuel. "A Clash of Civilisations?" *Foreign Affairs*, Summer (1993): 22–49.

Igreja, Victor, Wim C. Kleijn, Bas J. N. Schreuder, Janie A. Van Dijk, and Margot Verschuur. "Testimony Method to Ameliorate Post-Traumatic Stress Symptoms: Community-Based Intervention Study with Mozambican Civil War Survivors." *British Journal of Psychiatry* 184 (2004): 251–57.

Ilombe del Pozo Epita, Raquel. *Ceiba II (Poesía Inédita)*. Edited by Benita Sampedro Vizcaya and Baltasar Fra-Molinero. Madrid: Verbum, 2015.

Ingle, Sean, and Mark Hodgkinson. "When Did Football Hooliganism Start?" *The Guardian*, 13 December 2001.

International Monetary Fund (IMF). "Republic of Equatorial Guinea: IMF Country Report No. 15/260." September 2015.

Isidoros, Konstantina. "The Silencing of Unifying Tribes: The Colonial Construction of Tribe and Its 'Extraordinary Leap' to Nascent Nation-State Formation in Western Sahara." *Journal of the Anthropological Society of Oxford* 7, no. 2 (2015): 168–90.

Jackson, Lawrence. "President Barack Obama and First Lady Michelle Obama pose for a photo during a reception at the Metropolitan Museum in New York with Teodoro Obiang Nguema Mbasogo, President of the Republic of Equatorial Guinea, and his wife, First Lady Constancia Mangue de Obiang." White House, Washington, DC, 2009.

Jackson, Robert H., and Carl G. Rosberg. *Personal Rule in Black Africa: Prince, Autocrat, Prophet, Tyrant*. Berkeley: University of California Press, 1982.

Jiwani, Yasmin. "Trapped in the Carceral Net: Race, Gender, and the 'War on Terror.'" *Global Media Journal—Canadian Edition* 4, no. 2 (2011): 13–31.

Joseph, Suad, and Susan Slymovics, eds. *Women and Power in the Middle East*. Philadelphia: University of Philadelphia Press, 2001.

Joseph, Suad, and Susan Slymovics. "Introduction." In *Women and Power in the Middle East*, edited by Suad Joseph and Susan Slymovics, 1–19. Philadelphia: Pennsylvania Press, 2001.

Jubber, Nick. "Salaam's Story." *Sandblast*, 4 July 2012. http://sandblast-arts.blogspot .co.uk/2012/07/salaams-story-by-nick-jubber.html.

Kanaaneh, Rhoda Ann. *Birthing the Nation: Strategies of Palestinian Women in Israel*. Berkeley: University of California Press, 2002.

Kandiyoti, Deniz. "Islam and Patriarchy: A Comparative Perspective." In *Feminist Approaches to Theory and Methodology: An Interdisciplinary Reader*, edited by Sharlene Hesse-Biber, Christine Gilmartin, and Robin Lydenberg, 219–35. New York: Oxford University Press, 1999.

————. "The Politics of Gender and Reconstruction in Afghanistan: Old Dilemmas or New Challenges." In *Gendered Peace: Women's Struggles for Post-War Justice and Reconciliation*, edited by Donna Pankhurst, 155–85. London: Routledge, 2008.

Kaplan, Gisela. "Feminism and Nationalism: The European Case." In *Feminist Nationalism*, edited by Lois A. West, 3–40. New York: Routledge, 1997.

Kaplan, Temma. "Acts of Testimony: Reversing the Shame and Gendering the Memory." *Signs* 28, no. 1 (2002): 179–99.

————. "Female Conciousness and Collective Action: The Case of Barcelona, 1910–1918." *Signs* 7, no. 3 (1982): 545–66.

Katz, Cindi. *Growing Up Global: Economic Restructuring and Children's Everyday Lives.* Minneapolis: University of Minnesota Press, 2004.

Kennedy, Kerry. "Morocco Has Pressured UN to Ignore Western Sahara." *The Guardian*, 23 July 2015.

Khalil, Andrea. "Tunisia's Women: Partners in Revolution." *Journal of North African Studies* 19, no. 2 (2014): 186–99.

Khalili, Laleh. *Time in the Shadows: Confinement in Counterinsurgencies.* Stanford, CA: Stanford University Press, 2013.

King, Catherine. "The Politics of Representation: A Democracy of the Gaze." In *Imagining Women: Cultural Representations and Gender*, edited by Frances Bonner, Lizbeth Goodman, Richard Allen, Linda Jones, and Catherine King, 131–39. Cambridge: Polity Press, 1992.

Klein, Marian van der, Rebecca Jo Plant, Nichole Sanders, and Lori R. Weintrob, eds. *Maternalism Reconsidered: Motherhood, Welfare and Social Policy in the Twentieth Century.* New York: Berghahn Books, 2012.

Klinteberg, Robert. *Equatorial Guinea, Macías Country: The Forgotten Refugees.* Geneva: International University Exchange Fund (IUEF), 1978.

Klitgaard, Robert. *Tropical Gangsters: One Man's Experience with Development and Decadence in Deepest Africa.* New York: Basic Books, 1990.

Kontorovich, Eugene. "Economic Dealings with Occupied Territories." *Columbia Journal of Transnational Law* 53, no. 3 (2015): 584–637.

Kreutzberger, Kai. "Single Mothers and Children Born out of Wedlock in the Kingdom of Morocco." *Yearbook of Islamic and Middle Eastern Law* 14 (2008–9): 49–82.

Kugle, Scott Siraj al-Haqq. "Sexuality, Diversity, and Ethics in the Agenda of Progressive Muslims." In *Progressive Muslims*, edited by Safi Omid, 190–234. Oxford: Oneworld, 2003.

Kumar Srivastava, Pramod. "Resistance and Repression in India: The Hunger Strike at the Andaman Cellular Jail in 1933." *Crime, History and Societies* 7, no. 2 (2003): 81–102.

*La Vanguardia.* "Críticas al Gobierno por la invitación del Instituto Cervantes y la UNED al dictador Obiang." 20 March 2014. http://www.lavanguardia.com/contacto/index.html.

————. "Denuncia el secuestro de joven saharaui de acogida por su familia biológica." October 1, 2014. http://www.lavanguardia.com/local/valencia/20141001/544165271 23/denuncia-el-secuestro-de-joven-saharaui-de-acogida-por-su-familia-biologica .html.

Laclau, Ernesto. "Ideology and Post-Marxism." *Journal of Political Ideologies* 11, no. 2 (2006): 103–14.

Laclau, Ernesto, and Chantal Mouffe. *Hegemonía y estrategia socialista: Hacía una radicalización de la democracia.* Madrid: España Editores, 1987.

Lafarga, Alfonso. "Mariem Hassan, la voz que cantó la lucha del pueblo saharaui por el mundo." Por un sahara libre (blog), 24 August 2015. http://porunsaharalibre.org/ 2015/08/24/mariem-hassan-la-voz-que-canto-la-lucha-de-pueblo-saharaui-por-el -mundo/.

Larrú, José María. "Foreign Aid in Equatorial Guinea: Macroeconomic Feature and Future Challenges." Munich Personal RePEc Archive paper no. 25001, 2010, https://mpra.ub.uni-muenchen.de/25001/1/MPRA_paper_25001.pdf.

Laub, Dori. "Truth and Testimony: The Process and the Struggle." In *Trauma: Explorations in Memory*, edited by Cathy Caruth, 61–75. Baltimore: Johns Hopkins University Press, 1995.

Laurence, Anne. *Women in England, 1500–1760: A Social History*. London: Phoenix Press, 2002.

Law, Victoria. *Resistance Behind Bars: The Struggles of Incarcerated Women*. Oakland, CA: PM Press, 2009.

Lewis, Reina. *Gendering Orientalism: Race, Femininity and Representation*. London: Routledge, 1996.

Liddle, Joanna, and Shirin Rai. "Feminism, Imperialism and Orientalism: The Challenge of the 'Indian Woman.'" *Women's History Review* 7, no. 4 (1998): 495–520.

Limón Rivas, Laura. "La diversidad sexual en el Islam: El caso saharaui." *Perspectiva: Revista Trabajo Social* 18 (2008): 72–77.

Liniger-Goumaz, Max. *Guinea Ecuatorial: Memorándum; Medio siglo de terror y saqueo*. Madrid: Sial Ediciones, 2013.

Lippert, Anne. "Sahrawi Women in the Liberation Struggle of the Sahrawi People." *Signs* 17, no. 3 (1992): 636–51.

Lončar, Mladen, Vesna Medved, Nikolina Jovanović, and Ljubomir Hotujac. "Psychological Consequences of Rape in 1991–1995 War in Croatia and Bosnia and Herzegovina." *Croation Medical Journal* 47, no. 1 (2006): 67–75.

Lonely Planet. "Introducing Agdz." 2015.

López Ortega, Ángel Antonio. *La poesía oral de los pueblos de Guinea Ecuatorial: Géneros y funciones*. Barcelona: Ceiba Ediciones, 2008.

Lorch, Jasmin, and Bettina Bunk. "Gender Politics, Authoritarian Regime Resilience, and the Role of Civil Society in Algeria and Mozambique." *GIGA Working Papers*, no. 292 (2016): 1–41.

Lukes, Steven. *Power: A Radical View*. 2nd ed. Hampshire: Palgrave Macmillan, 2005.

Lunn, Jon. "Equatorial Guinea: A Quick Introduction." Edited by UK Parliament. London: House of Commons Library, 2011.

Lutgen-Sandvik, Pamela. "Take This Job and . . . : Quitting and Other Forms of Resistance to Workplace Bullying." *Communication Monographs* 73, no. 4 (2006): 406–33.

Machaqueiro, Mário. "Ambiguities of Seduction: Photography and the 'Islamic' Policy of Portuguese Colonialism." *Anthropological Quarterly* 88, no. 1 (2015): 97–131.

Mama, Amina. "Khaki in the Family: Gender Discourses and Militarism in Nigeria." *African Studies Review* 41, no. 2 (1998): 1–17.

Martín Beristain, Carlos, and Eloísa González Hidalgo. *El oasis de la memoria: Memoria histórica y violaciones de Derechos Humanos en el Sáhara Occidental*. Vol. 1. Bilbao: Hegoa, 2012.

———. *El oasis de la memoria: Memoria histórica y violaciones de Derechos Humanos en el Sáhara Occidental*. Vol. 2. Bilbao: Hegoa, 2012.

Martin-Marquéz, Susan. "Brothers and Others: Fraternal Rhetoric and the Negotiation of Spanish and Saharawi Identity." *Journal of Spanish Cultural Studies* 7, no. 3 (2006): 241–58.

―――. *Disorientations: Spanish Colonialism in Africa and the Performance of Identity.* New Haven, CT: Yale University Press, 2008.

Martino, Enrique. "Clandestine Recruitment Networks in the Bight of Biafra: Fernando Pó's Answer to the Labour Question, 1926–1945." *Internationaal Instituut voor Sociale Geschiedenis (IRSH)* 57, special issue (2012): 39–72.

―――. "Maoist China and Macias' Equatorial Guinea—write up of some of the notes of from [*sic*] fragmentary conversation with a secret and sort of expensive informant. Malabo, July 2013." 15 September 2013. http://www.opensourceguinea .org/2013/09/maoist-china-and-macias-equatorial.html.

―――. "Nsoa ('dote'), dinero, deuda y peonaje: Cómo el parentesco fang tejió y destejió la economía colonial de la Guinea española." *Endoxa: Revista Universitaria de Filosofía* 37 (2016): 337–61.

―――. "Touts and Despots: Recruiting Assemblages of Contract Labour in Fernando Pó and the Gulf of Guinea, 1858–1979." PhD diss., Humboldt University of Berlin, 2016.

Mason, Corinne L. "Global Violence against Women as a National Security 'Emergency.'" *Feminist Formations* 25, no. 2 (2013): 55–80.

Mazama, Ama. "The Afrocentric Paradigm: Contours and Definitions." *Journal of Black Studies* 31, no. 4 (2001): 387–405.

McAdam, Doug, Sidney Tarrow, and Charles Tilly. *Dynamics of Contention.* Cambridge: Cambridge University Press, 2001.

McClintock, Anne. *Imperial Leather: Race, Gender and Sexuality in the Colonial Contest.* New York: Routledge, 1995.

McDonald, Laura Zahra. "Islamic Feminism." *Feminist Theory* 9, no. 3 (2008): 347–54.

McFarland, Daniel A. "Student Resistance: How the Formal and Informal Organization of Classrooms Facilitate Everyday Forms of Student Defiance." *American Journal of Sociology* 107, no. 3 (2001): 612–78.

Medina-Doménech, Rosa. "Scientific Technologies of National Identity as Colonial Legacies: Extracting the Spanish Nation from Equatorial Guinea." *Social Studies of Science* 39, no. 1 (2009): 81–112.

Memmi, Albert. *The Colonizer and the Colonized.* London: Earthscan Publications, 2003.

Mercer, John. *Spanish Sahara.* London: George Allen & Unwin, 1976.

*Middle East Eye.* "Ban Ki-Moon Demands Western Sahara Mission Be Fully Restored." Middle East Eye, 19 April 2016. http://www.middleeasteye.net/news/ban-ki-moon -demands-western-sahara-mission-be-fully-restored-1606934184.

Minder, Raphael. "Spanish Soccer Team under Fire for Game in Equatorial Guinea." *New York Times,* 14 November 2013.

Ministry of Social Affairs and Promotion of Women. "Homepage." Accessed December 2015. https://www.minasige.com/.

Moghadam, Valentine. *From Patriarchy to Empowerment.* Syracuse, NY: Syracuse University Press, 2007.

Moghadam, Valentine N. "Nationalist Agendas and Women's Rights." In *Feminist Nationalism,* edited by Lois A. West, 75–100. London: Routledge, 1997.

Mohamed Lamin, Habibulah. "Amid Decreasing Aid, Sahrawis Seek Self-Determination." *Al-Monitor*, 25 May 2016. http://www.al-monitor.com/pulse/originals/2016/05/west ern-sahara-sahrawi-melhfa-civil-society.html.

Mohamed, Reem. "Women and the Arab Spring: Tough Choices to Make." *Open Democracy*, 25 October 2013. http://www.opendemocracy.net/arab-awakening/ reem-mohamed/women-and-arab-spring-tough-choices-to-make.

Mohanty Talpade, Chandra, Ann Russo, and Lourdes Torres, eds. *Third World Women and the Politics of Feminism*. Bloomington: Indiana University Press, 1991.

Mokhtar, Khadijatou. "La mujer saharaui en los campamentos de refugiados." Paper presented at the conference Jornadas de sensibilización sobre la cuestión del Sahara Occidental, University of Granada, 18 November 2014.

Mookherjee, Nayanika. "The Absent Piece of Skin: Gendered, Racialized and Territorial Inscriptions of Sexual Violence during the Bangladesh War." *Modern Asian Studies* 46, no. 6 (2011): 1572–601.

Morales Villena, Amalia, and Soledad Vieitez Cerdeño. "La Sección Femenina en la 'llamada de África': Saharauis y guineanas en el declive del colonialismo español." *Vegueta: Anuario de la Facultad de Geografía e Historia (Universidad de Granada)* 14 (2014): 117–33.

Morcillo, Aurora G. *True Catholic Womanhood: Gender Ideology in Franco's Spain*. Dekalb: Northern Illinois University Press, 2000.

Morgades Besari, Trinidad. "Antígona." *Arizona Journal of Hispanic Cultural Studies* 8, no. 1 (2004): 239–45.

Morris, Loveday. "In Western Sahara, Women Play Large Role in Forgotten Struggle for Independence." *Washington Post*, 7 July 2013.

————. "Women on Frontline in Struggle for Western Sahara." *The Guardian*, 16 July 2013.

Moya, Conxi. *Las 32 Batallas de Aminatu Haidar*. Madrid: Bubok, 2010.

Msimang, Sisonke. "African Feminisms II: Reflections on Politics Made Personal." *Agenda* 17, no. 54 (2002): 3–15.

Mundy, Jacob. "Autonomy & Intifada: New Horizons in Western Saharan National- isms." *Review of African Political Economy* 108 (2006): 255–67.

————. "The Dynamics of Repression and Resistance: Sahrawi Nationalist Activism in the Moroccan Occupied Western Sahara." Paper presented at the annual meeting of the International Studies Association, San Francisco, 2011.

————. "How the US and Morocco Seized the Spanish Sahara." *Le Monde Diploma- tique*, January 2006.

————. "Performing the Nation, Prefiguring the State: The Western Saharan Refu- gees, Thirty Years Later." *Journal of North African Studies* 45, no. 2 (2007): 275–97.

Murthy, Dhiraj. "'Muslim Punk' Music Online: Piety and Protest in the Digital Age." In *Music, Culture and Identity in the Muslim World*, edited by Kamal Salhi, 160–77. Abingdon: Taylor and Francis, 2013.

Ndongo-Bidyogo, Donato. "El Gobernador Faustino Ruiz González y el nacionalismo en Guinea Ecuatorial." Paper presented at the Seminario Internacional "Actores colo- niales españoles y espacios africanos SS. XIX–XX, University of Alcalá, 2–3 Decem- ber 2010.

————. *Historia y Tragedia de Guinea Ecuatorial*. Madrid: Cambio 16, 1977.

Negre Rigol, Jordi. "Sahara: España arria su bandera." *Diario de Barcelona*, 20 December 1975.

Nerín, Gustau. *Guinea Ecuatorial, historia en blanco y negro*. Barcelona: Ediciones Peninsula, 1998.

———. *La Sección Femenina de la Falange en la Guinea Española (1964–1969)*. Valencia: CEIBA, 2006.

———. *La última selva de España: Antropódagos, misioneros y guardias civiles*. Madrid: Catarata, 2010.

*New Vision*. "Africa's Longest-Serving Leader Re-elected." 28 April 2016. http://www.newvision.co.ug/new_vision/news/1423403/africas-serving-leader-elected-94-vote.

Nkogo Ondó, Eugenio. "La Guinea Ecuatorial: Reminiscencia histórica, experiencia de las luces y de las sombras de un proyecto político." Paper presented at the conference Between Three Continents: Rethinking Equatorial Guinea on the Fortieth Anniversary of Its Independence from Spain, Hofstra University, 2009.

Norris, Harry T. *The Arab Conquest of Western Sahara*. Beirut: Longman and Librairie du Liban, 1986.

Nsang Nguema, Maria Jesus. "Meeting for Women in the Equatorial Guinean Embassy in Spain." Government of Equatorial Guinea's Information and Press Office. 15 March 2013. http://www.guineaecuatorialpress.com/noticia.php?id=3607.

———. "Speech by the First Lady at the 5th Congress of the PDGE." Government of Equatorial Guinea's Information and Press Office. 21 April 2012. http://guineaecuatorialpress.com/noticia.php?id=2578&lang=en.

Nsang Nguema, Maria Jesus, and Reina Ngomo Avomo. "Return of Constancia Mangue de Obiang." Government of Equatorial Guinea's Information and Press Office. 20 June 2013. http://www.guineaecuatorialpress.com/noticia.php?id=3919.

Nsue Angüe, María. *Ekomo*. Madrid: UNED, 1985.

———. *Relatos*. Malabo: Centro Cultural Hispano-Guineano, 1999.

Nsue Mibui, Rosendo-Ela. *Historia de la Guinea Ecuatorial: Periodo Pre-Colonial*. Madrid: Gráficas Algoran, 2005.

Nugent, Paul. "States and Social Contracts in Africa." *New Left Review* 63 (2010): 35–68.

Nye, Joseph S. *The Future of Power*. New York: Public Affairs, 2011.

Nze Nfumu, Agustín. *Macías, verdugo o víctima*. Madrid: Herrero y Asociados, 2004.

Obiang Biko, Adolfo. *Equatorial Guinea: From Spanish Colonialism to the Discovery of Oil*. New York: O. Writers, 2010.

Obono Ntutumu, Trifonia Melibea. "Acerca de la mujer guineana: Un largo camino por recorrer." ASODEGUE, 8 March 2009. http://www.asodegue.org/marzo0809.htm.

Obono Ntutumu, Trifonia Melibea. *La hija de una soltera fang*. 2012. https://www.scribd.com/document/87524345/La-Hija-de-Una-Soltera-Fang.

Obono Ntutumu, Trifonia Melibea. "Guinea Ecuatorial: Misoginia en los partidos políticos." *Tiempos Canallas*, 8 March 2013.

Ocha'a Mve, Constantino. *Fuentes archivísticas y bibliotecarias de Guinea Ecuatorial: Guía general del administrativo, del investigador y del estudiante*. Madrid: Anzos, 1985.

Okenve, Enrique. "Equatorial Guinea 1927–1979: A New African Tradition." PhD diss., School of Oriental and African Studies (SOAS), University of London, 2007.

————. "'Wa kobo abe, wa kobo politik': Three Decades of Social Paralysis and Political Immobility in Equatorial Guinea." Paper presented at the conference Between Three Continents: Rethinking Equatorial Guinea on the Fortieth Anniversary of Its Independence from Spain, Hofstra University, 2009.

Ondo Ayang, Luis, Anacleto Bokesa Camó, and Max Liniger-Goumaz. *Nguemismo: 33 años de auto-golpes y torturas, corrupción nacional e internacional.* La Chaux, Switzerland: Editorial Tiempos Próximos, 2002.

Ondo'o Ayekaba, Mitoha. "The Politics of Gender Parity in Equatorial Guinea: Toward a more Sustained Political and Social Civility in the Twenty First Century." Paper presented at the conference Between Three Continents: Rethinking Equatorial Guinea on the Fortieth Anniversary of Its Independence from Spain, Hofstra University, New York, 2009.

Orgambides, Fernando. "La misión de la ONU llega hoy al Sáhara." *El País*, 20 November 1987.

Organization for Economic Cooperation and Development (OECD). "Development Aid at a Glance: Statistics by Region." 2015.

Ortega, Ines. "The First Lady Receives the Title of Doctor Honoris Causa." Government of Equatorial Guinea's Information and Press Office, 27 November 2013. http://www.guineaecuatorialpress.com/noticia.php?id=4529.

Ortner, Sherry B. "Resistance and the Problem of Ethnographic Refusal." *Comparative Studies in Society and History* 37, no. 1 (1995): 173–93.

Ostriker, Alicia. "A Wild Surmise: Motherhood and Poetry." In *Imagining Women: Cultural Representations and Gender*, edited by Frances Bonner, Lizbeth Goodman, Richard Allen, Linda Jones, and Catherine King, 103–7. Cambridge: Polity Press, 1992.

Paciello, Maria Cristina, Renata Pepicelli, and Daniela Pioppi. "Public Action towards Youth in Neo-Liberal Morocco: Fostering and Controlling the Unequal Inclusion of the New Generation." *Power2Youth Papers*, no. 5 (February 2016). https://unora.unior.it/retrieve/handle/11574/165777/19842/p2y_05.pdf.

Pardo Sanz, Rosa. "La herencia de la descolonización del África española." In *Europe face à son passé colonial*, edited by Olivier Dard and Daniel Lefeuvre. Paris: Riveneuve Editions, 2008.

Pélissier, René. *Los territorios españoles de Africa.* Madrid: Consejo Superior de Investigaciones Científicas, 1964.

Pérez Moreno, Heliodoro Manuel. "La Sección Femenina de la España de Franco (1939–1975) y sus Contradicciones entre 'Perfil de Mujer' y Medios Educativos." *Cadernos de História da Educação* 7 (January/December 2008): 77–92.

Peteet, Julie M. "Icons and Militants: Mothering in the Danger Zone." In *Gender, Politics and Islam*, edited by T. Saliba, C. Allen, and J. A. Howard, 133–59. Chicago: University of Chicago Press, 2002.

————. "Women and the Palestinian Movement: No Going Back?" In *Women and Power in the Middle East*, edited by Suad Joseph and Susan Slymovics, 126–34. Philadelphia: University of Pennsylvania Press, 2001.

Pohlman, Annie. "Testimonio and Telling Women's Narratives of Genocide, Torture and Political Imprisonment in Post-Suharto Indonesia." *Life Writing* 5, no. 1 (2008): 47–60.

Porges, Matthew, and Christian Leuprecht. "The Puzzle of Nonviolence in Western Sahara." *Democracy and Security* 12, no. 2 (2016): 65–84.

Power, Margaret. "Dictatorship and Single-Party States." In *The Oxford Encyclopedia of Women in World History*, edited by Bonnie G. Smith, 55–56. Oxford: Oxford University Press, 2008.

Pozo, Dani, and Susana Hidalgo. "Lo más duro es cuando escucho llorar a mi hijo." In *Las treinta y dos batallas de Aminetu Haidar*, edited by Conxi Moya, 91–94. Madrid: Bubok, 2010.

Qorvis Communications LLC. "Equatorial Guinea Reports Progress on Gender Equality, Elimination of Violence against Women." 14 March 2013. http://equatorialguinea info.blogspot.co.uk/2013/03/equatorial-guinea-reports-progress-on.html.

Rakowski, Cathy A. "Women as Political Actors: The Move from Maternalism to Citizenship Rights and Power." *Latin American Research Review* 38, no. 2 (2003): 180–94.

Rankin, Pauline L. "Gender and Nation Branding in 'The True North Strong and Free.'" *Place Branding and Public Diplomacy* 8, no. 4 (2012): 257–67.

Reporters without Borders. "Facebook and Opposition Websites Blocked Ahead of Elections." 14 May 2013. http://en.rsf.org/guinee-equatoriale-facebook-and-opposition-websites-14<HY>05<HY>2013,44618.html.

Rice, Xan. "Western Sahara Activist on Hunger Strike at Lanzarote Airport." *The Guardian*, 17 November 2009.

Richter-Montpetit, Melanie. "Beyond the Erotics of Orientalism: Lawfare, Torture and the Racial-Sexual Grammars of Legitimate Suffering." *Security Dialogue* 45, no. 1 (2014): 43–62.

———. "Empire, Desire and Violence: A Queer Transnational Feminist Reading of the Prisoner 'Abuse' in Abu Ghraib and the Question of 'Gender Equality.'" *International Feminist Journal of Politics* 9, no. 1 (2007): 38–59.

Río Joan, Francisco del. *África occidental española (Sáhara y Guinea): Memoria elevada al Excmo. señor Ministro de Estado por el comandante de ingenieros D. Francisco del Río Joan*. Madrid: Ministerio de Estado, Sección Colonial, 1915.

Rodney, Walter. *How Europe Underdeveloped Africa*. Washington, DC: Howard University Press, 1982.

Rodriguez Rescia, Victor. "Torture as a Form of Gendered Violence." *Essex Human Rights Review* 6, no. 2 (2010): 138–47.

Rose, Cecily. "The Application of Human Rights Law to Private Sector Complicity in Governmental Corruption." *Leiden Journal of International Law* 24 (2011): 715–40.

Ross, Michael L. "Oil, Islam, and Women." *American Political Science Review* 102, no. 1 (2008): 107–23.

Rowbotham, Sheila. *Hidden from History: 300 Years of Women's Oppression and the Fight against It*. London: Pluto Press, 1975.

Ruano Posada, Violeta, and Vivian Solana Moreno. "The Strategy of Style: Music, Struggle, and the Aesthetics of Sahrawi Nationalism in Exile." *Transmodernity: Journal of Peripheral Cultural Production of the Luso-Hispanic World* 5, no. 3 (2015): 40–61.

Saavedra y Magdalena, Diego. *España en el Africa Occidental (Río de Oro y Guinea)*. Madrid: Imprenta Artística Española, 1910.

Said, Edward. *Covering Islam: How the Media and the Experts Determine How We See the World*. New York: Vintage Books, 1997.

———. *Orientalism*. London: Penguin, 1995.

Salami, Minna. "7 Key Issues in African Feminist Thought." In *Ms Afropolitan*, 16 August 2012.

Salas Guirior, Jose. "Viaje a las Sombras de España." *ABC*, Madrid, 7 March 1976.

San Martín, Pablo. "Is Nationalism an Ideology? A Critical Exploration from the Asturian Case." 2007. Unpublished paper in author's possession.

———. "Nationalism, Identity and Citizenship in the Western Sahara." *Journal of North African Studies* 10, no. 3/4 (2005): 565–92.

———. *Western Sahara: The Refugee Nation*. Cardiff: University of Wales Press, 2010.

San Martín, Pablo, and Joanna Allan. "The Largest Prison in the World: Landmines, UXOs and the Role of the UN in the Western Sahara." Spanish Strategic Studies Group (GEES), Madrid, 2007.

Sands, William. "Equatorial Guinea: Legitimizing Obiang." Pulitzer Center on Crisis Reporting, 24 April 2012. http://pulitzercenter.org/reporting/equatorial-guinea-pres ident-teodoro-obiang-legitimization-corruption-oil-unesco-eiti-dodd-frank.

Sarkar, Sumit. "Orientalism Revisited: Saidian Frameworks in the Writing of Modern Indian History." In *Mapping Subaltern Studies and the Postcolonial*, edited by Vinayak Chaturvedi, 239–55. London: Verso, 2000.

Scafidi, Oscar. *Equatorial Guinea*. Chalfont St. Peter: Brandt, 2015.

Scholz, T. M. Linda. "The Rhetorical Power of *Testimonio* and *Ocupación*: Creating a Conceptual Framework for Analyzing Subaltern Rhetorical Agency." PhD diss., University of Colorado, 2007.

Schwartz, Adelaide. Email from adelaide.schwartz@stratfor.com to africa@stratfor .com. Wikileaks, the GI Files, 7 December 2011. https://wikileaks.org/gifiles/docs/ 28/2867601_re-africa-equatorial-guinea-uk-energy-ct-ukaccuses-eq.html.

Scott, James C. *Domination and the Arts of Resistance: Hidden Transcripts*. New Haven, CT: Yale University Press, 1990.

———. *Weapons of the Weak: Everyday Forms of Peasant Resistance*. New Haven, CT: Yale University Press, 1985.

Sears, Christine E. *American Slaves and African Masters: Algiers and the Western Sahara, 1776–1820*. New York: Palgrave Macmillan, 2012.

Seodu Herr, Ranjoo. "Reclaiming Third World Feminism: Or Why Transnational Feminism Needs Third World Feminism." *Meridians: Feminism, Race, Transnationalism* 12, no. 1 (2014): 1–30.

Sharp, Gene. *The Politics of Nonviolent Action: Parts 1–3*. Boston: Porter Sargent, 1973.

Shea, Maureen E. "Latin American Women and the Oral Tradition: Giving Voice to the Voiceless." *Critique* 34, no. 3 (1993): 139–53.

Shelley, Toby. *Endgame in the Western Sahara*. London: Zed Books, 2004.

Shepherd, Laura J. "Veiled References: Constructions of Gender in the Bush Administration Discourse on the Attacks on Afghanisation Post-9/11." *International Feminist Journal of Politics* 8, no. 1 (2006): 19–41.

Silverstein, Ken. "Obiang's American Enablers." *100 Reporters*, 14 December 2011. http://100r.org/2011/12/obiangs-american-enablers/.

Sipi Mayo, Remei. "Introducción." In *Voces femeninas de Guinea Ecuatorial: Una antología*, edited by Remei Sipi Mayo. Barcelona: Ediciones Mey, 2015.

———. "Ribocho. Identidad y encuentro." In *Baiso: Ellas y sus relatos*, edited by Remei Sipi Mayo, 1–53. Barcelona: Editorial Mey, 2015.

Sivakuman, Sandesh. "Sexual Violence against Men in Armed Conflict." *European Journal of International Law* 18, no. 2 (2007): 253–76.

Slyomovics, Susan. *The Performance of Human Rights in Morocco*. Philadelphia: University of Pennsylvania Press, 2005.

Smith, (first name unknown) (US Embassy to Equatorial Guinea). "Wikileaks Cable 09MALABO48_a: Equatorial Guinea Raw, Paper 6: Refining our Approach." Malabo, 21 May 2009.

Smith, Anthony. *National Identity*. Reno: University of Nevada Press, 1991.

Smith, David. "Equatorial Guinea Builds Luxury Resort for Week-Long Summit." *The Guardian*, Johannesburg, 7 June 2011.

Sola, Emilio. *Sahara Occidental: Viaje al país de la esperanza*. Madrid: Editorial Molinos de Agua, 1981.

Sola-Martin, Andreu. "Lessons from MINURSO: A Contribution to New Thinking on Peacekeeping." *International Peacekeeping Journal* 13, no. 3 (2006): 366–80.

———. *Peacekeeping and Conflict Resolution in Western Sahara*. Ceredigion: Edwin Mellen Press, 2006.

Solana Moreno, Vivian. "'No somos costosas. Somos valiosas.' La lucha de las mujeres saharauis 40 años después." In *Sahara Occidental: 40 años después*, edited by Isaías Barreñada and Raquel Ojeda, 81–91. Madrid: Catarata, 2016.

———. "'A Woman Is Stronger Than Our State': Performing Sovereignty on the Margins of the State." *Explorations in Anthropology* 11, no. 1 (2011): 57–70.

Soler, Bartolomé. "Cien días en el Sahara Español." Archives of the Institute of African Studies (Madrid National Library). Madrid, 14 January 1953, 43–58.

SOMAGEC Equatorial Guinea. "Homepage." Accessed December 2015. http://www.somagecge.com/.

SOMAGEC Morocco. "Homepage." Accessed December 2015. http://www.somagec.ma/e_acceuil.asp.

Spivak, Gayatri Chakravorty. "Can the Subaltern Speak?" In *Colonial Discourse and Post Colonial Theory*, edited by Patrick Williams and Laura Chrisman, 66–111. New York: Columbia University Press, 1994.

———. "The New Subaltern: A Silent Interview." In *Mapping Subaltern Studies and the Postcolonial*, edited by Vinayak Chaturvedi, 324–40. London: Verso, 2000.

Stehrenberger, Cécile Stephanie. "Folklore, Nation, and Gender in a Colonial Encounter: Coros y Danzas of the Sección Femenina of the Falange in Equatorial Guinea." *Afro-Hispanic Review* 28, no. 2 (2009): 231–44.

Stephan, Maria J., and Jacob Mundy. "A Battlefield Transformed: From Guerrilla Resistance to Mass Non-Violent Struggle in Western Sahara." *Journal of Military and Strategic Studies* 8, no. 3 (2006): 1–32.

Stucki, Andreas. "The Hard Side of Soft Power: Spanish Rhetorics of Empire from the 1950s to the 1970s." Paper presented at the conference Rhetoric of Empire: Imperial Discourse and the Language of Colonial Conflict, Exeter University's Center for War, State and Society, 2014.

Styhre, A., and U. Eriksson-Zetterquist. "Thinking the Multiple in Gender and Diversity Studies: Examining the Concept of Intersectionality." *Gender in Management* 23, no. 8 (2008): 567–82.

Sundiata, Ibrahim. *From Slaving to Neoslavery: The Bight of Biafra and Fernando Po in the Era of Abolition, 1827–1930*. Madison: University of Wisconsin Press, 1996.

Szeman, I. *Zones of Instability: Literature, Postcolonialism, and the Nation*. Baltimore: Johns Hopkins University Press, 2003.

Tabernero Chacobo, Hermenegildo. *Legislación de A.O.E.: Recopilación legislativa, por orden cronológico, de África Occidental Española (Territorios de Ifni y Sahara)*. Madrid: Selecciones Gráficas, 1947.

Taleb Mohammed, Asria. "'Influenciado por Occidente,' una acusación que funciona: Y seis lecciones que debemos aprender de Occidente." *Democracia Saharaui* (blog), 2 April 2017. http://lehdiamohameddafa.blogspot.co.uk/2017/04/influenciado-por -occidente-una.html.

Tarifa King, Sarilusi. "Celebration of International Women's Day in Malabo." Government of Equatorial Guinea's Information and Press Office. 11 March 2014. http:// www.guineaecuatorialpress.com/noticia.php?id=4907.

———. "Celebration of the World Day of Rural Women." Government of Equatorial Guinea's Information and Press Office. 18 October 2011. http://www.guineaecuato rialpress.com/noticia.php?id=1989.

———. "End of the Fifth Summit of Women, Gender and Development." Government of Equatorial Guinea's Information and Press Office. 25 June 2011. http:// www.guineaecuatorialpress.com/noticia.php?id=1693.

———. "Equatorial Guinea Women Make Progress in All Sectors." Government of Equatorial Guinea's Information and Press Office. 3 August 2011. http://www.guin eaecuatorialpress.com/noticia.php?id=1802.

———. "Meeting of the Wives of Government Members." Government of Equatorial Guinea's Information and Press Office. 15 May 2013. http://www.guineaecuatorial press.com/noticia.php?id=3795.

Tata Arcel, Libby. "Torture, Cruel, Inhuman and Degrading Treatment of Women. Psychological Consquences." *Psyke & Logos* 22 (2001): 322–51.

Tessmann, Günther. *Los Pamues (Los Fang). Monografía etnológica de una rama de las tribus negras del Africa Occidental*. 1913. Reprint, Alcalá de Henares: Universidad de Alcalá, 2003.

Thompson, Paul. *The Voice of the Past: Oral History*. Oxford: Oxford University Press, 1978.

Tillion, Germaine. *The Republic of Cousins: Women's Oppression in Mediterranean Society*. London: Al Saqi Books, 1983.

Tilly, Charles, and Sidney Tarrow. *Contentious Politics*. London: Paradigm Publishers, 2007.

Tohidi, Nayereh. "Modernity, Islamization and Women in Iran." In *Gender and National Identity: Women and Politics in Muslim Societies*, edited by Valentine Moghadam, 110–47. London: Zed Books, 1994.

Torfing, Jacob. *New Theories of Discourse: Laclau, Mouffe and Žižek*. Oxford: Blackwell, 1999.

Tortajada, Ana. *Hijas de la arena: Cartas desde los campamentos saharauis*. Barcelona: Debolsillo, 2004.

Trezenem, Edouard. "Notes Ethnographiques sur les Tribus Fan du Moyen Ogooué (Gabon)." *Journal de la Société des Africanistes* 6, no. 1 (1936): 65–93.

Tripp, Aili Marie. *Women and Power in Postconflict Africa.* Cambridge: Cambridge University Press, 2015.

Tsikata, Dzodzi. "Women's Organizing in Ghana since the 1990s: From Individual Organizations to Three Coalitions." *Development* 52, no. 2 (2009): 185–92.

UK Foreign and Commonwealth Office. "Equatorial Guinea: Current Conditions." 1979.

United Nations. "International Forum on the Role of Women in Population and Development." Warrenton, VA, 1974.

United Nations Development Program. "Human Development Report 2016: Human Development for Everyone. Table 4: Gender Development Index." 2016. http://hdr .undp.org/sites/default/files/2016_human_development_report.pdf.

United Nations High Commission for Refugees (UNHCR). "2015 UNHCR country operations profile—Algeria." 2015. http://www.unhcr.org/pages/49e485e16.html.

United Nations Women and International Development Cooperation of Spain. "Advancing Gender Equality: Promising Practices." 2013.

University of Granada Media. Video of Remei Sipi Mayo in conversation with Benita Sampedro, 20 June 2016. http://www.asodeguesegundaetapa.org/la-huella-de-la -colonizacion-espanola-en-las-mujeres-de-guinea-ecuatorial-remei-sipi-y-benita -sampedro-ugrmedia/.

United Press International. "Israeli Arms Companies Target Third World." 8 April 2011. http://www.upi.com/Business_News/Security-Industry/2011/04/08/Israeli-arms -companies-target-Third-World/29731302286121/.

US Department of State. "Country Reports on Human Rights Practices: Western Sahara 1999." 2000. https://www.state.gov/j/drl/rls/hrrpt/1999/423.htm.

———. "Country Reports on Human Rights Practices: Western Sahara 2000." 2001. https://www.state.gov/j/drl/rls/hrrpt/2000/nea/825.htm.

———. "Country Reports on Human Rights Practices: Western Sahara 2001." 2002. https://www.state.gov/j/drl/rls/hrrpt/2001/nea/8281.htm.

———. "Country Reports on Human Rights Practices: Western Sahara 2002." 2003. https://www.state.gov/j/drl/rls/hrrpt/2002/18292.htm.

———. "Trafficking in Persons Report: Equatorial Guinea." 2015. https://www.state .gov/j/tip/rls/tiprpt/countries/2015/243433.htm.

US Embassy to Morocco. "Wikileaks Cable: Moroccan Relations with Sub-Saharan African Countries—A Survey." Rabat, 3 June 2008.

Valenciano-Mañé, Alba. "Vestido, identidad y folklore. La invención de un vestido nacional de Guinea Ecuatorial." *Revista de Dialectología y Tradiciones Populares* 67, no. 1 (2012): 267–96.

Van Dijk, Teun A. "Contextual Knowledge Management in Discourse Production, a CDA Perspective." In *A New Agenda in (Critical) Discourse Analysis: Theory, Method and Interdisciplinarity*, edited by Ruth Wodak and Paul Chilton, 71–100. Amsterdam: John Benjamins, 2005.

———. "Principle of Critical Discourse Analysis." *Discourse and Society* 4, no. 2 (1993): 249–83.

Various. *Starry Nights in Western Sahara.* Cambridge, MA: Rounder Records, 2003.

Velloso, Agustín. "Israel starts business in Equatorial Guinea: Disaster Closes in Obiang Nguema's Regime." CSCAweb, 27 June 2005. https://www.nodo50.org/csca/agenda05/palestina/velloso_20<HY>06<HY>05.html.

Vickers, Jill. "Bringing Nations In: Some Methodological and Conceptual Issues in Connecting Feminisms with Nationhood and Nationalisms." *International Feminist Journal of Politics* 8, no. 1 (2006): 84–109.

Vines, Alex. "Well Oiled: Oil and Human Rights in Equatorial Guinea." Human Rights Watch, 2009. https://www.hrw.org/sites/default/files/reports/bhr0709web_0.pdf.

Vinthagen, Stellan. "Political Undergrounds: Can Raging Riots and Everyday Theft Become Politics of Normality?" Unpublished working paper, 2006.

Wallechinsky, David. "Dictator of the Month: Teodoro Obiang Nguema of Equatorial Guinea." 25 July 2011. http://www.allgov.com/news/us-and-the-world/dictator-of-the-month-teodoro-obiang-nguema-of-equatorial-guinea?news=843015.

Wenar, Leif. *Blood Oil: Tyrants, Violence and the Rules That Run the World.* Oxford: Oxford University Press, 2016.

———. "Clean Trade in Natural Resources." *Ethics and International Affairs* 25, no. 1 (2011): 27–39.

West, Lois A., ed. *Feminist Nationalism.* London: Routledge, 1997.

Wharton, Barrie. "Masters and Servants: The Spanish Civil War in Equatorial Guinea." *International Journal of the Canadian Institute for Mediterranean Studies* 26, no. 1 (2005): 39–50.

Whitaker, Brian. *Unspeakable Love: Gay and Lesbian Life in the Middle East.* London: Saqi Books, 2006.

White, Hayden. *The Content of Form: Narrative Discourse and Historical Representation.* London: Johns Hopkins University Press, 1989.

Wilson, Alice. "Household and the Production of Public and Private Domains: Revolutionary Changes in Western Sahara's Liberation Movement." *Paideuma* 58 (2012): 19–43.

———. "On the Margins of the Arab Spring." *Social Analysis* 57, no. 2 (2013): 81–98.

———. *Sovereignty in Exile: A Saharan Liberation Movement Governs.* Philadelphia: University of Pennsylvania Press, 2016.

Winter, Ida Sophie. "Many Moroccan Students Pursue Sex but Few Get Sex Education." *Al-Fanar Media*, 17 August 2015. http://www.al-fanarmedia.org/2015/08/many-moroccan-students-pursue-sex-but-few-get-sex-education/.

Wodak, Ruth, and Paul Chilton, eds. *A New Agenda in (Critical) Discourse Analysis: Theory, Method and Interdisciplinarity.* Amsterdam: John Benjamins, 2005.

Wodak, Ruth, Rudolf de Cillia, Martin Reisigl, and Karin Liebhart. *The Discursive Construction of National Identity.* Edinburgh: Edinburgh University Press, 1999.

Wolters, Stephanie. "Equatorial Guinea's Web of Wealth and Repression." Institute for Security Studies, 15 July 2014. https://issafrica.org/about-us/press-releases/equatorial-guineas-web-of-wealth-and-repression.

World Bank. "Migration and Remittances Factbook." 2010.

Yuval-Davis, Nira. *Gender and Nation.* London: SAGE, 1997.

Zuijdgeest, Nicolien. "Aminatou Haidar: The Sahrawi Gandhi." Blog, 15 March 2013. http://nicolien.com/aminatou-haidar-the-sahrawi-gandhi/.

Zunes, Stephen. "Upsurge in Repression Challenges Nonviolent Resistance in Western Sahara." *Open Democracy*, 17 November 2010.

———. "Western Sahara, Resources, and International Accountability." *Global Change, Peace and Security* 27, no. 3 (2015): 285–99.

Zunes, Stephen, and Jacob Mundy. *Western Sahara: War, Nationalism, and Conflict Irresolution.* Syracuse, NY: Syracuse University Press, 2010.

Zvan Elliott, Katja. *Modernizing Patriarchy: The Politics of Women's Rights in Morocco.* Austin: University of Texas Press, 2015.

# Index

colonial perceptions of Saharawi
women's relative freedom, 238n14
compulsory heterosexuality, 139
contentious politics, 164
Corisco Island, 74
coup d'états: of 1979 against Macías, 15;
allegedly against Obiang, 284n40;
and gender, 15
CPDS (Convergence for Social
Democracy), 215–17, 222, 289n116
CSR (Corporate Social Responsibility),
143
cultural relativism, 21
culture: colonial attempts to manipulate,
37; and cultural appropriation, 24;
and settler colonialism, 24; Women's
Section classes in the realm of, 44.
See also resistance tactics
curfews, 76, 88
custodial punishment: gendering of, 176
custody rights in Spanish Guinea, 74

Dahane, Brahim, 203
Dahbu, Shreisher, 34
Dahou, Mahfood 159–60, 162
Dafa, Lehdia, 21, 115, 118, 177
Dakhla, 32–33, 62
decontestation, 258n25
Deh, Shaya, 115, 118
demonization of Muslim men, 176
digital activism, 110, 115–18, 178
divorce: in cases of domestic violence in
Spanish Guinea, 73; and Catholicism,
70; facilitated by missionaries in
Guinea, 70; and Islam, 59; lack of
stigma for divorced Saharawi women,
59, 120; party, 121; in Saharawi society,
41, 43; in Spanish society, 59; unequal
rights to, 120; women's right to
initiate, 59
Djemaa, 45–46, 51, 58–59
Djimi, El Ghalia, 176–77, 279 n.140
domestic labor, 109, 110–11

Ebebiyin, 71
ebola, 215

education: advocacy for Equatoguinean
girls' access to, 89; demands for
reform of, 62; gendered, 47, 88;
grants, 45; for Guinean girls in Spain,
88, 89; for orphans in Spanish
Guinea, 7; POLISARIO promotion
of women's, 101; Quranic, 40, 45, 52;
Spanish colonial system of, in
Guinea, 33, 65; Spanish colonial
system of, in Sahara, 33, 39
EG Justice, 202
Ehseina, Maafiya Ment, 158
*Ekomo* (novel by María Nsue Angue),
74–75
electricity, 199. See also energy
Embarek Rahal, Baida, 104
embryonic movement. See Harakat
Tahrir
emotion: and history, 18; and resistance,
41, 163, 165
empty signifiers, 100
energy, 10, 27, 113, 199; solar energy, 113
enslaved peoples: conditions of, 34,
50, 239n25; labor of, 34; lack of
support for previously, 240n46;
sexual exploitation of, 34; Spanish
employment of, 34; Spanish solidarity
with, 36. See also slavery; slave
resistance
Envo Bela, Eulalia, 138
Equatorial Guinea: unequal wealth
distribution in, 193
equivalence: theory of, 83, 100
Errachid, Khalihenna Ould, 46
Errer Bouzeid, Aminetou, 115, 119
Esono, Nchama, 72–73
EU (European Union): in Equatorial
Guinea, 143; Fisheries Agreement
with Morocco, 187; in Morocco, 175;
POLISARIO versus, 26
Eyenga Mba-Oyana, Carmen, 88

FAFESA (Forum for the Future of
Saharawi Women in the Occupied
Territory), 184
Falange party: Spanish, 5

## Women in Africa and the Diaspora

*Holding the World Together: African Women in Changing Perspective*
Edited by NWANDO ACHEBE and CLAIRE ROBERTSON

*Engaging Modernity: Muslim Women and the Politics of
Agency in Postcolonial Niger*
OUSSEINA D. ALIDOU

*Muslim Women in Postcolonial Kenya: Leadership, Representation,
and Social Change*
OUSSEINA D. ALIDOU

*Silenced Resistance: Women, Dictatorships, and Genderwashing in
Western Sahara and Equatorial Guinea*
JOANNA ALLAN

*I Am Evelyn Amony: Reclaiming My Life from the Lord's Resistance Army*
EVELYN AMONY; edited with an introduction by ERIN BAINES

*Rising Anthills: African and African American Writing on
Female Genital Excision, 1960–2000*
ELISABETH BEKERS

*African Women Writing Resistance: An Anthology of Contemporary Voices*
Edited by JENNIFER BROWDY DE HERNANDEZ, PAULINE DONGALA,
OMOTAYO JOLAOSHO, and ANNE SERAFIN

*Genocide Lives in Us: Women, Memory, and Silence in Rwanda*
JENNIE E. BURNET

*Tired of Weeping: Mother Love, Child Death, and Poverty in Guinea-Bissau*
JÓNÍNA EINARSDÓTTIR

*Embodying Honor: Fertility, Foreignness, and Regeneration
in Eastern Sudan*
AMAL HASSAN FADLALLA